CATHOLIC LABOR MOVEMENTS IN EUROPE

PAUL MISNER

CATHOLIC LABOR MOVEMENTS IN EUROPE

SOCIAL THOUGHT
AND ACTION,
1914–1965

THE CATHOLIC UNIVERSITY OF AMERICA PRESS
WASHINGTON, D.C.

Copyright © 2015
The Catholic University of America Press
All rights reserved
The paper used in this publication meets the minimum requirements of American
National Standards for Information Science—Permanence of Paper for Printed
Library Materials, ANSI Z39.48-1984.

∞

Library of Congress Cataloging-in-Publication Data
Misner, Paul.
Catholic labor movements in Europe : social thought
and action, 1914–1965 / Paul Misner.
  pages cm
Includes bibliographical references and index.
ISBN 978-0-8132-2753-5 (cloth : alk. paper) 1. Labor—
Religious aspects—Catholic Church. 2. Labor—Europe—
History—20th century. 3. Labor movement—Religious aspects—
Christianity. 4. Labor movement—Europe—
History—20th century. I. Title.
HD6338.2.E8M57 2015
331.88094'090410—dc23   2015009766

*To my beloved Constance and
our daughter Danielle*

CONTENTS

	Abbreviations	ix
	Introduction	1
1.	Preparing the Ground, Sowing the Seed	5
2.	World War I and the Condition of Labor	15
3.	A White International?	40
4.	Social Catholic Analyses before *Quadragesimo Anno*: Common Aims, Diverse Paths	60
5.	Vitality in the Low Countries	88
6.	France: Controversies and Advances	106
7.	New Departures in Catholic Action: Youth Movements in the Working Class	121
8.	Women's Catholic Labor Movements	143
9.	Christian Labor in Weimar Germany	161
10.	Italy and Austria: Christian Labor at Grips with Authoritarian Rule	184
11.	*Quadragesimo Anno*, 1931: Its Controversial Reception	212
12.	France, Belgium, the Netherlands: Christian Labor in the Depression Years	231
13.	Labor and Catholicism under the Impact of World War II	255
14.	Working within Secular Pluralism	281
	Conclusion	293
	References	297
	Index of Names	331
	General Index	337

ABBREVIATIONS

AAS	*Acta Apostolicae Sedis*
AC	Action catholique; Azione cattolica
ACLI	Associazioni cristiane dei lavoratori italiani
ACO	Action catholique ouvrière
ACV	Algemeen Christelijk Vakverbond von België (see also CSC)
ACW	Algemeen Christelijk Werkersverbond (Belgian; see LNTC)
AP	Action populaire
ASS	*Acta Sanctae Sedis*
BASMSCI	Bollettino dell'Archivio per la storia del movimento sociale cattolico in Italia
BKF	Beiträge zur Katholizismusforschung
Carlen	*Papal Encyclicals*
Catholicisme	*Catholicisme: Hier, aujourd'hui, demain*
CFDT	Confédération française démocratique du travail
CFTC	Conféderation française des travailleurs chrétiens
CGIL	Confederazione generale italiana del lavoro
CGT	Confédération générale du travail
CIL	Confederazione italiana dei lavoratori
CISC	Confédération internationale des syndicats chrétiens (International Federation of Christian Trade Unions)
CISL	Confederazione italiana sindacati lavoratori
CSC	Confédération des syndicats chrétiens (Belgian, see ACV)
DBMOF	*Dictionnaire biographique du mouvement ouvrier français*
DC	Démocratie chrétienne; Democrazia cristiana
DGB	Deutscher Gewerkschaftsbund
DHFO	*Dictionnaire historique de la France sous l'Occupation*

DHGE	Dictionnaire d'histoire et de géographie ecclésiastique
DMR	Dictionnaire du monde religieux dans la France contemporaine
DS	Enchiridion symbolorum, definitionum et declarationum de rebus fidei et morum
DSMCI	Dizionario storico del movimento cattolico in Italia 1860–1980
DTC	Dictionnaire de théologie catholique
ECSC	European Coal and Steel Community
FIMOC	Fédération internationale des mouvements ouvriers chrétiens
GcG	Gesamtverband der christlichen Gewerkschaften Deutschlands (League of Christian Trade Unions of Germany)
Flannery	Vatican Council II: The Basic Sixteen Documents
FUCI	Federazione universitaria cattolica italiana
GCI	Gioventù cattolica italiana
GS	Gaudium et spes
HC	Histoire du christianisme des origines à nos jours
HDTFR	Historical Dictionary of the Third French Republic, 1870–1940
HJS	Honderd jaar sociaal: Teksten uit honderd jaar sociale beweging en sociaal denken in Nederland 1891–1991
HMOCB	Histoire du mouvement ouvrier chrétien en Belgique
IESS	International Encyclopedia of the Social Sciences
JCSW	Jahrbuch für christliche Sozialwissenschaften
JOC	Jeunesse ouvrière chrétienne
JOCF	Jeunesse ouvrière chrétienne féminine
KAB	Katholische Arbeiterbewegung
KAV	Katholieke Arbeidersvrouwenbeweging, Kristelijke Arbeidersvrouwenbeweging
KSL	Katholisches Soziallexikon
LNTC	Ligue nationale des travailleurs chrétiens (Belgian, see ACW; MOC)
LOC	Ligue ouvrière chrétienne
LOFC	Ligues ouvrières féminines chrétiennes
MEGA	Karl Marx, Friedrich Engels Gesamtausgabe
MM	Mater et magistra
MOC	Mouvement ouvrier chrétien

MPF	Mouvement populaire des familles
NDB	*Neue Deutsche Biographie*
NCE	*New Catholic Encyclopedia*
NDCST	*The New Dictionary of Catholic Social Thought*
NVV	Nederlands Verbond van Vakverenigingen
OC	Opera dei Congressi
OCCO	Oeuvre des cercles catholiques d'ouvriers
PP	*Populorum progressio*
PPI	Partito popolare italiano
QA	*Quadragesimo anno*
RHE	*Revue d'histoire ecclésiastique*
RKWV	Rooms-Katholiek Werkliedenverbond
RN	*Rerum novarum*
ST	Thomas Aquinas, *Summa theologiae*
StL	*Staatslexikon: Recht, Wirtschaft, Gesellschaft*
STO	Service du travail obligatoire
SWB	*Wilhelm Emmanuel von Ketteler: Sämtliche Werke und Briefe*
UTMI	Union des travailleurs manuels et intellectuels
VKAJ	Vrouwelijke Katholieke Arbeidersjeugd
VKZG	Veröffentlichungen der Kommission für Zeitgeschichte
WAZ	*Westdeutsche Arbeiter-Zeitung*
ZAG	Zentralarbeitsgemeinschaft
ZGiLB	*Zeitgeschichte in Lebensbildern: Aus dem deutschen Katholizismus des 20. Jahrhunderts*

CATHOLIC LABOR MOVEMENTS IN EUROPE

Introduction

In French, one often refers to the three decades following the Second World War as "les Trente Glorieuses" because of the vigorous postwar recovery (1945–75) that sustained itself with hardly a break until the first oil crisis.[1] And indeed, "les Trente Glorieuses" saw a most impressive economic boom in the Western democracies. Citizens experienced unprecedented peace and prosperity. If American nuclear-armed forces helped defend the peace and the American contribution in the form of the Marshall Plan catalyzed their prosperity, still, the Europeans themselves worked out the shape of both the peace and the prosperity that they began to enjoy. The "social state" or "welfare state" that they created bore the imprint of their own national and European histories.[2] The postwar Western European economies virtually achieved a central objective of the Christian social ideals upheld by Catholicism: the elimination of the stark inequality between the proletarian masses and the privileged class of capitalists.

How is one to account for this surprising result? How could the Catholic workers' movements in these countries play a significant part? After all, the three or four decades *before* les Trente Glorieuses, the decades commanding our principal attention here, would not seem to bode well for the next generation. Catholics for the most part held out hope for a good society only in one or another form of a revival of Christendom. For ultramontane Catholicism to come to terms with capitalism and socialism and to accept democracy, pluralism, and modernity as positive developments was a feature of a broader and equally unanticipated coming-to-terms with a "Secular Age." In his brilliant 2007 work, *A Secular Age*,

---

1. Piketty 2014, index.
2. Feldman 1993, 869n12, explains that the German term *Sozialstaat* has no precise English equivalent, since it encompasses both the welfare state and the system of industrial (labor) relations; see G. A. Ritter 1989, 10–28; Spieker 1989, 5:72–78; Piketty 2104, 477. See also Sheehan 2008, especially for the Europeans' newly definitive determination not to wage war with each other.

Charles Taylor points out that Catholic Christianity had built up its forces in an "Age of Mobilization" that stretched through the interwar years into the 1950s.³ In one historian's conceit, the thirty years when Catholicism flourished most conspicuously in civil society were precisely those that *preceded* the economic miracle in Europe.⁴ In the realm of social Catholicism a central preoccupation in the period between the two world wars was the mobilization of workers in labor organizations that vindicated their rights while not alienating them from their Christian faith. How did this favor integration into postwar Europe?

The focus of the present work, the first transnational account of Catholic labor movements in Europe by a single author, helps to understand this evolution. The Christian labor movements of the interwar period had a predominantly modernizing character within a Catholicism consciously set against modern times. As they adapted to new economic challenges, they brought the church at large gradually to appreciate some aspects of the troubled twentieth century. This was particularly the case with an acceptance, indeed an embrace, of pluralism in society, democracy in government, and a socially balanced capitalism in economic life.

Such inner-churchly effects fit broadly into the category of greater autonomy for lay initiatives and interacted with other modernizing developments in Catholic ecclesiastical history. From another perspective, however, that of labor history, these same movements contributed more than is generally realized to the model of social partnership between management and labor in Western European countries after World War II. To show how Christian labor organizations contributed to this positive outcome is an aim of this study.

The sources upon which the present account is based include the platforms, stands, manifestos, and programs that the Christian (predominantly Catholic) labor organizations published over the years. I investigate the struggles of activists to put such ideals into practice for the common good, the accommodations they made, and the opportunities they found. Similarly, on the ecclesial side, the documents and histories of church pronouncements provide a basis and context for the efforts of clerical advocates and lay educators of the rank and file. All the countries treated here (Belgium, the Netherlands, France, West Germany, Austria, and Italy) have been individually well served by historians.⁵ Such research by others has formed the principal resource for my synthesis

---

3. Taylor 2007, 423–72.

4. Hilaire 2010, 2:916: "Notons que les 30 glorieuses du catholicisme 1925/30–1955/60 ont précédé de quinze à vingt ans les 30 glorieuses de l'économie et de la démographie, 1945–1973. Cette réussite n'est pas due au hazard." See Launay 1990, 333–404, for international context and comparisons.

5. What these countries have in common is a previous tradition of Christian democracy followed by Axis dictatorship or occupation during World War II.

(see references). I have also made use of research that has recently appeared along comparative and transnational lines.[6]

Already in the biennium immediately following World War I, there were some promising developments tending in the direction of the social state. Even before 1914 a number of countries had introduced, for workers in at least some industries, one or another variant of the three core social security programs: accident insurance (workers' compensation), medical insurance, and retirement pensions. In stages, typically first during and just after World War I, then in the relative prosperity of 1925–29, and again at the end of the 1930s, these programs were extended to larger categories of people, and their benefits were improved.[7] New types of social benefits such as unemployment compensation came into being. Even the United States went beyond veterans' benefits to introduce broad-based Social Security during the Depression, while Sweden foreshadowed one particularly advanced form of the postwar welfare state. In Great Britain, during World War II, the Beveridge Plan was proposed, to be implemented by a Labour government after the war. Thereafter the welfare or social state became a hallmark of all advanced industrial nations in Western Europe.[8]

In moving whole societies from the severe economic inequalities of nineteenth-century industrialism to the provisional solution represented by the post–World War II social state, Catholics and Catholic culture played a discernible and significant role.[9] This is not to say that the welfare state in Western Europe turned out according to the plans of social Catholics, as outlined, for instance, in the 1931 encyclical *Quadragesimo anno* or as sketched along the lines of a "new Christendom" by Jacques Maritain in 1936—only that they helped bring about a state of affairs that they could recognize as corresponding to their historic social-justice aims. Not all features of this outcome were equally pleasing, of course. The mass consumer society that developed under the prevailing favorable economic winds, a society taking its cues more from

---

6. Note the valuable multiauthor works edited by Heerma van Voss, Pasture, and De Maeyer 2005 (led off by Pasture 2005b, which provides the most current state of the question), and Hiepel and Ruff 2003; see also Pazos 1993.

7. G. A. Ritter 1989, 88, 106, and 145–50; Pasture 2005a.

8. See Kaelble 1990, 13, 74–84, and 120–28; see also Alber 1982; Kaufmann 2000.

9. Among those commentators who acknowledge a Christian element in the postwar social policies is Tony Judt (2005, 7), who speaks of "the 'European model,' born of an eclectic mix of Social Democratic and Christian Democratic legislation and treaties"; see also his *Reappraisals* (Judt 2008, esp. 9–11; see also Judt 2010). See Nord 2010, 372–83, for France. A leading ecclesiastic, the cardinal-archbishop of Munich, Reinhard Marx, in his *Das Kapital: Ein Plädoyer für den Menschen* (2008; see Sen 1999), views a similar model of social capitalism as needful on the global scale, if human dignity is to be fostered. Recent studies also draw on this European model and apply it to American conditions—e.g., Steven Hill, *Europe's Promise* (2010, esp. 15–65) and Lew Daly, *God's Economy* (2009).

television than from any other cultural agent, was certainly not what the pioneers had in mind.[10] Nor was the permissiveness in socially tolerated mores that became evident particularly around 1968. But Pope John XXIII (in *Pacem in terris*, 1963) and Vatican II (in *Gaudium et spes*, 1965) had no difficulty recognizing that the emphasis on human rights in United Nations declarations, as well as in the democratic constitutions and practices of post–World War II states, corresponded to the traditional Christian ideals of justice and charity in a modern context.

The Catholic efforts that accompanied and contributed to this humane outcome are best known in connection with a political movement, that of Christian democracy.[11] Christian democratic (nonconfessional) governments gained and held power for a long time after World War II, particularly in Germany and Italy, but also in Austria and the Benelux countries. Christian labor representatives exerted varying influence in these parties. In the period we are examining, the interactions of Christian labor and political Christian democracy are significant and will be considered in some depth. The main focus will remain on the labor movements themselves and on the thinking and outlooks that influenced their undertakings.

Before commencing our account with the outbreak of World War I in 1914, a brief retrospective look at the nineteenth-century tradition of labor-oriented social Catholicism is appropriate. This I draw mainly from my 1991 study *Social Catholicism in Europe* (to 1914). It provides a baseline from which to understand the stands that social Catholic activists took, the continuities they strove to maintain, and the changed conditions they faced in the age of the world wars.

Besides presenting a roughly chronological narrative of events, this book also serves as a resource for reference purposes. Its indexes and references provide convenient access for inquiries in many fields, historical and cultural.

---

10. Scoppola 1986, 19, 81–110.

11. This was the proximate context for an early wavelet of studies on social and political Catholicism in English: Moody 1953; M. Fogarty 1957; and Vidler 1964. A sampling of more recent work is represented by Bokenkotter 1998; Becker and Morsey 1988; Cary 1996; Van Kersbergen 1995; Kalyvas 1996; and Kaiser 2007; as well as by the collective works of Lamberts 1997; Kselman and Buttigieg 2003; Kaiser and Wohnout 2004; and Kaiser 2007.

CHAPTER 1

Preparing the Ground, Sowing the Seed

Challenges of Industrialization

When population growth and the Industrial Revolution started rearranging how people had to make their livings, there was a new school of thought ready to interpret what was happening and to offer guidance on how society should respond. Mercantilism still had its practitioners, but the nineteenth century would belong to the liberal economic prescriptions of Adam Smith and other theorists of classical economics. Smith emphasized the virtues of a market economy in ways that have been confirmed again and again since his *Wealth of Nations* (1776). He also memorably pointed out the increase in productivity that comes from the division of labor, made possible by capital investments (hence finance) and entrepreneurial planning.[1]

Adam Smith's followers throughout the next century rather naively elevated his strictures against mercantilist government direction into a laissez-faire ideology. The division of economic agents into a small group of capitalists controlling enormous wealth and a mass of industrial workers vulnerable to being played off against one another and reduced to subsistence wages and a life of squalor was hardly known to Adam Smith. Where such contrasts did exist in prototype, they were land-based rather than money-based and implied a certain community of interests between landowner and farm workers—or they were in the mines, where Smith condemned such inhumanity in no uncertain terms. Property was capital, all the same, and the inherent tendency of capital to accumulate its returns in the hands of its owners over time grounded a

---

1. See Misner 1990 for the first (conservative Catholic) response on the continent; see Misner 1991, of which the present work is a sequel, for the whole chapter.

great inequality of income between the wealthy and the rest, who had to live off their labor.[2]

Great Britain was in the forefront of industrial development. Some leading lights of the Church of England worked out an accommodation between early industry and traditional Christian notions of economic relationships, even before a Christian socialist alternative was offered.[3] Early Roman Catholic observers of the British economy, such as Franz von Baader, Philippe Buchez, Alban de Villeneuve-Bargemont, and Charles de Coux, as well as Franz Josef von Buss and the Belgian Edouard Ducpétiaux, registered the impoverished condition of workers in newly industrialized regions with great concern and proposed measures to prevent the same from happening on a grand continental scale.[4] But T. R. Malthus and other liberal economists insisted on the futility of public poor relief and advocated industrial development without any restraints on capitalists.

While the Catholic figures just mentioned all found Malthus's original option (a kind of not-so-benign neglect) unacceptable, their own alternatives ranged from socialist (Buchez) to democratic (de Coux) to conservative-paternalistic (Armand de Melun). All, however, were bent on restoring the *association* of human beings with one another in their work lives. They aimed to put back together what had been set at odds by "industrialism": men and machinery, capital and labor, workers and their product. Baader in Munich, for example, deplored the formation of a "proletariat" before Karl Marx did: a class deprived of property and work would be abjectly dependent upon property owners and hence restive and hostile—in effect, antisocial. In the same period, the religious socialists in irreligious France and the irreligious reformers in Bible-reading Britain were trying out other formulas of association. One of the latter, William Godwin, was an early influence on Baader. Robert Owen's socialist ideas in the 1820s were contemporary with Buchez's. Men and machinery, they said, must be brought into a harmony. Self-governing workshops should federate together, so that the labor movement would take over industry by fair competition and then regulate it for the good of the working class.

This associationist character of embryonic social Catholicism would be retained, but "Christian socialist" elements would always be minoritarian if not altogether marginal. Not negligible was the "Christian democratic" movement of 1848–49 in Paris, but it was buried in the class tensions that soon rebounded with increased intensity. During the French Second Empire (1852–70),

---

2. See Piketty 2014, 238–46, for the historical development of the economic relationships of capital and labor since the eighteenth century in Europe (and America).
3. See Waterman 1991 and Christensen 1962.
4. See Misner 1991, index of persons.

the hostility between the church and the workers became fully cemented. On the one side, Catholicism grew more overtly anti-republican and reactionary, while on the other, conservative or reactionary bourgeois preachments tended to alienate workers.

In Germany, where Catholics, at least in the Prussian Rhineland, did not dream of monarchical favor but enjoyed, for a season, constitutionally guaranteed parity, things were not so bleak. A priest in Cologne, Adolph Kolping, and a bishop in Mainz, Wilhelm Emmanuel von Ketteler, responded energetically to the new possibilities of forming associations. Kolping invented a structure to which precariously employed journeymen could relate positively. He offered a way in which parish clergy and young, unmarried workingmen could collaborate in activities of professional training and mutual support. He did not try to bring employers and workers together in a paternalistic embrace as the concerned minority of French Catholic activists did, in an approach to overcoming class consciousness that often had the opposite effect. As a result, a positive rapport survived between clergy and artisans in sectors of Catholic Germany.

Bishop Ketteler promoted Kolping's efforts with the journeymen, but he came to see that a big gap was opening up between the church and factory workers. During the 1848 revolutions he had been a deputy to the pan-German constitutional assembly in Frankfurt. Already he sensed the social problem lurking beneath the political questions that everyone was debating so ardently. He delivered some sermons, published as *The Great Social Questions of the Present* (1848), that put forward a traditional charitable approach for their solution. Authentically traditional approaches were, however, greatly at variance with conventional ideas of the period. In his 1864 book *The Labor Problem and Christianity*, he grappled with the remedies proposed by the liberal Hermann Schulze-Delitzsch and the socialist leader Ferdinand Lassalle, leaning far toward the latter. He crossed another threshold in 1869 with a call for a British-style trade union movement to be supported by the clergy and laity of the Catholic Church in Germany. There followed the Franco-Prussian War of 1870 and the period of Bismarckian paternalistic as well as repressive social policy in the new German Reich. Neither the Catholic clergy nor labor organizations had much room to maneuver in the next twenty years; Ketteler's proposals were tabled until the 1890s, long after his death.

In France, too, the Third Republic, after about 1875, characterized as it was by a secular, liberal, anticlerical ascendancy, was not friendly toward labor or the church. A nasty separation of church and state had to take place in 1905 before a slow healing process between Catholics and republicans could make progress. Catholics, and notably French social Catholics, tended to be emphatic legitimists (monarchists), even more so after the Second Empire and the defeat of 1870. They dug in their heels against the Third Republic and hankered for a restored monarchy to recreate the conditions in which social justice could flourish in France. This remained the case for many even after the royal pretender had died and Pope Leo XIII called for a *ralliement*, a loyal acceptance of the republican form of government where it was firmly established. The two foremost representative figures of this stage of social Catholicism were Albert de Mun and René de La Tour du Pin. These few but dogged opponents of both the individualistic new status quo and its collectivist, statist, or anarchic socialist alternatives strove to work out applications of traditional Christian social ethics to modern economies in an international study group called the Union de Fribourg.[5]

Albert de Mun was the commanding figure at the head of the Oeuvre des cercles catholiques d'ouvriers (OCCO), which he founded in the aftermath of the Paris Commune in 1871. At a later date, he also founded the Association catholique de la jeunesse française (ACJF) for university students and graduates. He combined a genuine paternalistic concern for the welfare of workers with a conviction that the French liberal republican establishment simply incorporated all the diabolical qualities of the French Revolution. The only cure he could see for it was to annul the Revolution and all its effects. Although his counterrevolutionary prejudices prevented his organization from attaining any real influence among workers, his energy and combativeness led all the same to a flowering in the younger generation of educated Catholics of a less reactionary dedication to economic justice in modern society. All the same, social Catholics like Henri Bazire or, more conspicuously, the charismatic herald of democracy, Marc Sangnier, in the years before the Great War, had to contend with the fierce opposition of influential Catholics ("*intégristes*"), who imbibed the anti-modern rhetoric that de Mun shared with them.

A fellow captive with de Mun in 1870, sharing the same defeat and imprisonment at the hands of the Germans, was a scion of the greater nobility, de la Tour du Pin. He pursued the task of elaborating the social theory or "doctrine" that de Mun more or less took for granted. In Vienna, where he was stationed for a while, he encountered the corporatist, anti-capitalist ideas of the convert Baron Karl von Vogelsang, whom he considered the true heir of Bishop Ketteler. Then he injected these views on economic questions into the counterrevolutionary brew of the intransigent Catholicism of the OCCO, particularly through the *Revue de l'Association Catholique*.

Into this mix came Léon Harmel, a patriarchal textile manufacturer who by stages reconceived his relationship to the worker as emancipatory (and not

---

5. Paulhus 1994; Lamberts 2002.

permanently paternalistic). True charity would be to develop the workers' capacities to take their affairs into their own hands. Thus he became an important if improbable agent in the second Christian democratic workers' movement in the 1890s.

Christian Labor Organizations circa 1914

These and other efforts bore fruit in *Rerum novarum*, the social encyclical "on the condition of labor" of 1891.[6] Its effects on nascent Catholic labor movements came largely through galvanizing the scattered forces of social Catholics, just at the moment when industrialization was swinging into high gear for the sustained development of a new generation of industries (electrical, steel, chemical, automotive) in many parts of the continent. Coming out of a long slump that started around 1873, the industrial sector of the advanced European economies had to pay more attention to its treatment of workers. The labor movements on the continent also went into a phase of rapid development from being largely ineffectual to becoming a force to be reckoned with in the guise of organized trade unions. The encyclical cautiously endorsed the right of workers to organize on their own while omitting any condemnation of the right to strike. This, along with its denunciation of capitalist abuses and exploitation of labor, was a powerful encouragement for a new generation of activists. Clergy like Franz Hitze, Antoine Pottier, Romolo Murri, and Luigi Sturzo were involved; laity too, such as the miner August Brust and the entrepreneurs Léon Harmel and Franz Brandts, founder of the Volksverein, were involved.[7] (Other figures, especially from Belgium, will be named shortly.) Variations on the theme of labor solidarity were played by such participants as the influential Adam Stegerwald, leader of the German League of Christian Unions.[8] They each responded to the need to move beyond a paternalistic approach on the social question to a Christian democracy with some marked affinities to social democracy.

Rerum novarum called in no uncertain terms for the positive attention of the clergy and well-to-do laity to associations of workers and pointed out why and how governmental intervention in the labor question was sometimes necessary; but it did not mark any clear break with paternalistic presupposi-

---

6. See the studies by Shannon; there is an essay by Michael Schuck (2005) in *Modern Catholic Social Teaching*, ed. Kenneth Himes (Himes et al. 2005); see also Holland 2003 and Furlong and Curtis 1994. Of the many studies issued in continental Europe since its centennial, note especially *"Rerum novarum": Écriture, contenu et réception* 1997.

7. On Antoine Pottier, see Delville 2009a and 2009b; on August Brust, see Hiepel 1999; on Léon Harmel, see Coffey 2003.

8. Patch 1985; Forster 2003.

tions. In 1901 another encyclical of Leo's, *Graves de communi re*, took note of the "Christian democratic" movements. It endorsed the designation, not in a political sense, but as "beneficent Christian action on behalf of the people." In these circumstances the trade union question became the focus of bitter infighting among social Catholics of older (paternalistic) and newer (Christian democratic) stripes throughout the pontificate of Leo's successor, Pope Pius X (1903–14).[9] The two pathbreaking social Catholic organizations in France and Germany, the *Semaines sociales* led by Henri Lorin and the Volksverein in Mönchengladbach, came under heavy criticism for supporting workers' rights to organize by themselves.

To take the leading example, the Volksverein für das katholische Deutschland ("People's Association for Catholic Germany") ran training courses for citizens, prospective labor leaders, and clergy to deal with social policy so they could take full advantage of their rights under German social legislation. The priest and future minister of labor, Heinrich Brauns, conducted such courses for years. The Volksverein provided strong backing for the German Christian labor unions, which were interconfessional: largely Catholic, but not under hierarchical authority. Many in Rome, including Pope Pius X, frowned on such autonomy for workers and on their clerical advisers. Some bishops sought to discredit the Volksverein, while others supported its efforts discreetly in the years from 1900 to 1914.[10]

France, meanwhile, could not boast of such a robust organization with the broad reach of the Volksverein, but did have the noteworthy *Semaines sociales*, an annual gathering, an "itinerant university," as it was called, where for a week or two academics and activists shared their experiences and plans. The lectures were then published every year as a book. The institutions that sustained the *Semaines sociales* were in Paris, Lyon, and Lille. In addition to this, some Jesuits led by Gustave Desbuquois operated a center of training and publications in Reims aptly named Action populaire. Marc Sangnier's Sillon movement was condemned by the Vatican in 1910 for its advocacy of democracy, but its adherents stayed faithful to the ideals of social Catholicism. The *Semaines sociales* and the Action populaire also came under pressure during the labor union controversy under Pius X that heated up in the years just before World War I.

---

9. For the twentieth century, some historians, notably in their treating of Belgium, make a rather sharp distinction in their usage between "social Catholicism" (undemocratic, paternalistic) and the Christian labor movement, dubbed "Christian democracy." In this book the focus will be on the more democratic wing of Catholic social practice as exemplified particularly in Catholic working-class organizations.

10. On the Belgian unions and union federation spearheaded by Fr. Rutten and the lay union leaders he found already at work, such as Gustave Eylenbosch and René A. Debruyne, see especially Strikwerda 1997, 290–93 and 300–8; see Kwanten 1986a, 32–43.

Henri Lorin, a veteran of Catholic social thought, was the first target of conservatives, accused of social modernism. Given that Pius X in 1907 condemned "Modernism" as "the synthesis of all heresies," this was the worst accusation one could hurl at a fellow Catholic thinker. Lorin and Desbuquois, as Catholics, supported workers' organizations such as the SECI (Syndicat des employés du commerce et de l'industrie) for white-collar workers as well as the scattering of organizations for women working in shops or at piecework at home. These unions were religiously inspired, but they aimed primarily at the betterment of their members' economic welfare in the name of social justice. For this they incurred the same calls for condemnation as did the Volksverein.

The Italian situation displayed similar strains, although the conditions were different in its less industrialized economy. There had been considerable progress in previous decades toward a close-knit net of organizations to mobilize the Catholic population against the atomizing effect of anticlerical liberal forces, especially at the parish level. Nationally, Pope Pius X set up the Economic-Social Union to emulate in some sort the German Volksverein, but with tighter ecclesiastical control. It encouraged the expansion of cooperatives, credit unions, and workers' organizations to meet local needs. By 1909 the latter, dubbed Catholic "labor leagues," had about 100,000 members, many in agriculture. For example, Guido Miglioli organized the sharecroppers in the dairy industry around Cremona and went on to become the president of the national peasants' union until the Fascist crackdown. Such labor leagues represented workers in disputes with owners. In the first decade of the twentieth century, they handled 175 such known disputes, involving 80,000 workers. They claimed positive outcomes in 158 of them. Sometimes they resorted to strikes. Alongside these efforts, the leading Catholic theorist of social justice, Giuseppe Toniolo, ran "Social Weeks" after the French model from 1905 on, a week-long conference each year on a social theme. Conservative Catholics were not happy with such advocacy. Toniolo was reined in by the pope, but nevertheless could marshal enough friends of labor in high places in the church to stave off a threatened condemnation of such labor activism in the spring of 1914, in the final year of Pius X's pontificate.

After all, democratically minded social Catholics had laid foundations in all the countries we are examining—foundations that would sometimes need repair from the costs of war after 1918 but that could be rebuilt or built upon at that point. In Austria the Christian Social Party harbored a small labor wing under Leopold Kunschak. In Italy Romolo Murri, Giovanni Battista Valente, and especially Luigi Sturzo laid plans for democratic moves on behalf of the working class once Catholics were free to participate in national political mobilization. German Catholics had their Center Party, a minority party that was destined soon for greater responsibilities. There were representatives of Catholic peasant organizations as well as labor among the Center Party parliamentarians. Matthias Erzberger, for one, had been present at the 1899 founding of the national Christian union confederation (the League of Christian Trade Unions of Germany, representing 342,000 members in 1913). The unions and their confederation were *interconfessional* ("Christian"), hence not officially affiliated with the Catholic Church—a bone of contention that led to the controversies just noted.

In Belgium, the only Western European nation where a Catholic party had held sway in the late nineteenth century, Georges Ceslas Rutten, OP, was the pioneer instigator of the Catholic union movement.[11] But the union confederation in particular could not be and was not directed by clergy for long. Rutten raised the money, but René Debruyne did the actual organizing work involved in creating a national Christian union movement. Debruyne (1868–1941) originally worked in a bakery and was an activist in the "antisocialist" union headquarters in Ghent, the one town with a continuous double union movement going back to the nineteenth century.[12] He was the first paid union organizer in Rutten's secretariat from 1904 to 1914 and was president of the union right after the war and from 1923 to 1932, while serving in parliament.[13] After the social-ethical reflection of Abbé Antoine Pottier, Arthur Vermeersch, SJ (1909), offered practical information on the openings for social action created by legislation. There was a Flemish Social Week in 1908.[14]

Finally, the Netherlands: here industrialization came relatively late. Catholics had a distinctive relationship to the rest of society here. These two circumstances gave the state of their efforts at coping with the condition of labor (as *Rerum novarum* urged) a quite distinctive shape. A Calvinist leader, Abraham Kuyper, took the lead in addressing the problem.[15] In the 1890s, however, manufacturing picked up speed and with it the attraction of urban workers for socialism. Even in the Catholic south, in Eindhoven, to be exact, mass production of light bulbs and other electrical export items began in 1891 with the Phillips Corporation.[16] The five Catholic bishops would throw their weight behind social Catholic organizing efforts by the turn of the century, but until then they remained aloof from or averse to departures from customary ways of dealing with their mostly rural and small-town flocks, even after *Rerum novarum*.

---

11. See De Clercq 2007.
12. Strikwerda 1997, 42; see also 1995 and 2003.
13. *HMOCB* 1994, 1:130.
14. Gerard 1998, 127.
15. See Kuyper's address to a "social congress" in Amsterdam in 1891 in *HJS* 68–84; Van Til 2008, 619–26.
16. Kalb 1997, 81, 91.

Also, of all the nations here reviewed, the Netherlands would remain neutral in World War I. Hence we will reserve a fuller treatment of the early developments of Dutch social Catholicism until chapter 5.

To fortify the Christian labor movements across national borders, Adam Stegerwald, the leader of the German League of Christian Trade Unions, wished to emulate the socialist trade union example by setting up an international confederation of the Christian trade unions. In 1914, however, that aspiration was still in the works. Still, let us recall the international conference of Christian unions organized by Adam Stegerwald and held in Zurich in 1908.[17] A few dozen union representatives from eight countries conferred there on the steps toward such a confederation. Stegerwald offered his services as international secretary with a secretariat operating from his offices in Cologne. A continuation committee with a German, a Dutch, and an Italian member was also formed. The German, Johannes Giesberts, a former worker and labor journalist, now installed in Mönchengladbach near Cologne as the liaison person of the Catholic Volksverein to the labor movement, was its chair.[18] A small follow-up conference met in Cologne in 1911. The unions represented totaled 650,000 members. The comparable figure for the socialist workers' international of Berlin was over five million. The tensions in Germany between some bishops and Rome on the one hand and Stegerwald's Christian (interconfessional) unions on the other, however, took precedence over international contacts until the outbreak of World War I, which of course completely cut contacts between the Central Powers and the Allies.

Besides the trade unions, the other large branch of Christian labor consisted of the nonunion Catholic workers' organizations. These generally had a priest-chaplain and were the preferred place where union members and other working-class Catholics got their "formation" (training) in social justice issues from a religious perspective and could put it into practice organizationally. For such groups, in the narrative that follows, I have adopted terminology that comes from the Belgian usage in Dutch and French. An important if little-known priest who will figure in several subsequent chapters, Henricus Poels, seems to have been the first to define its contours in the Catholic vocabulary. His Dutch expression, *standsorganisatie*, simply means an organization of members occupying a certain *stand* or place in the socioeconomic order. In our case, the *stand* (plural *standen*: "estate") in question is the working class. The term "class" is avoided, however, because of the negative overtones of its use in conjunction with workers and because of the Marxist-influenced rhetoric of the "class struggle" or class warfare: class pitted against class. A difficulty

17. See Launay 1990, 244f; Misner 1994b and 2004b.
18. Brose 1985, 260–65.

arose in French (and English) usage, since there was no usable exact equivalent of the Dutch (and German) *stand,* and yet social Catholics in Belgium, France, and Italy also wanted to eschew class talk. So they chose *milieu*, which leads to our usage of the term "milieu organizations" as referring not to the given Catholic milieu or national milieu but to the social milieu. A further specification is that we do not use the expression *standsorganisationen* or milieu organizations for labor unions proper, but only for the para-union organizations that played so prominent a part in Catholic social-justice efforts. As will become apparent, the best known and most widespread of these organizations was that of the Young Christian Workers, the Jeunesse ouvrière chrétienne (JOC). In 1914 the most prominent examples were the Catholic Arbeitervereine for German adult workers. Across the border in Belgium, Victoire Cappe, with the encouragement of Cardinal Mercier, animated a league of Christian working-class women that also included some trade unions.[19]

Our story in this book begins with this base of fledgling labor organizations in several countries of industrialized Europe. The dedicated efforts of activists and supporters of Catholic labor movements over the next decades will make important, indeed indispensable, contributions to the social partnership model of post–World War II Western Europe. They will likewise play a key role in reconciling Catholic culture with modern economies and political and social democracy.

This was the situation when the Germans invaded Belgium on August 4, 1914. Starting at that point in chapter 2 of this volume, we follow the organizational and political engagements and intellectual and cultural developments in the history of Christian labor into the era of its greatest mobilization and influence. In this book the focus will be on Catholic social practice as exemplified particularly in European Catholic working-class organizations. The struggles of the interwar Catholic labor forces helped to prepare the ground for the prominent role of Catholics in the reconstruction of Western European political economies and civil societies after the Second World War.

19. Eaton 1955.

CHAPTER 2

World War I and the Condition of Labor

Pope Pius X died as war broke out between Austria, hence Germany, and Serbia, hence Russia and France. The conclave of cardinals elected the archbishop of Bologna, Giacomo Della Chiesa (1854–1922), as pope. He took the name of Benedict XV. The conclaves of 1914 and 1922 remained divided between the two tendencies that had prevailed throughout most of the nineteenth century at papal elections. It was a choice between a hard-line, anti-modernist course and the more supple and diplomatic variation of the same that Pope Leo XIII had pursued. The new pope, elected September 3, 1914, had the advantage of not having shown pronounced leanings for or against France or Germany, while being an experienced diplomat. He had served many years under Cardinal Rampolla, Leo XIII's secretary of state.[1] Although the integralist campaign against trade unions, which Pius X had abetted with his patronage, loomed large in the minds of some of the electors,[2] nevertheless the Great War became the focus and the dominating concern of the new pope's every act (his first message, *Ubi primum* of September 8, implored the warring parties to call a halt to the mass savagery).

Benedict XV

As expected, Benedict XV soon took care to chasten the hard-line integralist Catholics, who could always count on at least the moral support of Pius X. His appointments made an "out group" of Pius X's in group. He devoted *Ad beatissimi apostolorum*, his very

---

1. See Pollard 1999, 10–18, 59–65, for the biography of Benedict XV; see Kelly 2005, 314–16.
2. R. Aubert et al. 1978, 535.

first encyclical, to the three pressing issues of the war, social justice, and inner-churchly tensions in the wake of the modernist controversy. He took the occasion to admonish integralist Catholics that he was quite capable of speaking for himself in an authoritative way when necessary; but when the Apostolic See had not pronounced itself on a question, "no one should consider himself entitled to affix on those who merely do not agree with his ideas the stigma of disloyalty to faith or to discipline."[3]

This encyclical, like most of Benedict XV's work, has drifted into the backwaters of church history. As is also the case with Pius X's social teaching, Benedict's encyclical has not found its way into the canon of "social encyclicals" in the pertinent collections. Perhaps the reason for this is that he hewed closely to the intransigent (not "integralist") school of Catholic social thought, summing up a great deal of what Leo XIII and Pius X had in common. He did not add anything new apart from the parallel with the still more pressing problem of war and peace. His social teaching thus constitutes a representative expression of the post-Leonine magisterium. It also shows the important place of social teaching in the papal concerns, even as war began to rage. Sections 5–18 of *Ad beatissimi* take direct aim at the social question of the industrial countries, understood as the inequities in distribution of income that engendered class enmity and strife. For beside the ethnic hatreds that had just erupted, there was in each nation a battle for absolute hegemony—*class* warfare—that capitalists exemplified and that socialists elevated to a principle.

Ad beatissimi is also indicative of how little the cautious critique of paternalism in the ranks of the more progressive social Catholics had affected the thinking of the papal magisterium at this critical point. Benedict, an aristocrat of more secure and distinguished lineage than Leo XIII, firmly believed in *noblesse oblige*, the duty of the upper classes to attend to the needs of their social inferiors.[4] He had opted for the clerical calling in the time of the reactionary Pope Pius IX. The intransigent Catholic attitude toward modern society, reflected in the Syllabus of Errors of 1864, was deeply imbued in him.[5]

Hence he attributed the class struggle to the modern "liberal" (in a nineteenth-century continental sense) or positivist denial of a world beyond that which meets the eye. Once the leading classes had embraced this outlook and even propagated it widely by secular education, it could only be expected that the laboring classes would embrace it too and demand that their needs be fulfilled here and now, at the expense of others—those who held property. In this

---

3. *Ad beatissimi apostolorum*, no. 23, of Nov. 1, 1914; texts of papal encyclicals can be found at http://www.vatican.va, or in Carlen (here 3:148).
4. The *imperitum vulgus* of Leo XIII; see *Ad beatissimi*, no. 15.
5. Pollard 1999, 48–51.

view, socialist agitation merely drew out the implications of bourgeois materialism. Perhaps more tellingly even than this "liberal" ideology, the socialist approach tapped the power of the truly ineradicable (because God-given) desire of the human heart for respect and set loose the discontented masses against the forces of order in the Western world. By the alacrity with which the nations went to war with one another, one could see what a sham was the oft-claimed modern ideal of brotherly love. This was what came of surrendering "Christian wisdom."[6] Therefore, the remedy for the social question was a recognition that true happiness lies beyond the grave, with a commitment to justice motivated by a truly universal love. Otherwise one must reckon with the end of civilization.

Given this diagnosis of the predicament of contemporary society, one might not expect Benedict XV to show any favor to the highly controversial Christian labor unions formed under Catholic auspices in Italy, Germany, and elsewhere. But he did. Evidently a strike, distressing as it was, was not *ipso facto* a declaration of war on society in Benedict's mind, and he did not judge collective bargaining to constitute an offense against freedom and property rights. To be sure, Catholic workers needed their own separate Christian unions, apart from the unions whose socialist leaders propagated false and unacceptable principles.[7] Christian unions deserved the backing of church leaders, he felt, as long as they upheld religion, the family, and private property rights while claiming the rights of workers.

At any rate, as Aubert notes, the new pope did not "share his predecessor's prejudices on the subject of trade unionism, giving frequent encouragement to the development of Christian unions and assuring their leaders that he was with them 'wholeheartedly,' while exhorting the clergy 'not to regard social action, for all its economic connotations, as foreign to the sacerdotal ministry.'"[8] He knew and trusted his fellow Genoese, Giambattista Valente, who had worked among Italian laborers in Germany on behalf of the Christian unions there.[9] He appointed him to be secretary of the national Catholic Economic-Social Union in 1916 and approved his plans for a trade union federation on the German model for Italy. He also took an active part in the rehabilitation of the abbés Jules Lemire and Paul Six in the north of France, two of the most prominent of the *abbés démocrates*.[10] The pressure was off as well at Catholic centers

6. *Ad beatissimi*, no. 5.
7. *AAS* 12 (1920): 109–12; see Pollard 1999, 179 for important details of this anti-communist *motu proprio*, published in the *Civiltà Cattolica* of Aug. 21, 1920, at the height of Italy's postwar "red biennium."
8. R. Aubert et al. 1978, 543–44; Pollard 1999, 177–78.
9. *DSMCI* 2:653; Valente 1978, 136, 142.
10. See Mayeur 1968, 533–37; Talmy 1966, 159–60.

of labor activism, such as the German Volksverein and the Action populaire of the French Jesuits.[11] Indeed, the pope sent the latter a gift in December of 1918 to help the team reconstitute itself in new quarters near Paris, in Vanves.

There was also a changing of the guard in the ranks of social Catholicism, much of it apparently normal generational turnover, but some caused by war wounds and effects. Léon Harmel and his emulator in industry across the German border, Franz Brandts, died in 1915 and 1914, respectively. Whereas Harmel had gone into a well-deserved retirement on the social front because of age and Pius X's support of paternalism, Brandts had remained as the chief lay patron of the German Volksverein until his death. Albert de Mun died in 1914, as did Henri Lorin of the *Semaines sociales*, two leading figures in two succeeding generations of French Catholicism; so did Charles Péguy, in the battle of the Marne. Other pillars of the movement passed away by 1918: in Switzerland, Kaspar Decurtins; in Belgium, Victor Brants, Godefroid Kurth, and Arthur Verhaegen; in Italy, Giuseppe Toniolo. The redoubtable abbé Henri Cetty of Mulhouse succumbed in 1918, concurrently with German rule of the Alsace.[12] In Germany, Georg von Hertling, the chancellor of the Reich in 1918, and Franz Hitze, the leading Sozialpolitiker of the Center Party, died shortly after the war. Its most prominent social Catholic victim there, however, the Center Party politician who engineered a rapprochement with the social democratic parliamentarians in 1917 and signed the armistice in 1918, was Matthias Erzberger, assassinated in 1921 by nationalist fanatics. Marc Sangnier lost several of his closest comrades in the war, and the philosopher of the Sillon, Léonard Constant, was killed in 1923, when he came to the aid of a young man being beaten in the streets of Mainz. Henri Bazire, former president of the Association catholique de la jeunesse française, was expected to be the next political leader of Catholics, a successor of de Mun; but he was gassed at Verdun in 1917 and died two years later. He was not the only member of that key leadership organization to be a victim of the senseless slaughter that Benedict XV deplored.

To set this new phase in the Catholic social movement in context, before getting into further narratives of the 1920s, it will help to examine some elements of the interwar European situation on the basis of decisions that fell in or near the year 1919. World War I could not pass over the Catholic world without profound effects. As Jean-Marie Mayeur notes, two-thirds of all Catholics lived in the belligerent nations, 124 million on the Allied side and 64 million

---

11. On the Volksverein, see E. Ritter 1954, 333; on the Action populaire, see Droulers 1969, 404, 419.

12. Consult Misner 1991, index, on these figures. On Cetty (1847–1918), who organized a set of exemplary social institutions in Mulhouse (Mülhausen) and propagated them in French organs, see *DMR* 2:91–92, as well as Mengus 1991.

in the German and Austro-Hungarian empires.[13] The pressures of mobilization in each warring nation had bolstered democratizing tendencies in public life. These met up with and reinforced the democratic trend that was by now at home in social Catholic movements.

The liberal ascendancy, one will recall, had kept two groups in particular at arm's length: the labor movement, with its socialist party representatives, and "the Catholic movement" (with its own modest but not negligible contingent of organized labor). Both now worked their way into a degree of participation in establishment affairs that neither had enjoyed before. Socialist and Catholic politicians advanced to cabinet positions and even premierships in several countries where only liberals (including conservatives and some radicals) had ruled previously. Now, however, after the war, there would be no fruits of victory to share among their constituencies. To speak only of the nations on the Western and Southern fronts, the war tore holes in every community, every family relationship, in France, Germany, Austria, Italy, Britain, and Belgium. The enormous squandering of accumulated capital also made for unforeseen hardships; every class felt keenly threatened by ruin and fought hard to participate in or retain the gains, now thrown to the winds, of the *belle époque*. The Paris Peace Conference was at the center of many new determinations. It created new boundaries, international organizations, financial allocations, and obligations, and implicitly set new standards for national labor relations.

Nationalism, Corporatism, and Working-Class Advancement

One of the phenomena noted in each of the belligerent countries during the war was a closing of the ranks behind the patriotic war effort. Rival factions of all types laid aside their quarrels and united for purposes of the war effort. Thus the Burgfriede in Germany and the union sacrée in France saw labor and capital, church people and secularists, Catholics and Protestants rising above the barriers that separated them and joining with one another in the common effort.[14] One consequence of this was an equalizing one: social and political discrimination decreased markedly, whether based on class, party allegiance, religion, or region, while prejudices based on nationality became *de rigueur* (and internally unifying). This nationalistic fervor induced many observers to hope for a lessening of class tensions to continue and form a broader base in support of a peacefully integrated country after the war. Of course, this was

---

13. Mayeur 1990, 305.
14. Ruppert 1993, 199–201; McMillan 1995.

connected with the expectation of military victory in each case. Even so, the shock was great at the end of 1918 as workers in socialist uprisings showed great hostility to the previously prevailing order, not only in Russia but in the Central Powers, and unrest under socialist banners became troublesome and continued even in the victorious countries. For churchmen, of course, the rise to power of Bolshevist communism in Russia—and the hostile character of the workers' soviets, which attempted takeovers elsewhere—merely served to confirm the direst predictions of what socialist rule would be like.

The responsible leaders of existing working-class organizations and parties had cooperated loyally throughout the war and were not quick to hail the call to revolution thereafter. Hence they expected to sit at the table where important political decisions were made.[15] In fact, in all the warring nations, precedents had been set for postwar bargaining among interest groups important to the national economy. "Ministries of munitions had developed into economic planning agencies.... They extensively regulated the labor market and the allocation of scarce raw materials. They co-opted private business in this task, sharing public powers to increase the scope of regulation." Labor benefitted, relatively speaking, from this enforced cooperation of government, business, and trade unions. "Although wartime controls were not retained, the 1920s did not simply revert to the degree of market freedom prevailing before 1914."[16] Labor-management bodies were officially set up right after the war as a sort of peacetime version of these cooperative arrangements: *commissions paritaires* in France, Belgium, and the Netherlands and the "Central Partnership" or ZAG (Zentralarbeitsgemeinschaft) of November 1918 in Germany.[17] Because of the importance for future developments of the ZAG and its reflection of postwar vicissitudes in political economy, it is worthwhile to sketch here its origins and character.[18]

The armistice meeting in the railway cars near Compiègne on November 8–11, 1918, where the Catholic politician Matthias Erzberger represented the German parliament, took place against the background of mutinies in northern German ports and a revolt in Bavaria that led to the king's abdication. On November 9 the Republic of Germany was declared and the abdication of Kaiser Wilhelm was announced in Berlin. Worker-soldier "soviets" started to form in major cities the same day. The Majority Socialists, as the social democrats were called at this juncture, rushed into the power vacuum, with Friedrich Ebert, the future president of the Weimar Republic, as the central figure and

15. Nocken 1978, 45.
16. Maier 1975, 580–81.
17. On the *commissions paritaires*, see Kossmann 1978, 652, and Gribling 1978, 213–15.
18. See Feldman 1993, 106–10; Launay 1990, 195–97.

with left-liberal and Center Party support. The troops were starting to come home as fast as they could. War contracts that had kept factories going were dissolving. Local "councils of workers and soldiers" came together in many places under the communist banner. Sometimes they led to further revolts, and everywhere they appeared threatening to the bourgeoisie. The Allies occupied territory west of the Rhine and maintained a blockade of food and supplies until compliance with armistice demands was assured to their satisfaction. In these circumstances labor and industry spokesmen in Berlin who had dealt with each other during the war moved quickly—by November 15—to sign what was to become known as the Stinnes-Legien Agreement. (Hugo Stinnes was a leading Ruhr industrialist, and Carl Legien was the head of the national federation of socialist unions, called the Free Unions.) Adam Stegerwald of the Christian trade unions was also a signatory, having been intimately involved in working out the agreement.

The first point of the agreement was, "The trade unions are recognized as the competent representation of the workforce."[19] It thus called for continuing labor-management negotiation and cooperation; it provided for an *Arbeitsgemeinschaft*, literally a "collaborative" structure (or what might be called a "joint action committee") of union and industry representatives to carry this out during the demobilization and in the future. What came of this was known as the ZAG (in English, by Balderston, as the "Central Cooperating Partnership between Business and Labor").[20] It was based on labor-management parity and provided a forum for the discussion and negotiation of all economic and social questions affecting Germany industry. Subgroups would do the same for particular branches of industry. In the meantime, the industrialists acceded to certain longstanding wishes of the labor movement in return for immediate measures to cope with the problems of demobilization. In the former category were notable concessions: "recognition of unions, mandatory collective bargaining and wage contracts, worker committees in every plant with over fifty employees, the termination of employer support for yellow unions, and"—of greatest symbolic and immediate practical impact—"the introduction of the eight-hour day without any reduction in pay."[21] As shall be apparent, this agreement fell victim to the greater clout of the manufacturers even before its final burial with the Ruhr crisis of 1923.[22] Its provisions remained a symbolic goal of Catholic and other social policy shapers, however, and were partially restored after 1925.

The significance of this episode is brought out in view of analogous "corporatist" structures that revived in the later twenties and in the Great Depression

19. Schneider 1989, 426.
20. Balderston 2002, 5.
21. Feldman 1993, 107.
22. Schneider 1989, 426.

and the variations of social partnership that came to the fore in Western Europe with the more prosperous period after World War II. A terminological clarification in respect to the often ill-defined concept of corporatism will be of some help in understanding many trends and positions encountered in the history of social Catholicism. Philippe C. Schmitter has outlined a usable typology of the era's alternatives in political economy by first distinguishing and contrasting a pluralist from a corporatist political economy and then comparing "state corporatism" and "societal corporatism."[23]

The issue is how societies would institutionalize the representation of interests. Early liberal theory would have it that individuals negotiate and contract with each other to work out deals satisfying the greatest good of the greatest number. They organize themselves into a state, entrusting coercive means of keeping order to representatives elected by individuals deemed responsible members of society. The public realm would simply be that of state affairs, whereas all the other connections of civil society would be "private"—that is, dependent on the relationships freely entered into by individual citizens. As became apparent, however, people had interests that were not just those of individuals, but of groups and classes, especially under the influence of industrial capitalism.

To deal with such group interests, the approach here called *pluralism*, predominant in the Anglo-Saxon world, encouraged private associations of like-minded individuals. These came to represent group interests more effectively in civil society and, for instance, as trade associations or lobbying organizations, with the legislature and the bureaucracy of the state. The earliest exemplars of social Catholicism in the nineteenth century welcomed such an associationist orientation, as opposed to the unmitigated individualism of liberal ideology (think of Tocqueville in America). But there was also a strain of hankering for a restoration of the guilds, which would predispose social Catholics to lean toward corporatist arrangements.

The ideal type of corporatism constructed by Schmitter is nevertheless quite distinct from nostalgic dreams of preindustrial corporatism. Qua the system of interest representation in the twentieth century, *corporatism* is an alternative to pluralism, distinguished from it by several characteristics. A corporatist model supposes a relatively limited number of organized interest groups accredited to or by the government, representing the whole of a given segment of civil society (e.g., as previously, in the ZAG, the whole of heavy industry and the whole of its labor force). Unorganized or rival elements in their category simply go unrepresented or are represented by default; competition

23. Schmitter 1974.

of different groups within the category is excluded. On the other hand, no one belonging to the category may be excluded from the corporation that represents it; indeed, membership is virtually or legally automatic.

Thus far, the ideal type of corporatism is clearly differentiated from the paradigm of pluralism, but becomes a much more useful descriptive tool when its two main subtypes are distinguished: societal corporatism and state corporatism.[24] The difference can be summed up in a question. Do the corporatist organs determine their own policies and press them upon the state, or does the state create or suborn the organs of interest representation and subject them to its ends? In the first case the corporatism in question is of the societal subtype and in the second of the state subtype. One may note: the reason that the concept of corporatism (and its cognate in the Roman Catholic vocabulary in some languages, vocational order) went out of circulation after World War II was its incriminating association with authoritarian (Salazar's Portugal, Dollfuss's Austria) and fascist regimes. It was identified with the subtype of state corporatism.[25] The reason Schmitter and others brought the term back into circulation in a descriptive rather than pejorative sense was the need to label the distinctive character of post–World War II economies of Western European countries, the "Rhenish" or "Rhineland model." In several advanced industrial social states in Western Europe, the realities of public life and the way interest representation in fact functions have conformed much more closely to the model of societal corporatism than to the model of Anglo-Saxon pluralism.[26] Thomas Piketty refers to the "stakeholder model" of "Rhenish capitalism" in contrast to the "shareholder model" of Anglo-Saxon capitalism.[27]

If one surveys the previous history of social Catholicism and casts it in these terms, then the regimes in France and Belgium up to the 1850s were so liberal ("atomistic," in the judgment of its critics) as to be almost pre-pluralist; thereafter they became more pluralist. In German lands a sort of premodern

---

24. Ibid., 102–5.

25. See Giblin 1994a. One can spot the terminological aversion—e.g., in the 1942 Christian democratic Manifesto on the War, entitled, "In Face of the World's Crisis," *Commonweal* 36 (Aug. 21, 1942): 418: "Economic groups and the forces of labor especially have not found in modern institutions a proper representation nor means of expression proportionate to their importance and suited to their functions in the community. But it is not in the dictatorship of some corporatism, or of some state paternalism, that the answer will be found."

26. As distinct from the pluralist approach, in Western Europe the economic or social partners (business interests and representatives of labor), in consultation with a third party, the state, hash out important issues and policies with one another in an institutionalized set of forums. Such practices are referred to variously as a "social market economy" or Rhineland model, "policy concertation" or "consultation economy," or the "polder model" of the Netherlands; see, e.g., Berger and Compston 2002; Dyson and Padgett 2006; and Davids, Devos, and Pasture 2007.

27. Piketty 2014, 145–46.

state corporatism prevailed until the 1848 revolutions; thereafter a mixed system of the traditional system with pluralism developed.[28] With World War I, in all the warring countries, an emergency system of state corporatism superimposed itself on the pluralism that had prevailed. Thereafter it was dismantled again, but some degree of representation of the working class was retained. In some measure an upsurge of societal corporatism rushed into the vacuum of state power from 1918 to about 1921. Thereafter no one system of interest representation predominated until the onset of fascist or analogous authoritarian rule. Most Catholic theorists would lean toward a system of societal corporatism, but without great emphasis or conceptual agreement on some critical particulars. Often enough they were at home in the prevailing pluralism; they inclined against it in theory because of its liberal-individualist theoretical base and its rejection of the Christendom ideal while welcoming it in practice because of their apprehensions about untrammeled secular power.

In any case, the goal envisioned across most of social Catholic thinking was nicely caught by Henry Somerville.[29] Speaking of the embryonic moves toward industrial organization in Holland, he observed, "They represent progress to the ideal of industries organized for self-regulation instead of being regulated by the state and instead of being left to unrestricted capitalism."

In strictly political terms, for both Catholic and socialist candidates, World War I marked the threshold to becoming "contenders," by which I mean influential participants in the parliaments and cabinets.[30] They now took their place alongside the liberal politicians of more conservative or progressive leanings, who had conducted affairs up until then representing the *classes dirigeantes*. For Catholic labor forces this was a double emancipation occurring simultaneously. Both as supporters of a party of Catholics and as supporters of the more democratic left wing within it, they could now for the first time see their representatives in parliaments and cabinets taking an important, sometimes a leading role in the government of the nation.

A series of qualifications must be made to do justice to the complexity of the situation without nullifying the foregoing.[31] Of course there had been some socialist and Catholic members of parliament, even in Italy, where the Vatican had frowned on Catholic participation in national elections since the 1870s (the so-called *non expedit* policy). French Catholic members of parliament were spread over a number of parties or were effectively independents. In Belgium there was a Catholic Party that had actually been in power continuously since the elections of 1884—a unique case. It was a party of notables, however,

---

28. See Nocken 1978, 42; see also Crouch 1993, 295–311.
29. Somerville 1933, 103. 30. Durand 1995, 175–214.
31. Evans 1999, 143–230.

until some cabinet officers from the Christian democratic wing of the party had to be admitted from 1907 on. Now, after World War I, they were still in government, but not by themselves a majority.

In the Netherlands the Anti-Revolutionary Party of Dutch neo-Calvinists was formed before a specifically Catholic party. This latter, once formed, represented about a quarter of the voting population and entered into coalitions with the more powerful party of the Protestants from the end of the nineteenth century on.[32] The end of World War I (during which the Netherlands remained neutral) coincided with a "religious truce" (*Godsvrede*) between the parties, liberal and socialist, Catholic and Protestant. By its terms the government would support Protestant and Catholic schools with state aid equivalent to what public schools received, on the one hand, and pass labor legislation, in particular regulating the length of the workday, on the other. With this the Dutch found an early and durable solution to the issue of public versus religious schooling, a problem of cultural policy that continued to bedevil many other countries for a long time. Proportional representation with obligatory universal suffrage, including women, in the elections of 1918 resulted in a coalition government with, for the first but not the last time, a Roman Catholic prime minister, C. J. M. Ruijs de Beerenbrouck, and a Catholic lawyer, Petrus Aalberse, as the first minister of labor.[33]

What accounts for such political shifts and breakthroughs were not merely the wartime spirit and its subsequent disillusionment, but electoral reforms introduced widely during and after the war, combined with the underlying numerical strength of the socialist and Catholic electorates. Universal suffrage favored parties that appealed to the popular classes; suffrage for women helped, too, as it was introduced. The system of proportional representation (as opposed to winner-take-all elections with one deputy elected from each district) was definitely a plus for moderate parties who sought the center of the political spectrum.[34] With proportional representation, as refined particularly by Belgians, each electoral district would be large enough to elect several members of parliament, chosen according to an arrangement that would assure that no considerable body of voters would be unrepresented, even if it rarely or never constituted a plurality or majority in any one district. Thus the new Italian Popular Party won about a fifth of the votes and a fifth of the seats in the national assembly—not enough to form a government or name a prime minister, but enough to be reckoned with by any party that wished to do so. In the Weimar Republic, where Catholics were around one-third of the population, the Center

32. Mayeur 1980, 75–81; see Kossmann 1978, 715–20.
33. Brachin and Rogier 1974, 140–42.
34. Mayeur 1980, 106.

Party also commanded about a fifth of the vote total and got a fifth of the seats; their support was indispensable to every government coalition.

In Austria and Germany, in fact, Catholic parliamentarians and their constituencies came to the fore in the aftermath of the defeat and debacle of 1918, as in 1848, and as would be the case again in 1945—dramatically so. True, in the ranks of the German Center Party there had been enough collusion with and support for the prevailing policies of the Kaiserreich to make its war record a two-edged sword. At the bitter end of the conflict, a Catholic Center Party leader, Ludwig von Hertling, temporarily became a German chancellor, taking the highest political office of the Reich for the first time, and Matthias Erzberger's signing of the armistice was held against him and his party for a whole generation.[35] But Catholics, as good as unrepresented in the establishment that got Germany into the war, and the Center Party, with its modicum of labor representation tempering its basically bourgeois and agrarian makeup, felt no special responsibility for that establishment's failures. There was a feeling, as among the socialists, that their time had come. Even the lack of brilliant intellectuals, under which prewar Catholicism labored, with its all too evident *Bildungsdefizit*, seemed now to be lifting: had not one of the foremost philosophers of German academia, Max Scheler (1874–1928), embraced the faith? A spectacular convert, he lost no time working out the implications of Catholic thought for social and cultural philosophy and for "the mission of Germany."[36]

In Austria, the little Austria that the peace treaties left, the Christian-Social Party represented a camp just about as large as that of the Socialists, both trailed by more or less discredited liberal and nationalist groupings. "Red Vienna" was balanced by conservative strength in other districts. Ignaz Seipel, a priest-professor, adviser to the last emperor, quickly cast his lot in with the Republic and was elected to the legislature in February 1919 as the Socialists garnered a slim lead for a year. Soon he became undisputed leader of the party and, in 1922, chancellor.[37] In this respect, being a dominant party (one of only two), the Christian-Socials in the Austrian First Republic were quite differently situated than the Center Party in Weimar Germany.

The breakup of Austro-Hungary led to the organization of Christian social parties in several of the successor states.[38] But of more consequence for the development of social Catholicism in Western Europe were some coincidental

---

35. Erzberger remained a target the following year, when he supported acceptance of the one-sided Versailles Treaty—Erzberger, "who had led negotiations and who was a strong advocate of signing; prophetically, [Count Harry] Kessler predicted the minister would meet the same fate as Karl Liebknecht, who had been murdered a few months earlier"; McElligott 2014, 43.

36. See Scheler 1918; Lutz 1962, 26–47.   37. Wohnout 2004; Boyer 2005, 10–14.

38. Mayeur 1980, 141–43.

effects in Italy and France of the territorial acquisitions that the war brought them. Curiously enough, with the addition to Italy of South Tyrol and the Trentino, previously part of Austria, seasoned politicians (Alcide De Gasperi being the most notable) and a sort of party machine from the new provinces were prepared to ally themselves with the new Italian Popular Party of Luigi Sturzo, adding to its parliamentary clout.[39] In France, too, there was now a different kind of Catholic politician coming to Paris from Alsace and Lorraine, with experience and grassroots resources built up on the German Center Party model. The French democratic party "of Christian inspiration" benefitted from these recruits once it was finally organized in 1924.[40] In 1919 Marc Sangnier, the best-known activist because controversial, declined to take the lead in this direction, even though he enjoyed Benedict XV's confidence.[41] Perhaps one could say that he was unwilling to take up partisan stands against socialist workers' parties, just as he was opposed to the demonizing of Germany. In any case, most French Catholics continued to support parties to the right of such progressives.

Peace? Or Victors and Vanquished?

In contrast to the increased influence that Catholics gained in the national parliaments, there was next to no participation of interested Catholic figures in the tight little world of the victors' diplomacy in Paris.[42] The Vatican itself—at that point not a state, though maintaining diplomatic relations with an increasing number of countries—had been excluded by a prior agreement between Britain and Italy, when Italy decided to enter the conflict on the side of the West. Even Belgium, which had suffered the most from the German occupation, had to make its claims as best it could from the margins of the peace conference. Paris was nevertheless the focal point of internationalists' hopes until punitive treaties were forced on defeated Germany and Austria. Both were excluded from the League of Nations.

The idea of disarmament, of outlawing war and settling international disputes by negotiation, had been around especially since the 1890s in some radi-

---

39. See Canavero 1985; Vecchio 1987b; Campanini 1981, 2:157–68.

40. Although no Christian democratic party could be formed at the national level in France until 1924, the Catholic politicians in the region reannexed from Germany formed a regional party in 1919 and called it the Union populaire républicaine; see Baechler 1982, 239–57. They joined the new Parti démocrate populaire in 1924. In 1919, a number of decidedly Catholic deputies were elected as republicans, but not grouped in a particular party; see Paul 1967, 35–36. They included several Christian democrats—e.g., Marc Sangnier and Adéodat Boissard.

41. See Misner 1991, 300; Barthélemy-Madaule 1973, 231–36.

42. See MacMillan 2002.

cal and leftist circles. Catholics, however, not unlike the generality of Europeans, were few in the peace movement of the time. Suspected of being disloyal citizens for different but equally plausible reasons in both Germany and France, they were not inclined to provide pretexts to anti-clericals of any stripe to attack them for lack of patriotism.[43] Nor did their outlook induce them to favor the secular utopian worldview of those who dreamed of a world without war. As we have seen, in Germany and France they fell into line with practically all their fellow citizens in endorsing the justice of their nation's cause when war broke out, to the dismay of neutral onlookers. One of the latter was Pope Benedict XV (1914–22). From his inaugural encyclical, *Ad beatissimi*, on November 1, 1914, he took a negative view of the war as catastrophic in human terms and not at all a lesser evil in comparison with the possible alternatives. Though stopping short of calling for a unilateral surrender on either side, he did call insistently for a quick armistice and restitution of territory pending further negotiations.

Given the awkward situation of the pope vis-à-vis the Italian state, he was restrained in his pronouncements about Italy's entrance into the war in 1915, which he regretted.[44] But he kept up his efforts to bring the parties to the peace table.[45] In 1917, after the United States declared war on Germany, after Erzberger's peace resolution had been adopted by the Reichstag, and after a flurry of other peace feelers at the highest levels, Benedict XV tried to sum up and encourage the momentum. As recently as the beginning of 1917, President Woodrow Wilson himself had been calling for "a peace without victory." Hoping that the time had finally come for the war psychology to recede, the pope sent a diplomatic note "to the leaders of the belligerent nations," in which he moved beyond generalities to make several specific peace proposals that could serve as a basis for a cessation of hostilities.[46] The presupposition on all sides would have to be, he insisted, that the moral rule of right regain its role from the rule of sheer armed might, meaning that countries would consent to abide by the results of arbitration according to modalities and sanctions for noncompliance to be agreed upon. The central paragraphs laid out a way to a prompt armistice, but beyond that, to "a just and lasting peace."[47]

---

43. See, e.g., McMillan 1995.

44. On the old Roman question, see D'Agostino 2004, 53–57, 103–31.

45. These efforts ran parallel to those of a Lutheran prince of the church in neutral Sweden, Nathan Söderblom; see Lindt 1981, 39. In those early days of ecumenism, no one thought that there could be any cooperation between the two church leaders; their activities never intersected but ran on parallel and separate tracks.

46. Benedict XV, "Dès le début," note of Aug. 1, 1917, to the leaders of the belligerent nations, *AAS* 9 (1917): 417–20.

47. Pollard 1999, 123–28; text in Eppstein 1935, 217.

Let all obstacles to the free intercourse of people be swept away, in assuring by means of rules, to be fixed [through the instrumentality of a League of Nations], the true liberty of and common rights over the sea....

As to the damage to be made good and the cost of the war, We see no other way of solving the question but to lay down, as a general principle, an entire and reciprocal condonation, justified moreover by the immense benefits which will accrue from disarmament—the more so as the continuation of such carnage solely for economic reasons would be inconceivable. If in certain cases there are, on the other hand, particular reasons, let them be weighed justly and equitably.

But these peaceful agreements, with the immense advantages which flow from them, are not possible without the reciprocal restitution of territories at the moment occupied—consequently, on the part of Germany, a total evacuation of Belgium, with a guarantee of her complete political, military, and economic independence, as against any other Power whatever; similar evacuation of French territory; on the part of other belligerent Powers a similar restitution of the German Colonies.

As regards territorial questions—as, for instance, those pending between Italy and Austria, and between Germany and France—there is ground for hope that in view of the immense advantages of a permanent peace with disarmament, the disputants would feel disposed to examine them in a conciliatory spirit, giving due weight, within the limits of justice and feasibility, as We have said previously, to the aspirations of the populations, and, as occasion warrants, bringing their particular interests into harmony with the general welfare of the great community of mankind.

The most concrete place to start, if this appeal was to bear fruit, was directed to Germany, to indicate its willingness to return Belgium's independence, and then to Austria, to show movement on the issue of one of the territories Italy wanted. There was, tragically, not enough give in the positions assumed by the warring nations to permit them to draw back. Public opinion, still or again misled by maximalist ideas of how advantageously the war would turn out, was uniformly dismissive of the pope's proposals.[48] He had said of the war that it was increasingly evident that it was "useless slaughter"; patriots were still unwilling to hear it and governments decried it as engendering defeatism.

A celebrated instance occurred in Paris, December 10, 1917, in the church of the Madeleine, during a patriotic and religious service presided over by Cardinal Amette. The esteemed Dominican intellectual Antonin-Gilbert Sertillanges declared publicly, "Holy Father, we cannot for a moment go along with your appeals for peace." A "peace of conciliation" would simply not do; reparations, guarantees, the restitution of Alsace-Lorraine were nonnegotiable. The peace required was "a peace of power crushing violence, the peace of the soldier."[49] Sertillanges was subsequently censured for his expostulation by his

48. See Baadte 1985, 101–5.
49. Mayeur 1990, 311; 1993.

ecclesiastical superiors, but there is no question but that at the time he spoke as a tribune of the French people and with the approval of Amette. Among the Allied peoples, Benedict XV was written off as sympathetic to the Central Powers. Within Germany and Austro-Hungary, too, the pope had few admirers left.

After the war, particularly in his 1920 encyclical, *Pacem*, Benedict XV endorsed the Wilsonian idea of the League of Nations with its mission of reducing the need for armaments and armed conflict.[50] He obviously could not express a great deal of satisfaction for the other products of Versailles, inasmuch as the peace treaties did not try to weed out "the seeds of ancient discords." Instead, the economic consequences of the war were only aggravated by "the economic consequences of the peace," in the words of J. M. Keynes's famous 1920 book title. But the two peacemakers met in an unprecedented New Year's visit of the president to the pope (January 4, 1919).[51] Just before, on December 1, 1918, Benedict issued a mini-encyclical, *Quod iam diu*, asking for prayers for the peace conference that would shortly get under way.[52] It was an early sign of a Catholic peace movement that a significant number of Catholics did respond very positively to the proposals of an American president, the Presbyterian Woodrow Wilson.[53]

In Germany, the "Christian democrats" or social Catholics naturally belonged to the Center Party, but did not predominate. One of them, Matthias Erzberger, the Swabian journalist and former secretary to the Catholic workers' associations of Württemberg, had been a member of parliament since 1903 and a quite contentious one, given to mud-raking in his journalistic and parliamentary endeavors and always a champion of the masses and the Catholic minority.[54] This limited his influence in the upper strata of party and society; but the Great War opened up unprecedented tasks and responsibilities to this son of a tailor, who had only the minimal formal education, not at a university, of a primary school teacher. First he was called upon to organize a propaganda effort among neutral powers, among which he counted the papacy. By July 1917, perhaps knowing of the imminent papal note, he was thoroughly convinced that the self-deluding propaganda within Germany itself was counterproductive. He introduced the famous peace resolution that forced the issue of German war aims out into the open, at least in parliament; it called on the government to relinquish claims to Belgium and all other territorial annexations. This had tre-

50. Vecchio 1987a, 273–76. For the encyclical *Pacem*, see Carlen, 3:171–75.
51. See Peters 1959, 165.
52. Carlen, 3:161.
53. The signals that the Vatican saw real promise in Wilson's peace proposals are strong. Though they emanated from a source—Protestant and American, not traditional—unlikely to impress its writers, the *Osservatore Romano* pointed up the just and humanitarian nature of the Fourteen Points on several occasions in 1918; see Bressan 1990, 233 and 239; see also Musto 1986.
54. See Epstein 1959, 11; see also Morsey 1973.

mendous indirect consequences. It edged the parliament of the Reich closer to claiming the authority to set policy rather than simply serve as a funding mechanism. It set in motion the supremacy of the civil government over the military, which, true enough, was only acknowledged in the defeat of November 1918 and the forced abdication of Kaiser Wilhelm. For the first time it brought socialists (the Majority Socialists, to be exact) into a coalition with some national liberals and with centrists, the very coalition that was to shape and support the constitution of the Weimar Republic.

Erzberger's initiative in taking this step and dealing with its consequences also made him a marked man, accused of defeatism and later on, after the war, of having stabbed the fatherland in the back ("the *Dolchstoss-Legende*"). This was only reinforced when he accepted the thankless assignment of leading the delegation to the front on November 8–11, 1918, to sign what could, at that point, only be an ignominious armistice. As with his stands for the previous year or two, however, this was a matter of facing the facts and choosing the lesser of two evils. Germany stood at the crossroads between either abject surrender or actually being invaded and split up into weaker, defenseless states.

Then he hastened back to a Berlin in the hands of communist workers' soviets and pushed for quick elections to a constituent assembly, elections held under a government of "people's commissars" headed by Friedrich Ebert. The elections resulted in a substantial reflux to the bourgeois parties, including the Center Party. Catholics and Protestants were repelled by the zeal with which the socialists, who were in power in the states and in Berlin since the onset of the November revolution, had pushed to eliminate the influence of the churches from public life and from education.[55] Erzberger's prominence only increased, and his inborn optimism and ambition to assume responsibility led him to undertake further disagreeable tasks for which no one else had the stomach. In 1919 he was vice chancellor of the new republic and finance minister in a coalition government led by Gustav Bauer under the presidency of Ebert, the Majority Socialist leaders. The state of the exchequer was naturally catastrophic; Erzberger rammed through tax after tax, with something of a "soak-the-rich" character, arguing that the only Germans to have profited by the war should now pay as much as they could to foot the bill for the defeat. In the process he put the finances of the republic on a new basis, independent of its constituent states. This was the crowning achievement of his foreshortened career as a public servant. It made possible the financing of a modest democratic welfare state. He made good use of the solidarism of the then-current state of Catholic social teaching to guide the tax plan that he put forward.[56]

55. Hürten 1992, 55–56.
56. See Witt 2004, esp. 23: 217–18.

The humiliations of defeat were far from over, however. Matthias Erzberger had propagated the idea of a "peace of conciliation," a *Verständigungsfrieden*. His book on a Völkerbund, a League of Nations of the future, came out even before the war ended, in September 1918,[57] the same month the cooperating parties of the Reichstag pushed through a resolution endorsing such a forum of international arbitration. He continued to feed the Vatican information about the unrest and deprivations in Germany after the armistice. He had an understandable interest in keeping papal fear of anarchy and Bolshevist revolution alive, with a view to influencing delegates in Paris favorable to "Wilson's Fourteen Points as a basis of peace rather than the more severe demands of the French."[58] It fit in with the defensive strategy that Germany needed between the armistice and the peace conference. When Clemenceau and the Allies pushed through a punitive peace treaty, Erzberger persuaded the Center Party once more to act in a responsible manner. It entered a minority government with the social democrats as its only partner and reluctantly yielded to *force majeure*, ratifying the "brutal" Versailles treaty in mid-1919.[59]

Political Reform, Mass Politics, and Popularist Parties

Another aspect of the postwar scene conditioning social Catholicism in a new way was an evolution in continental political Catholicism. It not only regrouped in the form of Catholic parties in the prewar mold, but took on the form of mass parties, popular parties, predominantly democratic in character while insistently nonconfessional in the sense of not answering to church authorities. These parties inscribed social justice prominently on their manifestos in the tradition of the first and second movements of Christian democracy and of *Rerum novarum*.[60] They appealed to a broad Christian inspiration in setting their political line.[61] But as political parties claiming only the mandate of their voters in the temporal affairs of the commonwealth, not any commission from the church as such, they encountered difficulties in choosing their names. "Popularist" seems the label most apt to evoke this stage of their history, after the *popolari* in Italy.

After all, the Italian Popular Party presents the main instance of this new paradigm; it was the most original political formation of Catholics in the situation of 1919. Despite its short life, its example was to be an inspiration for other

---

57. Epstein 1959, 250–56.
58. Stehlin 1983, 46.
59. See Weitz 2007, 33–37; Morsey 1966, 180–95; 1988, 119.
60. On Christian democracy, see Misner 1991, 80–90 and 222–61.
61. See Mayeur 1980, 149–50.

Christian democratic parties, particularly after World War II.[62] Some sort of fresh start was sorely needed then in Italy, as the political abstention of Catholics in force since the 1870 taking of Rome was obviously counterproductive and had been increasingly hollowed out even under Pope Pius X (1903–14). In different circumstances or under different leadership, it might have taken the form of a conservative party of order, putting Catholic notables up for election on a program indistinguishable from their liberal-conservative cousins, except possibly for a plank about support of Catholic schools and the like. But several factors made the time ripe for a bolder new departure.

One element was the whole complex of events during the war that had raised the consciousness of the popular classes. With universal suffrage one had to break with old-style politics and appeal to the interests of the peasants and working classes. Another factor was the spread and vigor of a whole array of Catholic social organizations: credit unions tied into larger regional banks, agrarian and other trade unions, mutual-assistance programs, daily and weekly newspapers supporting Christian democratic proposals. Pope Benedict XV, unlike Pius X, did not sense insubordination in such activities and gave them his blessing.

Finally—and critically for the quality of the new political movement that was undertaken in 1919—was the presence of a figure of considerable experience and stature who had long reflected upon the political contours that a party of social Catholic inspiration should take in Italy: the priest Luigi Sturzo. Sturzo had already laid out his vision of what was necessary for the political well-being of the Italian nation in 1905.[63] He saw two blocs contending in the Italian political arena, the "liberal-conservatives" or bourgeois on the one hand and the socialists on the other. The former were grouped in several political parties, with little grassroots organization. The latter, divided into more and less radical orientations, served as the voice and anticlerical educators of the proletariat on the land and in the cities. What was missing was a democratic party for which Catholics could vote, one that would organize the lower-class part of the electorate that was currently unrepresented, the ones already partially organized in the Catholic movement.

Why not call it then a "Christian democratic" party? The term had been much bruited about and had even been the object of a papal clarification, *Graves de communi*, in 1901. Talk of "Christian democracy" generally implied a movement of church reform as well as societal or political reform.[64] Sturzo wanted to keep a clear separation between these two areas of reform. With such a distinction he would claim complete freedom and responsibility for the party's

---

62. Ibid., 109–17.
64. See Misner 1991, index, s.v. Murri.

63. See Misner 1991, 249–52.

political program, reform of the state and of government, while leaving all decisions concerning the interests of the Roman Catholic Church to the pope and hierarchy. So when it came time actually to name the party, Sturzo pointed to the name of the party that had operated in the formerly Austrian provinces and proposed the term "popular" for its distinctive name.[65] The Italian Popular Party (PPI, Partito popolare italiano) would not be "clerical," even though it had a priest for its political secretary and therefore, in actuality, at its head. It would be a secular party—"aconfessional" was the term, which Sturzo probably adapted from controversies about the German Christian unions—with a purely political program, leaving to the organizations of Catholic Action under the guidance of the hierarchy the cause of reforming society religiously.[66] In 1919 the accent was emphatically on the further democratization of political institutions in Italy and particularly in making the parliament an effective representation of the nation. Thus the party called for women's suffrage and proportional representation and counted on the universal manhood suffrage already in place to boost its electoral prospects.

Put to the test of elections, the PPI garnered 20 percent of the vote in November 1919, as has been noted. It continued to press for the causes enumerated in its founding documents.[67] Most of these were characteristic ideals of Christian democrats throughout Europe since the 1890s: they wanted to substitute for "the centralizing state, with its tendency to limit and police every organic power and every civic and individual activity, a truly popular state that keeps within its own limits, that respects the natural cells and organisms [of society]—the family, ways of life, local governments—that respects individual personality and encourages private initiatives." It insisted on religious freedom for individuals and also for the church, in particular freedom of education instead of a government monopoly, freedom of class organizations (of farm workers and other workers, of farmers and proprietors), without manipulation or discrimination on the part of officeholders, and freedom of local municipalities and regions (decentralization). It was very much in the mold of what we would today call liberal democracy with a developed social consciousness. (However, the terms "liberal" and "democracy" did not yet go together quite naturally in continental politics.)

Drawn up as it was during the Paris peace conference, the "Appeal to the Country" (addressed "to all persons free and strong," *tutti i liberi e forti*) endorsed the peace proposals made by Pope Benedict XV (without mentioning his name), and then by President Wilson of the United States (named). It supported

65. De Rosa's foreword in Sturzo 1992, xiii, or De Rosa 1979, 9.
66. See Molony 1977, 46–51.
67. Sturzo 1992, 39–44.

a "society of nations" that would acknowledge "legitimate national aspirations" and set up "international standards for social legislation, the equality of labor, and religious liberties against any sectarian oppression." Such a League of Nations should have the resources "to defend the rights of weak nations against the excesses of strong ones."

Its social program called for a sustained literacy campaign and economic development measures and mentioned that "urgent reforms" were necessary to raise the standard of living of the working classes—reforms "in the field of insurance and social assistance, in labor legislation, [and] in the encouragement of small holdings." All this made the PPI a party with its own contours and platform, easily distinguishable from its main rivals. These did not yet include fascism, whose ultra-nationalism and readiness to resort to violence would of course be repugnant to the PPI ideals; rather, they were the two ideologies against which social Catholicism had always defined itself: liberalism, here described as those "old sectarian liberalisms that employ the centralized state organism to resist new emancipatory currents," and socialism with its two faces, "anarchic upheavals of great fallen empires" in the communist version or "socialist democracies that attempt to reduce every ideal to the material level."[68]

In the middle of June 1919 the first party congress was held in Bologna in the midst of one of those waves of unrest that punctuated postwar Italy. The older and more bourgeois delegates wondered whether the congress could be held at all, with the city more or less strikebound, and if attempted, whether it could agree on anything, but the enthusiasm of the younger and less experienced seemed to carry it off.[69] Already the PPI had local committees operating in many

---

68. Some comparisons with the German situation may be noted—e.g., the Center Party stated the following in its hastily drawn up election platform of Dec. 30, 1918 (in Morsey 1988, 113): with the fall of the monarchy, a new form of government must be erected; it must be "not a socialistic republic, but a democratic republic" (democratic, i.e., not discriminating on the basis of property, education, religion or social status, as was the wont of those who styled themselves "liberal" or liberal-conservative). The platform also endorsed the Wilsonian idea of a League of Nations with arbitration powers (see Baadte 1985, 108).

To measure how great a leap was the German Catholic acceptance of even a democratic republic (instead of the monarchy), the letter of the German bishops of November 1, 1917, is enlightening. A broadening of the franchise in Prussia was in prospect; the bishops opposed this, fearing it would favor the socialists and endanger the legal standing of the church by separating church and state, as in France in 1905. They emphatically rejected the principle of sovereignty of the people (Morsey 1988, 101), declaring their adherence to the principle of monarchical authority. "The war has not loosened the old holy covenant between people and prince in Germany," they asserted, quite validly. "We were deeply indignant that one would offer us peace" as Wilson did, only on condition that "we were willing to play Judas in disloyalty and treason to the Kaiser" (102; see also Baadte 1985, 94). After the Kaiser fled and found sanctuary in the neutral Netherlands, of course, Catholic politicians helped construct the Weimar Republic. But some of the bishops, notably Michael Faulhaber, continued to regard the republic as an un-German mistake, a kind of contamination from the West.

69. De Rosa 1979, 23–26.

cities in Italy, especially in the north, where Catholic *opere* (associations, credit unions) were numerous and well-established. Prominent at the congress were Catholic labor leaders with their ideas on agrarian reform, backing up Sturzo's line.[70] Guido Miglioli, the populist farm-workers' leader from Cremona, was a strong but very left-wing supporter of peasants' rights ("the land to the peasants!" had been his cry since the end of the war). Achille Grandi, the head of a textile-workers' union, had worked from age eleven to twenty-four as a typographer until a job-connected disability forced him out. He gave the scheduled report on economic policy and presented motions that the congress, after debate and amendments, accepted by a large majority. His firm but moderate stance on labor issues remained a characteristic of the Popular Party and its emulators.

Grandi was by now a delegate of the Catholic labor movement, organized as a federation of unions the previous year.[71] The CIL (Confederazione italiana dei lavoratori or Italian confederation of workers, as it was called) was another product of the social Catholicism of the prewar years come to fruition at the end of the war. Given the explosive growth of these "white leagues" and unions at this time (in rivalry with the "red" or socialist trade unions), and given the common basic outlook between them and the PPI, it was naturally a source of strength for them both to cooperate. A foremost wish of Italian Catholic labor leaders was that the government would acknowledge them and deal with them as it dealt with the socialist union federation, a program plank that was already in the initial manifesto of the party. Grandi also got the endorsement of the party congress for a reform of farm labor contracts, for land reform, and for the "white international" of labor that was in process of formation (see chapter 3).

This new model of political party was congenial to Christian democrats, less concerned with the defense of the church than the parties founded in the nineteenth century and more focused on the national economy, from a particular political slant, neither individualistic nor collectivistic. Like certain tendencies in the German Zentrum, it was prepared to lose Catholic voters who would not agree with its particular political program. The PPI appealed to traditional Christian values while pursuing political ends on its own responsibility, without involving church authorities and without calling on them for support of its options. It directed its appeal also to those voters who might not be particularly concerned about church issues as such, and it espoused a "people's" or democratic line, anxious to give voice and participatory rights to those broad strata of the population who were still deprived of political representation.

In Germany, two of Erzberger's allies in the formation of the Christian trade union movement at the beginning of the century viewed the collapse of the

70. See Molony 1977, 55–57.
71. See *DSMCI* 1, part 1: 213–25.

imperial regime and came to conclusions similar to Luigi Sturzo's in Italy: that the time had come for a reform of parliament and a realignment of its palette of parties.[72] Adam Stegerwald, head of the League of Christian Trade Unions of Germany, and Heinrich Brauns, the priest and trainer of labor activists with the Volksverein in Mönchengladbach, wanted to see the Center Party transformed into a party with a greater Christian-democratic political consistency. That would entail nothing less than reshaping the whole landscape of political parties. It would no doubt lead to more conservative Catholics leaving for other parties. Stegerwald's and Brauns's past in the interconfessional labor unions, together with the wartime and postwar developments in industrial relations (e.g., the ZAG), led them to believe that there was need for a party that would fold their Center Party constituency into a much broader grouping. After all, the Protestant workers in the Christian unions would not vote for the Center Party as long as it remained a Catholic party; nor would they vote for secularizing social democrats; where they ended up was with a conservative or nationalist party with little time for workers' interests.

A center party, preferably with a new name, that was truly "interconfessional," might draw a whole range of reasonable, moderate, socially progressive backers now scattered across a senseless assortment of parties that did not represent them well. So besides a forthrightly democratic domestic-policy stance and a foreign policy of attempted cooperation rather than defiance of the victor powers, a reconstituted center party would have to be deconfessionalized in practice as well as in theory. It would continue to stand against the collectivist and anticlerical left from which the social democrats could not disentangle themselves, as well as against the reactionary (and perhaps clericalist) right. This would bring clarity into the political choices facing the voters and would encourage responsible democratic politics.

Erzberger personally was too much of an ultramontane Catholic to head or even be a prominent leader of such a party. Non-Catholics saw red when his name was mentioned; most Germans, unless they read a Center newspaper, were influenced by the calumnies spread abroad about him. Hence Stegerwald coolly proposed that Erzberger should stand aside permanently.[73] For the most part, though, party leaders opposed Stegerwald's proposal, out of calculations of risk that the cultural and political center might not hold, without the traditionally Catholic Center Party keeping its place in continuity with its tradition.

72. See Cary 1996, 45–99.
73. See Cary 1996, 78; in greater detail, Forster 2003, 306–11. In 1920 and 1921 Erzberger was defending himself against charges of treason and self-enrichment, but was preparing for a comeback as the charges evaporated on careful examination. Political assassins' bullets put an end to his career on Aug. 26, 1921. Ten months later, Stegerwald's industrialist ally, Walther Rathenau, would be killed by other rightist assassins; see Weitz 2007, 98–101.

The differences from the Italian case were two in particular. As there was no Catholic political party in Italy between 1870 and 1918, Sturzo's energetic initiative forestalled others. In Germany, by contrast, Erzberger and Joseph Wirth and other Center democrats were poised to take leadership of a party with its longstanding connections and supportive institutions. In any event, they reorganized the existing party in a modernized way at the federal level, starting national party congresses and the like that they had previously done without.

Such organizational developments were stimulated by a second difference. Whereas Italy already had a regime of parliamentary responsibility, the German Reich maintained the monarch's personal sovereignty in the sense that he could and did appoint the chancellor and his ministers independently of the will of the parliament. Only with the Peace Resolution of 1917 did the process of parliamentarization of power begin, which the Weimar constitution confirmed in the new republic after the threat of soviet-type rule was repulsed. In the elections that took place so rapidly one after the other in the first two years of the republic, it was the natural response to activate tried-and-true party procedures rather than attempting to force a virtually new party on the scene. Of course, this foreclosed a more thoroughgoing realignment of parties that would have obviated some of the difficulties of parliamentary government later on. But in the absence of any notable willing partners for the interconfessional party and of any groundswell of interest within the Zentrum, the time for a Christian democratic or popularist party had not yet arrived in Germany.[74]

The year 1919 marked the beginning of the interwar era of two decades' duration, in the prevailing reckoning. But the whole interwar period may also be seen as a more or less deceptive interlude hovering between war and peace, in outcome a mere truce in the second modern European conflagration after the wars of the French Revolutionary era, as the Thirty-Years' War of the twentieth century. In 1919 Franco-German understanding was not achieved, indeed was hardly even sought. Germany was deprived of its Austro-Hungarian allies, but was left basically intact in the territory of the Reich, resentful of being treated like a pariah. Forced to agree to crushing reparations to its foes to avoid occupations that were always threatened and sometimes carried out, resentment simmered. All political decisions of all European countries, whether in foreign or domestic policy, were henceforth governed by the specter of war breaking out again—or the hope of waging the next one successfully. The United States of America, having thrown its weight into the balance decisively in 1918, soon withdrew behind the broad moat of the Atlantic, to let down the drawbridge

---

74. Cary 1996, 90.

only in 1924 (with the Dawes plan for international credit) and only with minimal governmental involvement.

In economic terms, "the shocks of the period 1914–1945," with the Depression of the 1930s, devastated the wealth of the warring nations.[75] This brought about a highly unusual compression of the inequality between the classes, especially notable (if not generally remarked) in European countries. The long-term postwar recovery can only now be seen in adequate perspective.

Much more in the public eye were other developments. A quite new force, a new candidate for sociopolitical hegemony, made its appearance in Italy with kindred movements elsewhere: fascism.[76] Many would come to think that a fascist regime might have enough affinity with traditional values, and enough malleability underneath its brash upstart demeanor, to serve as a vehicle for other aims. Such aims might even include the reintegration of Roman Catholicism into European republics. Fascism's rise capitalized on the nationalistic feelings and resentments that the outcome of the war had only fueled, on the one hand; on the other, it seemed to be as emphatically opposed to individualistic "liberalism" and collectivist "socialism" as contemporary Catholicism was. It was certainly a threat and a rival to the democratic elements in social Catholicism, but democracy was not yet accepted as a political ideal by the normative authorities of the Roman Catholic Church.[77] Their noncommittal stance on the values of democracy, coupled with the illusory hope of using fascist rule for higher ends—ultimately for the re-Christianization of society with the aid of corporatism—set the stage for much testing of wills and forces. Within a few years, European Christian democratic movements were in exile or in the underground in several countries.

World War I and its aftermath broke apart the world in which social Catholics had struggled in the long nineteenth century. It also made imperative a greater attention to the international framing of connections and tensions that affected the cause of social justice and basic rights. There was a corresponding increase of efforts on the part of activists to keep pace with such developments, the subject of our next chapter.

75. Piketty 2014, 271.
76. Payne 1995; M. Mann 2004.
77. Durand 2002.

CHAPTER 3

A White International?

Before World War I, apart from the impulses communicated to and from the Vatican, there had only been occasional transnational contacts of Catholics interested in the social question and social justice (the most notable being the Congress of Liège in 1890). The only organization formally structured for international exchange and communication was the secretive, short-lived, and small "Union de Fribourg" (composed mostly of lay persons in both senses of the term—neither clergy nor trained specialists) who met annually seven times, starting in 1885.[1] New kinds of Catholic organizations, particularly those involved in the Christian labor movement developing in the industrialized and industrializing countries of Western Europe, called for international federations. And in fact, during the 1920s there was a blossoming of Catholic associations on the international level in two phases. The first burst was in the immediate aftermath of the war, while the second followed when a more stable period of peace and relative prosperity, however brief, set in from 1925 to 1929.[2]

Labor movements continued to be prominent among social Catholic concerns in this period. Internationalist initiatives by labor leaders from the prewar period came to fruition in 1920 with the founding of the CISC, the Confédération internationale des syndicats chrétiens, known in English as the IFCTU, or International Federation of Christian Trade Unions.[3] In the broader arena of electoral politics and public opinion, the leading figures

---

1. See the articles by Giorgio Rumi, Guy Bedouelle, and Philippe Chenaux, in "*Rerum novarum*" 1997; see also Paulhus 1983. Lamberts 2002 describes a sort of predecessor phenomenon from 1870 to 1878. For the Leonine period, see Viaene 2005 and the essay on Catholic Congresses included there, by Lamberts. See also Misner 1994b for the early steps of Christian labor across national boundaries after *Rerum novarum*.

2. The earlier foundations were recorded in Monti 1924; on the second period, see Mattiazzo 1983.

3. See Pasture 1999.

of internationalism in the Catholic world were Marc Sangnier in France and Luigi Sturzo, in particular, from Italy. The other main organizational form of the Catholic labor movement, the para-union Catholic workers' associations or leagues ("milieu organizations"), finally succeeded in giving itself an international federation in 1928 after its leaders met from time to time during the preceding years.[4] From this preview of the major groupings it is clear that the internationalism in question in the interwar period is still mostly continental or European. Today they might be called transnational instead.

For Christian labor the need to organize across borders became acute during the Paris Peace Conference early in 1919, when the International Labour Organization (ILO) was being created in association with the new League of Nations. Though far behind the socialist labor movement at both the national and the international levels, the Christian labor unions (with their predominantly Catholic component) were able to present themselves as an organized international federation in short order so as not to leave the international discussion of labor issues in the ILO entirely in the hands of socialist labor leaders and those of the American Federation of Labor.

The Formation of the CISC, 1918–20

Within each belligerent nation during the Great War, the social classes drew together in a *Burgfrieden* or *union sacrée*. For Catholics in Germany as in the French Third Republic, this represented a step up from second-class or suspect citizenship. Catholic labor leaders scrambled to take advantage of this double emancipation for their movements. A voice for workers and a voice for Catholics, neither willingly heard during the nineteenth-century liberal ascendancy, now could be raised. As far as Christian unions were concerned, as we have seen, the new pope, Benedict XV, showed a positive interest. All this created a more prominent platform for organized labor, whether socialist or Christian, to have its influence felt in society.

While the war dragged on, French and Belgian representatives discussed an international organization for Christian unions at a meeting at Le Havre in June 1918.[5] The head of the only French Catholic union of any weight, Jules Zirnheld of the clerical workers' union (SECI, the Syndicat des employés du commerce et de l'industrie), came back from German captivity in time to preside over an international conference held in Paris from March 16 to March 19, 1919. The

---

4. On the Catholic Worker International, see Vandeweyer 1981. The Young Christian Workers Movement or JOC (Jeunesse ouvrière chrétienne) spread rapidly from Belgium to France after 1925 and grew into an international movement; it will receive its own treatment in chapter 7.

5. Verstraelen 1966, 482–83.

Paris conference had delegates only from countries that had either been allies in the war (Belgium, France, Italy), had stayed neutral (the Netherlands, Switzerland, Spain), or were newly independent states (Latvia, Lithuania, Poland). Concurrently, the Germans, with their relatively large and solidly organized Christian labor movement, claimed to speak for the majority of Christian unionists when they joined with German-speaking Switzerland, Austria, and a second delegation from the Netherlands in a parallel conference in Lucerne. The two conferences did exchange telegrams. Further progress toward joining the movements of the two sides in one international federation required the diplomacy of the neutrals: the Swiss and especially the Dutch.

Meanwhile, the Italian Christian labor unions had come together in a national federation, the Confederazione italiana dei lavoratori (CIL), in March 1918.[6] Its first head was Giambattista Valente, who imbibed the principles of Christian unionism in Cologne as an organizer of Italian laborers for the German Christian unions before the war.[7] At the Paris Peace Conference there was a commission (headed by Samuel Gompers of the American Federation of Labor) set up to work out the treaty language concerning the International Labour Organization. Given the virtual absence of specifically Christian labor organizations in the Franco-Anglo-American alliance, there were no representatives of social Catholicism on it. All the same, the international Christian labor conference, which was meeting in Paris in March 1919, did submit a memorandum through one of their members, Giovanni Maria Longinotti,[8] who was a part of the official Italian delegation as an expert in social questions. In this way Catholic social viewpoints could make a small contribution to the 1919 Charter of Labor. This was Part XIII of the peace treaties concerning the labor question and the founding of the ILO.

In 1919, at Zirnheld's Paris conference, the CIL was by far the largest national confederation. By 1920, at the founding of the Confédération internationale des syndicats chrétiens (CISC), the Italians and the Germans each claimed to represent about 1,250,000 workers in their ranks. The Belgians, to be sure, had a greater proportion of organized workers in the Christian unions, but in a much smaller nation. The French lagged far behind. Although Zirnheld thought it most appropriate that Paris be the seat of the new international or-

---

6. See *DSMCI* 1, pt. 2:213–16, and vol. 2:651–59.

7. See Valente 1978, 139–55.

8. Giovanni Maria Longinotti (1876–1944) had come in contact with the pioneering agronomist Stanislao Solari during his university studies; he subsequently distinguished himself in Catholic rural and labor organizing in the area around Brescia. Winning a seat in parliament in 1909, he was reelected and served until the complete Fascist takeover in 1926. A founding member of the PPI (Luigi Sturzo's Italian Popular Party) in 1918, he served as undersecretary of labor in coalition cabinets from 1920 to 1922; *DSMCI* 2:314–18; see also Valente 1978, 247.

ganization, his national federation did not even exist until after the Paris conference. In November 1919, spurred on by the example of Italy and the other countries, France's CFTC (Confédération française des travailleurs chrétiens) came into being. It represented some 98,000 union members in several regions of France.

Despite the French Catholic labor leaders' conviction that they should take over from the Germans the leading international role in reconstructed Europe, it was the hour of the neutrals, in particular of the Dutch Christian unions, Catholic and Protestant. Just as the socialist International Federation of Trade Unions moved from Berlin to Amsterdam, so the secretariat of the CISC would move from its embryonic existence in Cologne to Utrecht.[9] P. J. S. (Petrus Josephus Servatius, or Jos) Serrarens (1888–1963), a graduate of a normal school and of Leiden University, still in his early thirties and already president of the Catholic union federation of the Netherlands, would become the leading figure as secretary general of the new International. As we shall observe in the following chapters, this constituted one element in the notable contribution to the history of Christian labor on the part of Dutch Catholics.

After all, this transnational collaboration was quite an accomplishment in such a short time after World War I.[10] The inadequate and controversial peace treaties had left deep resentments, even or especially in France and Belgium. At a preliminary session in Rotterdam (February 20, 1920), Theodor Brauer was one of the first German Christian trade union figures to meet face to face with Belgian and French counterparts. A Rhinelander who would end up after 1933 in American exile, Brauer had learned Dutch from his mother and French at school in Belgium and was the chief theoretician of the German League of Christian Trade Unions.[11] The Belgians suspected that the German unions he represented had supported the policy of deporting Belgian workers to Germany for forced labor during the war. He assured them that, apart perhaps from some few private individuals, his co-unionists deplored what had happened. He even promised an official declaration to that effect from the German union leadership at the founding Congress planned for the Hague. Upon arriving in the Hague, however, in June of 1920, Adam Stegerwald, at this point the welfare minister in Prussia, was unwilling to make any such statement. From Paris, meanwhile, Zirnheld brought with him to the Hague a demand of the French unions for a resolution approving "the just reparation of deliberate losses inflicted" in the war.[12]

---

9. Pasture 1999, 75–86; Verstraelen 1966, 483–84.
10. Launay 1990, 243–45.
11. Patch 1985, 57.
12. Quoted in Verstraelen 1966, 485.

With the question of war debts and reparations so inflamed, the cause of the international cooperation of Christian labor, even though it was the purpose of the congress (and an imperative need, if only in view of the creation of the International Labour Organization and the appointment of a French socialist to run it), threatened to take a back seat to nationalistic passions. Jos Serrarens chaired the sessions; he recalled later that in the course of a welcoming address, the head of the organizing committee read Brauer's statement from the minutes of the Rotterdam conference and thus inserted it into the acts of the Hague Congress.[13]

It was not a very elegant solution, but it was a solution.... The Germans suffered the loss of their dominant position in Christian unionism very keenly, given the strength of their movement at home. This was especially the case since their delegation was headed by Adam Stegerwald, the previous international secretary, now a minister in the Prussian government; while the French were led by Jules Zirnheld, an aviator shot down behind German lines and condemned to death by reason of his Alsatian birth; even though the sentence was suspended, he still had to spend a year and a half in a prison cell.

Serrarens, writing in 1946, went on to remark that, after five years of German occupation, he now understood "the mentality of certain delegates better than we understood it in 1920, we who had been neutrals."[14]

There were ten countries represented at the Hague in 1920 at this first congress of the CISC. Belgium, the Netherlands, Germany, Austria, Switzerland, Italy, and France were joined by delegates from Spain and from the new states of Czechoslovakia and Hungary. As president the delegates chose the executive secretary of the Swiss Central Association of Christian-Social Organizations (interconfessional) in Sankt Gallen. Joseph Scherrer remained president of the international federation until 1928; Serrarens stayed on as secretary general while playing a significant role on the Dutch labor scene until 1952, when he became one of the first judges in the European coal and steel community's court of justice. As treasurer until 1939, a man from the Protestant labor union federation of the Netherlands was chosen: Herman Amelink.

The CISC consolidated itself well enough to weather the loss of the Italian unions in 1923–24 and the German ones in 1933, both suppressed by totalitarian regimes. The Austrians were expelled in 1934, as well, with the advent of state corporatism.[15] Four congresses were held between the Hague and the 1933 Nazi takeover. After meeting in Innsbruck in 1922, a move back to neutral territory was necessitated by French-German tensions over fulfilling the

13. Ibid.
14. Cited in ibid., 489.
15. Pasture 1999, 171–82.

terms of Versailles; the third congress was held in Lucerne in 1925. The spirit of the Locarno treaties of 1925, however, eased international tensions sufficiently that Munich was chosen as the site for the 1928 congress. Bernhard Otte was chosen to succeed Joseph Scherrer as president. Otte had previously been head of the German Christian textile workers' union, of the international textile union federation, and was now also successor to Stegerwald as secretary general of the *Gesamtverband*, the national federation or League of Christian Trade Unions (GcG). The CISC also held four international conferences of women labor unionists in its first decade. Women's unions were unique to Christian trade unionism.[16] Three seats on the CISC board were reserved for female union leaders.

While the Christian unions held to the ideal of interclass harmony or cooperation, this did not prevent them from recognizing the very real class interests that employers and workers did *not* have in common. The success of the Christian trade unions in forming and sustaining their international ties with each other so soon after World War I, though modest, appears more remarkable when one compares it with the difficulties and frustrations encountered in other sectors of political economy in the "hollow years."[17]

The next congress in Antwerp in 1932 was poorly attended as a consequence of the Depression's effects on labor generally. The congresses planned after Antwerp were often not much more than expanded executive committee meetings. The membership represented had sunk from over 3,000,000 to less than a million by 1934. Before Otte died in late 1933 in an automobile accident, he had had to resign from the CISC as a consequence of the Nazi takeover of the German unions. Jules Zirnheld and Henri Pauwels took the reins provisionally until Zirnheld became president in 1937. But the more significant developments took place within the national movements, as we shall see in subsequent chapters.

Catholic Labor and the ILO in Geneva

From the 1920s, the CISC was a factor to be reckoned with in the ILO.[18] The ILO director, Albert Thomas, showed himself to be favorable to a truly inclusive policy and wanted to integrate Christian labor unions within the purview of the ILO. A socialist himself, he cultivated the friendship of Catholic as well as socialist labor leaders, including two monsignori with high governmental responsibilities: Heinrich Brauns of Germany and Willem Hubert Nolens of the Netherlands. Thomas dispatched deputies to the congresses of the CISC.

16. Launay 1990, 87.
17. To cite E. Weber 1994.
18. See *International Labour Organisation* 1931, 336–38.

In 1926 he prevailed upon Gustave Desbuquois, SJ, the director of the French Action populaire, to put at his disposition an experienced Jesuit, André Arnou, to be the liaison person at the Geneva headquarters of the ILO with the Catholic labor movement.[19] In 1928 Thomas addressed the CISC Congress in Munich in person, validating their claim and that of the Catholic social outlook in the tradition of *Rerum novarum* to be an integral part of the worldwide labor movement of the twentieth century.[20]

But Thomas could not set policy, which was determined by the annual conferences of delegates from member states of the League of Nations. For the 1921 conference the Netherlands appointed P. J. S. Serrarens as one of its delegates representing labor after consulting with the five major labor federations of the country. Four agreed on Serrarens; the fifth—socialist and the largest, though still not representing by itself a majority of unionized Dutch workers—did not. At the ILO conference itself, the International Federation of Trade Unions of Amsterdam (IFTU) challenged Serrarens's credentials. Eventually the case went before the Court of International Justice, which ruled in the Netherlands government's (and Serrarens' and the Christian unions') favor.[21] Similarly, when the ILO organized the World Economic Conference of Geneva in 1927, the socialist-dominated IFTU wished to have a monopoly of the labor representation. However, Emile Vandervelde (1866–1938), a rare socialist Belgian foreign minister in coalition cabinets for thirty months, saw to it that Henri Pauwels got a seat on the preparatory commission.[22] At the World Conference itself, Serrarens and nine other Christian labor unionists took part.[23]

It was really the Belgians and particularly the Dutch, given the strength of the organizations they represented at home, who as social Catholics exercised the greatest influence in international labor affairs through the ILO. Like others, the Dutch government was invited to send a delegation to the first ILO conference in Washington later in 1919 (before the negative American response to the League of Nations and its adjunct, the ILO, was given). The Dutch cabinet minister for labor affairs was the Catholic lawyer and politician Petrus J. M. Aalberse, a Christian democrat whose long involvement in labor issues

---

19. Droulers 1981, 126.
20. See Letterhaus 1928, in Klein, Ludwig, and Rivinius, 1052–53.
21. *International Labour Organisation* 1931, 336; Verstraelen 1966, 496–97; see also M. Fogarty 1957, 214.
22. Pauwels (born 1890) was secretary of the Christian union federation Algemeen Christelijk Vakverbond von België (ACV; see chaps. 5 and 12 of this volume) of Belgium from 1920 to 1932 and its president from 1932 until his death in 1946. (He was traveling abroad in connection with his duties as president of the World Labor Confederation, the successor to the CISC after World War II, when he died suddenly in Canada.) On Vandevelde, see Polasky 1995.
23. Verstraelen 1966, 498.

and organization qualified him for the post now that the Catholic party formed part of the governing coalition.[24] In turn he appointed a priest, W. H. Nolens, to head the Dutch delegation to the ILO conference, where the great question was the eight-hour day. (He was one of the two government delegates; besides these every member state was to send an employer delegate and a labor delegate, the latter being the socialist labor leader Jan Oudegeest. Serrarens went along as a technical adviser.)

Nolens was a natural choice, having long been active in representing the coal mining area of South Limburg in parliament through his service on the board of the Dutch State Mines and his already considerable international experience in the area of labor and working conditions. Nolens simply knew more about the issues that the ILO would deal with than most other delegates and presented well-worked-out draft proposals; hence he was a leading figure at this and later conferences.[25] The Serrarens affair in 1921 (when the Netherlands replaced Oudegeest with Serrarens as the labor representative) did not improve relations with the socialists, who of course constituted a strong majority in the labor group at the Geneva conference. Even so, Nolens was finally chosen to preside at the ILO conference in 1928 (he died in 1931).

The interaction and mutual support of the CISC with other labor currents, especially through the ILO, are especially apparent when one considers the platform of the CISC adopted in 1922 at Innsbruck. A first part, laying out the philosophical foundations of the Christian labor movement, adopts the basic thrust of social Catholicism in steering a course between the individualistic extreme of "the liberal economic school" and the collectivist tendencies of socialist or Marxist doctrine. The presupposition is the unsurpassable human dignity of each person, realizable only with the orientation of each one to the common good. Property is natural, private ownership is a good thing, but "the forms of property can vary according to cultural differences, whereas the acquisition and the use made of property are subject to moral obligations incumbent on all."[26]

The second part, on the social economy, identified the most pressing problem as the sharp tensions existing between the providers of capital and the providers of labor, with management for the most part representing capital. Labor too should have a role in management and a part in the profits of the common enterprise. Here are reflected the ideas, often summed up in the expression "co-determination" (in German, *Mitbestimmung*) or "co-responsibility," that were present in each country, forged by the ideological struggle with capitalist control on the side of the employers and socialist ideas in the labor movement at large.

24. Kossmann 1978, 660.
25. See Gribling 1978, 268.
26. Otte 1932, 822; see Pasture 1999, 109–12.

In other national venues, the *Semaines sociales* of France had emulators in Italy, Belgium, Spain, and other countries; there was even a German one in Mönchengladbach in 1932, bringing the development full circle.[27] The *Semaines catholiques internationales*, held in Geneva in 1929, 1930, 1931, and 1932, came about from the example of the eighteenth *Semaine sociale de France*, held in Le Havre in 1926.[28] The Fribourg-based "Union catholique d'études internationales," founded in 1920 and headed by Gonzague de Reynold, sponsored these international *Semaines*.[29] They attracted some hundreds of participants to hear what Catholics might have to say on the burning international issues of the day (1929), contemporary Catholic thought on peace (1930), the League of Nations itself (1931), and moral disarmament (1932). Each year's presentations were then published by the Action populaire's press in Paris, Editions Spes. Antonio Gramsci learned about them in prison from an article in the *Civiltà Cattolica*.[30] As was his wont, Gramsci took Catholicism in its popularist version seriously; he remarked that here "*una Internazionale laica*" was manifesting itself—a laity that communists like himself would have to reckon with, even after fascism was gone.[31]

This was just one example of a multitude of peace activities that went on in the Catholic world parallel to the diplomatic and other efforts of the 1920s. The French Jesuits of Action populaire followed, reported on, encouraged, and engaged in many of these efforts.[32] Most of the social and political Catholic groups with which Fr. Desbuquois was in contact supported the idea of a European fatherland and an end to the German-French enmity. He also made contact with like-minded German Catholics to start to dismantle the hostile feelings left by recent events.

Marc Sangnier's Initiatives for Peace and Justice

The charismatic founder of the Sillon had been forbidden by Pope Pius X to link politics and religion. The effect would be to relegate his social democratic programs to realizations exclusively in the realm of secular politics instead of considering them also as part of his Christian vocation, as was his wont. Pope Benedict XV, in contrast, encouraged him privately in 1916 to champion democratic and republican ideals as compatible with Catholicism.[33] But he declined the offer to stand at the head of a small Christian democratic party, which con-

---

27. See Schoelen 1982, 542.
28. See Mattiazzo 1983, 143–44. The proceedings of the eighteenth *Semaine sociale* de France appeared as *Problème de la vie internationale* 1927.
29. Yerly 1999, 131.   30. Brucculeri 1933.
31. Gramsci 1977, 70.   32. Droulers 1981, 320–36.
33. Barthélemy-Madaule 1973, 232–36; see Dreyfus 1988, 110.

sequently did not materialize in France until 1924. After military service during World War I, he was persuaded to stand for a seat in parliament, as did a number of other social Catholics, in a larger electoral grouping known as the *bloc national*. However, he soon found himself out of place there on the right; after serving as a deputy from 1920 to 1924, he could not find a base from which to be reelected: for the left, he was too Catholic, and for the Catholic electorate, he was too leftist—and insufficiently nationalistic.

In fact, he stood out for his admiration of the original Fourteen Points laid out by President Wilson as a proper basis for a real peace. He considered the Treaty of Versailles' clauses à propos of German war reparations payments to be unrealistic, vindictive, and unjust. He was perpetually at odds with the majority in the chamber, particularly with the *bloc national*, whenever nationalism versus French-German reconciliation was at issue. Public opinion was so aroused during and after the peace conference that Georges Clemenceau, the French premier who dug in his heels against Wilson, lost the election for president of the Republic, in part because the French were persuaded that he had let Germany off on overly generous terms.

In this atmosphere Sangnier turned his efforts more and more to preparing the ground for peace through international understanding. He played a prominent part, not just among Catholics, in the greening of pacifism that took place after World War I. In France Aristide Briand was the politician most associated with postwar reconciliation; Briand received the Nobel Peace Prize in 1926 along with Gustav Stresemann. Yves de la Brière, S.J., of the Jesuit periodical *Etudes*, was the most notable propagandist of the papal guidance and commitment in respect of peace between nations. Sangnier did most to influence public opinion and encourage the rising generation to support the League of Nations and seek still more effective ways of ensuring world peace.[34]

In December 1921 his newspaper, *La Démocratie*, hosted the first of the annual international conferences that he would spearhead from 1921 to 1931 devoted to democracy and peace. It was the first congress held in Paris to which delegates of the vanquished enemy countries were invited—quite a risky undertaking. Held for maximum public effect, it highlighted addresses by Sangnier and Max Josef Metzger (1887–1944) at the closing session, which attracted an attendance of 3,000. Echoing the preamble of the Charter of Labor from the 1919 peace treaties, it sounded the theme "There is no international peace without social justice."[35]

The next two such congresses were held in Vienna (Austria) and in Freiburg (Germany), the latter in 1923, right in the midst of the occupation of the Ruhr

---

34. See Barry 2012 also for Sangnier's subsequent peace-making efforts; see Farrugia 1992.
35. Barthélemy-Madaule 1973, 249.

by French and Belgian forces and of the economic collapse that accompanied it. The enthusiastic participation of German youth despite everything stimulated Sangnier to take special measures to get the youth of the recently belligerent nations together. A large estate, Bierville, which he had bought with an inheritance left to his wife, provided the setting for an enormous gathering of youth from all over Europe in July and August of 1925. For a month, after converging on Paris in special railway cars and being transported to Bierville in buses, 6,000 young people lived in tents provided, ironically enough, by the defense ministry. They flocked to three aircraft hangars placed end to end for the plenary assemblies when they were not following courses on subjects like those offered in a *Semaine sociale*, engaging in open-air theater and musical evenings, and coming to know each other across national barriers. From that time on, youth conferences and youth hostels engaged a major part of Sangnier's energies. In 1928 a peace conference at Bierville with a visit to the Geneva headquarters of the League of Nations and the International Labor Office was held for young people. Again in 1929, youth treks from all directions, converging on Bierville, attracted the attention of the public.[36]

Another international theme occupied their 1927 congress of Wurzburg: colonialism. In a remarkable resolution, the congress called for colonial policy to be oriented toward the political independence of the colonies and for the League of Nations to assert stricter control, while expressing "full sympathy for the peaceful work of liberation of all oppressed peoples."[37] Certainly few policy proposals could have been more important for the future peace of the world.[38]

Sangnier represents a recurrent development in the Catholicism of the period, an effort to venture "out of the tower" of organizations linked exclusively to the Roman Catholic Church.[39] For some time to come, Catholicism would still play its public roles as a fairly compact and separate subculture. Hence the issue of the autonomy of Catholics' cultural, social, and political organizations from the jurisdiction of the hierarchy would remain a delicate one, never far from their leaders' minds. Luigi Sturzo was a prime example.

Luigi Sturzo and the SIPDIC

To Marc Sangnier's "first international democratic congress" (as the spectacular conference of December 1921 was styled), Luigi Sturzo, the head of the Popular Party of Italy (PPI), sent a letter in the care of the two PPI delegates.

36. Ibid., 255–59.
37. The resolution is cited in full in ibid., 257–58.
38. See also *Semaines sociales de France* 1931.
39. To use the expression of Julius Bachem, "Wir müssen aus dem Turm heraus"; Bachem 1906; see Morsey 1973, 1:36. For more on Sangnier, see Delbreil 1997, 1999.

Sturzo's fate would be to live and work in exile from 1925 until 1945.[40] Deprived of a platform in his native Italy, Sturzo deployed his considerable talents in the international arena. Among his projects was the creation of a white international for political parties of Christian democratic inspiration.

Sturzo and other members of his party had a pronounced supranationalist and conciliatory bent. Although under time constraints to mount campaigns for the elections in September 1919 and again already in May 1921, the party put international contacts with other parties of like orientation on its agenda at its very first conventions.[41] Indeed, the twelfth and last point of the party program called for an international order supported by a formal organization—in other words, for a development of the League of Nations that would include international courts, "the abolition of secret treaties and obligatory conscription," and universal disarmament.[42] Stefano Cavazzoni was one of the first *popolari* (as party members were called) to travel abroad; he was at an international trade conference in Paris in May 1920 on behalf of the government and, after touching base in Rome, betook himself again to the founding congress of the CISC at the Hague in June, where Valente and a railroad union representative named Cuniolo participated for the Italian unions.[43] There he met the Catholic Party politician C. J. M. Ruijs (or Ruys) de Beerenbrouck, the Dutch prime minister. Ruijs de Beerenbrouck was only the first of a number of leading Christian social or Christian democratic politicians of various European countries with whom PPI emissaries would confer in person in the next two years.[44]

Don Giulio De Rossi (1877–1925), head of the PPI press office, made a trip to France in the same summer to cover the *Semaine sociale* of Caen and stir up interest in international communications, running up against the hypersensitivity of the French at that period. They were irritated by what they saw as Italian Catholic leanings toward the Germans; they were not prepared to accept criticism of their attitudes in regard to the Versailles treaty. Moreover, French Catholics were scattered among different political parties. De Rossi recognized that it would not be easy to persuade them to collaborate in a Christian democratic international organization of any kind. His reasons for hoping that they would come around in the end reveal a prewar outlook that was only reinforced during the "red biennium" in postwar Italy: "Faced with a powerful Masonic International, an even more powerful Jewish and financial International, and a violent red International, the political parties that are inspired by the Christian school of social policy in all the countries cannot remain disconnected. This would be tantamount to a death sentence."[45]

40. Mayeur 1980, 151–52.
41. Vecchio 1987a, 276.
42. See Sturzo 1992, 42–44.
43. Robbiati 1981b, 260.
44. See *DSMCI* 2:100–106.
45. Vecchio 1987a, 281.

As a model of a Catholicism equipped with the resources to play a leading role in the public life of a country, German Catholicism, with its Volksverein, its trade unions, and its Center Party—all operating autonomously and apart from any hierarchical chain of command or delegation—was undeniably more attractive to the *popolari* than were the comparatively unorganized French Catholics. So it is no surprise to learn that the major international effort undertaken by the PPI (before the rise of fascism made them concentrate on survival at home) was a trip to Germany in September 1921, three months before Sangnier's first congress could take place in Paris.[46] The small party accompanying Sturzo was well covered in the party press of Germany and Italy. Alcide De Gasperi and Konrad Adenauer first met on this occasion, when the group visited Cologne, part of occupied Germany. In Berlin the delegation of *popolari* met a number of Catholic politicians, including Joseph Wirth, who was head of a government that ruled with the combined support of his own Center Party and the Social Democrats.[47] This example of a center-left coalition in the democratic spirit of Matthias Erzberger, who had just been assassinated, impressed the Italian party leadership—even those like Cavazzoni and Filippo Meda, who were viscerally distrustful of socialism.

The PPI was represented, as we have seen, at the "first international democratic congress" organized by Sangnier and *La Jeune République* in Paris in December 1921 (by De Rossi, for whom it was a repeat visit, and by Fulvio Milani, a *Popolare* member of parliament). Sturzo was convinced that Italy had a specific contribution to make in the difficult postwar context. This was a major theme of his utterances in Germany. "Of all the nations, I believe that Italy is the best situated to promote understandings, contacts, and voluntary organizations in the political arena, because Italy occupies an intermediary position today between the states that only yesterday were at war with each other. It is one of the victor states, without however pursuing imperialistic aims in politics and the economy; and it suffers from the crisis of the countries that lost the war, without being counted among the antagonists or harboring a spirit of resistance."[48]

These initial contacts turned out to be the only initiatives that the PPI could develop in its short period of growth (1919–22). They were enough, however, to prompt a warning shot across the bow from Cardinal Pietro Gasparri, Benedict XV's secretary of state. In a newspaper interview he complained that the

---

46. Vecchio 1987a, 284–86; Molony 1977, 101.

47. The tour and contacts in Germany seem to have been arranged by Carl Sonnenschein, a priest most noted for his work with Catholic students in Berlin, who had gotten to know Luigi Sturzo when both were seminarians in Rome at the turn of the century. In fact, Sturzo had attended an unusual international gathering of Catholic students organized by Sonnenschein in Rome in 1900; see *ZGiLB* 4:94.

German junket could only lead to trouble; any attempt to form a "White International" was an unwanted complication in the foreign relations of the Vatican, which alone could act responsibly in such a delicate field.[49] Besides, he observed, "Catholicism [itself] is the true 'white international,' with its own mechanisms of discipline and oversight."[50] Sturzo had tried to forestall such a reaction with the distinction on which his whole effort stood or fell: it was not a "*Catholic* international" at which he was aiming, but an "*internazionale popolare*," that is, one of similar *political* parties and groups.[51]

After Sturzo was forced into exile,[52] circumstances seemed paradoxically more propitious for the foundation of such an international organization of Christian parties or, more precisely (since the parties in question all identified themselves not as churchly but as political formations, with complete autonomy from ecclesiastical control), of "parties of Christian inspiration." After touching base with Catholic politicians in Germany and the Low Countries, he arrived in Paris for a meeting on April 4, 1925, with leaders of the new French party founded along the lines Sturzo had drawn for the PPI. He saw this party, the PDP (Parti démocrate populaire), as constituting the indispensable French link in the international political ties that he had been wanting to establish. He proposed to them that they take the initiative in forming what became the Secrétariat international des partis démocratiques d'inspiration chrétienne, or SIPDIC.[53] After the French sent out invitations to party headquarters in other European countries, based on Sturzo's rather elaborate proposal, the initial meeting was held in Paris near the end of 1925, bringing representatives of five nations together: France, Germany, Italy, Belgium, and Poland. The next meeting, in Brussels in May 1926, still did not see any representatives of the Dutch Catholic Party appear, but thereafter they came rather regularly. Written contacts at least were established with Austria, Czechoslovakia, Lithuania, and Switzerland.

The cumbersome name of the organization corresponds closely to the new phase of European Catholic politics ushered in by Sturzo's PPI.[54] "Democratic" did service also for "popular" in the sense understood by the Italian and French social Catholics as indicating an orientation to the left and to social justice.

---

48. Cited in Vecchio 1987a, 285.
49. Molony 1977, 102.
50. Scoppola 1971, 491.
51. Vecchio 1987a, 301.
52. Molony 1977, 192
53. On the PDP, see Delbreil 1990, 259–64 and 270–71. On the SIPDIC, see W. Kaiser 2007, esp. 72–118. Besides Delbreil 1990, several recent studies of the rise and difficult existence of SIPDIC have appeared, each the fruit of independent research in the periodicals and archives of the period: Papini 1988 was first published in Italian in 1986 (English translation 1997); Vecchio 1987a, 269–310, and Hanschmidt 1988 followed; then Papini 1995 and 1997. See also Pulzer 2004, 10–24, and Guido Müller 2004, 252–64.

The phrase "Christian democracy" was avoided because Pope Leo XIII had fixed an apolitical, purely social sense on it for church usage. It was a matter of political parties, not parties organized primarily for the defense of church interests, hence not "Catholic" parties, despite the Dutch party of that name that eventually joined. In the loose coalition that was the Catholic party in Belgium, only one of its components joined SIPDIC: the Workers' League, which behaved much like a political party of its own.[55] The democracy in question was "of Christian inspiration"; this is what constituted the specific difference from other parties of the left or center. The name ("democratic parties of Christian inspiration") also reflects the difficulties the parties had over international tensions. The adjective "democratic" indicated a firm stand demanding parliamentary government and opposing fascist and other dictatorships. When the Belgians, Dutch, and French parties declined to expel the Austrian Christian-Social Party with the advent of the Dollfuss authoritarian state in 1934, Sturzo felt that SIPDIC had failed to stand up for its principles.

The Catholic Worker International

Returning to organizations of workers, one must recognize that Christian trade unions, prominent as they were, were only part of the labor component of social Catholicism between the wars. Many unionized Catholics also belonged to Catholic workers' milieu associations: Arbeitervereine or "workers' leagues," as they have been called in English.[56] These were strictly Catholic organizations for workers, men and women separately, just as there were other such organizations for students or women or other special categories of church members. The early, extremely paternalistic form of Catholic workers' clubs initiated in the France of the 1870s by Albert de Mun had sunk into insignificance, while Austria, Belgium, Germany, the Netherlands, and Switzerland had national (supra-diocesan) Catholic workers' associations by the 1920s alongside the Christian unions. In fact, an international federation of such Catholic milieu organizations was discussed already at the Lucerne conference of Christian trade unions of 1919 mentioned earlier.[57] In any event, only Belgium, Germany, and the Netherlands would contribute significantly to establishing such an international connection.

The raison d'être of a parallel set of Catholic organizations for workers alongside the Christian unions was clear in the minds of their proponents and leaders—priests like Otto Müller in the Rhineland, Carl Walterbach in Bavaria,

54. See W. Kaiser 2007, 42–65.
55. Gerard 1994c, 2:612.
56. M. Fogarty 1957, 207 and 215–16.

and especially Henri Poels in Holland and laymen such as Poels's close collaborator Hendrik Hermans (1874–1949) and Joseph Joos, the labor journalist from Mönchengladbach who was also a leader of the Center Party. The case for unions (Dutch: *vakorganisatie*) was one matter. The case that Poels made for nonunion Catholic labor organizations (Dutch: *standsorganisatie*) was another. Christian trade unions separate from their social democratic counterparts were necessary, but only conditionally, as long as socialist labor organizations undermined church membership and discriminated against Christian workers. As this was the case everywhere on the continent, however, the need for Christian labor unions was recognized by most Catholics in any way involved with the labor movement. After all, labor unions as such had their own intrinsic validating purposes, which were primarily economic, not religious. They pursued, legitimately enough, class interests. They welcomed members who had no connection to the Catholic Church or any church, but who supported social-policy aims such as codetermination with no admixture of Marxist doctrine. They could hardly be effective in their own spheres if they were expected to propagate a "confessional" religious worldview that insisted on Catholic loyalties.

Therefore, the core contribution that only the church could make to the societal common good would have to be structured more directly for such foundational work: a patient and thorough formation of Christian workers for long-term beneficial influence through faith development and education that would meet the challenge of their situation as workers. In modern Europe this formative religio-cultural task of the church would have to be differentiated according to class.[58] Just as employers, academics, and bourgeois generally should have a religious socialization appropriate to their needs, so also the Catholic labor movement should provide means of religious development, socioeconomic formation, and public influence adapted to the requirements of the workers' milieu.

This rationale for the coexistence of Christian trade unions and Catholic workers' associations left an opaque area of overlap between them. The primary purpose of the unions was to defend and advance workers' economic interests. The Catholic workers' associations took charge of the milieu-specific spiritual and cultural formation of workers. Where did that leave the mobilization of the democratic political force of working people? Both the Christian trade unions and the Arbeitervereine wished to counter the rise of socialism with a positive alternative approach to social injustice in industrial society. How the two Christian movements were to collaborate or divide their tasks in the crucial

---

57. See Mattiazzo 1983, 118–19, and Verstraelen 1966, 499–504.

activities of *political* formation and mobilization was a recurrent question with no easy answer.[59] In the Netherlands and elsewhere, as we shall see, the issue kept raising its head in various guises, connected with other questions of religion, politics, and class struggle.

At any rate, the Dutch champion of the *standsorganisatie* model, Msgr. Henri (or Henricus) Poels, pushed for an international organization bringing together the whole labor movement qua Catholic in this form.[60] Things were far enough along to plan for the first international congress in Wurzburg in 1923; then came the occupation of the Ruhr by the French and Belgian forces and the precipitous drop of the German mark, which made international exchange virtually impossible. After Wurzburg was called off, two further small conferences were held in Antwerp, in 1924 and 1926, also attracting some participants from France, Italy, Spain, and Czechoslovakia. (A Catholic workers' association in Argentina also reported in at some point.)[61] A standing committee in view of establishing a Catholic Worker International included the principal figures, half clergy and half lay persons: Henri Hermans (Dutch) as president, with Poels and Adrianus Cornelis De Bruijn also for the Netherlands; Louis Colens and Hendrik Heyman, representing Belgium; Otto Müller and Joseph Joos for Germany; Johannes Antonius Schutte, of the Dutch Catholic central labor office in Utrecht, was a sort of corresponding secretary.[62]

The Catholic Worker International had a short life after this extended period of incubation.[63] Of its two congresses, the first, in Cologne in the middle of June 1928, was almost spectacular; the second, in Utrecht in 1931, was already under the twin shadow of Depression and Nazism; the reinvigoration of the Catholic labor idea signaled by the encyclical of 1931, *Quadragesimo anno*, could not have immediate organizational effects at this level. In 1928 Joseph Joos was elected president by 350 delegates from ten European countries.[64] Eugenio

58. Vandeweyer 1981, 61–63.

59. For Joos's perspective, see Wachtling 1974, 138–45; likewise Wachtling 1973, 1:239: "Joos did not work in the interconfessional trade unions led by lay persons and principally concerned with the material improvement of the worker's lot, but in the Arbeitervereine under the leadership of clergy. It was in the latter, he was convinced, that the decisive formative task in the religious, social, and political area was carried out. The function of the Catholic workers' associations was above all to enable the workers to take their place in society as an 'estate' beside the other 'estates' [or 'classes': *Stände*]. For Joos, the *Westdeutsche Arbeiterzeitung* that he edited was not an instrument of battle, but primarily an organ of formation and education; its task was not to stir up resentment over social distinctions, but to awaken 'the desire for commonality between the confessions, the worldviews, the 'estates,' classes and parties."

60. Vandeweyer 1981, 63–70. Poels gave an important address in 1921 to a Catholic workers congress in Nijmegen on "The Catholic Standsorganisatie in Industrial Society"; see *HJS* 290–99 for major excerpts.

61. Wachtling 1974, 143.   62. Verstraelen 1966, 501.
63. Aretz 1978, 18–19.

Pacelli, still the nuncio to Germany but soon to be a curial cardinal and, on Pope Pius XI's death in 1939, himself pope, sent a letter of encouragement to Msgr. Otto Müller on the occasion.[65] Adenauer, the lord mayor, laid on a festal reception. Carl Sonnenschein gave the main public address, also broadcast by radio. Rarely at a loss for a telling phrase, he consigned laissez-faire to the past: "Victory in the world will belong either to (Pope) Leo's Rome or Lenin's Moscow."[66] Bernhard Letterhaus summed up the unfulfilled hopes of industrial wage-earners in the demand for "economic democracy."[67] This would require a fairer distribution of wealth, perhaps through employee stockholding or profit-sharing, as well as a say in management decisions.

The founders had not thought it appropriate or necessary to seek permission from the Vatican for the International. According to Poels's conception, such workers' associations were "Catholic, but not church organizations."[68] The following year, after Pius XI and Mussolini sealed the Lateran Pacts, they went to Rome to visit the pope on the occasion of his fiftieth anniversary of ordination. They submitted for his consideration a memorandum on the church and labor, among other things asking for a new papal message on the subject. The memorandum described the newly established Catholic Worker International with the expectation that the pope would approve. The pope did not seem to see their federation as particularly helpful to his own grand scheme for re-Christianizing Italy and the Western world. At any rate, they were taken aback when their undertaking seemed to be treated as undesirable interference in delicate affairs.[69] Although they were received kindly as pilgrims, their status as representatives of a large international Catholic organization was not recognized. Poels would later say, "They showed us the door."[70]

This may have been partly due to its transnational or supra-diocesan character, but principally because of its relative autonomy and its structure, which involved lay co-leadership. A clear departure from the papal perspective of the time was that it was not directly subject to hierarchical chain of command. When Cardinal Gasparri reluctantly, after repeated requests from the German embassy, acknowledged the memorandum signed by Joos and Carl Walterbach, the priest-president of the Bavarian Arbeitervereine, he could have been thinking of what he had said about Sturzo's more political efforts in 1921: "Catholicism [itself] is the true white international, with its own mechanisms of oversight and control."

64. Verstraelen 1966, 502–3; see W. Kaiser 2007, 92–96.
65. Klein, Ludwig, and Rivinius 1976, 2:1013.
66. Wachtling 1974, 145.
67. Aretz 1982, 2:183; Klein, Ludwig, and Rivinius 1976, 2:1059.
68. Wentholt 1984, 48.
69. Vandeweyer 1981, 75; see Wachtling 1974, 145–47.

What was the yield of all these efforts at Europe-wide consolidation and mutual support? Given the ascendancy of the totalitarianisms, in the 1920s in Italy, then in 1930s Germany, a hiatus loomed at the level of trade union transnational structures until 1945. As tokens of Catholic presence, not only did priests in governmental positions such as Nolens of the Netherlands (1928) and Brauns of Germany (1929) preside over the annual conferences of the ILO, but Serrarens himself also served as deputy member of its greatly hampered administrative council between 1934 and 1951.

As for the political parties' secretariat (SIPDIC), the contacts it promoted (or upon which it was based) during the interwar period assume world historical significance in retrospect, involving as they did such founding figures of the future European Union as Adenauer, De Gasperi, Georges Bidault, and Robert Schuman.[71] Even during the 1920s the efforts to create some more effective structure were at least the occasion for a number of democratic Catholic politicians from neighboring countries to meet one another. It is enough to underscore that during the visit of the PPI delegation to Cologne in 1921, the future leaders of democratic Italy and Germany, Konrad Adenauer and Alcide De Gasperi, met for the first and possibly the only time until they did so as prime ministers after World War II. And at the SIPDIC congress of Cologne in 1927, Adenauer and Robert Schuman, the foreign minister of France after whom the Schuman Plan for the European Coal and Steel Community was named, made each other's acquaintance.[72] Leading politicians (Josef Wirth, Heinrich Brauns, Joseph Joos, Franz von Papen, C. J. M. Ruijs de Beerenbrouck, Luigi Sturzo, Ignaz Seipel, Richard Schmitz) and less prominent ones (Maurice Prélot, Francesco Luigi Ferrari) strove to overcome the isolation of nationalism. Although it was completely unequal to the challenges of Fascism, Nazism, and the authoritarian state in Austria, some of SIPDIC's participants were ready after World War II to take up Christian democratic challenges in changed circumstances, having learned from the past.

It is noteworthy that the elements of political Catholicism that spearheaded the international contacts in this period were predominantly those in the left or labor wing of their respective parties. The trade union International itself, the CISC, revived and became the World Confederation of Labor after World War II.[73] It was a positive part of the manifold influences that led Western Europe to the social and democratic political economy of the post–World War II period. The earlier generation of Catholic politicians responded courageously to the situation created by the First World War. They defended the gains made by the working class before, during, and just after the war through times when

70. Verstraelen 1966, 503.
71. Papini 1988, 39–41.   72. Ibid., 36.

adversity threatened them. And when crushed by *force majeure* in the 1930s, their successors emerged from the devastation of the Second World War in the form of Christian democracy and its social outlook after 1945.

At the 1933 conference of the International Labour Organization (ILO), the Nazi regime paraded the CISC president himself, Bernhard Otte, as a kind of hostage, soon to be disowned.[74] It had no effect on the remaining leaders of the CISC. The federation did not depart from its resolve not to give credibility to the unfree labor organizations of any totalitarian or "corporatist" regime, not even the Austrian *Ständestaat*.

Bernhard Letterhaus was involved in the conspiracy of July 20, 1944, to assassinate Hitler. After it went awry, he decided to remain at his post in the army in Berlin and not to seek refuge with his Dutch associates in the former Catholic Worker International. He was arrested, tried, and hanged on November 14, 1944. Otto Müller had already died in prison. Nikolaus Gross, labor journalist in succession to Joseph Joos, would be executed January 23, 1945.[75] Joos survived Dachau and recalled some of his fellow prisoners there, including French Catholic workers.[76]

73. Bendiner 1987, 45; Pasture 1999.
74. Patch 1985, 224; Pasture 1999, 162–68.
75. *ZGiLB* 3:202 and 4:170; Gross was beatified in 2001.
76. Joos 1958.

CHAPTER 4

Social Catholic Analyses before *Quadragesimo Anno*

COMMON AIMS, DIVERSE PATHS

In this chapter I provide a baseline in the theoretical and doctrinal assumptions, arguments, and issues that were broadly shared in the 1920s among Catholics concerned with social justice, particularly as regards the relations of the propertied and propertyless classes. Several typical examples of the consistency of the social Catholic stances have already been encountered. Here we wish first to examine the theorists. It will be helpful to indicate where on an ideological spectrum the different schools or orientations of social Catholicism placed themselves—how they differed from and related to one another. Equally important is the correlative question as to what set them apart from other views in a family relationship and made them a part of Catholicism. Here the work of Heinrich Pesch will be the focus of special attention. After all, it has a strong claim to be considered as the most authoritative and comprehensive expression of Catholic (neo-Thomistic) thought in social theory and economics between *Rerum novarum* and *Quadragesimo anno*. To fill in the picture, we will take a look at some other authoritative and representative samples of Catholic social teaching, especially the compendium known as the *Code Social de Malines* (Union internationale d'études sociales [UIES], 1927). A brief comparison with points of view reflecting the authoritarian mindset still so influential at this time helps to understand what this generation of Catholic social theorists was up against. In closing this chapter we will take up one further issue that arose in the 1920s, an issue that the theorists did not yet address. In the simplest terms, this was the question of whether to mobilize Catholic forces by social class, the approach of the milieu organizations, or by age and gender, the approach of Pope Pius XI's Catholic Action.

The two approaches were not necessarily mutually exclusive in practice, as Joseph Cardijn would show (see chapter 7). But they were representative of two ecclesiologies, one (that of Catholic Action) focused on hierarchical authority and the other requiring a theology of the laity that had not yet surfaced, but that underlay Henri Poels's stress on the autonomous engagement of the faithful in their respective social milieus.

All this will serve as relevant context for the narratives that follow of events at the level of individual national settings.

The Catholic Spectrum

Catholic social thought was characterized by the conviction that it was quite distinct from liberalism and socialism as views of society. The very title of Heinrich Pesch's 1901 collection (translated in 2000 as *Liberalism, Socialism, and Christian Social Order*) is a telling example. This remained the case with minor exceptions after World War I. Many others outside of Catholicism were also seeking such an alternative, and corporatist varieties of social thought were prominent in the quest for a Third Way beyond capitalism and socialism in the wake of World War I, with the liberal project regarded by so many contemporaries as having failed, all false promises. Corporatist ideas in one form or another will also be found all across the Catholic spectrum. Corporatism, however, is too diffuse and in some cases too loaded a concept to be the leading idea of our description of the social Catholic spectrum of the 1920s.

A typical case, rather, was an authoritative book in francophone Catholicism that reached its sixth edition in 1921: the *Cours d'économie sociale*, by Charles Antoine, SJ.[1] Its seventh chapter is devoted to "the social question" of poverty and need among the working classes. The eighth and ninth treat the two dominant secular approaches offering prescriptions to deal with it, the liberal school and the socialist school. The tenth chapter presents the Catholic school of social and economic thought, including the two rival Catholic outlooks of Liège and Angers as included in the overall Catholic school.[2] These were not portrayed as mere variants of socialism and liberalism within the Catholic pale, but constituted aspects of a unitary and original view of how modern society should be reshaped from a perspective anchored in the Catholic tradition. In this view, both liberals and socialists started from a truncated social philosophy that prevented their actual plantings from bearing good social fruit.

In claiming that *the* Catholic school was united in regarding society as a moral organism, Antoine was at one with "all professors of Catholic philosophy

---

1. On Antoine, see *DMR* 1:26.
2. On Liège and Angers, see Misner 1991, 190–94 and 208f.

who have published their courses," including the representative names he cited in this connection: Heinrich Pesch, SJ, Theodor Meyer, SJ, Albert Maria Weiss, OP, and Giulio Costa-Rossetti, SJ.[3] They were one in their intransigent opposition to the Enlightenment's individualistic social contract theory that was at the base of both liberalism and socialism. One can name others who agreed, as well: Leo XIII,[4] along with Matteo Liberatore, August Lehmkuhl, and Victor Cathrein, all Jesuit moral philosophers writing in the 1880s and '90s, and two more Jesuits, Belgian and somewhat younger, Arthur Vermeersch and Albert Muller. All of them had a communitarian perspective—that is, they saw society as analogous to an organism (a moral organism inasmuch as it was composed of relatively self-determining persons who were also ends in themselves)—as opposed to the one-sidedly individualistic teachings of doctrinaire nineteenth-century continental liberalism.

Antoine classified the various tendencies and emphases in rivalry with one another within this common framework. His fourth edition reflects the development subsequent to *Rerum novarum*.[5] He saw three groups. The conservatives carried on in the line of the school of Angers, seeing little need for governmental intervention in economic affairs. (Antoine might have termed them liberals, except that that epithet would have implied that they had so far departed from Catholicism as to share the individualistic attitudes of others of their social class.) The reformers (in the line of Liège) saw the need for society to intervene for the improvement of the lot of the working class, by legislation if necessary. The newer third grouping, the Christian democrats, strove for an alliance of the people and the church for social justice by organizing the masses without waiting for the political elite to bestow justice on its own initiative.

The Italian layman and social economist Giuseppe Toniolo (1845–1918) also belongs here, firmly ensconced in Antoine's second subgroup, with affinities also to the first and third.[6] His *Trattato di economia sociale* (1907, repr. 1949) pulled together a life's work in sociology and economics that stressed the ethical and cultural component. His was a Thomistic understanding of human activity, but one with a strong historicizing trait picked up in part from the German historical school of economics with which he was familiar, as well as his own studies in economic history. He was acquainted, in fact, not only with Austrian and German scholarship, but with leading French and Belgian proponents of the revival of Thomism (such as Désiré Mercier in Louvain) and with his Catholic colleagues in economics, as well.[7] The *Rivista internazionale*

3. Antoine 1908, 115.
4. See Schuck 1991, 67–69 and 87, with notes.
5. Antoine 1908, 254–92; for the previous period, see Schuck 2005.
6. See Antoine 1908, 264; Pecorari 1991, 59–62.
7. Spicciani 1984. On Mercier, see Acerbi 1988, 83–85.

delle scienze sociali e discipline ausiliarie that he founded with Salvatore Talamo in 1893 was a truly international journal of high quality. It served as one of the principal organs of theoretical discussions within social Catholicism.

Another important perspective on the inner-Catholic divergences was what they thought of capitalism. Goetz Briefs, who was not altogether content with the polemical attitude he noted among his fellow Catholics toward both capitalism and socialism, drew attention to this.[8] A negative view of capitalism in one sense or another was almost a defining characteristic of self-conscious Catholicism because of its association as an economic doctrine and practice with liberalism—that is, areligious individualism. Capitalism's apologists tended to exhibit an exalted sense of human freedom that was not balanced by any positive appreciation for solidarity with other persons in society at large. But such solidarity, although it necessarily implies some restraints and social obligations, constitutes an essential element of human worth, and not just at the level of intimate family ties. The problem was not with the formation and investment of capital—most Catholics stoutly defended the private ownership of property, including productive property—but with the systemic capital*ism* that conferred on persons in possession of sufficient capital the virtually unrestricted domination of the economic process.[9]

Within the bounds of this general disinclination to spring to the defense of capitalism, however, the spectrum of opinion that Briefs surveyed displays quite a variation. An example of the more positive assessment that was possible, if not dominant, is furnished by a wartime essay looking toward the postwar prospects of Catholicism in Germany.[10] Even Franz Keller presented the spirit of capitalism negatively as characterized by individualism, unbridled competition, and the lack of any but a survival-of-the-fittest social conscience. But he emphasized the separable moral achievements of capitalism that should be preserved and enhanced: its spirit of enterprise and responsibility for the things of this earth, its ability to contribute as no other economic system to prosperity, its respect for capital as the material basis for an ethical utilization of goods. The Catholic ethos, Keller argued, should not exhaust itself in anti-capitalism, but should appreciate the contribution modern business can make to the integration of sound economic practice into the whole of the Christian life.

The Jesuit moralists whom we've already named, and to whom we shall return in the person of Heinrich Pesch, were all middle-of-the-roaders. They remained for the most part unwilling to attribute the virtues just so positively

8. Briefs 1921.
9. A point of view also articulated in *QA* 106f.
10. Keller 1918, 362–66.

assessed to capitalism, though they appreciated entrepreneurs, at least those who could carve out a business niche for their firms that allowed them to treat their employees humanely. At the other end of the Catholic spectrum from Franz Keller were some Austrian theorists (none with the name recognition of Joseph Schumpeter or Friedrich von Hayek) concentrated in the so-called "Viennese orientations" (*Wiener Richtungen*).[11] They grew from roots in the theories of Karl von Vogelsang. The most consistent and most vehement anti-capitalists among them were the radical Vogelsangians around Anton Orel, who ensouled a romantic monarchist youth movement during this period of the blossoming of youth movements. The gifted Ernst Karl Winter remained true to this basic orientation, though in a chastened form. Orel went so far as to belittle *Rerum novarum* as inadequate and hardly authoritative, a rare occurrence in social Catholicism. But he was also among those Austrian Catholics who were opposed to the exclusive connection of Catholics with any one political party.

In contrast, the Christian labor movement in Austria under Leopold Kunschak took *Rerum novarum* as its guide, or at least its point of departure. Karl Lugmayer was the theorist of this tendency. He helped draw up a labor union platform, the *Linzer Programm* of 1923. It insisted, unlike most other Austrian Catholic positions, on maintaining the democratic political institutions that came with the First Republic (1920–34) and called for anti-capitalist corporatist economic reform within this framework. The goal sought was the reconciliation of "industrial control and the worker community." Like the Orelians, this labor wing held the conventional wage contract to be beneath human dignity—it had to be replaced by some sort of partnership relationship between employer or firm and employees.[12]

A third Wiener Richtung pulled in still another direction. Othmar Spann was a social philosopher (1878–1950, at the University of Vienna from 1919), who developed a theory diametrically opposed to individualism called "universalism." Although little known in the history of social thought that is written about in America today, Spann formed a school of neo-Romantic social philosophy and exercised a significant attraction among Catholics in Austria and Germany, including Eugen Kogon.[13] He was responsible in large part for the renewed attention paid to Adam Müller's early nineteenth-century political thought after World War I.[14]

Spann spoke of "the whole" of society as logically and even philosophically preexistent to individual persons, who are "members" and not themselves a

11. See Weinzierl 1980, 2030–32, and, in context, Weinzierl 1983, 1:471–74.
12. Diamant 1960, 121, 214–20.   13. Hürten 1992, 154.
14. Misner 1991, 35–39.

whole. True, society does not exist apart from its members; it is not present as such except in and through them; but no individual comes into his or her own except through others.[15] On this reading, the social connection between people is a basic precondition of each one's life as a human being. The ancient idea of society as a body—and individuals as the members of this body—played a background role in Spann's updated philosophical-sociological construction. One may note the strong expression of neo-Romantic organic thinking, with a concomitant stress on the principle of authority, in the best-selling book by Karl Adam, *The Spirit of Catholicism*, in the same period.[16]

In most circumstances political-party considerations precluded talk of a Christian socialism. Stereotypes flourished: socialists lumped Catholics together with all the other retrograde forces, hostile to the destiny of the working class, while Catholics regarded all socialists as materialists out to establish the dictatorship of the proletariat. However, there were exceptions, especially where the revisionist controversies within socialism were carried out prominently, as in Germany.[17] At any rate, for a short time during the November Revolution of 1918, a number of Catholics claimed the label of Christian socialism for Catholic social teaching. Even Heinrich Pesch put out a pamphlet in the 1918 run-up to the elections for the National Assembly with the title "Not Communist, but Christian Socialism!" Otherwise, however, he conceded the term to his ideological opponents. Max Scheler, too, wrote an article in *Hochland* (1919) that set up the alternative between "Prophetischer oder marxistischer Sozialismus."

Theodor Steinbüchel was the exception, a Catholic author who did not give up in the attempt to redeem the concept. Influenced by Scheler, the future professor of moral theology at Tübingen published his *Socialism as a Moral Idea* in 1921. He found in Johann Plenge, a sociologist at the University of Münster, a dialogue partner with a communitarian interpretation of the socialist idea. And a circle of religious (Catholic) democratic socialists managed to form and present their ideas to the public in dialogue with Marxist thought—but this was a little later on.[18]

There was no lack of mutual critique and disagreement among the Catholic tendencies, of course. In particular, the Jesuits, with Heinrich Pesch as their leading authority, developed a theory called solidarism that involved a rejection of the more extreme tenets of the *Wiener Richtungen*. To stay with Austria

---

15. Baumgartner 1977, 31–37; Stegmann and Langhorst 2000, 716–20.
16. See Karl Adam 1929; originally published in 1924 as *Wesen des Katholizismus*; see Krieg 1992, 1999.
17. Stegmann and Langhorst 2000, 720–27.
18. See Knapp 1975; see Baumgartner 1977, 131, and Focke 1978, 71–174.

for the moment, this moderate tendency had been represented in Innsbruck by the Jesuit Josef Biederlack; he carried on a running battle with Vogelsang's rejection of interest as usury—his book *Die Soziale Frage* went through ten editions between 1895 and 1925. For that matter, Heinrich Pesch himself, in an early work in the Innsbruck Jesuits' periodical, had developed a theory that justified departing from the old prohibition of pure interest on a loan.[19] Although the church had long since relaxed the prohibition in practice, it was not yet clear on exactly what grounds. Pesch proposed that lending money be conceived as rendering an economic service, which, like any other service, could claim its price. The price would not normally deviate far from a level indicated by the market; this would be a perfectly legitimate rate of interest as such.[20] The classic Aristotelian theory of money gave rise to recurrent suspicions that any modern economy depended essentially on an intrinsically sinful practice: usury. Pesch invalidated that suspicion with his new perspective.

In Vienna itself the influence of social policy meliorism had made itself felt since the death of Vogelsang in 1890 and the publication of *Rerum novarum* in 1891. This meliorist approach was a matter of gradualist social change, referred to as *Sozialpolitik*, with government intervening where helpful, rather than a radical project of remaking the system from stem to stern, called *Sozialreform*.[21] One of Vogelsang's priest-disciples, Franz M. Schindler, became professor of moral theology at the University of Vienna and started a line of social thought more like that of the Jesuits.[22] His successor was Ignaz Seipel, the future chancellor of the First Republic. Then there was the young Johannes Messner, for whom a position in social ethics at the university was created in 1934, and who worked with two prelates influenced by Biederlack, Sigismund Waitz and Ämilian Schöpfer.[23] A largely lay movement also gained ground and spread a moderate doctrine modeled on that of the German Volksverein; this was the Austrian Volksbund, propelled by a talented journalist, Richard Schmitz. The social Catholic perspective prevailing elsewhere thus prevailed also in Vienna, despite the radical *Richtungen*. Schindler, Schmitz, and Messner were still opposed to capitalism "in its liberal phase," but could easily accept a duly tamed capitalism.[24] Johannes Messner and Josef Dobretsberger of Graz were moderate "solidarists," the former at least with a greater appreciation of market economics than Pesch himself evinced.

Around social Catholicism proper, with its activists and theorists, there

---

19. Pesch 1888.
20. Pesch 1905–25, 5:721–31.
21. See Mueller 1984, 87–90 and 103, on the role of Franz Hitze in favor of legislating step-by-step improvements in the conditions of labor.
22. Boyer 1995, 298–321; 2010, 413–16.   23. Weiler 1992, 122.
24. To quote Briefs 1951, 1:159.

was a much broader communitarian current or upsurge in the years after World War I. While Romano Guardini was savoring the public reception of *The Spirit of the Liturgy* (1918) and Martin Buber was still writing *Ich und Du* (1923) or *Die Chassidischen Bücher* (1927), an older book by the sociologist Ferdinand Tönnies was enjoying an extraordinary vogue in the 1920s. This was his famous comparison and contrast of community (organic, face-to-face, solidary, typically small and rural, associated with the Romantic outlook) and society (contractarian, individualistic, a product of Enlightenment rationalism as much as of anonymous urban masses), entitled *Gemeinschaft und Gesellschaft* (1887). It met a keenly felt need, just as the youth movements of the same period did in their own way. The possibility of felt community seemed to provide an answer to the cultural despair that was another characteristic of the time, and not just in the countries that were defeated in the First World War (as in Oswald Spengler's *Decline of the West*, 1918).[25]

The attraction of Romantic art, literature, and music went along in the public mind with a renewed respectability for certain longstanding traditions, such as monarchy or Catholicism or the Baroque (as, for instance, in the Salzburg Mozart festivals). Catholics could also see themselves as heirs of a tradition once again conceivably in the avant-garde, buoyed up as they were in Germany by Max Scheler's championing of Catholic thought. Romano Guardini engaged his immense genius in church and academia at this juncture, celebrating the "awakening of the church in souls" through Catholic youth encampments and by fostering the liturgical movement in parishes. Given also the arrival of Catholic politicians, along with socialists, to a share in governmental power, there was hope that a new beginning could be made and that a Third Way compatible with Catholic social ideas might well take shape.[26]

The evocation of Gemeinschaft (community) would play a prominent role in the cultural and political life of the interwar period in many an involved connection. It is interesting to note that the leading Dutch Catholic intellectual journal between the wars was called *De Gemeenschap*. (Its counterpart in the United States was not so different: *Commonweal*.) The Catholic subculture of the German-speaking countries in particular gravitated around the appeal of community. It often served also as an anti-Semitic rallying cry (especially in the combination Volksgemeinschaft), just as the very appellative "Christian"

---

25. Stern 1961.

26. Both French and German Catholics spoke of the preceding half century as a time of "exile," exile in their own land. Among those who hailed the dawn of a *Rückkehr aus dem Exil*, notions of a restoration of past glories seemed to predominate over creative adaptations to new circumstances; Hürten 1992, 65; Komonchak 1999. But see Schloesser 2010, based on his 2005 work, for Maritain's use of Thomas Aquinas to foster the latter course in a somewhat analogous ultramodern direction.

did (as in Christlich-soziale partei), a connotation that one can unfortunately not ignore.[27] But the basic semantic function of Gemeinschaft in the present context was to mark off an understanding of social reality distinct from contractarian or collectivist (liberal or socialist) notions of Gesellschaft. More fully than the latter, it could nurture the conviction of the human dignity of each human person; better than the former, it could bring to expression an organic idea of persons in community. It nourished the dream of recombining these two elements, which belonged together, after they had tragically come apart and found themselves pitted against each other.

The Solidarist Middle Ground of Heinrich Pesch

Among those who fostered the postwar openness to communitarian values such as the common good was Heinrich Pesch (1854–1926). In his irenic way Pesch laid out his philosophical objections to Spann's anthropology and to Orel's corporatist rejection of private ownership of natural resources and industry at several places in his massive *Lehrbuch der Nationalökonomie*.[28] But he was much more concerned with setting forth a sound philosophical anthropology that would serve as a basis for all the social sciences and for economics in particular. He devoted his whole first volume to this task, developing solidarism as a theory of social philosophy, before entering the field of his chosen discipline, economics itself. Then, in the second volume, he compared and contrasted economic theories, properly speaking, and proposed his own. Beside or beyond economic liberalism and socialism there was room for a better-founded and more humane economic order or system, if not quite an economic model or Third Way. He called it the social labor system, itself often referred to as solidarism.[29]

As was already true of his earlier work, Pesch takes a decidedly neo-Thomistic approach, in accord with his Jesuit predecessors and conspicuously also with Leo XIII's encyclicals.[30] However, in social ethics neo-Thomism did not simply represent an extension of the standard moral theology of the scholastic manuals, where, for instance, the issue of justice was generally confined

---

27. Pauley 1992, 150–64.
28. Pesch 1905–25; see, e.g., on Spann's "universalism," ibid., 1:447; on Orel's radicalism 1:215–18 and 2:241–44. A good brief recent treatment is found in Stegmann and Langhorst 2000, 727–45. On Pesch himself, see Ruhnau 1980; Rauscher 1988b, 4:362, and Rauscher 1979, 3:136–48, as well as Mueller 1980; 1994a; and 1994b. For more on Pesch's economics, see also Mulcahy 1952. Indications of his influence in American Catholicism are found in McGreevy 2003, 142–47. For Rupert J. Ederer's translation of the *Lehrbuch* into English, see Pesch 2002.
29. An English translation, Pesch 2008, 147–55, provides a quasi-popular précis of the argument.
30. See, e.g., Pesch 1901.

to commutative justice (that is, in transactions between individuals as private persons).[31] The Pesch of the economics textbook (his five-volume *Lehrbuch*), writing since the turn of the century, was one of the scholastic pioneers in recognizing the relative autonomy of the social sciences. He entered into dialogue with one of them, economic theory, so as to relate Christian morality to that field more competently and authoritatively. He recognized that one could not pronounce on social justice without taking into account contemporary analyses of economic life and structures.

Pesch's neo-Thomism made itself felt in structuring the relationship between economics and the ultimate meaning of human existence according to the paradigm of nature and grace. Pesch's overall scheme for understanding economic reality involved relating it to philosophical first principles. This is most evident in his elevation of Aristotle's final cause—the purpose of a thing or an operation—to the determinative theoretical point of reference for his whole system. One also sees the scholastic mind at work in the effort to make needed distinctions at every step along the way. Philosophically, he insisted that work was central to being human; economic activity was oriented to the good of humankind. Human beings were hylomorphic, composed of body and soul, and had needs that could only be met by work. This provided him with his point of departure in economics from the material wants and needs of human beings, but with a subtle difference from classical theory. For him economics was not a "dismal science" focusing on the disposition of scarce commodities,[32] but a matter of understanding how human activity, at the level of material goods and services rendered for compensation, was intrinsically oriented to and fitted for the satisfaction of human needs in community.

In the history of economic analysis Heinrich Pesch follows in the wake of the so-called Kathedersozialisten or academic socialists. This grouping was a wing not of socialism—their nickname originated among their liberal critics—but of the historical school of German economists. In particular, he saw one of his teachers in Berlin, Adolph Wagner (1835–1917), as a pivotal figure, since he was interested in working out a theory that would provide a coherent alternative to individualism and socialism. He missed the mark, as Pesch saw it, for want of an adequate (that is, Thomistic) political philosophy and a consistent systematic perspective, and strayed into "state socialism."[33] Pesch was in tune with the leading economists of his generation, who were already convinced of the shortcomings of liberal economic theory while unwilling to jump on the Marxist bandwagon.[34] To Pesch, therefore, his teachers practiced a discipline

31. See Gallagher 1990.
32. Carlyle 1849, 672.
33. Pesch 1905–25, 2:202–12; see Ruhnau 1980, 263–68.
34. Schumpeter 1954, 766.

in search of an explicit theoretical basis. Pesch was anxious to provide this with his teleological (purpose-oriented) approach.[35] In this endeavor he was not hampered, as one might expect of a scholastic of his generation, by an ahistorical understanding of natural law. On the contrary, he became keenly aware of the changes and shifts that take place from one period of human history to another. He did not expect the natural-law precepts of solidarity, the common good, or justice to give rise to the same institutions in the twentieth century as in the thirteenth or sixteenth.[36]

Solidarism offered the necessary comprehensive social-philosophical horizon of which the historical school, despite the historicist allergies of some of its representatives, stood in need. It placed "the human person in the midst of society" as the organizing perspective at the center of all the social sciences; the special object of economic researches would be "human beings at work, as masters of the cosmos, in the midst of society."[37] Thus economists could and should always survey their material with an eye to material human needs (and the ethical imperative to satisfy them), but without reducing their notion of human persons to that of unconnected atomistic individuals.

Pesch's view of the person in society, pivotal for his whole enterprise, was meant to be in stark contrast with the liberal view prevailing since the Enlightenment and in harmony with the general communitarian tendencies of pre- and counter-Enlightenment thinkers such as the German Romantics and Romantic Idealists. However, he did not simply choose a starting point diametrically opposed to liberal individualism, as did Othmar Spann.[38] In fact, he

35. Ruhnau 1980, 270.

36. In Pesch's time the historical school of economics, like theology and law, was racked by controversies over "historicism." "Historicism" took on the implication of an inherent tendency of positivist historical research to engender a pervasive relativism of values and norms, including ethical norms. Max Weber solved this problem for himself and many others in a neo-Kantian way by declaring value judgments to be out of place in the social sciences. The only role they play in research is the liminary one of guiding the scholar in the choice of lines or topics of research. At the other end, once the value-free research is published, the unscientific but public-spirited moral side of those involved in or utilizing the research for private purposes or public policy was to take charge again. While in the lab, so to speak, social scientists were to ignore value judgments; not so, however, in their capacity as responsible members of society, where their advocacy was not a matter of "science" but of personal conviction; Wittkau 1992, 142–46.

It seems that Heinrich Pesch played a peripheral part in the controversies that swirled around historicist relativism and Max Weber's solution to it; Pesch 1905–25, 1:121–24. At the meeting of the Social Policy Association in 1909, Eugen von Philippovich spoke approvingly of Pesch's teleologically and ethically oriented approach in political economy and provoked Max Weber's vigorous rejection of any such mixing of science and ethics. Weber's view would prove more congenial to the secular mind, but during the decline of liberalism between the world wars, many Catholics and others were confident that the times were propitious for a modern, ethically guided social science.

37. Pesch's formulation already in 1899 as cited by Ruhnau 1980, 270; see Pesch 1905–25 1:1–17 and 2:215.

38. Pesch 1905–25, 1:447.

implicitly allied himself with, for instance, Kant (but more pertinently with the whole Thomistic school) in treating the human person not as a means or a mere part of a whole, but as an end.

And yet he was just as emphatic in insisting that human beings are not just accidentally, but inherently, connected with other persons in a common life, for which they are morally responsible agents.[39] This does not merely constitute a fact of life: mutual dependence. Rather it is a principle: the principle of solidarity. Personal human dignity is essentially related to the recognition of the human dignity and responsible freedom of other agents besides oneself—a recognition extending to all other instances of the species.[40] One is not just an individual, facing the pleasant or unpleasant task of coming to some tolerable arrangements for living in society; nor is one just a member of society, suffering from a psychological need for some private space, control, fulfillment. Instead, the human person in society is and always has been both at the same time. Hence, mutual assistance both given and received is a law of human life. This, at least, is what should be clear to Christians from the biblical interpretation of humanity as created for the shared destiny of union with God.

What this means for the understanding of political economy is, first, to underscore the finality (or purpose) of economic activity in general: it is to serve the needs of the population, to raise the national standard of living, to see to it that the available resources are best used to subserve both the individual and the community needs of a people. The key factor to be attended to and developed is labor. Adam Smith focused on the division of labor as the key to increasing wealth. Heinrich Pesch welcomed this focus and pointed out that such division of labor calls for and can promote better-developed bonds of solidarity.[41] As one person receives work from another and passes it on to a third in an ever more highly organized process of production, distribution, and consumption, social connections are laid down on which a humane society can capitalize. Working and enjoying the fruits of one's labor are the humanizing and socializing factors that loom the largest in most persons' lives.

From this follows a key axiom of the solidarist approach that Pesch commended to his contemporaries: "socialization of persons," not of things.[42] The socialist theorists had, as usual, got it half right: the economy needed socialization. The kind of socialization to pursue, however, was not by taking (all) the means of production out of private hands and into the hands of the state, but rather by organizing and developing the capacities of human beings to work cooperatively. They, after all, are the ones who run the economy and benefit by it. What he had in mind with this advice will become clearer as we proceed.

39. Ibid., 1:1–20; see Pesch 1988, 11–26.
41. Ibid., 3:421–38.
40. Pesch 1905–25, 1:33.
42. See ibid., 2:219; see Pesch 1988, 153.

The principle of solidarity places into a broader, more adequate context the principle of economy, which normally governs the science of economics.[43] Certainly, in microeconomics (or what Pesch referred to as the private economy), the principle of economy holds unchallenged sway—that is, the dominant issue is marshaling and husbanding limited resources for maximum effective output. True and valid as this is, Pesch maintained that at the national level, in a fully functional political economy, the principle of economy must be tempered by and subordinated to the principle of solidarity. In other words, just as in political society, weaker members may not be cut off or denied their rights for the greater effectiveness of the state, so weaker economic participants may not be put at further disadvantage in the name of higher productivity or greater gross national product. Since a country's economy is ordained to fulfill the purpose of satisfying the country's needs, the principle of solidarity must complement and if necessary correct the operation of the principle of economy.

This solidarity, which is so basic to human identity, is present in different forms and levels. The references made thus far have been quite general: to the universal solidarity of the whole human race and to the solidarity that connects all citizens (and residents) of a state with one another. Pesch naturally does not think highly of the class solidarity of the bourgeois in one camp and the workers in another—that is, a group loyalty that creates walls and makes any perpetrator of interclass solidarity a traitor to one's class. He also ruled out any racial or national solidarity that would offend against the all-encompassing universal solidarity of the human species.[44] Affirmatively, the characteristic emphasis of solidarism is upon two other levels: the family and the industry or occupational group (as in the insurance industry, the dairy industry, the aircraft industry, or the advertising community).[45] The family was, of course, to be held in respect as a natural community in the strongest sense: as required by the (moral) law of nature for the propagation and education of children. Organization by occupational groupings was not a matter of natural law in that strong sense, but was natural in the sense of a healthy development in an organically sound advanced society.[46]

As a system of social philosophy, therefore, or as a coherent view of society, Pesch sets forth the distinctive features of solidarism in the following terms:

Solidarism is a social system that validates the solidary connection of human beings as such [that is, "one for all and all for one"]. [It acknowledges their] membership

---

43. Pesch 1905–25, 1:35–36; Pesch 1988, 149–51.
44. Pesch 1905–25, 2:594–96.
45. Ibid., 1:432–34.
46. Ibid., 1:442. In this connection, Pesch 1905–25, 1:411 refers also to Émile Durkheim's parallel considerations.

in the natural communities of Family and State in accordance with the nature of the respective community, while also grounding and advocating as rich a development as historical circumstances permit of cooperative, representative and corporative associations. [Such associations as arise] on the basis of place in society and occupation (*nach Stand und Beruf*) maintain their vigor by virtue of the public spirit of their members, but they also may enjoy legally recognized status.[47]

The difference from individualistic and socialistic societal ideals is sufficiently plain to obviate any long further explanations. "Catholic solidarism," in the words of Matthew Lamb, "aimed at transposing pre-modern understandings of natural law, of human beings as essentially social, and of society itself as organic and cooperative, into the modern contexts of industrialized societies with complex exchange economies."[48]

The Solidarist Labor System

Within this comprehensive view of human nature and society, Heinrich Pesch went on to develop a theory of how an economy that he called the social or solidarist labor system, as distinct from the liberal (that is, actually existing capitalist) and socialist economic theories, should be structured in the twentieth century.[49]

If society is most adequately regarded as a moral organism, then it would stand to reason that it should have organs at its disposition, not only in the cultural sector (schools and school boards, academies, accrediting associations, churches, zoos, art galleries, musical groups) and in the political sector (cities, counties, states, federal government, with legislative, judicial, and executive functions), but also in the economic sector (shops, firms, trade associations, labor unions, chambers of commerce, serving consumers through production and distribution). It was Pesch's conviction that a defective organic development in the socioeconomic sector, imbalanced to the detriment of labor (working people), meant that concerns proper to the economy were left to the government to deal with bureaucratically, with the crude tools of coercive intervention. What was needed was a set of organs beyond the marketplace that would permit the economic actors themselves to face and deal with economic issues of import to society—in other words (to translate a bit crudely and rapidly into more familiar terms), a comprehensive set of trade associations including shareholder, management, and labor representation.

The interaction among these national organizations at the summit would eventually have to be organized; Pesch did not shrink from speaking of an

---

47. Ibid., 1:432.
48. See Lamb 1994, 908.
49. Pesch 1905–25, 2:213–84.

"economic parliament" as the logical central clearing-house of this decentralized organic development.[50] In the typology we have borrowed from Schmitter, we can speak of a theory of "societal corporatism."[51]

The aim of unburdening the state and its coercive power from overmuch regulation of the economy, let alone engaging in a command economy, did not go so far as to banish government from any role in the social labor system, as earlier liberal doctrine would have it. For one thing, the cooperation of the state would be needed to sanction the formation and activities of the trade associations in the socialized market (or the social market).[52] And courts of law would always be needed, at least to adjudicate conflicts that would arise from the very operation of the social market. But Pesch cherished the hope that the vast administrative and regulatory oversight required in an advanced economy could be done more effectively and efficiently on a basis of properly promoted cooperation than in the mode of coercion proper to government or of competition proper to unsocialized markets.[53]

Hence he was careful to allow for state intervention only to the extent that it was truly helpful and necessary. This was to be judged on a case-by-case basis, for the most part. Thus, in a discussion of when a given industry might legitimately be nationalized (for instance, as an alternative to a private monopoly), he proposed several criteria to consider.[54] Will the state monopoly be technically and economically feasible? Financially supportable and necessary? Would a regulated (private) monopoly serve the purpose just as well? Behind all such questions stood the conviction that the government's inherent purpose was not to satisfy the economic needs of the population, but to create the framework of order, freedom, and justice in which a people's cultural and economic life could thrive.[55] His idea of the range of competence of government had always gone far beyond the stereotypical liberal night-watchman state, but it included cultural and economic aims only indirectly. As the last barrier against chaos and civil war, the state had to provide for emergency situations and breakdowns of other societal institutions, but should not take over their functions without necessity.

In such discussions Pesch implicitly proceeded according to what his disciple, Gustav Gundlach, SJ, was soon to dub "the principle of subsidiarity."

50. Ibid., 2:259.
51. Schmitter 1974.
52. To borrow a term from Bruyn 1991; Waters 1994.
53. At the same time, Pesch was realistic or cautious enough to judge that attempts to erect a thoroughgoing corporative regime in the prevailing circumstances would do more harm than good. Hence he recommended that one work to open existing institutions and associations, which could function in the current economy, to solidarist horizons and a cooperative social spirit; Ruhnau 1980, 317–23.
54. Pesch 1905–25, 2:253–56.
55. Ibid., 1:183–84; 3:744–838.

That is, the state as the broadest all-inclusive organized level of society should be ready to offer aid and assistance (Latin *subsidium*) to smaller units within it, but only in case of need; governmental agencies should not supplant intermediary bodies that are capable of meeting social needs.[56]

Pesch applied this principle even at another level, where it has been rarely noticed, but where its presence helps clear up much obscurity—namely, in his rather diffuse explorations of vocational order or corporative organizations.[57] For all Pesch's advocacy of vocational organs that would serve the body politic by removing much of the burden of economic and market regulation from the direct responsibility of government, he deliberately refrained from calling for a complete corporative regime sanctioned by law. (To anticipate, this means that he declined to go so far in this direction as the encyclical *Quadragesimo anno* of 1931 would go.) Despite his openness to an eventual *Wirtschaftsparlament* as cited earlier,[58] he was also and decidedly open to a plurality of vocational groupings, some official and others voluntary.[59] And his reasoning was his typical appeal to the principle of subsidiarity (without the name): only in those cases where specific reasons indicated the necessity or benefit of governmental involvement should the legislature authorize or set up an organization to represent a given industry.

Another reason was the absence of any historical example in the modern world of a successful overall system of vocational order (corporatism, functional representation) or even of a plausible outline of one that would not severely, unduly limit freedom. (Pesch thought primarily of entrepreneurial initiative, since forced labor did not seem to be what advocates of a corporative regime before World War I were contemplating.) It is clear that in Pesch's mind, trade associations should encourage and promote, rather than supplant, honest initiatives—for instance, by stabilizing markets.[60] As an alternative to direct governmental regulation, his view is that such bodies should lean "more to restraining and controlling than to positive direction and planning."[61]

But without official standing, what sort of beneficial influence did Pesch expect vocational groups to exercise? Of course they could function as pressure groups or lobbying organizations for their members. This, within moral

---

56. See Ederer in Pesch 1988, 2–3; Ruhnau 1980, 117–19; see also Rauscher 1986. The American constitution, according to which all tasks not assigned to the federal government remain with the several states, is an instance of this principle. Oswald von Nell-Breuning (1970, 6:115) cites Abraham Lincoln's 1854 formulation (*Sacramentum Mundi*, article on "Social Movements") as follows: "The legitimate object of government is to do for a community of people whatever they need to have done but cannot do at all, or cannot so well do for themselves in their separate and individual capacities. In all that people can individually do as well for themselves, government ought not to interfere."

57. See Ruhnau 1980, 310–16.
58. Pesch 1905 25, 2:259.
59. Ibid., 3:505.
60. Ruhnau 1980, 328–29.
61. Briefs 1951, 1:159.

bounds, was legitimate enough, but by itself hardly constituted a contribution to the good of society that was the raison d'être of solidaristic vocational organization in Pesch's scheme of things. Besides the defense of the group's interests (for instance, those of a footwear industry trade association), narrowly considered, a properly motivated and oriented vocational organization would pursue other goals for the shoe industry (including employees, management, stockholders, distributors, retailers) as occasion demanded, both within the industry and outside. Commissioning of research projects, cooperation on the development of products, joint marketing agreements, training programs, pension fund management, and the like would be the sort of economic services such an organization could offer its members internally. Lobbying or studying proposed legislation and making contacts, engaging in public relations and education, facilitating international trade, or at least contributing to such activities in the framework of a more comprehensive association such as a chamber of commerce are examples of external functions an industry council might undertake.

Such activities, of course, are carried out today by trade associations, as they were in Pesch's Germany. Pesch, however, could point to the model of consultation and cooperation between labor and industrialists that had arisen during the First World War and that was codified just afterwards as the ZAG (Central Working Partnership of Employers and Employees). He saw it as pointing the way for all the trade associations, as "communities of/at work" (*Arbeitsgemeinschaften*), to promote positions common to labor and capital, rather than having the chambers of commerce take one side on every issue and labor unions the other. The vocational groups' central task, it would then appear, was to formulate the respective interests of labor and capital and then to mediate between them so as to regulate the market, to render markets socially productive, in a way that sheer competition would not.[62]

In all of this Pesch was aware that no stable examples of what he ideated were at hand. He had to content himself with pointing to developments that seemed to go in the desired direction. What was that direction? It was to embody the solidarity of a whole group engaged in the same economic activity, joined together by the sharing of their productive efforts. This solidarity would

---

62. Pesch 1921, 43. But the market is a phenomenon that exercised on Pesch a quite meager fascination (see Pesch 1905–25, vol. 5). This is where his distance from classical economics is most evident. Contrast Adam Smith's *Wealth of Nations*, I.ii.1, on the pivotal role of "the propensity to truck, barter, and exchange one thing for another"; A. Smith 1976. This goes together with Pesch's neglect of consumer representation among the stakeholders in the trade associations. Although he emphasized that the whole purpose of economic activity is to serve the needs of human beings, Pesch saw socialization of producers rather than consumers as the priority. Perhaps this was a tacit acknowledgment of the benefits of a competitive market economy, after all.

encompass both those who direct the enterprise and those who work with (for) them.[63] Would this not mean the accession of employees, even laborers, to share the kind of say and status that their employers already generally enjoyed? Pesch seems to have seen this potential in the ZAG model, enhanced as a solidarist labor system.

Thus, for all the sympathy and length with which Pesch treated the question of vocational order, and for all the deference he paid to his predecessors in Catholic social thought, such as Vogelsang and Hitze, he shied away from clothing the ideal skeleton of solidarism with much organizational flesh in this regard. In particular, having once (in the 1890s) been mightily attracted to Baron von Vogelsang's schemes of a complete reorganization of the economy along corporatist lines, and having come to appreciate the depth and unpredictability of historical change on social forms, he foreswore any prospect of designing a vocational order.[64] His social labor system was something more modest and more a matter of principles than of applications. It was, all the same, he held, more soundly based than the prevailing ideologies of liberal individualism and Marxist socialism.

Other Standard Works

In the tradition of Antoine, Toniolo, and Pesch, Albert Muller in Antwerp also published a political economics text from the perspective of Catholic social doctrine. Based on the course that he gave to Jesuit seminarians, it first came out in 1927; hence we did not examine it here to establish a baseline of standard Catholic teaching circa 1920. All the same, it reflects the same general emphases and self-placements in contrast to liberalism and socialism.[65] Muller would be involved at least to some extent in the drafting of *Quadragesimo Anno*.[66] Earlier, Muller had collaborated with Arthur Vermeersch in another genre of influential and standard-setting social Catholic literature—namely, the social manual or guide. The Vermeersch *Manuel social* went back to 1900 in its first edition and went into expanded and revised second (1904) and third (1909) editions in two volumes.[67] It was not the first of its kind, however; that honor seems to belong to Léon Dehon in 1894; his *Manuel social chrétien* gave firm support to the nascent and embattled Christian democracy in the wake of *Rerum novarum*.[68]

The subtitle of Vermeersch's manual reveals its particular orientation: *La législation et les oeuvres en Belgique*. It is first of all a description, a catalog or

63. Ruhnau 1980, 311.
65. Muller 1933.
67. Vermeersch and Muller, 1909.
64. Ibid., 319 and 326.
66. Droulers 1981, 152–55.
68. Ledure 2005.

inventory, of the social legislation and associations of Belgium. Thus it offered concrete information for anyone confronting a social problem and wishing to know what the legal situation was and where to turn for further assistance. Second, it gathered together statistical data on the dimensions of the social problems of the time. Beyond that, it at least implied a program of action or a set of goals to be pursued, with sage advice on how to engage oneself in the effort as a public or private person.[69] The principles were those Vermeersch laid out scholastically in a seminary course, published in Latin in 1901 as *Quaestiones de Justitia ad usum hodiernum*. The manual itself was nothing if not close to the current situation in law and social organizations. In Flemish, a periodical, *De Gids op maaatschappelijk (sociaal) gebied*, offered guidance since its inception in 1902.

In France the Action populaire of Gustav Desbuquois and his Jesuit confreres, starting in 1905, included an annual *Guide Social* among their educative and publishing activities. It contained a collection of articles and *enquêtes* by various authors providing for French Catholicism a resource comparable to Vermeersch for Belgium.[70] In 1914 they published a 1,200-page *Année Sociale Internationale 1913–1914*. It truly was a mine of data and current developments of all sorts covering the industrialized world. Of course, it reflected the perspective of progressive Catholic social thought of the era. After World War I the annual publication of the *Guide social* was replaced by a smaller but more frequent periodical, the *Dossiers de l'Action Populaire*, backed up twice a month by a simpler, more directly practical bulletin called the *Cahiers d'Action Religieuse et Sociale*.[71]

Finally, another summary statement of authoritative Catholic social doctrine, in one rather slim, almost catechetical, volume, was the *Code Social* of Malines (Mechlin).[72] It was a project of a transnational association for Catholic social ethics, the Union internationale d'études sociales (UIES), called the Union de Malines, for short, founded in 1920 under the presidency of Cardinal Mercier.[73] A Louvain professor, Maurice Defourny, was its secretary, and Eugène Duthoit, the dean of law at the Institut Catholique of Lille and president of the Semaines sociales de France, may be regarded as its leading spirit.[74] The *Code Social* was rapidly translated into six languages, including German and English. The Catholic Social Guild published it as *A Code of Social Principles* (Oxford: 1929).

69. Gérard Cooreman, in his preface to Vermeersch and Muller 1909, 8.
70. Droulers 1969, 86.
71. Droulers 1981, 50.
72. See Union international d'études socials 1927.
73. See Monti 1924, 58; see De Maeyer 2003, 112–14.
74. On Duthoit, see *DMR* 4:216–19; Caudron 1991; see also Droulers 1981, 182.

Revealing the undergirding perspective of the whole project, Defourny stated that to bring about a mutually positive and effective relationship among the disparate initiatives of individuals and private firms or other groups, it is preferable, as a rule, to operate through the social bodies of which we are naturally a part, rather than to bring the coercive powers of the state directly into play.[75] This statement extolling intermediary bodies may be regarded as another prefiguration of the principle of subsidiarity as well as the basis for all the corporatist schemes that social Catholics sketched between the world wars. Figuring explicitly among these bodies were the family, the professions (Pesch's vocational organizations), voluntary associations, and the church, but also the League of Nations. Even though, as emerges from the last item, German Catholics were not represented in the UIES—Mercier after all was a leader of the Belgian resistance to the German occupation, and both Louvain and Lille were devastated by the Germans—one can see that the common ground between German social Catholics and their colleagues to the west far outweighed any nationalist differences. Even the contemporary preoccupation with organization by *Stand* is reflected in the section (articles 51–52) on "the Christian organization of classes." It has the same (modest) view of the place of class-based representative bodies or organizations with a goal of interclass harmony and mutual respect that characterizes Pesch's discussions. Defourny highlights this doctrine and common teaching about the intermediary bodies in his preface; the *Code* itself does not treat them in a special section of their own.[76]

The first nine of the 143 short articles or sections that make up the book lay out the anthropology of Catholicism. As in Pesch, this was contrasted with the individualism that so infects modern outlooks. But it finds the absolute priority accorded to society by socialist and positivist sociologists (Durkheim?) equally wrong, since society exists ultimately for the sake of its members qua persons. Other common themes, mostly Leonine ones, resound as well. The church has a legitimate role to play in calling economic agents to task. All sectors of society must cooperate to maintain the vigor of family life. The purpose of the state is to provide for the common good; since this includes private initiative, the state is not to provide for everything itself, but proceed according to the principle of subsidiarity (article 45; the term itself is not yet known). The essential equality and dignity of all persons set strict bounds to authoritarianism.

In the section on economic life (articles 57–134), a large number of issues are addressed in some detail, with pros and cons weighed and a mediating

---

75. Union international d'études sociales 1927, 27.
76. Durand 1995, 114, avers that later editions of the *Code social* were vetted of corporatist elements. I have found this "Preface to the First Edition" also in a translation of the third revised edition in Union internationale d'études sociales 1952, 12.

position taken. Certainly trade associations would be appropriate, as well as permanent bodies representing labor and management to supervise (and improve) wage settlements. Something like a national economic council is needed. Benedict XV is cited on war and peace at the level of international relationships. The League of Nations is also an appropriate embodiment of the world of many nations on the civil side, as the church is on the spiritual plane. What Catholicism has to offer in the last analysis is not any specific political or economic model, but the insistence that however they are shaped, they do not militate against justice and love (article 142). For alone among human institutions, the church knows the true source and nature of the dignity and freedom of the human person.

It seems then that the leading articulators of social Catholic thought in the 1920s acknowledged after all that there was not really a Third Way, in the sense of a single Catholic social order to be proposed and defended, much less ideologically required. They were clear that neither liberalism nor socialism, as they understood them, could welcome the traditional communitarian values that alone gave hope for a just society. All the same, such values or principles—the dignity of the human person in community or the social solidarity of all with all—could find realization in a number of social settings and systems. With this nuance, they could and did agree with all their predecessors that the church had a social mission, that they would not allow religion to be made altogether into a private affair.

In practice they adapted to the rules of a pluralistic democracy without as yet a theoretical framework to justify this accommodation beyond the axiom of preferring the lesser evil. Such a framework would be unavailable except in fragmentary form throughout the interwar period. Building on the accomplishments of nineteenth-century Catholic revival in a secularizing world,[77] they advocated organization—association—as the main prescription to stem social deterioration and strengthen the sinews of society as a moral organism. This could go as far as the pillarization of the Netherlands, where adherents of each worldview could build for themselves rather complete subcultures while sharing the helm of the ship of state. Or it could remain on the level of strictly voluntary organizations. In any case, Catholics would represent a compact group in the public square; social Catholics would press, perhaps in tactical coalition with moderate socialists, for measures to alleviate social inequalities, raise the standard of living of the working class, and provide social services to women, families, and other underprivileged groups.

77. See Taylor 2007, 423–72, on the "Age of Mobilization." I consider Charles Taylor's perspective and periodization of the relations between Catholicism and modern culture to be a fundamental insight for framing the developments treated in the present work. See also Hürten 2003.

A question that would soon arise was this: How were Catholics to respond to a new social and political force that arose alongside Catholicism and socialism in the divided anti-liberal camp?

And Fascism?

Fascism is often regarded as a movement of such flexible ideological content as to make its doctrinal borrowings and expressions purely arbitrary. Since the national community and its aggrandizement is in every case the inspiration of the movement, in each country it is pitted against its counterparts elsewhere. But Zeev Sternhell has made the case for the existence of a fascist ideology with the same consistency and self-sufficiency as socialism and liberalism. This ideology was already formed before World War I, hence it is not to be thought of as a simple reaction to that war in the losing countries or to the red scare that followed.[78] A sympathetic but critical reviewer registered the important point that the ideology ("first fascism") behind the movement did not hold up, but had to be changed to come to a position of actual power, as in Italy ("second fascism"), so as to appeal to conservatives.[79] Further on, we shall note several such alliances, such as the *clerico-fascisti* in Italy; for now, however, comparing apples with apples, let us examine what two out-of-power systems of thought, the solidarist and the fascist, may have had in common.

Early fascist ideology was a product of the coming together "of nonconformists from two disparate intellectual camps in Latin Europe: integral nationalism and revolutionary syndicalism," the most radical wing of the labor movement.[80] They found common ground, still according to Paxton, in five areas:

both rejected the materialism which underpinned progressive reform efforts, socialist as well as bourgeois; both hated democratic individualism as the dissolvent of any kind of community élan; both dreamed of replacing bourgeois complacency by heroic grandeur; both admired producers and entrepreneurs while condemning financiers and speculators. They could even find common ground in a commitment to "revolution" once some dissident syndicalists were ready to alter revolution's goals from the redistribution of wealth and power to the redemption of human moral fiber.

If one compares this summary with the *Code Social* (Eugène Duthoit wrote a good deal on vocational order) or with the social economics of Antoine or Pesch, one notices at once that the shared opposition to liberalism and socialism resulted in certain conspicuous parallels. Precisely the rejection of their materialism springs to the eyes, as well as the dissolving of community ties by

---

78. Sternhell 1994.
80. Ibid., 51.

79. Paxton 1994, 53.

individualism and the moral disqualification of market speculations. Yet one conclusion to be drawn is that whatever positive affinities there were between Catholicism and fascism, they had no basis in the writings of standard social Catholic authors. A third-party observer such as Antonio Gramsci spotted the gulf between the positive "spirituality" of the Jesuit theorists and the fascist ones, even though both were sworn enemies and critics of his own Marxism.[81] In a fascist outlook, one's worth derives from the self-assertion of one's nation; in Catholic social ethics, human dignity is grounded in God's creation. Even integralist Catholics, for their part, turned their back on violent revolution; and heroic grandeur was only to be sought for the sake of the church and hence for supernatural ends, not merely nationalistic ones. As for democracy, our standard solidarist authors did not fear it—quite the contrary. This is not to say that they spoke for the tone-setting circles in Catholicism; but it might be said that Catholic authorities finally came to terms with a chastened liberalism, during and after World War II, as both cultures gained an appreciation for the merits of democracy.

To be sure, there were circumstantial connections between the positions of certain social Catholic spokesmen and tendencies that would become, in exaggerated form, features of fascist outlooks. Albert de Mun, for example, was well-known as a forceful advocate of Catholic social thought, but also of revanchism or nationalistic militarism.[82] René de La Tour du Pin was more than sympathetic with the proto-fascist Action française because of its anti-republicanism—that is, its support of the monarchical principle. Beyond a certain mutual distaste for liberal parliamentary regimes, however, his elaborate social thought had little in common with fascist ideology. With Joseph de Maistre (1754–1821) the case may well be different.[83] But the precocious fascist elements in de Maistre's thought hardly counted in the received version of de Maistre honored by later Roman Catholics. They certainly played no role in any of the Catholic subgroups that Antoine and others recognized as such. Some of the Viennese orientations displayed a greater susceptibility, it is true, as we shall note in the narration of developments.

What Catholicism and fascism, after its initial socialist leanings were excised, had in common was a stance opposed in each case both to liberalism and to socialism. But what the two social orientations, Catholic solidarism and fascism, had against socialism was different in each case. Fascism jettisoned the socialist demand for equality. Social Catholicism—apart from the authoritarian impress Pius XI would make on it with *Quadragesimo anno*—objected to the takeover of the state and the broad use of its coercive powers to crush op-

81. Gramsci 1977, 66–70.   82. See Martin 1978.
83. See Berlin 1990, 91–174.

position and enforce unity of action by dictatorship, whether of the proletariat or of the strong man, whether in the name of class domination or national power. That is what emerges from the examination of the doctrine of the early Catholic solidarists in its Austrian (Messner), Italo-Belgian (Toniolo, Pottier, Vermeersch), French (Antoine), and German (Pesch et al.) representatives.[84] Need it be said that doctrine's influence on practice has never been absolute? When it came to a choice of actual alliances with either socialists or fascists, the decisions could and did fall either way. Solidarism would show its limitations in practice and theory over the next few decades; but it would be rash to say that it steered Catholic social teaching onto the wrong path for its time. I would say to the contrary that solidarism, with its person-centered communitarian thrust, constituted its sound and authentic core.

Workers' Leagues or Catholic Action? Two Models of Mobilization

Given an ideal of solidarity—that is, of free persons in mutually supportive community—what were the most effective ways in which Catholics could move society toward this goal? That was a question that occupied the minds of Catholic activists and leaders. Beyond the family, the basic unit of society, how were Catholics to mobilize so as to "re-Christianize" society, to make it "Christian again," to quote the oft-used slogan of the time? And how did the unfavorable situation of the lower economic classes figure in this aspiration? Banding together was key to a solidary society. To bear good fruit, it had to be accomplished in a disciplined Christian but also contemporary way.

Toward the end of chapter 3, we saw two such contemporary manners brush up against each other, only to part without having reached an understanding. The elected officers of the recently founded international federation of workers' milieu organizations came to Rome in 1929 to present this new Catholic body to the pope. However, they got the distinct impression that their initiative was unwelcome in the Vatican. To understand why this was so and its broader significance in the story of Christian labor, it may help to compare these two approaches to mobilization.

The differences stemmed in large part from different practices that had sprung up in different national settings. In Germany, Belgium, and the Netherlands, exemplified most clearly for present purposes in the Dutch case, the

---

84. Antoine Pottier (1849–1923), a diocesan priest of Liège, published his tract *De jure et justitia*, based on his seminary courses, in 1900; see Jadoulle 1991 and 1992; see also Delville 2009a and Tedeschi 2005 and 2008; Abbé Pottier played a significant role in Italian and even Spanish social Catholicism after he moved to Rome around the turn of the century.

pattern was according to occupational groupings: *standen*.[85] As previously indicated, the Dutch Catholics used this term for social class that was free of the negative overtones of "class." In French and English, another expression had to be used: "milieu." Organizations formed on this pattern we call *standsorganisaties* in Dutch and milieu organizations in English. The next chapter will examine these developments in the national context.

In Italy a somewhat different evolution was taking place. It influenced the model that Pope Pius XI adopted for his key program of Catholic Action. Here one organized the Catholic laity in distinct groupings for adults and youth, male and female, without much regard for social standing or occupation. The primary categories were age and gender. A very important branch of Catholic Action in Italy as elsewhere had to do with young people. By the early twentieth century, Catholics had developed a strong national federation known as the GC (Gioventù cattolica, Catholic Youth). By Pius X's time, many bishops and the Vatican had blessed the Italian Catholic Youth organization, along with the parallel organization of university students and graduates, the FUCI (Federazione universitaria cattolica italiana), with the designation of "Catholic Action," without as yet formalizing the relationship canonically. What Pius XI inherited in Italian Catholicism was a multitude of associations, some pious, some activist, and some dedicated to the formation and strengthening of the Catholic tradition in the various strata of Italian society.[86] The pope wished to expand and systematize Catholic Action. Given the presence of hostile trends even more threatening after World War I—Bolshevism and ultra-nationalistic fascism appealing to the idealism of discontented youth—he felt it imperative to gather forces in closed ranks for the re-Christianization of society.

In contrast with the Netherlands, the Italy that confronted Pius XI when he was elected pope in February of 1922 was riven with threats to civil order. Both communism and fascism were striving for supremacy, the supremacy precariously still held by a liberal and mostly anticlerical parliamentary government. By October 1922 Benito Mussolini had major cities in his power and staged the "March on Rome." The king dismissed the prime minister and commissioned Mussolini to form a cabinet. In another month the king and parliament granted Mussolini dictatorial powers for the following year. Confidence that parliamentary politics could cope with the crisis after a period of suspension was not widespread.

Meanwhile, papal intransigence in opposing secularistic liberalism and socialism had not waned. Many Catholics, the new pope included, saw a possible opportunity opening up to regain influence with the help of this new

85. See Damberg and Pasture 2010, 58–60.
86. See Traniello and Campanini 1981, in *DSMCI* 1, pt. 1:ix.

Fascist rival to the same hostile modern forces. Mussolini gave indications that he could work with the influence of the church and rein in the anticlerical impulses of his followers. Fascist paramilitary squads were wreaking havoc on competing movements (socialist ones, but also such as the PPI and the CIL [see chapter 2], and even Catholic youth groups that seemed allied with such democratic organizations). Pius XI was not sold on democracy as a likely solution; he thought that a cautious detente with an authoritarian party or regime could well be of mutual benefit for Italy and for the church.

Pope Pius XI was determined in any case to move Catholicism's defense against modern secularism to a new level.[87] He promulgated his first encyclical, *Ubi arcano Dei consilio*, only at the end of a tumultuous 1922.[88] In it he staked his pontificate on Catholic Action, "the collaboration" or "participation of the laity in the apostolate of the hierarchy."[89] So it is to be expected that he shaped his perspective on various social Catholic undertakings according to this overall plan. It is a recurrent theme in the developments of Catholic social apostolates.

One can compare two features of Pius XI's plan of Catholic Action with the one put into play according to the ideas of Henri Poels. One has to do with how the groupings of the lay body of the church are conceived in view of the Christian apostolate, and one concerns the relationship of the lay activity to the authority of the hierarchy. To take the latter issue first, we will see how the Dutch bishops did not shrink from exercising their authority over the shape of the Catholic action (in a broader sense) of the laity in the Netherlands. At the same time, Poels, the champion of the milieu organizations, was anxious to emphasize that the task of bringing about a society in accord with the gospel of Christ was shared between the clergy and the laity. The fields of economics, politics, art, and culture, he said, do not predominantly belong to the clergy to make Christian, but to the laity involved in those areas.[90] He took for granted that the bishops would determine what was required or permissible for Catholic organizations, but wanted to stress the initiative of the laity in the Catholic movements as their own Christian responsibility.

In the Italian Catholic scene there was a comparable dynamic of clerical and lay leadership in the church's social action. It resulted, however, in a more authoritarian tone. The time had come, it seemed to Pope Pius, to assert the leadership role in society that belonged to Christianity in its Roman Catholic incarnation. It also seemed obvious that this mission of the church was the

---

87. Pollard 2009, 176. John Pollard's other works are also highly informative in regard to Catholicism and Fascism; see particularly Pollard 1985, 1996, and 2008. On Pius XI, see also Chiron 2004, 198–205. On Italian Catholic Action, see especially Casella 1992; on Pius XI's reform, ibid., 67–143.

88. Chiron 2004, 143f.   89. Casella 1992, 16; Barral 1996.

90. Wentholt 1984, 49.

responsibility of the hierarchy. The novelty of Catholic Action was to associate the laity formally with the hierarchy in the latter's apostolate. The role of the laity was therefore defined in a strictly top-down manner. Pius XI spelled this out in the reform of Catholic Action in Italy that he promulgated in September 1923, but it was already forecast in a circular directive that Cardinal Gasparri sent to the bishops of Italy dated October 2, 1922. When an official *Manuale di Azione Cattolica* was published, it did not play down this dependence of the lay members and leaders on the directives of the hierarchy, but instead put it rather more starkly:

> Catholic Action is *participation, collaboration* in the apostolate of the Ecclesiastical Hierarchy. Thus there is in the Church the hierarchical apostolate, which is the principal one, the true and proper apostolate ... ; and the apostolate of lay people, which is secondary, an *auxiliary* of the first.

Its author, Msgr. Luigi Civardi, an authority on the lay apostolate in Italy comparable to Msgr. Poels in Holland, went on to stress that lay activists in Catholic Action organizations were "not called upon to act on their own. Their job is simply to *aid* the hierarchy in any way that is needful, in any way that they can."[91]

The other feature mentioned earlier concerned the branches into which Catholic Action was organized—to wit, by social milieu in the Netherlands; in Italy primarily by age and sex. The milieu organizations were specialized according to the occupational *standen* (workers, farmers, middle class employees or middle-class employers, and upper classes). The four main branches of Catholic Action according to the Italian model of Pius X and Pius XI were simply those of men, of women, of young men, and young women. With the incorporation of the university students (FUCI, as just mentioned, male and female associations), the result was six branches or categories of Catholic Action in Italy.[92] The leaders and the clergy assistants of each of the six groupings sat on the Central Board (Giunta centrale) in Rome, which oversaw and guided the analogous diocesan boards throughout Italy. Later on, as we shall see, influenced by Cardijn, the pope welcomed a shift to a more specialized model of Catholic Action categories by occupation or milieu.[93] In either form, Pius XI returned regularly to his overall project of a universal Catholic Action under the impulsion of the hierarchy. Especially notable were his letters to cardinal primates in different countries in 1928 and 1929,[94] in addition to repeated commendations in his pronouncements over the years.

As already adumbrated, the advent of Fascism in Italy conditioned the

91. Ferrari 1989, 34–37, here 35.
93. Chiron 2004, 135 and 202–5.
92. Casella 1992, 15.
94. Ibid., 205f.

growth of Catholic Action there. Pius XI was adamant that Catholic Action, like the hierarchy itself, must remain distant from politics (read: parties in parliaments). He withdrew all support that the church had been giving to the Partito popolare of Don Sturzo, thus removing a center of opposition to a Fascist regime as Mussolini was consolidating its hold on power. The similar fate of the Catholic labor unions will occupy us in due course. For now, let us turn to Catholic movements geared to improving the lot of workers more at the grass roots, country by country, starting in the Netherlands and Belgium.

CHAPTER 5

Vitality in the Low Countries

Both Belgium and the Netherlands developed vigorous Catholic labor movements in the 1920s. Belgium preceded the Netherlands in industrial development and in regard to social Catholicism by several decades in the nineteenth century, but some Dutch Catholics also became active in the labor field before World War I.[1] To fill in this part of the picture, we begin this chapter with the Netherlands. The two neighboring Catholicisms had much in common, including their use of the Dutch language in the northern part of Belgium. Belgium was a Catholic country, however, whereas Reformed churches were historically predominant in the Netherlands. By 1920, however, the biggest difference in the respective national contexts came from the effects of World War I. Belgium had been invaded and occupied, whereas the Netherlands remained neutral and somewhat sheltered from the war's chaos.

In the Netherlands

Before and during World War I

Dutch industrialization was a quite gradual process; the Netherlands remained a predominantly agricultural and trading country until after World War II. Pioneers were few but notable.[2] *Rerum novarum* converted a Catholic priest-politician, Herman Schaepman (1844–1903), from an opponent to an advocate of some government intervention in aid of social justice.[3] Schaepman arrived at the same formula as the French social Catholic Léon Harmel in

---

1. For prewar Belgium from the social Catholic angle, I refer the reader to my previous exposition: Misner 1991, 106f, 193f, 222–26.
2. Luykx 1994, 123–26.
3. Georgi and Heerma van Voss 2005, 229.

enunciating an axiom that would guide the Dutch Catholic labor movement: "Everything done for workers must be done through and by workers."[4] I call this the anti-paternalist principle; its relatively early formulation in the Dutch Catholic context was to be indispensable to the formation of an authentic labor movement.

For another priest-leader, Alfons Ariëns (1860–1928), the encyclical was a real godsend; already in 1889 he had organized some exclusively workers' groups, embryonic unions, in the textile industry in the north of the country.[5] With the backing of the bishop of Haarlem in North Holland, he helped found the Catholic Social Action (KSA) in 1904 with the idea of imitating the organizing success of the German Volksverein. A Catholic lawyer, Petrus J. M. Aalberse (1871–1948), served as head of this effort—his maiden speech in parliament in 1897 had invoked *Rerum novarum* in the cause of social justice.[6] If the idea of the KSA was to form a mass organization of Catholics like the Volksverein, this did not come to pass. The KSA did, however, encourage Catholic tradespeople, farmers, and bulb-growers to form their own Catholic associations instead of just joining nonconfessional groups—a trait particularly characteristic of the Netherlands.[7]

The tardily exploited coalfields in Limburg in the southeast, a solidly Catholic area, represented a new opportunity. The priest-politician Willem H. Nolens (1860–1931) was a member of parliament from Venlo, South Limburg, when the coalfields were first developed. The mines were all owned by the state and leased to operators. Nolens, the de facto head of the Catholic caucus, exerted as much influence as he could on the Mines Act of 1901, successfully insisting on the principle of governmental regulation of working conditions. He consulted with leaders of the Christian trade unions in neighboring Germany and encouraged the Limburg miners to form their own interconfessional unions on the Cologne-Mönchengladbach model, even organizing a federation of eight locals in 1903.[8] When a priest named Poels arrived back from the United States, Nolens got him to take over as spiritual guide of these unions, as he himself was more than occupied with parliamentary work and a part-time professorship in Amsterdam. In 1911 Poels started a foundation, Ons Limburg, which was able to deal creatively and positively with the administration of the mines to transform the hovels of the miners into town housing that blended in with the countryside. In 1913 Nolens was appointed head of the board of the Dutch State Mines,

4. *HJS* 57.
5. See Ariëns, in Roes 1982, 27–46; 1985a; see also *HJS* 138; Kossmann 1978, 489–90; R. Aubert 1978, 153.
6. Luykx 1994, 125.
7. Van Marrewijk 1994, 21–26; Duffhues 1992, 177–90.
8. Gribling 1978, 100–4.

from which position he could all the more effectively protect the freedom of the mineworkers to organize and press their demands,[9] while also favoring cooperative arrangements between the local clergy and the mine administration. Limburg became a model for modern industrialized Europe.[10]

Henricus A. Poels (1868–1948) had, as it were, two successive careers. Before he was a labor priest in his native Limburg, he had been a scripture scholar at the Catholic University of America.[11] Ordained a priest of the diocese of Roermond in 1891, he earned his doctorate with a dissertation in Old Testament studies at Louvain in 1897. After teaching in a Belgian seminary from 1897 to 1899, he was abruptly assigned to a parish in Venlo as assistant pastor.[12] Even though some confreres thought his views were dangerously advanced, he was appointed to Pope Leo XIII's new Biblical Commission in 1901; subsequently he taught at the young Catholic University of America from 1904 to 1910. Removed from teaching as a result of the Roman Catholic modernist controversy in 1910, he became parish priest and chaplain of the social works at Welten in the same year and promptly took the measure of the local situation.[13] Even before going to Washington, he spoke at Catholic congresses in 1899 and 1903. On the latter occasion he criticized those conservatives who saw in Catholic workers' organizations only a sort of dam against socialism and who wished, as he put it, to plant the banner of reaction in their ranks. He did not want to see materialistic socialism dominate labor in the newly exploited mining region, to be sure. But he was just as fierce against capitalistic exploitation of workers as if they too were but natural resources. He had to parry many a blow in controversy from the side of economic liberals and conservatives.[14]

In the course of the First World War, Netherlands, though neutral, was under pressure partly because of the threat of invasion, but more directly because of the breakdown of trade: unemployment reached worrying levels. There was as yet no unemployment compensation plan, but emergency relief programs were launched. The unions, socialist and Christian, were allowed to participate in distributing such aid to their out-of-work members. This association of labor unions with public authority was a highly significant precedent. It was followed in 1917, as a reward for worker loyalty and an inducement to maintain it, by the introduction of the so-called Ghent system. This meant that public moneys would match the unemployment funds that a union built up and distributed, making it a distinct advantage to workers faced with possible unemployment to join a union. This created a related precedent for state aid

9. Ibid., 96.
10. Coleman 1978, 42; for a less favorable view, see Kreukels 1986.
11. See G. Fogarty 1989; Nuesse 1990; and Poels 1982.
12. Colsen 1955, 13–250.   13. Brachin and Rogier 1974, 146–48.
14. Hebben 2001.

programs during the 1920s and '30s: unions became the normal conduit for government assistance to workers in the Netherlands as in Belgium.[15]

At first the Dutch economy was not too badly affected, though there were dislocations painful for certain sectors. The pragmatic measures taken by the government, together with the basically neutralist sentiment of the people, whether working-class or bourgeois, kept popular unrest at bay. Politicians signaled their intention to pass universal manhood suffrage, duly introduced in the "pacification" or "accommodation" of 1917.[16] The other main element of the compromise was full state subsidizing of church schools. But harder times descended as the war went on and discontent grew. Nevertheless, the elections of July 1918 returned a moderate if splintered parliament. Liberals lost seats, socialists gained them, but the confessional parties had half the house between them and were able, with difficulty, to form a coalition government. The new cabinet (with for the first time a Catholic for prime minister) took office in September, just before the German war effort crumbled. Aalberse took on the new position of labor minister; he successfully insisted on a labor-friendly legislative program as a condition of accepting the post.[17]

Then, for a few days in that fateful November of 1918, the socialist leader Pieter J. Troelstra (1860–1930) displayed disastrous political judgment by calling for the revolution of the working man and the overthrow of the constitutional monarchy. In reality, not that many working people were anxious to overthrow a democratically elected government, even if social democracy had not prevailed. Nor did Troelstra's fellow socialist leaders think that a revolution in a country plainly in the process of democratization made much sense. Troelstra's rhetoric, all the same, put the Protestant and especially the Catholic unions and political leaders on guard; they quickly organized massive demonstrations "in support of the queen," which were much appreciated by the army and the political classes in general. The upshot was a black eye for the socialists and corresponding admiration, grudging or otherwise, for organized Catholicism. A side benefit did accrue to the working class as a whole: "the unrest created by Troelstra enabled the confessional government quickly to carry its Christian democratic programme of social measures into effect. Both in the eyes of the frightened masses and of the higher classes this social policy was a guarantee against a repetition of what had seemed for one tense week the start of revolution."[18]

Significant legislation took place, especially in 1919, under the aegis of the

---

15. See Van den Berg 1995, 40–44; see also Windmuller 1969, 41–45, and Strikwerda 1997, 260.
16. Kossmann 1978, 553–57; Brachin and Rogier 1974, 139–43.
17. HJS 244–45.
18. Kossmann 1978, 560.

Catholic and Protestant parties. Hard on the heels of universal male suffrage, women's suffrage followed in 1920. With voting compulsory, the Christian parties enjoyed a virtual lock on parliamentary majorities. Their coalitions, referred to as "the confessional government," held power from 1919 to 1940, since the liberals and the socialists were relegated to minority positions in parliament. Socialists were left with just a part of the working class as its electorate. Aalberse took advantage of the red scare and the brief postwar recovery to implement an act of 1913 compelling some industries to finance disability insurance for their workers. He pushed through legislation contributing to a pension plan and establishing an eight-hour day (in a forty-five-hour week), long a socialist demand.[19]

Aalberse's signal achievement was the establishment of the Supreme Labor Council, also in 1919. This was a permanent advisory committee of between forty and fifty members appointed by the minister of labor, consisting of representatives of employers and unions in equal numbers, with some independent experts and higher civil servants.[20] This committee, though advisory, represented a corporatist element in the state and fit well into Aalberse's Peschian solidarist perspective. It remained a factor to be reckoned with during the whole interwar period in Dutch politics and economics. Unlike the similar institutions that appeared at the same time in other European countries, only to fade soon into innocuous desuetude (for instance, the ZAG in Germany), the Supreme Labor Council became more prominent in the Depression. Johannes D. J. Aengenant, a priest adviser (1873–1935), Nolens, and Jos Serrarens, the head of the Catholic trade union confederation in Utrecht, served on this board when it began work in February 1920.[21] All three major branches of the union movement (Socialist, Protestant, and Catholic) benefitted from these developments, with peaks and valleys of membership figures corresponding to economic conditions in the 1920s, but holding their constituencies steady in the 1930s Depression era.

The Catholic Trade Union Movement

The Catholic unions had lower membership numbers but more solid finances than the *standsorganisaties* until 1918, when each federation counted 97,000 members. After that, the unions took the lead, rising to 150,000 in 1920 and 1921, before shrinking to 93,000 in 1925.[22] In 1920 a fifth or more of unionized workers in the Netherlands belonged to Catholic unions.[23] This figure

19. See *HJS* 159, 244.
21. Gribling 1978, 213–15.
23. See *HJS* 784–85.

20. Kossmann 1978, 660.
22. After Roes 1985a, 41, table 1.

sank to 18.5 percent in 1925 before rebounding under the vigorous leadership of Adrianus Cornelis De Bruijn, in charge of the finally established RKWV (Rooms-Katholiek Werkliedenverbond, or Catholic Workers' Federation of the Netherlands). Between the bishops' insistence on collaboration between the two wings of Catholic labor and the other *standen* and the competitive pressure from the socialist movement, the labor leaders and the bishops agreed upon a pragmatic compromise in the course of 1924.[24] The national structure that was set up combined the diocesan *standsorganisaties* for the working class and the Catholic labor unions, each maintaining its own federation, in a joint umbrella organization, the RKWV, with the power of the purse. As the Catholic political party got itself better organized, the labor contingent won influence. By the end of the 1920s, labor representatives were assured of four seats in parliament out of the Catholic Party's thirty, as well as a couple of senators, one being Jos Serrarens.[25] Catholic unions proved to be as effective for labor concerns as their rivals; membership grew to almost a quarter of the total of unionized workers in the 1930s, with a peak membership approaching 200,000 in 1932.

The salient feature of the Dutch Catholic labor movement was the existence side by side of the two types of labor organizations, to each of which the Catholic worker was expected to belong. For each worker this meant two memberships and two dues payments. Even though a relatively high percentage of free riders still stayed out of Dutch unions, this did not seem to impair the effectiveness of the national Catholic trade union movement as much as one might suppose. There were forerunners of this sort only in German and Belgian Catholicism; and only in the Netherlands were the respective aims of the sibling movements formulated so clearly, along lines laid down by Msgr. Poels. Elsewhere, Catholics tended to found unions and confide the whole worker question to them without trying to complement the unions with another membership organization such as the workers' leagues (in Germany the Katholische Arbeitervereine; in Belgium the ACW, or Algemeen Christelijk Werkersverbond, and in the Netherlands the RKWV).

Among the Dutch working-class lay leaders was the collaborator of Henricus Poels, Henri Hermans, director of a Catholic (diocesan) social secretariat in Limburg since 1904; he initially promoted the formation of the interconfessional unions that were coming into existence there, and he continued to play a major role in the RKWV.[26] On the union side of the RKWV, Cornelis Johannes Kuiper (1875–1951) was a member of the board from 1925 to 1941, representing the Catholic metalworkers while also writing the history of the Catholic

---

24. See ibid, 341–54.
25. Roes 2004, 87; Van Meeuwen 1998, 301, 399–404.
26. On the interconfessional unions, see Winkelman 1966, 379.

labor movement.[27] The labor union federation had its own secretary general, Jos Serrarens, who served in the same capacity for the International Federation of Christian Trade Unions (the CISC) from its foundation in 1920, was hired in 1916 to be the secretary of the federation of the *standsorganisaties* once the bishops decided to go national.[28]

The Veraart Episode

An experiment with a still more frankly corporatist scheme was connected with the name of Johannes Antonius Veraart. It had little success in his time, but it played a role in eventually affecting the ideology of the Third Way in the Netherlands.[29] Veraart was the principal theorist of a Catholic alternative to the prevailing capitalist economic system. Right after World War I, a debate began "between socialists and Roman Catholics on the theme of 'socialization' versus 'industrial organization'" (to wit, "*bedrijfsorganisatie*"). Kossmann continues:

During the war Veraart had successfully mediated in the printing trade: at a time when fierce competition was causing disastrous wage cuts he had managed through collective wage and price agreements to set the industry on its feet again. In effect membership of the employers' unions and of the trade unions became necessary for enterprises wanting to survive.... Veraart, having been appointed to a chair in the Technical High School at Delft, ... devoted the whole of his life to substantiating the thesis that this system, if applied to the economy as a whole, would solve all the social problems of the time. Here, he argued, was a truly Catholic principle, a corporatist doctrine originating from a new school of economic research. Moreover, the system would cut the state down to its proper size. It had to give the boards representing the various branches of industry the necessary legislative powers and recognize them as organic parts of the state itself. But once this was done, the various branches of industry could themselves be made responsible for most of the intricate fabric of social insurance, and labour legislation could be limited. Consequently, it would be possible drastically to reduce the number of civil servants. Veraart dreamt of an economy controlled by a large number of industrial boards, with equal representation of employees and employers within each branch of industry, and with an executive nominated by the government. These boards would meet regularly to take binding decisions on labour conditions, prices, the organization of the individual enterprises, their expansion or contraction.... Solidarity of the classes, the unity of capital and labour, the profound calm and harmony of a society that had recovered its organic structure were the foundations of Veraart's vision, conjured out of his experience in just one branch of industry over a brief period.[30]

27. Kuiper 1951–53; first published 1924–27.
28. Roes 1985a, 43.
29. See Georgi and Heerma van Voss 2005, 233.
30. Kossmann 1978, 595–97.

Conjured as well, as Kossmann hints, from a background in Catholic social thought like that of Heinrich Pesch, without the gradualism or meliorism that generally characterized that school of thought.[31] We may note that Pesch himself dropped his guard enough in 1919 to speak briefly of Christian socialism and to envisage the possibility of a thoroughgoing overhaul of the existing order. At any rate, Veraart launched a continuing discussion of this system of works councils and industry-wide boards.[32] It was put forward as another alternative, a third way, between industrial capitalism and the nationalization of key industries that socialists advocated, notably in a report on socialization issued by the Dutch Socialist Party in 1920. Veraart made an initial splash in April 1919 by procuring the backing of the four more-or-less organized *standen* of Roman Catholics for the so-called "Easter Manifesto."[33] In this document the Catholic associations "undertook to introduce in their own enterprises the system which Veraart considered the ideal solution for the Dutch economy as a whole."[34] In hindsight this was certainly quixotic, and yet Veraart's proposal foreshadowed the development of the milder legally sanctioned representation of interests that obtained a remarkable purchase on several economies of northwestern Europe since World War II in the forms of *Mitbestimmung* (most often referred to in Dutch as *"overleg,"* literally "consultation," or later on in French as *"concertation"*).[35]

In practice the organized *standen* came to function as interest groups, as intermediary bodies in a modified capitalist economy rather than as harbingers of a radically revised economic system. When business went into a postwar economic slump, the employers saw industrial democracy as placing them in an unfavorable competitive position; they formally opted out of the Veraart plan by the end of 1922. The Catholic workers and their leaders who had committed themselves to this realization of the Catholic social ideal had to be disillusioned, and the membership statistics temporarily suffered more than those of other unions as a result.[36] But they recouped, and when they did, it was with a pronounced class consciousness and self-confident leadership that enabled it to hold its own in comparison with the socialist and other labor movements. Christian labor's ties to and influence with the confessional government let the workers feel that their interests were well represented in such unions. In many

---

31. See *HJS* 282–89.

32. Roes 2004, 89; for a contemporary account by a British social Catholic, see Somerville 1933, 103.

33. Cf. Brachin and Rogier 1974, 195, and Versluis 1949, 55–57; also *HJS* 731, 265–71.

34. Kossmann 1978, 598.

35. Philippe Schmitter (1974) categorized all these as instances of "societal corporatism," to be distinguished from "state corporatism," as we noted briefly in chapter 2.

36. Roes 1985a, 45.

a rally two weeks after May Day, on the anniversary of *Rerum novarum*, speakers reminded the rank and file that Pope Leo XIII had spoken out for workers' rights. The name of the encyclical, so it was said, was Latin for "Workers, unite!"[37]—which, if not philologically correct, was nevertheless not completely amiss.

From the side of the socialist and smaller Protestant labor movements one could also perceive an incipient willingness to lay aside ideological (not organizational) differences so as to advance common goals. On the side of Catholic proponents of social justice, the various thrusts of the period following World War I—Aalberse's insurance legislation and Supreme Labor Council, Veraart's scheme for an alternative economic system, Poels' *standsorganisatie*—all contributed to the stock of experiences that would nourish thinking and activity during the Depression and the Nazi takeover and would continue to influence developments after World War II.

With a plethora of insurance plans for health care and pensions, and with highly developed programs in education and formation, the social Catholic movement was solidly grounded before the Depression hit and the second major papal pronouncement on labor questions, *Quadragesimo anno*, came out in May of 1931. Pope Pius XI congratulated Aalberse in person in that year for having put *Rerum novarum* into practice, favoring the harmonious interaction of classes rather than their mutual enmity. The social Catholic movement certainly contributed to the formation of a strong Catholic subculture or "pillar" in Dutch society. It had contributed as well to the realization of social justice in the shape of deproletarianizing the working class and enabling its voice at least to be heard, however toned down, in the corridors of power.

In Belgium

As Martin Conway remarks, "Belgium in the pre-1914 years appeared almost as a Catholic paradise in which control of political power combined with a strong Church and a flourishing network of schools and social organizations protected the faithful from the twin horrors of atheistic liberalism and Marxist socialism."[38] During the war Catholics formed a government in exile together with liberals and socialists; it operated out of Le Havre, while Cardinal Mercier became the soul of the moral resistance within the occupied country.[39] The Catholic party maintained a prominent political position after the war—its leaders constituted the indispensable coalition partners in every succeeding

---

37. Luykx 1994, 130.
39. Tihon 1990, 541.

38. Conway 1996, 192.

government—but the party was gripped by a long-lasting crisis nevertheless. After all, being forced to seek coalition partners was a comedown after thirty years of sole rule. King Albert took advantage of the spirit of 1919 to endorse democratizing political reforms, especially universal manhood suffrage. This gave greater leverage to the lower classes, socialist and Flemish, and resulted in about a third of the electorate voting Catholic, a third socialist, and a fifth or less for the main liberal party. The introduction of universal manhood suffrage was a new development that the old-fashioned Catholic party had to deal with. Under pressure, its leaders allowed the democratic or workers' wing to propose and vote for socially progressive legislation that most of the bourgeois notables in the party opposed. There was also a well-organized agricultural or peasants' constituency with its deputies in government, who represented its own sometimes divergent interests.[40]

Though overall Catholic political dominance was taken down a peg, the clout of the Catholic working class had the potential to become significantly greater than heretofore. This potential had to be mobilized, however, against the resistance of the bourgeois political class and the rival socialist Labor Party. Not until 1936, after workers (Flemish and Walloon, Catholic and socialist) went out on a massive general strike, did Catholic labor unions achieve acceptance as a legitimate social partner from some other Catholics, from public authorities, and particularly from their socialist rivals. Thus after World War II, instead of merging into a unitary labor movement as was often the case outside the Low Countries, the Christian labor movement in Belgium reconstituted itself on the bases reached in 1939–40 in (fairly cooperative) rivalry with the socialist labor movement.[41] By 1960 the Christian labor movement had drawn up to and overtaken its socialist older sibling in membership;[42] to this day it maintains its place in Belgian society, no longer dependent on the church or a Catholic pillar. This in some ways atypical development lends special interest to the history of the Belgian Catholic labor movement.

Labor Organizations

In the 1920s certain clerics still played important roles from time to time in the institutional history of Christian labor. Georges Ceslas Rutten, OP, was the pioneer instigator of the Catholic union movement in prewar Belgium.[43] After

---

40. For a short history in English of the interwar Catholic party in Belgium by an expert in the subject, see Gerard 2004b.
41. Pasture 1992.
42. Tihon 1990, 545; Pasture 1994c.
43. On the Belgian unions and union federation spearheaded by Fr. Rutten and the lay union

the war he attempted to guide the fortunes of the social apostolate by convening the priest heads of diocesan social offices together with the priest advisors of national lay associations or movements.[44] He became a senator in 1921 and remained an eminent figure of the Catholic political elite throughout the interwar period. On the side of the milieu organizations, Louis Colens, whose death in 1936 coincided with the breakthrough of Christian union recognition, from 1921 on founded and shepherded the National League of Christian Workers (ACW/LNTC) as its general secretary as well as its spiritual adviser. In 1925 Joseph Cardijn (1882–1967, who was made a cardinal in 1965) founded and guided the Young Christian Workers movement (JOC) through its remarkable development (see chapter 7).

Occupying a less prominent but nevertheless influential position in the Confederation of Christian Trade Unions (CSC/ACV) was Joseph Arendt (1885–1952).[45] This son of a French-speaking industrialist from Ghent assisted Fr. Rutten before World War I; after the war he entered the Jesuits and was ordained in 1926. In 1928 René Carels, a young lay intellectual who had done noteworthy work in clarifying the points at issue with socialist ideology and approach to labor questions, died suddenly. The lay leadership of the trade union confederation then asked for Arendt to be head of its study department.[46]

The mention of lay leadership in this Confédération des syndicats chrétiens (CSC; Flemish ACV, Algemeen Christelijk Vakverbond) shows the necessity of relativizing the role of the prominent priests in the movement as a whole. (As the reader notices from the alphabet soup, in Belgium, besides the highly developed associationism that characterized modern Catholicism since the nineteenth century, there is also the need to have two names for each organization with two corresponding abbreviations, one Dutch and one French.) Clergymen did play indispensable roles in stimulating and supporting the Christian labor movement, which was for so long the Cinderella in the household of labor as in that of the faith. Also valued was the liaison that clergy maintained between the working-class Catholics and the bishops and Catholic lay political leaders, especially in the early years. It was particularly positive that Rutten had the confidence of Cardinal Mercier (1851–1926) and Cardijn that of the next head of the Belgian hierarchy, Cardinal Ernest Van Roey (1874–1961). But the union confederation in particular could not be and was not directed by clergy for long. Even before the war Rutten raised the money, but René

---

leaders he found already at work, such as Gustave Eylenbosch and René A. Debruyne, see especially Strikwerda 1997, 290–93 and 300–308; see also Kwanten 1986a, 32–43.

44. Gerard 1990; see also Gerard 1994b, 150.
45. Pirotte and Zelis 2003, 462–64; Kreins 2003.
46. *HMOCB* 1:210; Mampuys 1994, 2:179; Kwanten 1986a, 63.

Debruyne did the actual organizing work involved in creating a national Christian union movement. Debruyne (1868–1941) originally worked in a bakery and was an activist in the antisocialist union headquarters in Ghent, the one town with a continuous double union movement going back to the nineteenth century.[47] He was the first paid union organizer in Rutten's secretariat from 1904 to 1914, and was president of the ACV/CSC right after the war and from 1923 to 1932, while serving in parliament.[48]

The schoolteacher Hendrik Heyman also joined Rutten's team in 1911 and went on to become a cabinet minister for labor and industry, as we shall see. The foremost labor leader of the period, however, as secretary general of the ACV/CSC under Debruyne and president from 1932 to 1946, was Henri Pauwels, whom we have met previously as head of the CISC (see chapter 3). An exceptional autodidact, Pauwels began his working life at the standard school-leaving age of fourteen with a menial job at a paper mill in 1904. After eight years of this, he helped organize unions south of Brussels for Rutten's office.[49] It was as a prisoner of war in Germany that he learned German—and Dutch!—and was able to read up on the theory and practice of Christian labor. A fellow prisoner of war who assisted him in this study was Fr. Louis Barde of the Action populaire center of the French Jesuits.[50] Thus he came out of the war as an exceptionally well-trained Christian unionist, a Belgian layperson of working-class background who could speak both French and Dutch. Flemish cadres had to, and could, when necessary, speak French as well as Dutch. Pauwels, however, was virtually the only Walloon in the category of leading Christian labor leader, since the Flemish preponderance in the movement regularly left monolingual francophone candidates at a disadvantage.

We introduce the personnel of the labor unions here, not only to balance the role of clergy with that of lay working-class leaders, but also to make clear the distinction between labor unions as such and the rest of the Belgian labor movement under Catholic auspices. Among the many associations making up the world of Christian labor, the unions were the key ingredient, to be sure. To union members, whose unemployment benefits and wage negotiations were in the hands of their union confederation, the unions were no doubt the institutions with the most tangible impact on their lives. On the other hand, there were many working people who did not belong to a union. The Christian labor movement aimed to improve their lives, as well, just as the Catholic Boerenbond did for the Flemish farming population in general. If the Catholic broader working class were not to benefit from the movement in some way, or

47. Strikwerda 1997, 42.
49. Ibid., 2:178.

48. *HMOCB* 1:130.
50. Droulers 1981, 344.

worse yet, were alienated from the unions, then the union federation would be in an isolated and ineffective position. Mobilizing this broader constituency, undergirding and surrounding the unions proper, called for a cohesive organizational connection that would reach up and into parliament and the cabinet, if possible, just as the socialist Belgian Labor Party was able to integrate services and political power from bottom to top in an effective way. Here is where the leadership role of a priest from West Flanders, the afore-mentioned Louis Colens (1877–1936), came in. In 1921 he proposed the coordination of all the labor-oriented Catholic institutions in an overarching umbrella organization; he was able to bring it about shortly thereafter.

The formation of this National League of Christian Workers (ACW/LNTC) brought together the unions and the Christian workers' associations, male and female, Flemish and Walloon.[51] The same *standsorganisatie* also included the mutual-aid societies that provided insurance for sickness and accidents, the saving banks, and the cooperative stores. Bundling these forces together, the ACW ("W" for *Werkersverbond*, workers' league or association, as distinguished from ACV with a "V" for *Vakverbond* or trade union federation) was able after some ten years' time to provide a plethora of services and leadership training opportunities with the financial strength to survive hard times. And indeed it withstood even the Depression of the 1930s.

In this climate the Catholic peasants' and workers' leagues asserted themselves. Predecessor organizations had existed previously in Belgium; they served as a stimulus to the analogous formation of workers' and peasants' associations in the Netherlands. The term *standsorganisatie*, on the other hand, with its connotations of emancipatory class consciousness, seems to have found its way to Belgium from the Dutch Limburg in a reciprocal process. But whereas the Belgian *standsorganisatie* of the working class in Colens's design was "a copy of the socialist party," in the Netherlands Poels had seen to it that it did not include labor unions, but operated alongside of them with a predominantly educational mission.[52] Of course, after the 1925 coordination of the two Dutch movements under the overall leadership of A. C. De Bruijn, the *standsorganisaties* of the two countries came to resemble each other more closely.

Bourgeoisie and Labor in the Belgian Catholic Pillar

The prewar Catholic elite retained their electoral organization, the Federation of Circles, and their pretensions of leadership in Belgian political Catholicism.

51. See Gerard 1994c.
52. Gerard 1990, 13.

Now, however, under the system of one man, one vote, they were dependent on an electorate mobilized in the *standsorganisaties* of peasants, workers, and middle class, and hence had to allow representatives of the latter organizations to be placed on the ballot and elected as members of parliament. In 1921 this state of affairs was formalized in a new party structure in which each of the four groupings "had an equal part in the selection of candidates and elaboration of policy."[53] In practice this meant that the labor *standsorganisatie*, the ACW/LNTC, enjoyed "political autonomy"—that is, it pursued its own socioeconomic policies and legislative strategy in election campaigns and in parliament, as did the Peasants League. In matters of Catholic emancipation (education, cultural subsidies, family policy, church-state issues), it made common cause with the other groupings in the party, which was called the Belgian Catholic Union.[54] Will Rogers in the United States said he belonged to no organized party, being a Democrat; his contemporaries in Belgium could and did make similar remarks: "There are now Catholic groups rather than a Catholic party."[55] Emmanuel Gerard asserts that the Catholic Union was a mere "caricature of a party."[56] What held it together was the Catholic pillar in which it operated and what, with all its inner social tensions, the party represented politically. (Only in 1936 was the party reorganized, with individuals rather than class organizations as members, and with the basics of party discipline such as its own policy-making structure.)

In this structure Catholic workers had in the ACW/LNTC a *standsorganisatie* with growing political clout. For all practical purposes it was a counterpart to the Belgian Labor Party. It had to be self-sufficient financially so as to be strong and call its own shots. Hence, besides the dues of the members, Colens built up the cooperatives and savings banks that already existed and formed them into what was to become a powerful financial support of the Catholic labor movement, the COB (Coopération ouvrière belge), in this as in other respects playing catch-up with the socialists.[57] Like them it already had its representatives in parliament, except that the Catholic labor deputies belonged to an interclass parliamentary party not uniformly supportive of labor interests. On the other hand, the Catholic party regularly formed part of a coalition government, providing entrée for its labor deputies to hold cabinet positions not usually available to socialist politicians. The Catholic conservatives chafed under this loss of prestige and power in their party. Some former Christian democrats of the French-speaking bourgeois elite, like Carton de Wiart of Brussels, allied

53. Conway 1996, 193; see also Gerard 1994c, 2:575–78.
54. Evans 1999, 175.
55. Cited in Somerville 1933, 117.
56. Gerard 1994c, 2:575–77; Gerard 2001, 104, or Gerard 2004b, 98.
57. Kwanten 1994, 318–20.

themselves with the conservatives in the face of a new coalition of peasants and Flemish-rights activists.[58]

Tensions and polarization grew especially acute in French-speaking Belgium (Wallonia). An exemplary case occurred in Charleroi. Catholic conservatives there hoped to preserve or rebuild a paternalistic relationship between bourgeois and working-class Catholics and resented the autonomous political influence of organized Catholic labor.[59] Because it illustrates the presence and significance of the ACW/LNTC within the Belgian Catholic pillar and because it actualizes the issues that were typical of the situation, a closer look at this controversy will be worthwhile.[60]

A local Catholic party secretary, Georges Michaux, was unwilling to give the Catholic workers' association in the Charleroi area any say in party affairs. Prior to the 1929 election, while trying to keep labor representatives off the party's list of candidates, he was also determined to prevent them from appearing on an independent slate of candidates. The latter course would have been a last resort of the Christian democrats, since it would have created much ill will against the Catholic left in Catholic Belgium at large. Much to the conservatives' chagrin, however, a young Christian democratic lawyer, Jean Bodart, forced his way onto the Catholic party list and was elected to parliament. At the same time, the mutual insurance associations that had existed for some time, like other Catholic *oeuvres*, were federating at the national level while also establishing organizational ties with the ACW/LNTC, the labor *standsorganisatie* that exerted such unwelcome influence as a constituent element of the Catholic party. To counter this mobilization and accumulation of resources under LNTC auspices, Michaux embarked on a two-track strategy. He induced several mutual-aid societies in his district to withdraw from affiliation with the LNTC. He also bethought himself of the program of Catholic Action, so insistently urged by Pope Pius XI and of great appeal to many apostolic-minded Catholics. An argument calculated to carry much weight with the bishops was then put forward to the following effect.

Are the Catholics of Belgium as a whole to be constrained to support a system that binds institutions for the benefit of workers to the particular political program and electoral activities of the Belgian Christian Workers' League? Does any given Catholic grouping have the right to claim a monopoly on the social apostolate in the working-class milieu? In other words, must it be impossible for a Belgian Catholic to collaborate in working-class betterment without at the same time strengthening the political position of representatives of the Christian Workers' League?[61]

---

58. Gerard 1994b, 1:157.   59. Gerard 1990, 29–30.
60. The following is based on based on Gerard 1986; 1990, 22–31, 170–76; and 1994a, 1:192–94.
61. Cited in Gerard 1990, 172.

These rhetorical questions, representing Michaux's position, were formulated in a note written in January 1931 by Ceslas Rutten, OP. He sent this note to the diocesan priest-directors of social works to coordinate a concerted response to the threat from Charleroi, as he saw it. To the argument that Rutten summed up as above, his own first reply was simply: No, the social apostolate could of course not be a special group's monopoly; contributions from all quarters were needed to make Catholic institutions thrive among workers and to fight against the paganizing influence of the socialist labor movement.[62] But Rutten prefaced this concession with an account (of special interest to us) of just what the "social works" in question (*oeuvres sociales ouvrières*) amounted to, and he followed it up with considerations meant to impress bishops and others of the folly of trying to split the Catholic labor movement. His tally started with the over 200,000 members of the Christian labor unions as such. The mutual insurance societies that belonged to the Catholic national federation covered 330,000 heads of families; 140,000 women workers belonged to their national association. The Young Christian Workers organizations (Joseph Cardijn's JOC) numbered 100,000 members. Both the JOC movement and the Christian unions were in a phase of rapid growth. As Conway notes, during the early 1930s "a mood of spiritual renewal was evident within Belgian Catholicism."[63] It was "not a religion in decline." In fact, at the workers' level, the Christian trade unions had grown from a mere 50,000 members in 1919, compared with a socialist union membership of 500,000. By 1939, alongside the socialists' 600,000, there would be some 350,000 organized in Christian unions.[64] In Charleroi and environs, however, churchgoers were a distinct minority and had been for some time.[65]

What about the charge of monopolizing the social apostolate and opposing other initiatives? Rutten pointed out that all these highly beneficial activities and institutions flourished as well as they did in great part because they were connected in a strong umbrella organization. The training programs, in particular, supplied well-schooled young men and women who could staff the social secretariats that were to be found in practically every larger town. These in turn could depend on the regional and national offices for organizational support, know-how, and materials. Isolated local initiatives would stand no chance of competing with their socialist counterparts—in fact, it was the centralization of the various Catholic *oeuvres* as promoted by Colens that accounted in large measure for their attractiveness and effectiveness. Another socialist feature, adequate compensation of paid League officers and employees, was also necessary for the Catholic counterpart, which by this time was in many respects

62. Ibid., 173.
64. Gerard 1998, 132.
63. Conway 1996, 189.
65. Tihon 1990, 548; see also 543.

the equal of the socialist network.[66] What the socialist labor movement did not have, of course, was another characteristic of the ACW/LNTC that Rutten was at pains to state explicitly: every affiliated organization had its priest-adviser who reported to priest-directors at the district and diocesan levels or functioned as advisers attached to the various national offices.

Who would wish to dismantle this network built up with such effort over forty years? he asked.

It has served our workers well in terms of religious and intellectual benefits as well as economic ones, as everyone will admit. It helps to reinforce the Catholic party; after all, what would the party amount to if, alongside of the associations of the farmers and the petite bourgeoisie, there were no strong labor organization?[67]

Rutten was now ready to rephrase the question about monopolizing in a more practical light—namely, how best to counter the de-Christianizing tendency of the socialist labor movement. How were Catholics "to keep the confidence of the members of Christian labor and gain the adherence of others?" Could it be done without a well-organized national movement that would wield "an influence and strength comparable to that" of the socialist movement? And if bourgeois paternalists would succeed in launching a parallel movement, what would this mean if not trouble and weakness? For one thing, the clergy would have to withdraw so as not to take sides. Christian labor now had enough lay leaders and resources to go it alone, without the chaplains and advisers. Was that what the church wanted? Besides, when it came to nominating candidates for political office, the two Catholic labor movements would operate from opposed policy viewpoints. Inevitably the ACW/LNTC would secede from the party to form its own electoral bloc, an independent democratic labor party, which, in coalition with the socialist deputies, could form a labor government after the subsequent election and cast the Catholic party into the unaccustomed role of the opposition. After that, who could know what would ensue?

This quite realistic threat had already been uttered earlier in the controversy, but now it was taken up by the two labor priests par excellence, Rutten and Colens.[68] Colens was the least clerical of the clerics and did not see the ACW/LNTC as part of official Catholic Action at all.[69] Rutten, too, saw through the lofty rhetoric of much of the criticism: "What they always want us to refrain from is not politics but democratic politics."[70] The foreseeable practical conse-

66. See Gerard 1994c, 2:578–87.
68. Gerard 1986, 219–23.
67. Gerard 1990, 172.
69. Gerard 1994a, 1:191.
70. Cited in Gerard 1983, 128; 1990, 25; and 1994b, 1:191. Pasture (2001b, 231–32) states, "In the mid-1920s Christian labor had to resist attacks from Catholic Action, ... a movement of lay apostolate under clerical authority. It tried to bring the lay apostolate, actually in particular the leadership of the Catholic social works, under clerical control.... Moreover, Catholic Action emphasized

quences, however, were sufficient to impress ecclesiastical leaders, Van Roey most of all, and lead them to protect the Christian labor movement in its prevailing structures from attacks by its integralist Catholic critics. What is striking here is the pragmatic character of the argumentation of the clerical defenders of the labor movement.[71] Arguments in principle, from human rights, or the desirability in principle of democratic participation, were not yet available in prevailing Catholic social teaching that could be used with bishops.

As the 1930s unrolled, however, the electioneering of the ACW/LNTC would come under increased criticism, even from chaplains devoted to the cause of Christian labor. The more strictly political activity would devolve increasingly upon the Christian unions proper and especially upon the Catholic party, which would develop its own structures of campaigning and party discipline.[72] But this is a part of the next phase of the story, after the onset of the Depression and the updating of papal social teaching in *Quadragesimo anno*.

Belgium and the Netherlands were the leading interwar labor exemplars of the "Age of Mobilization" preceding a fully Secular Age, as in Charles Taylor's paradigm[73] (which our introduction proposed as a leitmotiv). Next, a comparison with an equally vibrant case—that of France, where church life had suffered greater losses—adds other accents to the Catholic workers' scene.

Catholic unity and opposed separate social works for different social classes, especially workers.... It combated Christian labor, since according to Catholic Action Christian labor introduced the class struggle into the heart of the Catholic world.... What they opposed was democratic politics. In fact they believed democracy and workers' emancipation were expressions of secularization and moral decay. Catholic Action thus revealed itself as, on the one hand, an offensive movement of Catholic re-Christianization, education and renewal, and on the other hand as a reactionary, anti-democratic movement and a mortal enemy of Christian labor. It was no accident that the major francophone Fascist party in Belgium, Rex, had its roots in a Catholic Action publishing house."

71. Gerard 1990, 31.
72. Gerard 2004b, 103–10.
73. See Taylor 2007, especially 423–72.

CHAPTER 6

France

CONTROVERSIES AND
ADVANCES

Like the challenge mounted in Belgium in the late 1920s against Catholic organizations for the working class, a contemporary struggle in France gave evidence of sharp differences among Catholics. It too ended with a vindication for the workers, but it was much more notorious and protracted. A Catholic employers' organization, the Patrons du Nord, stoked the controversy against a Catholic labor union. Among the differences between Charleroi in Belgium and Roubaix to the west in French Flanders, two factors immediately stand out. One was the complication arising from a more sensational *affaire* in the religio-political realm—namely, the papal reprimand in 1927 of the Action française, the reactionary movement founded by Charles Maurras. Pius XI went so far as to impose an excommunication on regular readers of its daily paper of the same name. The French hierarchy counted in its ranks a number of stout Action française sympathizers, since the AF opposed the anti-clericalism of the left. The papal intervention threw Catholics who supported this ultra-nationalist and anti-democratic political movement onto the defensive while energizing progressive activists and movements.

Another factor was a matter of social culture. The phenomenon of pillarization, as it came about in the Low Countries and to some extent elsewhere, never developed a foothold in France. Hence the Christian labor unions in France, in contrast with those in the Low Countries, had to struggle to maintain a presence and deploy their union activities without the support of a broader Catholic workers' association tied in with a national political party. In certain regions, nevertheless, there was a *"chrétienté,"* a Catholic subculture that generated a network of credit unions, insurance organizations, and cooperatives. In such regions—Alsace-Lorraine, Lyon, Brittany, the Nord—as well as in certain manifestations at the national level, French social Catholicism displayed real vigor.

French Social Catholicism in the 1920s

Though in no way comparable in associational density to the Catholicism of Belgium or the Netherlands, the national institutions of French Catholicism gained in numbers and influence after World War I. Anticlericalism in parliament let up, as the patriotism of Catholics could hardly be impugned after World War I. The short-lived Cartel des Gauches in 1924 renewed the threat long enough for General Edouard de Castelnau to put together the FNC (Fédération nationale catholique), a durable religious right focused on conservative church interests, within the framework of the republic. The large French hierarchy did not have a conference of bishops, but formed a sort of coordinating committee of cardinals and archbishops. There were only a few bishops who were not "timid, unsure, or even hostile" as to labor activism.[1] One must remember that since the separation of church and state of 1905, bishops were quite dependent on the good will of moneyed benefactors to support the pastoral and educational works in their dioceses. They hesitated to challenge the mentality requiring sole and unchallenged authority over their workforce; employers insisted on remaining, as they said, "*maître chez soi.*" Even magnanimous factory owners still shared this outlook with their class and regarded it as nonnegotiable. The clergy component of the democratic wing of social Catholicism remained essential and received some reinforcements from the experience of the trenches. The Action populaire, the center for social justice that the four French Jesuit provinces founded at the time of the Séparation, moved from bombed-out Reims to Paris (Vanves) after the war and resumed its publications and training programs.[2] The bishops of Paris, of Lille in the Nord, of Lyon and Grenoble appointed priests to advise Christian unions and to head "social secretariats" (roughly, social-concerns offices assisting cooperative and self-help projects). The social Catholicism of formerly German Alsace and Lorraine continued with hardly a break and contributed to the national associations that were being formed or revivified. Its representatives in parliament—for instance, Robert Schuman (1886–1963)—could occasionally exert some helpful influence.

The *Semaines sociales* resumed in 1919 by meeting in Metz (Lorraine), where German Catholics had gathered in 1913 for their *Katholikentag*. The

1. Droulers 1981, 105.
2. Misner 1991, 288–98; Droulers 1981.

period from 1919 to 1939 saw these *Semaines*, annual conferences of social Catholics with serious lectures published subsequently in book form, achieve a status of considerable authority within the church. Eugène Duthoit, the law professor at the Catholic Institute of Lille, took the place of Henri Lorin at its head. Progressive thinkers in the Catholic community gave short courses to ground and guide the Christian outlook and activism of the participants. Every year there would be a letter of encouragement from the Vatican secretary of state in the name of the pope. Such attestations, evidently well informed about the tendencies within the *Semaines sociales*, served to offset to some degree the identification of Catholicism with the bourgeois class and its interests.[3]

Catholic trade unionism crossed a threshold in November 1919 with the founding of the Confédération française des travailleurs chrétiens (CFTC), a national federation of most of the relatively small regional Christian trade unions that existed at that time.[4] Its president, Jules Zirnheld, and secretary general, Gaston Tessier, had long experience of Christian unionism as leaders of a Parisian clerical workers union. We have noted earlier Zirnheld's role in the International Federation of Christian Trade Unions (CISC). For some time, the CFTC would count among its members only a negligible portion of the industrial workforce of France (14,500 textile workers, 10,000 miners, 8,000 metalworkers, 7,000 construction workers). Its strength was in the railways (36,500) and especially among clerical workers (43,000). At its founding in 1919, the total of dues-paying adherents was some 125,000.[5] Its unions could rarely function as a collective bargaining agent. Its actual role and significance came largely through its educational activities and training of activists and in its persistent attention to legislative proposals until its bargaining potential could come to fruition in the labor conflicts of 1928 and 1936. The eight hundred locals of its affiliated unions were a factor in some regions, particularly around Paris, Grenoble, Lyon, St. Etienne, and in the Nord and Alsace. In comparison with the major union federation (the Confédération générale du travail, CGT), women always had a more prominent part in the CFTC's organization and programs.[6] Throughout, Christian formation and social outlook of the members was a priority.

In its founding documents, the French Confederation of Christian Workers declared itself in the line of *Rerum novarum*.[7] Catholics could not support anticlerical labor organizations and hence should form their own. Class struggle might be necessary defensively, but there was a better way. In a setting of private industry, government could certainly be more even-handed, recognizing

---

3. Lécrivain 1990; 1993.
5. Launay 1986, 64.
7. Ibid., 431.

4. Rollet 1955, 201; Pierrard 1984, 521.
6. Ibid., 41–42.

and supporting workers' rights, but workers and employers also had to deal with one another. This could happen most efficaciously through *commissions mixtes*—that is, by negotiations, not between individual employers and individual workers but between representatives of employers' associations on the one side of the table and labor representatives of the unions on the other. By this means the organized economic partners could obviate the most negative effects of unregulated competition in the markets for goods and for labor. While strikes were certainly admissible as a last resort, "revolutionary" means and aims were eschewed. The CFTC unions were meliorist: they aimed to transform capitalist industrial society gradually, by democratic means, rather than overturn it abruptly. The employers' and workers' *syndicats* would each enjoy complete independence and autonomy and come to the table with their respective claims and interests. Any one-sided hegemony, whether on the labor side (as the socialist unions would have it) or on the employers' side (as was most often the case), was categorically rejected. What the CFTC aimed for was a recognition of the social rights of labor, not a dictatorship of the proletariat. "Corporative organization," declared the CFTC at its first annual congress in 1920, "has to group the different elements of production in separate associations possessing absolute independence but connected by mixed commissions. Such organization is indispensable to assure the balance and harmony of the productive forces and the due assessment of their rights."[8]

The unions made incremental progress. They retained the loyalty of workers for whom the social Catholic worldview was important, who consequently could not feel at home in the secularist and anticlerical ambience of the CGT, even in its reformist wing. The transcendent calling of human beings, created by God and destined for life eternal with the Father, the Son, and the Holy Spirit, gave meaning to their lives. They responded to the formation offered by social Catholic institutions.[9] In becoming militants, they soldiered on in the cause of re-Christianizing society. Their employers could often simply refuse to recognize them or talk with them when they did not have the numbers to strike. In some cases employers would talk with them and settle issues without labor trouble. When this happened, however, the Christian unions would not get credit for the concessions from their socialist rivals. They would appear to be pawns in paternalistic moves to put the damper on labor militancy.

8. Cited in ibid., 436.
9. Ibid., 256–73.

The Controversy with the Patrons du Nord

In one region, however, the Nord (including Roubaix and Tourcoing on the Belgian border within the Lille conurbation), a long, drawn-out confrontation between textile mill owners who were mostly practicing Catholics and the Christian unions required a mobilization of solidarity that had two remarkable effects. It demonstrated to the anticlerical workers that Catholic unions were not "kept" unions and would stubbornly defend workers' interests; and it resulted in a formal public declaration from the Vatican in 1929 that repudiated the Catholic employers' complaints about Christian unionism while validating labor's claims to negotiate wages and working conditions.

Starting in 1919–20, the Association catholique des patrons du Nord was folded into a broader nonreligious organization, the Textile Consortium. Heedless of warnings that arrant paternalism would not go over after the Great War,[10] these Catholic employers, with the blessing of their Jesuit adviser, adopted the proposals of one Eugène Mathon, diametrically opposed to consultation with organized labor.[11] A Catholic himself, he never belonged to the professedly Catholic association, but was quite close to Archbishop Chollet of Cambrai; both were inclined to regard the Action française as on the whole a healthy development. It was, after all, the most forthrightly monarchist, anti-liberal and anti-socialist party on the horizon. Mathon's ideas about the proper economic development of France skewed in an authoritarian direction, but were at considerable variance with both René de La Tour du Pin and Georges Valois, a corporatist theorist of the Action française.[12] At any rate, the Textile Consortium came into being with the express policy of not dealing with unions, only with individual workers. A new government policy superceded that private policy, however. Employers had to deal with labor representatives. Forced to comply, the members of the Textile Consortium accepted Mathon's plan to avoid direct negotiations. The consortium appointed an administrator to conduct its labor relations. This was one Désiré Ley, who would become infamous in Christian labor memory.[13] Class solidarity among the owners was to reign supreme. As if in response, a communist faction, the CGTU ("*les unitaires*"), broke away from the main CGT and won the adherence of a majority of textile workers in the Nord.

While Mathon and Ley conceded that they had to deal with the red unions, reluctantly and as adversaries, they were not prepared to do so with the small Christian unions. What business did Catholics have engaging in class warfare,

10. Talmy 1966, 136–40.
11. On Eugène Mathon, see Caudron 1990, 351–52.
12. On La Tour du Pin, see Misner 1991, 175–81.
13. Caudron 1990, 329–31.

after all? They should respect the bosses' authority. If they would stay in their place, they could enjoy regular subsidies from the employers as a loyal workmen's association.[14] After all, the owners were Christians, too, and did not want their workers destitute, just obedient. Had they not instituted generous "family allocations" and other social aid that required a payment on their part to the consortium of an extra 6.5 percent of payroll?[15] These family allocations increased according to the size of the family; they would permit an older child to stay home to look after the rest and help assure a local workforce into the future. In all this the principle was that it remained the sole prerogative of the business owners to determine the types of assistance to be offered and the level of expense the industry could afford—and it must be remembered that such beneficent sharing was not a matter of justice but of charity. No claims on these extras could be made as entitlements on any legal or moral grounds.

There was an initial skirmish with the CFTC local or, more precisely, between the consortium and the clergy affiliated with the *sécrétariat social* of Roubaix, in February of 1921. The consortium's Ley announced a unilateral decision to revoke a cost-of-living increase. The pretext was that a previous increase had been made unilaterally, so in changed economic conditions it could also be unilaterally withdrawn—this in the face of two successive collective agreements since the end of the war. The workers were up in arms. At this tense moment the old labor priest Jules Bataille, now a pastor in Roubaix, wrote a pulpit announcement to be read also in the other churches.[16] When apprised of it, Bishop Quilliet (bishop of Lille, 1920–28) saw to it that the consortium's decision was reversed overnight so as to forestall the reading of the announcement. The text itself supported collective agreements on wages and working conditions in the name of Catholic social teaching. It also called for a permanent mixed commission of union and employer representatives (some months before the CFTC did so in its declaration) to discuss such issues, rather than unilateral pronouncements. Bishop Quilliet, like Archbishop Chollet of Cambrai, was sympathetic to the right in general and the Action française in particular. The fact that he did not support the consortium's stand encouraged Alphonse Debussche, the priest whom the previous bishop had just recently appointed to the new position of labor chaplain as director of a *sécrétariat social* in Roubaix.[17] Debussche let each bishop know that he considered it his task to help set up a union of textile workers completely independent of company unions. He was not isolated among the clergy; the bishop did not squelch his initiatives. De-

14. Launay 1986, 128, reports such offers; see Talmy 1966, 165.
15. Talmy 1966, 162.
16. Caudron 1990, 49–51.
17. Ibid., 142–43.

bussche took the opportunity of his new position to acquaint himself with the leading figures of the *Semaines sociales* when they met at Metz; he also went to see how the Belgian labor institutions under the aegis of the LNTC operated.

Désiré Ley, from his office in Roubaix as secretary general of the Textile Consortium, resented being overruled. Here he was, charged with the labor relations of a mostly Catholic body of textile manufacturers, and Christian democrats (as he referred to them derogatorily) were spoiling his project. As Launay explains, the red union was a clear and present danger, out to dispossess capitalists—an easy target.[18] There was no doubt in any employer's mind that a firm and united front against them was necessary. The CFTC, however, were Catholics; they might appeal to their Catholic employers to put their common faith ahead of their class interests on occasion. This would ruin the solid front that the consortium formed against democracy in the workplace. It would overturn the relationships of command that were so strictly maintained between the managers and the wage-earners of the firm. It would threaten the prerogatives of the former. The CFTC manner of gentle persuasion rather than raucous demonstrations appealed to one or another Catholic industrialist already; it could weaken employers' resolve to hold out against working-class demands. Ley proceeded to stymie the Christian unions of the Nord at every turn. This was not the prewar paternalism of concerned employers any longer; this was still a policy with benefits, but one predicated on class dominance, on crushing worker autonomy and participation.[19]

His targets held their own, however. CFTC unions were founded, and clergy support for them did not wane. Soon after the war, Abbé Paul Six was brought out of rural exile and appointed director of social works for the whole diocese of Lille.[20] He proceeded to coordinate and stimulate the work of new and existing *sécretariats sociaux*, as in the textile towns of Roubaix and Tourcoing. He had the close cooperation of Eugène Duthoit of the Catholic university of Lille.[21] Other intellectual activists, such as the theology professor Pierre Tiberghien, taught at the training courses for labor organizers in Lille (the École normale ouvrière) and later at the program set up to train priests (*missionnaires du travail*) to work in proletarian milieus.[22] Abbé Six recruited workers to lead unions. Such were Georges Torcq, a white-collar CFTC unionist, and Léon Viellefon, who founded and led a union of railway workers.[23] Charlemagne Brou-

18. Launay 1986, 126.
19. Talmy 1966, 163.
20. Caudron 1990, 433–35, for Paul Six (1860–1936); see also Misner 1991, index, for Six and other activists named and their prewar roles.
21. Caudron 1990, 216–19.
22. Ibid., 448.
23. On Georges Torcq, see ibid., 449; on Léon Viellefon, see ibid., 475.

tin worked in the railroad yards around Lille with Viellefon and like him belonged to the CGT until 1912, when they left to found a Christian union.[24] In the 1920s Broutin was head of a regional office of the CFTC in the Nord that gradually linked over a hundred locals. Debussche's successor in the Roubaix social secretariat in 1923, Pierre Lesage, would carry on in the same spirit during a long career as labor chaplain.[25]

Over Christmas of 1923 Mathon sent a letter to Cardinal Sbarretti of the Congregation of the Council. He must have had some advice from clergy so as to address it to the place where it would receive attention. The clergy who most esteemed him were those sympathetic to the Action française, such as Archbishop Chollet and Cardinal Louis Billot, SJ, in Rome. Mathon obviously did not know that the new pope, Pius XI, wished to come to a modus vivendi with republican France and that the Action française was falling out of papal favor. It would take a number of years for Pius XI to bring the French episcopate around to accept this second *Ralliement*, as it is called.[26] Mathon, as an anti-democratic royalist opponent of the Third French Republic, must have thought that his complaints (first, about the labor chaplains, and second, about the Christian labor unions) would get a sympathetic hearing and that he need not be too concerned about the accuracy of his specific charges.

They were indeed taken seriously. Sbarretti asked the local bishops about the matter, but he also confided in Msgr. Gaston Vanneufville in Rome in a bid for advice. Vanneufville, from Roubaix, a long-time supporter of *abbés démocrates*, was the Roman correspondent for *La Croix*. Vanneufville asked Eugène Duthoit in Lille to supply information. More officially, Sbarretti also commissioned Achille Danset, SJ, of the Action populaire center, to investigate the situation thoroughly and report back with findings and recommendations. Both Duthoit and Danset sprang from the bourgeoisie of the Nord, Duthoit from Lille and Danset from a family of industrialists in Halluin.[27] Both were well placed to supply inside information. Danset devoted the months from March to December 1925 with his charge. Duthoit wrote when Vanneufville requested help, the last time in January 1928, actually proposing a draft response of which the Congregation of the Council made large use.[28]

The tendencies and institutions that Mathon wanted reined in, as it hap-

24. Ibid., 90–91.   25. Ibid., 323.
26. Paul 1967.   27. Caudron 1990, 135–36.
28. Why the long delay? Apart from whatever other reasons there may have been, in 1926 and 1927 the pope's priority in regard to France was a sort of "second Ralliement" so that Catholics would work within the republic's institutions. This involved countering the grip that Charles Maurras and Action française had over the political outlook of so many Catholics. It also forced Jacques Maritain to abandon his approach of upholding both worldviews (those of Maurras and of Pius XI) in the years from 1925 to 1929; see Prévotat 2001, 299–302 and 415–22.

pened, were the very ones that Duthoit had been promoting since the 1890s: Catholic labor, *Semaines sociales*, *sécrétariats sociaux*, the training of clergy and lay leaders in Catholic social doctrine and action.[29] Danset, for his part, was part of Desbuquois's team at the Action populaire; he was a specialist in economics and had advised and promoted Catholic unionism for years.[30] Before joining the Jesuits, he had worked in the family firm in Halluin, so he knew the terrain from many angles. From the reports of both Duthoit and Danset it was clear that the consortium altogether failed to recognize the right of Catholic workers to organize and was pushing them into the arms of the socialists and communists. Despite its steps to ease their lot by supplements for workers' families and other social benefits, the consortium under the administration of Ley refused to talk to union leaders about wages or benefits unless forced, and then only with the red unions. At all costs, Ley and Mathon wanted to prevent the formation of a labor elite who might be able to hold its own with Catholic employers on the common ground of reformist Catholic social teaching. Hence, they also wanted Rome to suppress or limit the activity of the labor chaplains in the social secretariats so that they would not develop working-class leaders.[31] They conjured up an inevitable communist threat as inherent in the advocacy of unions.

Further instances of this same reactionary policy occurred as the matter was under consideration. Sbarretti naturally hesitated to offend the generous Catholic employers of the Nord in Désiré Ley's organization. Events in the Nord, however, particularly the consortium's handling of the long and bitter strikes in Halluin in 1928 and 1929, would overcome these hesitations. When Bishop Quilliet resigned for health reasons in early 1928, the Congregation of the Council was ready to act. Arthur Vermeersch, SJ, supplied a catena of papal texts since 1891 relative to labor unions and employers' associations. The congregation made these the first part of its reply to Mathon. Then it judged the situation in the Nord in the light of these teachings. It rejected the complaints alleged against the Christian unions and the labor chaplains. Some were exaggerated; "others, the most serious ones, which attributed a Marxist spirit and a state socialism to the unions, are entirely unfounded and unjust."[32] It also

---

29. See Ribaut 1991, 367; Duthoit was the guiding spirit behind the *Code social* of Mechlin, as noted in chap. 4 of this volume.

30. Droulers 1981, 115–16 and 141–52.

31. Talmy 1966, 186–87.

32. *AAS* 1929, 21: 500. The official published text of this important document, dated June 5, 1929, appeared on August 9, 1929, in the *Acta Apostolicae Sedis* 21 (1929): 494–504, in the form of a letter signed by the prefect of the Sacred Congregation of the Council, Cardinal Sbarretti, to Bishop Achille Liénart of Lille, in French with a Latin title referring to a labor conflict in his region. The second part is excerpted in Rémond 1996, 27–30, which also contains press comments on the affair; it attracted much attention (in *La Croix*, *Osservatore Romano*, *Études*, *L'Action Française*, and elsewhere).

went out of its way to praise rather than condemn the appointment of priests as labor missionaries to assist union members spiritually as well as to point out the implications for Christian morality of workplace issues. Following as it seems a suggestion of Msgr. Vanneufville, it voiced the wish that bishops in other industrial regions would imitate this example. An apostolate such as this "will not only protect the populations against the evil of indifference and of the socialist and communist danger, but it will also be a witness of the maternal care that the Church lavishes on workers."[33] Thus the consortium, for all the praise of its social assistance programs, found its leader's main charges against the CFTC of the Nord completely disavowed—formally dismissed after a careful investigation.

What had happened was this. Cardinal Sbarretti's information-gathering requests were a fairly closely guarded secret. The lay union leaders apparently knew nothing of all this. Ley continued to manage the consortium's industrial relations in his customary authoritarian manner. Relations between the consortium and some of the clergy became more heated and public. In a case in the national press, the perfume magnate François Coty, who had bought *Le Figaro* to support reactionary causes, praised the consortium and accused the Christian democratic clergy of the Nord, including the ex-scripture professor and pastor in Roubaix, Achille Liénart, of aiding and abetting communism.[34] In March 1928 a strike broke out at the Sion plant in Halluin, where Arthur Houte had founded a Christian union after the war and had entrée with the Sion family managers.[35] Now, however, Sion joined the consortium, and the door was slammed shut. The strike, led by the CGTU, nevertheless ended in May. The company gave in to the wage demands, for the present, but Ley had achieved the rupture he so ardently desired between Sion and the CFTC union.

Shortly thereafter the Congregation of the Council deemed it time to reply to Mathon's suit of 1924 on the basis of the intelligence it had gathered. Under date of June 5, 1928 (note the year), it sent the letter it would make public in 1929 to the apostolic administrator of the diocese of Lille to be communicated to the interested parties. (Bishop Quilliet had resigned; Bishop Liénart was not yet appointed.) Not until Liénart's appointment was announced (in October 1928) did the administrator pro-tem forward the Vatican response to Eugène Mathon. Ley made copies for industrialists who heard about it.[36] It does not appear that the *sécrétariat social* of Roubaix or any of its union associates received a copy. But from the industrialists' side, word would leak out.

33. *AAS* 1929, 21: 503.
34. *Figaro*, March 15, 1927, as cited in Talmy 1966, 201; see Masson 2001, 90.
35. On Arthur Houte, see Caudron 1990, 281–82.
36. Talmy 1966, 213–21.

Meanwhile, a second hard-fought strike broke out in Halluin on September 20, 1928. The CFTC union under Houte called for arbitration while returning to work, which Ley turned down. In view of the hardship on the workers and their families (and in view of the dwindling numbers of Christian union members), the new bishop, Achille Liénart, demonstratively headed the list of contributors to a fund to alleviate the distress in Halluin (this in February 1929). The strike went on. Disgruntlement with the consortium's handling of labor relations was developing also among some employers. Somehow, Liénart managed to get Ley to talk to the Christian union leaders—perhaps the still unpublished Vatican letter was having some effect after all.[37] It was agreed to avoid retaliations against labor agitators and to remove some objectionable parts of the new work rules that Ley had promulgated. The pay issue was left where it stood. The gates were open on April 5, and by April 11 even the CGTU called its members back to work.

It was at this juncture that someone in the Vatican decided that the response sent privately the year before deserved to be rebaptized as a letter to Bishop Liénart and issued publicly as a clear statement of Catholic social teaching on unionism. Taken in conjunction with the pope's personal interest in the choice of a bishop for Lille and in the cardinalate that he bestowed a few months later on Liénart, the forty-six-year-old bishop of a young diocese,[38] it is not much of a leap to attribute all these decisions to Pope Pius XI. It was a vindication of the CFTC, to be sure, and a new stage in the magisterial support given to the labor movement. It was also a vindication of Duthoit's direction and of priests such as Bataille and Six, and of the Action populaire against its detractors inside and outside the Society of Jesus. Pius XI was determined to break the pretensions of the extreme right in France to an exclusive alliance with Roman Catholicism. In the Catholic world at large, it could at least serve as a straw in the wind that the pope was not going to bend Catholic social ethics to fit the Italian mode, even if he had let Mussolini suppress the Catholic unions in Italy without a protest.[39] Though he was without any appreciation for political democracy himself, the pope found the Christian democratic development of social Catholicism more responsive to his vision of Catholic Action than were the reactionaries.[40]

37. The meeting was during Holy Week 1929; see Launay 1986, 165.
38. Masson 2001, 88–93, 131.
39. Duffy 1997, 259–61.
40. Equivocations remained in Vatican policy at this time. In the very same years, 1928 and 1929, that the Nord dispute reached its climax, the "Catholic Worker International" (see the end of chap. 3 of this volume) could not get recognition from the Holy See. The Catholic Worker International was composed of strictly Catholic "confessional" workers' associations, not unions, and its co-leader, Joseph Joos, was a strong proponent of interclass harmony. But he was a lay person, and the International was not under the supervision of the hierarchy in the Catholic Action mode.

The outcome of this crisis caused a stir in France.[41] In the world of social Catholicism in which Duthoit, the Action populaire, and the CFTC moved, the denouement of the "social war of the Nord" in the 1920s was simply stunning. Although one tried not to gloat, the letter to Bishop Liénart gave more immediate satisfaction than the much longer and weightier social encyclical that followed two years later. Indeed, in France (but not elsewhere) the letter was treated like a social encyclical. An ambivalent or hostile attitude toward labor unions had prevailed in Catholic circles. Now a strong endorsement of unions, confessional and anti-socialist, to be sure, but defenders of workers' rights, deprived their Catholic opponents of any objections in principle. Two suggestions were especially telling (the magisterium would insist firmly upon the principles of social progress that it enunciated, but only suggested certain more technical, changeable applications that seemed particularly appropriate). After commending the CFTC unions for the emphasis they placed on the formation of their members, the letter stated, "On this topic, in view of a fuller and better adapted education of the youth in Christian social teaching, the Sacred Congregation suggests that one impart a social instruction adapted to the understanding of young people in the patronages and other educational institutions. This is done in some dioceses with excellent results."[42] Left unstated was the fact that this suggestion countermanded the policy formulated by the bishops of the Nord in 1925 to keep such controversial topics out of the educational programs of the church. The second such detail concerns the relations of employers and unions more directly: "The Church wishes that the labor and employer associations be instruments of harmony and peace; toward this end it suggests the institution of Mixed Commissions as a means of union between them."[43]

All in all, a fuller vindication of the CFTC's stands and of Christian unionism in general could hardly be expected. An official Vatican statement had finally taken aim directly at the stubborn integralist campaign against unionism.[44]

Other Centers of Social-Justice Advocacy

The Nord was not the only theater of social Catholic activities in the 1920s, just the most dramatic. Developments in Alsace, Brittany, and the Lyon region should be noted. The Alsatian region along the Rhine boasted a historic archbishopric and university in its capital, Strasbourg. From 1870 to the end of the First World War, it had been incorporated into the German Reich. The factors

---

41. Rémond 1996, 39; Droulers 1981, 150–52.
42. *AAS* 1929, 21: 501.   43. *AAS* 1929, 21: 497.
44. To fully appreciate why this ruling came as such a relief to French Catholic union sympathizers, one must be aware of the pre–World War I history of this campaign; see Misner 1991, 175–81.

of language, French and German, and increasingly, education on the German model, together with the example of militant German Catholicism, combined to create a different environment than in the rest of France. After all, it had been cut off from the metropolis for the whole history of the Third Republic. This did not mean that Alsatians felt fully accepted as German citizens—far from it. But in the period under Reich rule, they had become more self-consciously Catholic, as had been the case, analogously, with other subject populations like the Irish or the Polish. To the surprise of French officials, they did not want to see their state-supported confessional, German-language primary schools turned into secular schools with French teachers from the interior.[45] For the history of social Catholicism in France, what is significant is that this highly organized Catholicism entered into the Catholic world of France, one with its own challenges, and changed the complexion of the latter at least marginally during the interwar period. The Alsatians' own regional political party and other organizations, formed more or less after the Volksverein model, supported and affected the national associations. The existing Alsatian Christian labor unions joined and strengthened the CFTC.[46]

In Brittany, at the opposite end of France, regional pride and Catholic religion also tended to reinforce one another since the French Revolution. Despite the coolness of the successive bishops of Rennes, the signal success of the Christian democratic movement around the daily *L'Ouest-Éclair* continued after World War I.[47] On the coast, at Saint-Malo, two priests and their young recruits attacked the severe economic problems of the fisherfolk with a *secrétariat social* maritime and the founding of a Jeunesse maritime chrétienne in 1928. The priests were Georges Havard and Louis Lebret, OP.[48] Lebret would later help draft the 1967 encyclical *Populorum progressio*. Given the ability of Christian democratic candidates to be elected to parliament in both Alsace and Brittany, these regions were prominent in the PDP (Parti démocrate populaire). This party, formed on the pattern of Luigi Sturzo's PPI (as noted in chapter 3), had members from other regions, as well, but never gained the adherence of a substantial bloc of Catholic voters nationally. It remained a minor if sometimes effective force in the Assembly.[49]

In the years leading up to 1930, something like a national lobbying campaign brought together all the social Catholic institutions plus the FNC. From the Action populaire and the *Chronique* social groups of southeastern France to

45. Gaines 1993.
46. See Vogler, in *DMR* 2:26; see also Delbreil 1990, index s.v. Bilger and Meck.
47. Ford 1993.
48. See Lagrée 1992. On Lebret, see Delprat and Pelletier 1994; Pelletier 1996; Calvez 2006, 2:39–59; Lavigne and Puel 2007.
49. McMillan 1996; Delbreil 2004.

the *Semaines sociales* and the CFTC, the numerous local social-concerns offices and the deputies of the PDP, along with the women's groups, all worked to sensitize public opinion in support of the most important piece of social legislation proposed in France following World War I. This was the law establishing a first national policy on social security, endorsed in principle by the Assembly since 1924 but resisted by many rightists.[50] By dint of much patient lobbying and publicity, they won the support of the FNC (the mass "religious defense" society called the Fédération nationale catholique).[51] Referred to as *assurances sociales*, this policy entailed state subsidies added to contributions from employers and workers for old-age pensions as well as health and injury benefits and maternity care. Key aspects were voluntary, which is why the collaboration of the FNC's broad conservative organization was so important. Potential beneficiaries had to sign up for the program and make contributions. Along the lines of the system prevailing in Alsace-Lorraine and Belgium, the funds could be administered by nongovernmental bodies authorized for this purpose. Many Catholics from left to right could and did agree to this system, which lasted until replaced in 1946, despite warnings of creeping socialism and unbearable financial burdens.

The mention of the *Chronique Social de France*, a periodical and a whole aggregation of social Catholic formation and activism, brings us to Lyon, its headquarters. The most prominent person here was Marius Gonin (1873–1937), who would head the *Chronique Social* until his death. Originally a clerk in one of the silk factories, he got into social Catholicism by peddling *La Croix* on the streets and in the surrounding villages around the time of *Rerum novarum*. Along with forming circles, encouraging unions, and being in charge of the *Chronique Social*, in 1904 he became the founding secretary general of the *Semaines sociales*, the first of which was held in Lyon. In partnership with Henri Lorin of Paris until 1919, thereafter with Eugène Duthoit of Lille, he kept the organizational reins of the *Semaines sociales* in hand through 1936.[52] Gonin was a figure who did not make a splash like the charismatic Marc Sangnier, nor did he ever provoke church authority. The Lyon movement, though democratic in the social sense, escaped censure when the Sillon was condemned in 1910. It was nevertheless distinctly opposed to the fiercely nationalistic and antimodern outlook that the Action française spread among Catholic youth.[53] Bernard Comte sums up the character of the *Chronique Social* movement as a social Catholicism of "integralist" roots, not separating church and social action, while also pursuing an approach of "open" Catholicism, out of a Franciscan love of the people and the age of the people.[54]

50. Droulers 1981, 158–60; Delbreil 1990, 238–42, 250–51.
51. McMillan 1996b, 41–43; 1996a.
52. Durand 2006.
53. Ponson 1994.
54. Comte 1992, 385–88.

Adding to and drawing on such impulses, resisted by strong liberal and conservative influences in Lyonnaise Catholicism, many other initiatives sprang up.[55] Of special note as time passed was the stimulus given and received by the three ecclesiastical faculties in Lyon: the seminary, the Institut catholique, and the Jesuit scholasticate of Fourvières. Another lay *Chronique Social* figure, Joseph Vialatoux, taught and wrote philosophy while animating and teaching social Catholic study circles in the region.[56] He was ready with one of the first defenses and commentaries on the papal opposition to the Action française when it was announced in 1926. (He had published his first criticisms of Maurras's positivism in 1908 and 1909.) Prominent at the *Semaines sociales* between the wars, he linked together progressive and Blondelian thinkers such as the Jesuits Auguste Valensin and Henri de Lubac with others in Lyon's vibrant intellectual and social-justice community. The CFTC was also strong in the area. Maurice Guérin (1887–1969) was a former Sillonist who lost a leg in the war.[57] Thereafter he settled in Lyon and was the main organizer of CFTC unions in the region. With Gonin, he started a journal, *La Voix Sociale*, and joined the PDP at its foundation in 1924.

Between World War I and the economic crisis of the 1930s and before *Quadragesimo anno*, social Catholicism continued to root itself firmly and to democratize itself in northwestern Catholic Europe. It gained adherents and force. It put representatives in the new, more broadly based legislative bodies and governmental cabinets as well as in labor relations boards and the like. It struggled with nonrecognition from the socialist labor movement as well as from bourgeois Catholicism. Next to some small victories and many small setbacks, there were some major breakthroughs to mark. Already prior to *Quadragesimo anno* in 1931, social Catholics knew they had a powerful advocate in Pius XI, even if he lacked appreciation for the Christian democracy that many activists cherished.

Meanwhile, new departures were taking place in the mobilization of and by persons who were previously too much taken for granted and who deserve sustained attention: the young people and women in factories and workshops.

55. Comte 1992.
57. Voog 1994, 6:220–21.

56. See Chenaux 1999, index.

CHAPTER 7

New Departures in Catholic Action

YOUTH MOVEMENTS IN THE WORKING CLASS

Young people, "youth," grew into a much more distinct demographic category between childhood and adulthood in the nineteenth and twentieth centuries, long before one spoke of teenagers. The Catholic world, like Western culture at large, devoted considerable attention to its members in this age group, with some distinctive developments. A sound custom assigned the responsibility of rearing children and youth to the Christian family and the Christian school, but for those who had left school, the need was clear for supplementary Christian influence. The work that the YMCA and YWCA undertook in the Anglo-Saxon and Protestant world was the province, in the Catholicism of Western Europe, principally of the *patronages*, typically parish youth groups, separated by gender.[1]

As to youth of the working class, in 1912 two social-activist priests, Henri Poels in the Netherlands and the younger Joseph Cardijn in Belgium, independently of each other, crossed decisive thresholds toward the Young Christian Workers movement of the future. Poels determined the social placement of the movement conceptually, while Cardijn was experimenting with an approach that would prove to be of pivotal importance for its effectiveness. Poels diagnosed the situation in terms of his general program of *standsorganisaties* (milieu organizations) (see chapter 5) for the re-Christianization of modern society. His particular interest was, of course, in the *standsorganisatie* of the Catholic working class.

1. See Cholvy 1985a; 1985b; Fouilloux 1990a, 225; Cholvy 1999; see Cholvy 2000; Roux 1995.

But he realized that among workers, the young school-leavers who entered the workforce were not quite ready to deal with adult responsibilities and yet were expected to fit into the adult work environment from day one. They could not and would not be treated like children or yet like fully mature persons who needed no special attention.[2] They needed to be among others of their own age. Their situation thus required that the church recognize the need for a *standsorganisatie* of their own. Neither the existing youth groups nor the (adult) labor movement were in a position to deal appropriately with working youth, since the former did not take account of their embeddedness in a social class with its own pressing problems—and the latter would not validate their youthfulness. Recognition as a *stand* with their own *standsorganisatie* was the only appropriate response in the circumstances. Two Dutch dioceses set up an organization, De Jonge Werkman; however, it did not correspond fully to Poels's intuition and for a number of reasons did not take off with the same élan that Cardijn's JOC displayed especially after 1925.

In addition, other Catholics were wary of the two declarations of independence that Poels made on behalf of adolescent workers. In a pattern that would repeat itself in the history of the JOC, established or barely established union federations of Catholic men and women would want to fold the youth into their own ranks without further ado, while from the direction of the clergy, many a priest and bishop wished to have a single organization for Catholic youth as a whole, whether working or continuing their schooling. They did not want to see a class organization where young Catholics might even be prone to adopt revolutionary attitudes. These were formidable obstacles to overcome.

In Wallonia, for example, the Association catholique de la jeunesse belge (ACJB, with its feminine counterpart, ACJBF) was founded shortly after the war under the banner of Catholic Action, understood as participation of the laity in the apostolate of the hierarchy.[3] A particular impetus came from the encouragement of Catholic Action in the form called for by Pope Pius XI in his 1922 encyclical *Ubi arcano*. On the one hand, this signaled the pope's recognition and warm approval of the enhanced role lay Catholics had been taking in the mission of the church in the modern world. On the other, it sought to consolidate these lay forces firmly under the control of the hierarchy and, of course, in the ultramontane church in the image of Vatican I, under the command of the pope. It connoted at the very least some strong clerical guidance of any project undertaken as Catholic. Unlike the French ACJF, which was started by laymen and which had been engaged in the Christian democratic movement for social justice since at least 1903, the Belgian ACJB was an official church

2. Colsen 1922, in *HJS* 300–305; Peet 1987, 37–38.
3. Pirotte and Zelis 2003, 335–68, esp. 342–44.

movement whose chaplain was its director. It was francophone and sought its lay leaders primarily among the educated classes of youth, not workers. Like Pius XI's Catholic Action in Italy, it steered clear of any electioneering. It was not affiliated with the Belgian Catholic political establishment.

Cardijn and the Jeunesse Ouvrière Chrétienne (JOC) in Belgium

Meanwhile, in the outskirts of Brussels, Joseph Cardijn was getting the long-sought opportunity to try his hand at inspiring pride and an apostolic spirit in some young working-class parishioners. Because of its international pioneering history in social Catholicism, the Belgian and French beginnings of the JOC (Jeunesse ouvrière chrétienne) deserve detailed scrutiny.[4] Cardijn had the heart and missionary zeal to attempt a decisive breakthrough in bringing the gospel to the largely alienated working class of industrialized Europe—and he had the background, training, position, and charisma to mobilize young workers themselves to do it effectively.

Himself the son of Flemish domestic workers near Brussels who gathered enough together to run a neighborhood coal-delivery business, but who never could aspire to propertied status and died poor, he was an avid student. His father was quite illiterate, but his mother was able to read and instruct the children with Bible stories. She and his father expected him to go to work to help support the family when he finished his studies at fifteen or sixteen. Two years of secondary school was as much extra education as they could afford for him. Without previous discussion, however, he made the unusual request to study for the priesthood at that point (1897). His father took the surprise piously, much as St. Joseph must have taken the news of Mary's pregnancy. Six years later the father died, while Joseph Cardijn was still in seminary.

Cardijn's first vacations at home left an indelible impression of the effect on his comrades of the transition from school to factory. Children he had grown up with now regarded him as having gone over to the other side, that of the bosses and the francophone establishment. In Belgium education to the age of fourteen had recently been made compulsory, so at fourteen practically the whole cohort in working-class neighborhoods trekked off to work. Many of them lived at home for some years and commuted to their jobs in another town or city by rail every day. It was hardly the case, however, that this assured them a healthy environment for their moral growth and development. Cast unknowing and unprepared into the labor market, neither they nor their parents were in any position to insist upon decent working conditions or humane

4. See Wynants and Vanneste 2000, 1254–80.

treatment. The prevailing clerical approach was bafflement over an alien environment that had grown practically without Christian influence. The response had been to create islands of a protected Catholic world as best as one could in the patronages and pluck more or less willing adolescents from their situation, their *milieu*. The JOC created and realized a new approach, not to isolate young workers but to equip them to work actively in and on their working-class milieus at work, in the family, at recreation, and in prayer. The method, famously summed up in the triad "See—Judge—Act" was the product of Joseph Cardijn's interaction with young workers in Brussels from 1912 on.[5]

The basic breakthrough, away from sheltering paternalism and toward apostolic engagement in society, was really unprecedented in its daring combination of entrusting the development of youth to the young themselves (with training), of targeting young workers by themselves, and of firing them with a mission that only they themselves could carry out. Nevertheless, it was one that had several partial forerunners in the history of modern Catholicism.[6] Cardijn himself actively sought out precedents and came to know several from personal contact. Even before entering the major seminary, he was engaged in the Flemish (*flamingant*) movement. He attended rallies addressed by the populist priest Adolf Daens (the one who so shocked the bourgeoisie in Catholic Party circles in 1896).[7] Upon his ordination in 1906, he asked Cardinal Mercier if he could study social economics under Victor Brants, the Louvain social scientist.[8] Here he learned the method of doing surveys, "*enquêtes*," after the manner of Frédéric le Play, to ascertain social facts and conditions.

With Brants's recommendation he obtained modest travel grants to investigate the various flourishing social undertakings and organizations of the Rhineland, effectively coordinated by the Volksverein in Mönchengladbach. In France he interviewed Léon Harmel, the grand old man of Val-des-Bois, from whose lips he may have heard the golden rule of Christian democracy: anything undertaken *for* the workers must happen "*with* and *through* the workers," never without their input and participation. He met Marc Sangnier at the *Semaine sociale* at Amiens in 1907 and acquainted himself with the study circles of Sangnier's Sillon in France, a movement of still quite young adults assuming a mission as Catholics to push Christian democratic ideas further to the left. A trip in 1911 to England and close observation of and discussion with trade union leaders there was perhaps even closer to what he was searching for: working-class pride and clout nourished out of Christian conviction and dedication. He was perhaps most impressed by their emphasis on training working-class activists

---

5. Vos 1994, 452–56; Alaerts 2004, 83–91.
7. Fiévez and Meert 1978, 18.
6. Misner 1991, 192, 241, 288–303.
8. Ibid., 26–30.

to assume leading roles. He met Lord Baden-Powell in the first flush of establishing the Boy Scouts and admired the scope for youth action and self-respect that characterized the movement.

For the time being (1907–12), Cardijn was assigned to teach Latin in a boarding school. But this gave him the chance to go about asking people about their work life in the towns and villages of the French-speaking part of Brabant where the school was located. During the vacations he continued his social investigations and travels. Finally, he was able to move to an urban parish ideally situated for his further development, in Laeken (Brussels), where the working-class parishioners spoke Dutch and those with more education spoke French, but where evidently there was much bilingualism on the part of the speakers of Dutch. Young Father Cardijn was put in charge of the female associations: charitable endeavors, prayer groups, and a patronage for girls of thirteen years of age and up who might be in school or working locally. Assisted by some of the parish's *demoiselles*, devout young unmarried women of the leisure class, he soon gave it an unwonted new direction.[9] At his arrival in April 1912 he knew of the unionizing efforts of Victoire Cappe and wanted to encourage them; before a year was out, Cappe had come and given a talk to the Needlework Union that had been formed in the meantime.[10] With the assistance of Madeleine De Roo and others, not only was the needlework local established, but by 1914 a section for the youngest seamstress apprentices came into being.[11]

The amazing thing about all this was the way Cardijn went about it, emphasizing and practicing the principle of worker autonomy and self-governance more consistently and methodically than other socially progressive priests. He did this to the extent it was possible (while always expanding the ambit of the possible) not only with the *demoiselles* and needle workers, but even with the apprentices, girls from the patronage, and their like. His chosen instrument was the well-known and innocently named study circle. In Cardijn's hands it would become a study circle with a difference! Combined with the *enquête* and a tremendous apostolic urgency, he turned it into a method of investigation, self-education, and planning for action with enormous potential.[12] He started to develop the method at once, by August 1912, to sensitize and train a score or so of the young bourgeois women helping out at the patronage. Then they practiced the method with the working girls, divided into two levels by age. The

---

9. On the *demoiselles*, see B. Smith 1981.

10. Just previously, in 1911, Victoire Cappe had founded a study circle of young bourgeois women in an industrial area west of Liège; it led to the founding of a working-class women's league that tapped into existing trade-union and credit-union organizations; see Eaton 1955, 88–90. On Cappe and other women activists and activities, see chapter 8 of this volume.

11. Bragard, Fiévez, and Meert 1990, 1:38; Joret 1990, 1:61–67.

12. Joret 1990, 1:68–69.

girls were encouraged to compare notes on working conditions in their various jobs. A process of mutual education set in. Perhaps a guest would speak of unionizing or of conditions in other lines of work or of the social services that were even then available. This could lead to suggestions for services that workers could render to one another.

Results of this patient guidance and dosed challenges were not long in showing themselves. The girls of the patronage previously rehearsed for a holiday show for their *dames patronesses* according to preconceived scripts, which they mouthed dutifully if listlessly. Now the ladies were entertained by self-confident young women who were excited to present a modest production for which they themselves took responsibility. To keep up an active program, a central study circle was set up that met weekly to stimulate the broader membership—and little by little this central study circle was taken over by the more active and engaged members themselves. This institution, a sort of coordinating committee at the parish level that was intent on self-education and promoting "the apostolate of like by like," would become the pivot on which the whole JOC movement turned at its various levels after its founding in 1925. The only adult present would be the chaplain.[13]

Cardijn's pastor in Laeken and his bishop, Cardinal Mercier in Mechlin (Malines), did not quite know what to make of this young priest with his unorthodox methods. They acknowledged the results, however, so they let him proceed. Out of study circles arose unions, and the unionized workers were more professional: nicely groomed, more polite, more reliable, more interested in improving themselves. Madeleine De Roo headed the new social secretariat for women in Laeken with its own locale, courses in practical subjects, a job service.[14] Then, in August 1914, the Germans invaded Belgium. A year later Mercier gave Cardijn the extra job of director of social works for the Brussels area. In November 1915 the patriotic Mercier had Cardijn preach a sermon at a service for the civilian and military victims of the war, in the course of which he denounced collaborators. A year later he was arrested for the first of two stretches in prison, the first for seven months and the second for the last few months of the war in 1918. Though he suffered from asthma, he was able to write and even to remain in contact with his young parish leaders during these months. In the case of the second imprisonment, he had been caught passing information on train movements to a spy network and had to face the real possibility of a death sentence.

After the war he threw himself into organizing work among the working class of Brussels, in view of the need to reorganize the Christian unions and get

13. Ibid., 73.
14. Fiévez and Meert 1978, 40–41.

out the vote in the crucial 1919 elections. He had dreamed of a Young Christian Workers movement in prison, however, and even laid plans for it. It was not to be strictly tied to participation in union affairs and still less to party politics. Before the war some young male workers of the parish had sought him out and asked to be initiated into his method of the study circle. One, Fernand Tonnet, then spent the war on the front plus some months with the victorious armies in Germany. When he showed up again, Cardijn enlisted him as his secretary in his capacity as director of social works in Brussels, a charge that he had hardly been able to carry out during the war. In a letter Cardijn wrote to Tonnet at this time, when Cardijn was on a forced health furlough, one gets a glimpse of the spirituality that motivated him. He saw the suffering Christ as present in the working class of modern Europe, in need of liberation from its affliction.[15]

Soon another prewar lad, Paul Garcet, appeared. By 1923 the third of the JOC's founding trio, Jacques Meert, was on board, as well. Between them, from 1919 on, they had started groups of young male workers in Brussels and other French-speaking areas. To help train the new study circles by plunging them into their tasks, Cardijn developed a questionnaire of five hundred items.[16] This "Enquête sur l'adolescence salariée," or survey on wage-earning workers of both sexes between the ages of fourteen and twenty-one, gave those who wrote down and discussed the answers a much better sense of their own situation. By 1925 many groups had gathered the responses teenager by teenager and summarized the data. Thus they learned in great detail about the problems facing their comrades and shared it with other study circles through their reports. Already in the early 1920s there was a first periodical of the movement, a monthly called *La Jeunesse Syndicaliste*, like the movement itself. A major preoccupation was the deplorable lack of any guidance in placement. The paper carried stories of adolescents who had no idea what they were getting into when they took a job. This left the door wide open for unscrupulous employers, for example, to assign dangerous tasks to unprepared and utterly dispensable young workers. In Brussels, accordingly, Paul Garcet set up a placement service to guide boys through the procedures of the Office of Professional Orientation and the job exchange; less formal word-of-mouth efforts elsewhere were propagated.

At first these groups were called "Young Unionists"—La jeunesse syndicaliste.[17] Their threefold aim was to aid and protect young workers at the level of one's job, one's social status, and one's moral development. Meanwhile, in Antwerp, another priest in charge of youth groups, Joseph Bloquaux, had spent

---

15. Walckiers 1970, document 1.
16. Fiévez and Meert 1978, 60–61; Joret 1990, 1:72–73.
17. Walckiers 1970, xviii–xx; Joret 1990, 1:70–80; and Vos 1994, 434–36.

part of the war as a refugee in the southern Netherlands with the Belgian troops he had been serving. There he discovered the new organization of union youth, De Jonge Werkman, trying to realize the program Poels had outlined. On his return and appointment to the Antwerp social-concerns office of the huge Mechlin archdiocese, he also noticed the straits to which the Catholic youth groups and the union federation, the ACV/CSC, had been reduced during and since the war. The socialist unions, less centralized than the Catholic ones in 1913, rebounded much more quickly in the postwar confusion and attracted many former members of the Christian unions. Bloquaux heard Cardijn present the Jeunesse syndicaliste project at a diocesan meeting of social concerns directors (later "chaplains") in the spring of 1920 and launched De Jonge Werkman for the Antwerp region over the next few weeks. Like scouting and other youth movements of the time, it aimed, beyond the stated ends of improving the young workers' lot, to create a group life, or, as we might say, lifestyle. The young males took pleasure in sports, putting on shows and parades, and camping out together. As a movement of Flemings it supported the *flamingant* program of Frans Van Cauwelaert, which wished to make Dutch the recognized language of business and bureaucracy in Flanders. It put out a monthly paper of the same name for its 1,500 members and another 1,500 to attract broader support. It became as much a rural youth organization as one of young industrial workers, embracing also any other young people who fell into the cracks between the labor unions and the Peasants League (Boerenbond).

In fact, the trade-union self-identification of both Jeunesse syndicaliste and De Jonge Werkman became a bit troublesome and limiting.[18] Around 1924 one knew of quite a few groups in both Flanders and Wallonia that developed a group life and a self-education program for young working-class men and women that were not limited to (prospective) union members.[19] A national (Flemish) federation of such youth groups, the KAJ (Catholic Worker Youth), was formed at a meeting in Brussels under the watchful eye of Bloquaux and Cardijn. Young workers became its officers, with at first just one, Jan Schellekens, an old Cardijn recruit, serving in a full-time salaried position. The KAJ committee asked Bloquaux to become their chaplain. He turned their request aside, saying it was up to the bishops to make such appointments. Thus, by accident or by design, the way was open for Cardijn, in due course, to assume national leadership of both the Flemish and the Walloon sections of the JOC/KAJ.

The next step was obviously to set up the federation for Brussels and the south of the country. In May 1924, on the occasion of a study day for priests, Cardijn won many of his colleagues in youth work in Wallonia for the project of

18. See Vos 1994, 441.
19. Vos 1994, 437–43.

an autonomous Catholic organization of young workers. He expressed the logic of his argument to Abbé Aloïs Douterlungne, the longtime influential director of social works for the diocese of Tournai, in these terms:

You know even better than I the moral and religious plight of our young workers. A movement of adults is not suitable to their age, and a broad youth movement does not take sufficient account of their mentality and their special needs. "La jeunesse ouvrière" will have ties with these two movements, all the same.[20]

From the subsequent collaboration of these priests and the founding trio at Cardijn's Brussels office (Tonnet, Garcet, and Meert) a phenomenal explosion of JOC groups took place throughout Wallonia.[21] The movement had found its name (no longer "unionist" but simply "worker" youth: Jeunesse ouvrière chrétienne).

The Young Christian Worker Movement and the Design of Catholic Action

Serious difficulties arose at this point with official Catholic Action and to a lesser extent with the adult Catholic labor movement.[22] The bishops, always solicitous to maintain the solidity of what was not yet called the Catholic pillar, could be troubled by intramural controversy and call a halt to any radical new departures. In many respects, of course, what ensued was not much more than a turf war between the upstart claims of Cardijn, on the one hand, and the clerical leaders of existing structures, on the other. These included the youth organization of Catholic Action (the ACJB, led by Canon Abel Brohée, from Tournai, and Louis Picard, a priest of the Namur diocese, and its lay president, Giovanni Hoyois), the regional federation of youth patronages under another priest, the labor unions, and the broader labor *standsorganisatie* (the ACW/LNTC) that was the brainchild of Louis Colens. The latter, because it exercised considerable political clout in elections and through its representatives in parliament, did not consider itself to be a Catholic Action organization, although it was definitely Catholic. (Recall Poels's attempt at a formal distinction between "Catholic" and "churchly" organizations.) Hence the controversy involved some never definitively solved issues of modern Catholic Action, issues of church authority in a pluralist society. The resolution or compromise that was found would also have enduring effects on the character of Jocism and social Catholicism as a whole.

20. Walckiers 1970, 33; see 100.
21. Vos 1994, 437.
22. Vos 1994, 440–44; see Gerard 1994a, 189–91.

All parties to the controversy were agreed on the objective of re-Christianizing society. Indeed, the labor contingent (JOC and ACW/LNTC) were clearer on this, if anything, than the bourgeois components (the ACJB and conservative clergy). The popes of the new century extolled Catholic Action as the best strategy to accomplish this goal. Poels, Colens, and the labor chaplain Jan Belpaire committed themselves to the principle of milieu-specific organizations, hence also to what would soon be called specialized Catholic Action. In a note addressed to Pius XI in 1923, the three activist priests insisted that lay persons had to "bring the Catholic spirit to bear in their own social milieu and in their own class, so that that spirit can Christianize contemporary civil and economic structure.... Catholic Action should be specialized according to the prevailing realities of today's society."[23]

Pius XI defined Catholic Action as the organized participation of the laity in the hierarchical apostolate of the church so as to re-Christianize society, transcending party politics. Where did this leave class distinctions? Now the clerical leaders of the official youth movement reminded Cardinal Mercier of the papal outlook and the practice in Italy, where Pius XI withdrew the Italian Popular Party, led by a priest, Luigi Sturzo, from action so as to come to a modus vivendi with a dictator, Mussolini. Catholic Action "Italian style" was definitely nonpolitical. Political democracy was not valued, and hence neither were autonomous Christian democratic labor organizations. Church-state issues would be reserved to the pope and the duce, since in Italy they involved the settling the Roman Question arising from the liquidation by force of the Papal States in 1870, hence an issue of international relations. With that issue removed from the concerns of the Italian Catholic laity, Pius XI reasoned, Catholic Action could turn its energies with all the more focus on the formation of Catholic men and women, adult and youth, into citizens of a future Christian social order.

Of course, in Belgium there could be no question of dispensing with elected Catholic politicians in the parliament. Cardinal Mercier did not have to deal with a dictator. There still lingered, all the same, some unrealistic hankering for dealing with notables rather than elected representatives of the populous classes with their own left-leaning demands. We are reminded again of Fr. Rutten's observation: "What they always want us to refrain from is not politics but democratic politics."

Canon Brohée alerted Cardinal Mercier to two dangers or deviations in the Cardijn formula. Both had to do with the fact that the new movement would be just for working-class youth. This would introduce class distinctions and even

23. Cited in Gerard 1981, 44.

class resentments into the structure of Catholic youth groups, a separatism that savored of Marxist class struggle (Cardijn's questionnaires). To make matters worse, Cardijn was determined to keep his movement autonomous, to be sure, but nevertheless affiliated with the ACW/LNTC, a milieu organization claiming a political role. Support for Cardijn's side came rather unexpectedly from another quarter. Fr. Eduard Luytgaerens, general secretary of the by now well-established Catholic farmers' *standsorganisatie*, parried Picard's and Brohée's arguments indirectly. He proposed an organization for Flemish young people that would emphasize the need to represent their great social interests. Meanwhile he encouraged Cardijn to build up such an organization among workers in industry as the Boerenbond was doing in the countryside before the ACJB could interfere.[24]

Mercier pondered. At this juncture Cardijn decided to go to Rome and seek an audience with the pope himself. As he later told it, he had little idea of Vatican protocol but found himself miraculously in the presence of the pope for a private audience.[25] It stretched out to an unusual length as the pope found someone after his own heart, fervently desiring to dedicate himself to the salvation of the working-class young people. Pius XI exclaimed, in words printed conspicuously in the front-page story of the fortnightly *La Jeunesse Ouvrière* of April 5, 1925, that the need of the hour was to restore to the church "the working masses which she has lost."[26] The pope's enthusiasm for Cardijn's "holy ambition" turned in this conversation on the question of "the masses" versus "an elite." "Everyone else talks to me of an elite. What is needed is an elite in the masses, the leaven in the paste."[27] Cardijn thereafter made annual visits and reports to Pius XI and always came away with blessings and encouragements.[28]

A good part of the mutual appreciation rested on the dynamism of the JOC. Pius XI wanted action, and Cardijn, for his part, always insisted that a movement worthy of the name had to generate motion.[29] One could not rest content with study circles that did not lead to action, to conquest. The question at issue about what kind of movements could claim the quality of Catholic Action was

24. Van Molle 1990, 228.
25. De La Bedoyère 1958, 65–68, but see Tihon 1996, 648.
26. Fiévez 1990, 1: 94–95.
27. De La Bedoyère 1958, 67.
28. In 1929 Pius XI would go so far as to pronounce Cardijn's JOC as the "complete" (*parfait*) form of Catholic Action; Scholl 1966, 3:266. Scholl's view is that Cardijn struggled to formulate a theology of the lay apostolate combining the movement's autonomy with hierarchical coordination and direction—and that to articulate this combination consistently was not possible in the available ecclesiological frame of reference. See Tranvoucz 2011b, 73–84, for a recent analysis of this squaring of a circle.
29. Bragard, Fiévez, and Meert 1990, 1:35.

not settled by this papal encouragement, but it made the JOC an entity, or better, a movement that had to be accommodated one way or another in churchly circles. Since class was such a neuralgic topic, and the French language had no usable equivalent for the Dutch euphemism (*stand*), one habitually spoke of the social milieu of the worker, which was to be validated and transformed on the way to a Christian society. This then led to the concept, soon generally accepted, of a legitimately specialized Catholic Action—specialized, that is, according to social milieu.[30] Thus the JOC was specialized for young workers, and the ACJB, the umbrella association, reluctantly and unofficially became specialized for youth with secondary and higher education. The further development of Catholic Action, especially in France, would lead to special organizations for young Christian students, young Christian farmers, young Christian seamen, and so forth.

But in April 1925 the timing was right for the founding congress of the national federation (Walloon) of the Young Christian Workers. It took place on Easter Sunday in Brussels, a glorious culmination of the preceding organizational activity in the regions and a powerful impetus for its next stage. Would Mercier welcome this new movement, which did not result from his own initiative and did not quite correspond to his expectations? The question presented itself in the very month when the Catholic party had lost 100,000 votes to the socialists, resulting, after extended birth pangs, in a short-lived coalition of Christian democrats and socialists, the Poullet-Vandervelde cabinet.[31] The bishops and conservative circles were chagrined at this development, given the anticlericalism of the socialists and the labor clout in the coalition. At the same time they were sobered by the clear signs of discontent in the ranks of Catholic labor, who deserted the Catholic party in droves.[32] So they were happy to see signs of a younger generation of workers who might reverse the tide. All the same, Mercier still worried about the potential divisiveness of a working-class youth movement and would not give his imprimatur to Cardijn's JOC *Manual*, ready for the press in May, until October. Only when he died in February 1926, to be succeeded by his vicar general, Jozef Ernest Van Roey, were episcopal reservations dropped. Van Roey, archbishop until 1961, was a pragmatic if conservative Fleming and friend of Luytgaerens and the Boerenbond. In the meantime, Cardijn was stressing more and more the educational, religious, and milieu-oriented aspects of the JOC and letting the Catholic trade unions and the electoral campaign organizations fend for themselves.

The materials in the 1925 *Manuel de la JOC* were among the painstaking and extended preparations for the founding congress, where the statutes and pro-

30. Gerard 1990, 190.
32. Gerard, 1990, 254–73.
31. Conway 1996, 193–96.

gram of the JOC were briefly discussed and approved, having been distributed earlier. Substantially based on Cardijn's prison prayers, ruminations, and writings, it proved to be an effective tool, along with the many other publications of the central office, in the spread of the movement. It opens with a memorable sketch of the problem of working youth, drawn from official statistics and from the questionnaire *enquêtes* that had been compiled. About 500,000 Belgians in the industrial workforce of 1,800,000 were said to be between fourteen and twenty-one years of age. Each year tens of thousands left school at fourteen to work in factories or offices. The conditions described, including such matters as hours, heat, light, ventilation, and sanitary facilities, were deplorable. School-leavers were left entirely on their own, quite unprepared for what faced them, although often with pocket money for modern entertainments. This was to be their life and milieu. To remove a few from the milieu was not the answer; rather, they must be enabled to influence their milieu—that was the call that the JOC issued, with prophetic earnestness. These young workers were after all destined for eternal life with God in Christ; they deserved to be able to live as brothers and sisters of Christ in their life as workers. For this they desperately needed support and education, both adapted to their work life.[33]

Every zealous organizer for a cause hopes for a contagious effect like that which crowned the JOC's initial efforts in Brussels and Wallonia. Six hundred delegates representing 3,000 or 4,000 members appeared at the founding congress in 1925, while by the end of the year one counted 6,000. Before the end of the decade there were over 20,000 male Jocists swelling the ranks of the ACJB by their affiliate membership. Added to them were the 10,000 young Flemish workers in the KAJ and at least 10,000 on the feminine side, which was just starting its own growth curve.[34] These were all dues-paying members, supporting the services and publications of the central office and paying the wages of the full-time organizers ("propagandists"). With the help of a well-disposed priest, the organizer would gather a few young industrial workers who were still known to the parish and explain to them the nature of the JOC. He would press a copy of the *Manuel* or some other literature into the hands of those who were receptive and conduct a few sessions with them. Then it was up to them to approach another comrade in the apostolate of like to like and invite them to a study circle or a convivial evening event of some kind.

Once a section got under way, such person-to-person contacts were continued and broadened, while a spectrum of activities (educational, religious, remonstrative) developed. The terrain was rocky and unwelcoming. In many of the larger industrial plants of Wallonia (at that time the heavily industrialized

---

33. See Debès and Poulat 1986, 230–34.
34. Vos 1994, 498; see also Wynants and Vanneste 2000, 1259; Alaerts 2004.

part of Belgium), a regime of "*Rouge ou pas de pain*" was in effect: "Red—or no bread" (Flemish: *Rood of geen brood*). Knowing that in union there was strength, the socialists were determined to retain the monopoly of labor representation as the (sole) party of labor. Should a worker be hired who declined to join the union, there would be trouble on the shop floor: slowdowns or even a walkout of the workforce. The owners, often Catholic, would let the offending worker go.[35] The industrialists could not dislodge the socialist union, but used their connections with the hierarchy to prevent Catholic workers' organizations from becoming militant. In fact, the adult CSC always remained quite small and weak in Wallonia, in contrast to the ACV in Flanders. Everywhere, however, young workers were isolated in a world of work that the outside world never penetrated. Cardijn pictured a big sign hanging over the entrance of every factory, workshop, and office: "No entrance for parents, teachers, pastors! Workers only past this point."[36] In the *Manuel* there was a contact list of the twenty-five government inspectors of factories for the whole country, pointing up implicitly the insufficiency of the effort. The superficial inspections that did take place paid no particular attention to the training or safety of young workers.

Jocists sought various expedients and remedies to penetrate this opaque barrier between the working-class reality and the bourgeois consciousness and—the other side of the coin—to raise the consciousness of the working youth themselves. The *enquête* was the principal tool. Allied student and clergy conferences brought the reports from the worker front to a broader audience. In 1925 and annually thereafter, the central office prepared coordinated *enquêtes* focused on one or another aspect of the life of young workers. The local sections asked the questions, noted the answers, discussed and digested them, and reported back. Cardijn took advantage of public addresses to excoriate the disparity that existed between two classes of youth, those who enjoyed education at the secondary level or beyond and their age-mates in industry and commerce. If the methods in force for young workers were applied to boarding-school students, he wrote in 1926, "the whole national press would shout scandal and call for sanctions." In 1928, at the April congress, he homed in on the church:

With splendid dedication, thousands of priests and teachers undertake the great work of education of bourgeois youth. The state, the Church, the families spend millions to this end. How regrettable it is, then, to have to admit that no comparable effort has been made to date for the education of a half million young wage earners between 14 and 21 years of age.[37]

35. Fiévez and Meert 1978, 63.
37. Ibid., 125–26.

36. Bragard, Fiévez, and Zelis 1990, 1:134.

Among the actions, besides publicity, that the movement unfolded were two that sought to ease the transition from school to work. In schools where permission could be obtained, a kind of club was formed to prepare the children in their last year for finding a job and keeping their head above water while in the first months. A major part of this was establishing contact with Jocists in the home parish or in the workplace. This was called the Pré-JOC. The other action that was methodically encouraged, which was referred to as *la tutelle jociste*, was for JOC members in the workplace to take new young workers under their wings.[38]

JOC activity was bound to arouse the opposition not only of the Catholic and liberal industrialists but also of the socialist union leaders and members. Even when the Jocist coworker retained his membership in the socialist union, which Cardijn, to the horror of many clergy, did not absolutely rule out, such a worker had to brave the strong implication that he was a traitor to his class. This was a hopeless position for one standing alone and shunned. Only with the group life and backing of one's fellow JOC members could one persevere. And thousands did persevere! There were even conversions of young persons whose good worker parents could only shake their heads and wring their hands—these conversions were not connected with an escape from the working-class existence but with increased dedication to its transformation.

When young workers began to become conscious of their situation, they became aware at the same time of the shortcomings and incompleteness of their education, their intellectual formation. This put them at a severe disadvantage in dealing with officialdom of all sorts and also with making the case for social justice before the court of public opinion, first of all among Catholics of the middle and upper classes. In 1930 a regional president made a stirring presentation on "the intellectual plight of the young worker" at the JOC congress in Brussels.[39] Cardijn's emphasis on reflection on the gospel message and on observing and judging the contrasting factors in their own daily lives obviously met a real need. The JOC central office in Brussels scrambled to provide printed material and programs that responded to this need. One of the most characteristic programs was the annual *enquête* theme, the same for all local sections and regions. In some years it was intensified into an *enquête-campagne* on a specific issue—for instance, on industrial safety or unemployment.

---

38. Ibid., 129.
39. Ibid., 144; see also 137–48.

The JOC in France

The working class in many parts of France was still more distant from Christianity than it was in Wallonia. A parish might still shepherd a goodly number of boys and girls through their First Communion, which was then also their last. In France children were still legally allowed to quit school and go to work at the age of thirteen. Naturally, the loss of so many children to Catholic practice was much noted. The youth patronages were reinvigorated before and especially after World War I. During the war itself, many priests and seminarians had served in the armed forces and came face to face with the youth of France across the gulf that separated so many of them, of all classes, from any shred of Christian church life.[40] Much has been made of the inadequacies of the patronages. However, they were changing, adopting many of the characteristics of the other burgeoning youth movements of the time, including organized sports leagues, outings, and rallies; they would grow and become or remain an influential Christian leaven in a largely laicist—that is, militantly secular—France.[41] In fact, many of the militants of the French JOC would cut their eye teeth in a patronage. Moreover, the degree of commitment required by the JOC or even the French Scouts (founded 1920) was beyond the reach of many a young person who nevertheless felt at home in a less demanding youth group.[42]

The ACJF (Association catholique de la jeunesse française), founded by Albert de Mun in 1886, saw the accession of the young Charles Flory and Georges Bidault as president and vice president from 1922 to 1926.[43] They succeeded in recruiting about 10,000 young workers in their 160,000-strong association. All the same, the need for a much more focused effort was apparent to those lay and clerical activists who were not willing simply to write off the working class and its youth in the industrial centers. This accounts for the French interest in Cardijn's JOC as early as 1926. In the working-class "red belt" around Paris, in Clichy, to be exact, a priest ordained the previous June, Georges Guérin, was wondering how to do something more apt for the youth than the stagnant patronage. Abbé Guérin was of working-class background himself, but found himself as a thirty-five-year-old priest unable to lift the miasma surrounding his young working people.[44] His deeply Christian parents had moved to Paris after he was born in 1891, where father and eventually son worked for a chemical processing plant, melting down old jewelry and separating the precious

---

40. Susan B. Whitney's 2009 book, *Mobilizing Youth*, compares communist and JOC efforts in France after World War I; see her third chapter for an insightful treatment of the emergence of the JOC; Whitney 2009, 82–89.
41. Pierrard 1984, 518.
42. Cholvy 1982; for the historiography of JOC's beginnings in France, see Cholvy 2000.
43. Pierrard 1984, 526–28.
44. Launay 1985, 223–25; Debès and Poulat 1986, 15–25; Pierrard 1997, 91–96.

elements for reuse by jewelers. Before going to work, however, he went to the Christian Brothers school attended also by many other future Christian labor union activists of Paris. A chaplain, Charles Fichaux, brought up the possibility of a priestly vocation. Guérin became an activist in the Sillon, visiting poor neighborhoods.[45] Guérin had no contact as yet with the ACJF, the main Catholic Action movement of the 1920s.

Guérin (1891–1972) had decided upon a priestly vocation when the war descended upon Europe, extending the period of military service that he had begun in 1912. The chaplain of his battalion was Achille Danset, SJ (1877–1935), one of Fr. Desbuquois's collaborators in the Action populaire of Reims, who reinforced his priestly calling. After catching up on his secondary education while recuperating from war wounds, he was admitted to the Seminary of St. Sulpice. There the social orientation of the Christian Brothers was reinforced especially by his frequent and intimate contact with an unusual professor, the Sulpician Pierre Callon (1882–1959). Callon would have been accused of being a "social modernist" had he published his views. As it was, he brought in speakers from the Action populaire and elsewhere and encouraged Georges in his concern for the working class.

Guérin was deeply convinced of the need and benefits of frequent communion. At Clichy he extended the Eucharistic crusade that was propagated among schoolchildren to the young apprentices he could reach. Building on this spiritual base, he tried to do something also for their social consciousness. Making contact with the CFTC element in the parish, he met Georges (a.k.a. Maurice) Quiclet (1899–1981), an alumnus of the patronage, who was interested and contacted other young union members. Casting about for an effective way to proceed, Guérin paid a visit to Danset at the Action populaire headquarters, now in Paris (Vanves), where he learned about the new JOC of Brussels. He read the *Manuel* of the JOC and wasted no time getting in touch with the Brussels central office. He learned that there already was activity in the Nord of France (Lille), started after one of the young workers who crossed the French-Belgian border so often, Fernand Bouxom, joined a Belgian group. Guérin was not immediately convinced that the approach described so concretely in the *Manuel* was the way to go for his young men. Georges Guérin was no Joseph Cardijn. Retiring, humble, diffident, he was nevertheless not timid. When the responsibility for

---

45. The Sillon was disbanded before the war; afterward, its leader, Marc Sangnier, focused on creating international ties among youth, particularly for the purpose of reconciling the youth of France and Germany and preventing future wars. The Equipes Sociales of Robert Garric, another Silloniste, counted sixty groups of students and young workers in Paris in 1924. Pierrard states that Guérin knew Garric's writings, but that the program was geared to cultural exchange between the classes, not to attacking the problems of life specific to the young workers; Pierrard 1984, 524; 1997, 90 and 98.

the JOC in France came to rest largely on his shoulders, he would fight with determination to see that it had the requisite autonomy to provide a structure in which young workers could run their own organization.

First, however, he brought the JOC material to Quiclet and his three younger companions. Without an ACJF study circle for workers, such as Flory had initiated in other parishes, Guérin's informal group studied the new Belgian model in the priest's room. One evening in July 1926, after such a session, they were having a drink in the patronage and one of them lifted his glass and toasted, "*À la santé de la JOC!*" They looked at each other and another asked, "Shall we try it?" That was the birth of the JOC in France, as Guérin would later say.[46] He would insist he was not its founder; the young workers themselves were. Be that as it may, it is clear that Cardijn intensified his involvement in these birth pangs to the point that he could be regarded as the indispensable man in the launching of the French JOC as well as the Belgian.[47]

They did try it. They made up and duplicated a little handwritten notice to distribute to potential members, inviting them to a discussion of what they could do to help the youngest new workers "become excellent workers and proud Christians, too." With all the ideas of the Belgian *Manuel* to offer, they were hopeful they would not disappoint their guests. After closer study of the JOC materials, they put on a better prepared meeting at the patronage hall in October 1926. Of six or seven hundred invitations sent out, they drew some sixty young workers and plunged into the never-ending phase of training, organizing, and retreats that were the meat and potatoes of the JOC diet. Everyday realities such as wages, working conditions, the specific problems of apprentices were to be addressed. How could a serious young worker not enter into a pointed discussion of such matters?

The crucial issue of worker autonomy presented itself to Guérin as to Cardijn in these first years and was officially resolved in 1927 (in August for the Belgians and in September for the French JOC). The autonomy in question was not autonomy from the church or the chaplains, but from the tutelage of the bourgeois, whether clergy or laity. Not that many of the JOC chaplains were of working-class origins, but what mattered in their case was their dedication to the workers' autonomy. Some could identify with their cause and some could not. Those who could functioned like labor intellectuals, necessary allies of the working class. Whereas in the Belgian case the ACJB was not yet well established, but anxious to be *the* Catholic Action category for youth, the French ACJF *was* the paragon of civic nonpolitical Catholicism in France ever since Albert de Mun founded it in 1886, and particularly since its "democratic" turn in

46. Debès and Poulat 1986, 33–35; Pierrard 1997, 111–12.
47. Cholvy 2000, 115.

1903. The ACJF was already active in the arena of working youth. It had its study circles and used the approach of *enquêtes*. It paid homage to the principle of "among themselves, by themselves and for themselves." So, the question soon came up, would it not be better for the embryonic JOC to ally itself with the solidly established ACJF and avail itself of its considerable influence in Catholic France?

Guérin sought support and approval for the fledgling movement among his fellow clergy. The Jesuits of the Action Populaire provided it unstintingly.[48] Besides Danset and Desbuquois, Guérin soon met Jean Boulier (1894–1980, a Jesuit only until 1932), assigned to the Action populaire for the two years preceding his third year of Jesuit novitiate. Boulier had received his previous Jesuit training in Belgium, only a half-hour from Brussels by rail. He and his friend Jacques Leurent, SJ, became acquainted with Cardijn around 1923 and followed his movement closely. Like the Sulpician Callon in this, he was instinctively opposed to clericalism. This gave him an additional reason to be suspicious of close links with the ACJF, since the ACJF always had a Jesuit chaplain, at the time one François Corbillé, of a distinctly bourgeois-clerical bent. Guérin also belonged to a support group of young priests who had known each other in the seminary. Other encouragement came from social priests such as Jean-Emile Anizan and most notably from Pierre Gerlier (1880–1965), former president of the ACJF as a young layman, currently director of social concerns as a priest of the archdiocese of Paris, future archbishop and cardinal of Lyon. Guérin wanted the JOC, as an eminently apostolic undertaking, to receive the approval of the hierarchy. An independent organization would need, for one thing, two priests delegated full-time to assist him in guiding the national movement, and local chaplains would have to be appointed, as well. All this required good will on the part of the bishops. But relations with the youth organization already in place, the ACJF, would have to be settled for that to be gained.

In meetings with Corbillé and François de Menthon, the new lay president of the ACJF, whom Corbillé dubbed "the president of the workers," Guérin concluded that they did not "get it"—that is, did not grasp the necessity of autonomy from an organization of bourgeois leadership. Reinforced by Boulier and Cardijn, Guérin insisted that the new movement have its own headquarters in Paris, distinct from the ACJF, and that no ACJF commission have any real say over JOC operations. Otherwise, the ACJF personnel would fatally reduce "our elites" to a subordinate role.[49] Though some elements in the ACJF were distinctly favorable, it seemed for months as if no agreement on these terms was possible. Desbuquois, who got it early on, and Gerlier swung into

---

48. Droulers 1981, 274–82.
49. Guérin, as cited in Debès and Poulat 1986, 211.

action supporting Guérin's rationale and conditions in visits and letters to the Jesuit superiors. They arranged for Corbillé to yield while saving face for the ACJF. Boulier was rusticated for his third year of Jesuit novitiate. Corbillé was quietly replaced a year later as ACJF chaplain by another Jesuit. As in Belgium, formal ties were maintained between the two organizations. In practice, the ACJF acknowledged the JOC as its labor wing and left off trying to organize its own labor sections.[50] While this was going on, Gerlier introduced Cardijn and Guérin to Cardinal Dubois of Paris; he paid a visit to the second study day of JOC leaders in November of 1927. (At the first national congress a year later, the cardinal would elicit a laudatory letter from the papal secretary of state, thus serving notice that the French JOC had arrived, ecclesiastically speaking.)

At the same time that the way was thus cleared for the JOC's expansion as the young workers' own national federation, Jean Boulier delivered the manuscript for a small book that was to give it a mighty boost. *L'Appel de la JOC* appeared anonymously, the first publication of the Paris headquarters except for a modest periodical, *La Jeunesse Ouvrière*.[51] Until 1930, when a full manual was published for France, *L'Appel de la JOC* served as the guidebook for the French JOC. Its significance lay also in its spiritual message of embarking on a social conquest for Christ. To borrow a phrase, "happy warriors" translates a good part of the slogan, "*Fiers, purs, joyeux et conquérants*."[52] *L'Appel* powerfully evoked the sense of a vast collaborative enterprise of social reconstruction in which each Jocist had an important part to play.

When the JOC works on the shop floors and stirs a holy enthusiasm for an ideal of moral beauty and Christian justice, you [*tu*] can say that a new springtime is on its way... a season whose divine breeze already caresses your souls and makes a mysterious sap rise up in vigorous sprouts, the sap of an immense Vine of which you are the young shoots.

So we're mystics? Yes, indeed. But also realists.... The JOC works in the insurance plans, in the unions, in the cooperatives, in the dowry programs, in the League for Public Morality, in the apprentices' lunch rooms, in the vocational courses, in the amateur sports leagues, in the thousand institutions of social progress where workers acquire the knack for saving and providing for their own future.

True social progress demands men who do not spare themselves and whose conscience is raised above all self-serving ploys. The JOC, for its part, has to form and furnish such persons.

... The world is before us and we are the future. It will be what we make of it. We shall be the relief crew.

50. Debès and Poulat 1986, 124 and 136.
52. Debès and Poulat 1986, 166–68.

51. See Arnal 1987.

It seemed that a method had finally been found that had a real chance of fulfilling the dream of Leo XIII and the other intransigent Catholics, to take the modern individualistic, materialistic social disorder and reconstitute it into a new Christian order. "We shall make our brothers Christians again," was the watchword.[53] Such hopefulness, coupled with practical measures to improve the worker's lot, was infectious, "as was their courage in openly witnessing to their faith whether through badges, public prayers, or the downing of tools at 3 o'clock on the afternoon of Good Friday."[54] It is no wonder that the influence of the Young Christian Worker movement was determinative of many of the new developments that would mark social Catholicism for decades to come.

Throughout the struggles of this period in the history of social Catholicism, a dominant theme continues to be emancipation, autonomy. The striking feature of this drive for autonomy that emerges in the 1920s is the differentiation that took place in the Catholic labor movement. Young people responded to their own special movements, distinct by age, class, gender, and, in Belgium, by language as well. An accompanying salient feature was the emphasis on popular education so characteristic of social work of the period. All this grassroots ferment profited from some coincidental events in the years 1926–27 that indirectly assisted the emancipatory movements, particularly the succession of Van Roey to Mercier in Belgium and the Vatican's condemnation of the Action française.

The rise of the JOC was the most prominent but not at all the only factor to force a broad differentiation between the sociocultural and socioeconomic aspects of social Catholic activism, along with a sharper sense of class adherence. As we shall see in the next chapter, women constructed their own associations and unions, as well. The trend among Catholics engaged in the social question focused on "the specificities that enable a person to engage in self-education: age, sex, social milieu."[55] This led by the 1930s to the general acceptance of so-called "specialized" Catholic Action. In terms of Catholic Action, what took place in the 1920s was the emergence of a second model in Belgium and France, organized along what we might call lines of affinity. The older model of organization according to age and sex alone held its own in Italy, Austria, and the Iberian world. This seemed more appropriate for Catholic countries, whereas in mission countries or in de-Christianized terrains such as liberal academia or the working class, Pius XI welcomed the specialization by "social milieu."[56]

---

53. Ibid., 1986, 219.
54. McMillan 1996b, 51.
55. Fayet-Scribe 1990, 125. See Tranvouez 2011b, 64, for a helpful overall graph of the institutional development of specialized Catholic Action in France from 1926 to 1975.
56. Barral 1996, 600–603.

The theme that "the church has lost the working class" and that something had to be done about it was sounded in many quarters.[57]

Thus a working person might identify consciously with a socialist (class struggle) or a social-reconstructionist (democratic or bourgeois or aristocratic, often corporatist) worldview, or even with a conventional middle-class liberal-conservative outlook. Within the Catholic persuasion, he or she would belong to one set of organizations for socioeconomic interests (a labor union, a savings institution, a mutual insurance organization, a cooperative, a farm league, other professional organizations) and often enough to another parallel set for sociocultural advancement, including religious formation. The bishops kept in touch with all these organizations of the variegated Catholic labor movement by manifold contacts, organizationally through the numerous chaplains that they appointed. The head chaplains performed a key service of providing channels of communication up and down the Catholic hierarchical ladder alongside their primary function of stimulating the religious self-formation of the membership and the leadership cadres of the organizations.

Eventually, better educated lay leaders of the movements would rely less and less on their chaplains for guidance in economic and political decisions. Before World War II, however, and to some extent thereafter, the autonomy that the organized Catholic working class sought so assiduously was not *from* clerical oversight, but *with* labor chaplains *from* socialist or communist hegemony of the labor movement on the one hand *and from* Catholic upper-class hegemony on the other.[58]

There was as yet little or no allowance among militant Catholics for a plurality of worldviews or religious faiths in an ideal society. Social Catholicism derived from the will to work for a society based on a Christian model, different from modern society based on liberal individualism, materialist values, and a secular morality. This Christendom ideal differed also from the equally materialistic and secular socialist alternative. Within the Catholic family, all the same, by a process of interaction between the faith and the age, working-class people were finding their voices and raising them in church and society. A significant new element after World War I was that the distinct voices of women and young unmarried lay people, male and female, joined those of adult males.

---

57. In the March 1934 manifesto *Pour le bien commun*, drawn up by Jacques Maritain, a familiar quote of Pius XI appears: "The greatest scandal of the nineteenth century is that the Church in fact has lost the working class." Maritain (see Jacques Maritain and Raïssa Maritain 1982, 5:1030) notes: "This saying, reported by abbé Cardijn, in whose presence it was made [ca. 1925], has been cited often since then."

58. Whitney 2009, 104–6.

CHAPTER 8

Women's Catholic Labor Movements

The women's movements of the modern period had their counterparts in organized Catholicism, particularly after the turn of the century. Catholic women structured their movements along the patterns of mobilization that had developed in the various countries and encountered the typical frictions and turf battles. Given the role expectations that prevailed for women in European society as a whole and in Catholic circles in particular, the efforts of some pioneers that led to lasting organizational results are revealing as to the possibilities that they envisioned and the obstacles they faced.

Our focus will be on the activities of Catholic women primarily in and for the working class. These were the persons subject to compounded discrimination and marginalization on the basis not only of gender but of class and religion. To the extent that they were practicing Catholics, their Catholicism often seemed alien to working-class and feminist aspirations. In the case of working girls, their youth was another disadvantage, along with their meager schooling. The prevailing gender separation, however, also sometimes worked for greater autonomy and leadership roles for Catholic women than women had, say, in the socialist labor movements. Trade unions exclusively of and for women arose mostly in the context of Christian labor movements. They had to contend with the masculine model dominant in the social and labor world of the times.[1] Much of social Catholic feminism is therefore not as well documented as the male side.[2]

Educational endeavors, "formation," constituted a predominant element in efforts to mobilize underprivileged groups for

1. Chabot 2003, 5–7.
2. Bard 1993; see Offen 2000, 196–200.

self-improvement. This was certainly the case with women, whether bourgeois or working-class, married or single, adult or younger. In the Catholic world the stress on formation was a matter of enabling women to deal with the practical challenges of modern life. At another level it aimed at arming the faithful against the modern ideologies fostered by liberal or republican educational policies that hoped to raise up a new humanity emancipated from the oppressive traditions of Christendom.[3] The same was also the case in regard to the socialist challenge appealing to the lower classes from the same materialist base. With the aim of reconstituting society on Christian bases, these social Catholic women chose educational activities beyond the usual elementary level of schooling as the arena in which they could best lay the foundations of a Christian society.

The organizational development of these Catholic women's movements grew stronger especially in the decades just before and after World War II. Their roots stretch back, however, to notable predecessors in Germany and France.

Pioneers of Women's Labor Movements

In Italy, one Adelaide Coari carried on in Pius X's time after the Vatican disavowal of Romolo Murri's Christian democratic movement in 1902 in which she was involved.[4] She edited the periodical of a women's organization in Milan that "conducted literacy courses for women employed in factories and agricultural work."[5] This undertaking came under fire as the anti-modernist campaign heated up with the issuance of the 1907 encyclical *Pascendi dominici gregis*, whereupon she went back to her occupation as a schoolteacher. Later, as an inspector for seven hundred rural elementary schools in Lombardy, she imbued many of the female teachers with her views of educational method and aims through her visits and writings.[6]

Armida Barelli, also in Milan, showed a remarkable gift for organization. She enjoyed the esteem of the archbishop, Cardinal Andrea Ferrari, as well as that of his successor as archbishop, Achille Ratti (the future Pope Pius XI from 1921 to 1939). Her work took a decidedly religious approach to the groups of young female workers she had gathered together as early as 1912. Later, in Fascist Italy, she led the most numerous and important component of Italian Catholic Action, the women's organization, independent of the men's groups. Already in 1919, however, at its foundation, its youth wing had 50,000 mem-

3. Fayet-Scribe 1990, 189–90.
4. Misner 1991, 253–54.
5. Dawes 2011, 484–526, here 514; see for context Gaiotti de Biase 2002.
6. Colombo 1982.

bers, and the adult women numbered some 70,000.[7] Barelli brought many working-class young Catholic women into her movement, but did not turn the running of the local groups, much less the central organization, over to the workers themselves. They remained part of an interclass women's movement after Pius XI's pattern of Catholic Action.

Apart from Catholic Action, however, and leaving only scant traces in accessible sources, we know that some Catholic women's labor unions existed before 1918, when they were among the founding federations of the Confederazione italiana dei lavoratori (CIL). According to the official documents edited by Angelo Robbiati, the organizer of the founding convention, Giovanni Battista Valente, invited a "signorina Scanni" (not identified further) to give a report on the Catholic women's organizations.[8] Scanni was subsequently elected to represent them on the executive committee. It is not clear whether she came from the national federation of seamstresses (headquartered in Milan) or the clearly feminine national union of tobacco workers (Rome), or perhaps from the ranks of the Italian Textile Union (Como).

A prominent concern, perhaps dominant in the early phases of female unionization, was to come to grips at the level of knowledge and insight with the dire situation of women workers. Their special needs, not least those of the sheer numbers of women who worked at home in the clothing industry, attracted Europe-wide attention in the first decade of the twentieth century.

In Germany the newly founded middle-class Catholic women's association in Germany turned its attention to the working woman under the leadership of Hedwig Dransfeld. The Katholischer Deutscher Frauenbund was started in 1903 due to the advocacy of Elisabeth Gnauck-Kühne after her conversion to Catholicism; she had previously initiated the Protestant women's movement in an address to the Evangelic-Social Congress of 1895.[9] She was an eloquent spokesperson for the rights of women. Though she did not play a direct role in founding any specific labor organizations, she contributed much to raising the consciousness of Catholic women with regard to the conditions of female industrial workers. The Frauenbund strove to work with and coordinate the many particular Catholic organizations for working-class women and girls that were already on the scene. The Catholic Volksverein also claimed this as its own task, which led to frictions between the two umbrella organizations. After World War I, however, the Frauenbund increased and the Volksverein decreased.[10]

---

7. Dau Novelli 1998, 122.
8. Robbiati 1981b, 16–17 and 51–52; 1981a.
9. Baadte 1979.
10. See *ZGiLB* 1:129–36; 3:106–22, 223–34; Pankoke-Schenk and Mehrle 1986. Two leaders of the movement, Dransfeld and Helene Weber (see Ferber 1973 and Morsey 1979), traveled to the

Religious congregations of sisters and charitable organizations devoted themselves to alleviating the disadvantaged of the industrial economy. In the broad spectrum from individual charity through all aspects of social work to political pressure and legislation for social change, some figures stand out. Such were Gnauck-Kühne in Germany and, later, Hildegard Burjan in Austria. In the early 1890s Gnauck-Kühne, who as a woman was not officially allowed to be admitted to a university until 1895, nevertheless was invited by famed economist Gustav Schmoller to attend his seminar. She also did sociological research on the spot in a Berlin cardboard factory as a single middle-aged wage-earner for three months. Then, using a carefully worked-out questionnaire (like the Le Play–style *enquêtes* that Cardijn would later employ), she did a sociological analysis of the living conditions of seventy-two women workers in the Berlin paper industry (published in Schmoller's *Jahrbuch*, 1896). With her unusual command of academic training in social science, she was an instigator of social action in the women's movement.[11] Heinrich Pesch cited her writings several times in his *Lehrbuch*.[12] Not until 1912 did an analogous figure appear in Austria: another convert, named Hildegard Burjan (1883–1933). In the course of her unusually inspiring life as a member of the prosperous bourgeoisie, in 1912 she founded a Christian alliance of women who worked in Viennese couture from their homes.[13] At the same time she planned and worked to form a group called the Caritas Socialis, which numbered one hundred fifty at the time of her early death. These were unmarried women who dedicated their lives to aid women and children in the most miserable economic circumstances.

Movement in France

Amid the new growth of feminist publications in 1890s France was one edited by Marie Maugeret from 1896 to 1899, courageously entitled *Le Féminisme Chrétien*. In its pages she focused on women's right to work. "We admit no restriction, no limitation, no regulation of this freedom, and we protest with all our energy against any law that, under the fallacious and hypocritical pretext of 'protecting' us, takes away our right, the most sacred of all, to earn our living honestly."[14] Expressed in these terms, it remained a minority view for decades. However, as we shall see, "equal pay for equal work," often coupled with measures to restrict factory work for women, became a standard demand in social Catholic circles.

United States in the inflation year of 1923 to raise money for the needs that the Frauenbund was trying to meet. They could count on the support of an emulator organization in the States, the National Catholic Women's Union; Moloney 2002, 183; Spael 1964, 97–98.

11. Baadte 1979, esp. 111–14.
13. Greshake 2008.
12. E.g., Pesch 1925, 2:523ff.
14. Cited by Offen 2000, 197.

A pioneer of actual labor unions for working women in France was Marie-Louise Rochebillard (1860–1936). Her middle-class family had come down in the world, so she had to work to support herself. Thrown into the working-class world from 1876 on, but impressed by *Rerum novarum*, she was eventually able to hold courses for women under the auspices of the Catholic university of Lyon. In 1898–99 she organized three local women's unions.[15] Even more than the educational courses for working-class women, it was quite a departure to opt for labor unions (*syndicats*). Her motive was simply that unions were necessary to fight for the freedom of women to work for their living honestly, with self-respect. Otherwise the isolation and dependence that threatened the females in the working force made them prey in an unjust system. Her unions, for commercial employees, for garment workers, and for workers in silk in and around Lyon, could not change the system at once, but they gave hope to the women who took the vocational courses offered by the unions and gradually supported militants to carry on the struggle. "The best way to help people," she wrote, "is to teach them how they can help themselves. This has been the basic idea of our *syndicats de femmes*."[16]

The *syndicats* were separate—no men or bosses allowed. The educational offerings, however, brought the social classes together, inasmuch as Rochebillard recruited young ladies and older notables of the city to lead the training, whether in accounting, French, or needlecraft. In the longer haul, Rochebillard's ambitious undertakings did not develop beyond promising beginnings. It made no headway in the larger mills, where the CGT, the Confédération générale du travail, prevailed among the workers. However, its combination of autonomous female militancy and services to the members supported by educated and better-off women was a model for other Catholic women's unions.

Prompted by one of Rochebillard's talks in 1901, a young woman not of working-class background got involved in her ever-changing projects. This was Andrée Butillard (1881–1955). She tried her hand at organizing similar unions in Marseilles and Grenoble, where she met Emile Guerry (1891–1969), a priest-founder of women's unions. Never very confrontational, such unions nevertheless embraced the feminist principles: equal pay for equal work and the pursuit of career paths otherwise reserved just for men.[17] Their moderation made them the occasional beneficiaries of an awakening social consciousness evident here and there among ladies of the leisure class. The Catholic feminist association L'action sociale de la femme, founded by Jeanne Chenu, for exam-

---

15. Dumons 1994; Chabot 2003, 9–24.
16. Cited by Chabot 2003, 16, from a 1904 brochure by Rochebillard published in the Jesuits' series *L'Action populaire*.
17. Ibid, 20, 32.

ple, held a lecture series in Paris in the winter of 1903-4 on "the education of our daughters in family, work and society."[18] Most "feminists" among French Catholics did not yet advocate women's suffrage (which France did not put into effect until 1946), but there were three small Catholic women's rights organizations in France in 1900.[19]

In 1908 Andrée Butillard made her way to Paris armed with letters of introduction to two upper-class social Catholics, the young Joseph Zamanski of the ACJF and Henri Lorin of the *Semaines sociales*.[20] Soon she was acquainted with the whole Parisian Catholic network of people involved in social thought and action. Lorin used her knowledge of working conditions to help draft a bill setting minimum piecework rates for sewing garments at home. This bill was introduced by de Mun in 1909; its major provisions finally were passed in legislation of 1915. In 1911, assisted by Jean Verdier, the Sulpician head of the Institut catholique of Paris and later archbishop and cardinal (1929-40), Butillard initiated a more ambitious version of Rochebillard's courses in Lyon. She inaugurated a curriculum of training courses for women interested in social service taught by her acquaintances in the Catholic office-workers' union, Lorin's highly theoretical Union des études, the Action populaire, the ACJF, and the *Semaines sociales*. This program, initially under the auspices of the Institut catholique, was called the École normale sociale (ENS). In the 1920s it would provide professional training for numbers of women, both bourgeois (*promotrices*) and working-class (*propagandistes* or *militantes*). With their improved French and knowledge of the avenues of recourse available to mothers and working people in general, many of these latter were elected to the arbitration panels set up in the various industries (*conseils prud'hommales*). Diébolt notes that Butillard took advantage of legislation in 1920 that gave a woman the right to join a union without the approval of her husband to press for the growth and the federation of women's unions.[21]

Before and concomitantly with all this, Butillard had already started in 1908 to realize a novel project—namely, organizing isolated and demoralized women who worked at home for pitiful wages as pieceworkers.[22] Starting by gathering a few such seamstresses in a discussion group, she communicated to them the prospect of getting organized under her (initial) leadership to deal with the system that exploited them. She even set up a workshop and served as a kind of cooperative business agent for them, taking orders from department

18. Fayet-Scribe 1990, 95.
19. See Hause and Kenney 1984, 41-42; 1981, 11-30; Diébolt 2000, 223-35; see Black 1989.
20. For Butillard, see *DMR* 6:90-91; Rollet 1960, esp. 41-71; Black 1989; Fayet-Scribe 1990, 112-17; Cova 1992; Pedersen 1993; and Chabot 2003, 47-59, 90-101.
21. Diébolt 2000, 233.
22. Rollet 1960, 45-55.

stores. Then she got another group together and another, taking care of their own orders. There were 240 seamstresses in her union in 1913. There was also a union for office workers.[23]

For women who worked for a regular employer, unions had sprung up in different places. Two religious congregations of sisters in Paris helped women workers in the garment industry get started.[24] The Catholic unions in and around Lyon were important. Christine Bard has discovered the weight of women members in the Nord in the CFTC.[25] This is notable in view of the conspicuous lack of welcome shown to women in the socialist and communist unions of the era. Not that women had an easy time of it in Christian labor: the dominant ideal of the woman as homemaker was challenged by the very existence of single women making a career in labor organizing. The possibility of combining such a role with marriage and motherhood was still more remote. Nevertheless, as early as 1912 Andrée Butillard addressed the *Semaine sociale* at Limoges on "the formation of *promotrices* in the trade-union idea."[26] Still earlier, the Jesuits of the Action populaire had published many an article by and about women in an industrial society.

One of the union members Butillard came to know in Paris, Maria Bardot, serves as an exemplary case of an organizer in the Christian women's unions.[27] Maria Bardot left a sisters' school at the age of twelve in 1895 and became an apprentice to a Parisian couturier. Making the most of what training was available, she became one of the most skilled garment workers in the trade, while at the same time mobilizing her fellow workers in one of the Catholic unions for garment workers. She became its president in 1909 at the age of twenty-six. At that time, given the demands of her union office, she left her employer and set herself up as a home worker. At the same time she drank in the outlook of social Catholicism after *Rerum novarum*, having come into contact with Butillard, who saw exceptional potential. She appeared briefly on the international stage at a Congress of Catholic Social Action held in April 1911 in Paris. Père Desbuquois of the Action populaire organized the four-day conference, which attracted hundreds of participants, many from neighboring countries (Hilaire Belloc was among them). Maria Bardot also attended and was on a panel chaired by Andrée Butillard.[28]

In 1916 the Catholic women's unions of Paris formed a federation (one of two, actually; Catholic unions in France found it hard to link up with one another). One federation hired Bardot as a full-time propagandist; she stimulated courses for the formation of other workers. These militants already had

23. Black 1989, 177–78.
25. Bard 1993.
27. Chabot 1993; 2003, 100–113.
24. Launay 1986, 29; Chabot 2003, 25–46.
26. Chabot 1993, 9.
28. Droulers 1969, 139.

experienced the study circles, which they then replicated where they worked. The two federations joined the national confederation of Christian unions (the CFTC led by Jules Zirnheld and Gaston Tessier) at its founding in 1919.[29]

Taking advantage of labor legislation, Bardot led the way into the official *conseils prud'hommales* when workers elected her to such a garment industry arbitration panel in 1920. She squeaked by the CGT candidate with a 97-to-92-vote result. In 1926, after a needleworkers' strike in Paris in 1923 in which the Catholic unions were active, she handily won reelection with 273 out of 379 votes. Some of the social Catholics who followed her progress faulted her for her fiery rhetoric as being unduly one-sided in her defense of strikers in the industry. By virtue of her formation, however, she was able to negotiate effectively for an agreement by collective bargaining that regulated the working conditions of thousands of garment workers. She was a member of the governing bodies of several unions and of the CFTC. Upon her premature death in 1927, she quickly became celebrated as the role model of a new type of Catholic woman, the single young labor militant. Other women in the Christian labor movement used her example to show Catholics, male unionists, and others that a woman could legitimately use her life to make a social contribution in public affairs even outside the home.[30]

The federations organized "union weeks," as well: a sort of annual convention or retreat to nourish the militants' dedication. By the 1930s intensive annual three-week training courses took place for those who had the vocation of propagandist. Here, under the guidance of social Catholic experts and of experienced propagandists, one learned how to launch actions in favor of concrete reforms. The key was formation, resulting in knowledge of Catholic social teaching and competence in dealing with industrial relations. This responded to the felt needs of working-class women as wives and mothers without neglecting the professional education of office workers, the problems of factory workers, or the cooperatives that made the lives of seamstresses more tolerable.[31]

Then, although women's suffrage had been stymied in France and the anticlerical left had prevailed in national elections, Andrée Butillard broadened her sights from unionism to the political (civic) formation of working-class women. In 1925, again with the encouragement of Canon Verdier, she founded the Union féminine civique et sociale (UFCS), which aimed at stimulating the activism of women not employed outside the home, primarily in neighborhood and local affairs. Naomi Black sees the UFCS, which had a long future ahead of it, as a leading example of social feminism comparable in some ways to the

29. See Launay 1986, 103.   30. Ibid., 239.
31. Ibid., 238–40, notes other prominent women leaders in the history of the CFTC, especially Eugénie Beeckmans, Marguerite Lafeuille (423), and Marie-Louise Danguy (346).

Women's Co-operative Guild in Britain and in others to the League of Women Voters in the United States.[32] Others find its feminist credentials more ambiguous.[33] There is no question, however, of its matrix of social Catholicism with its concern for the welfare of women of the working class. Hence it is no surprise to find Père Desbuquois of Action populaire advising and assisting Butillard and her coworkers, since he was already regularly involved in their training center (at ENS) and women's unions.[34]

More surprising is Desbuquois's intense interest in the feminist movement as such and in Catholicism's need to face it and adapt. His life's work was dedicated to the social question, which was then understood clearly to refer to labor issues. And yet he held that "the most important social movement" of his time was "feminism, more important than the economic social question."[35] In this regard he was of course anything but typical, though not quite alone in clerical circles. Antonin Sertillanges, OP, published his *Féminisme et christianisme* in 1908. An indication of the attention paid to the question at this stage is that it was reprinted many times. In what would be one typical moderating stance of progressive Catholics, he defined his position in this way:

If by feminism you understand a struggle of the sexes, hence individualism, an egoism on the part of women, and finally a tendency to suppress the division of human labor by removing women from their family roles so as to throw them *ex-aequo* with men into public life, then we are not feminists. But if by feminism one means the progressive emancipation of the feminine moral person, her augmented value, her more intense deployment in all occupations in relation to her aptitudes and duties, in the full breadth that these duties allow and that her aptitudes enhance, in this case we are feminists.[36]

After the war the papal line changed from Pius X's disapproval of women's suffrage to Benedict XV's approval; Catholic opinion generally concurred, it seems, but at least in France did not take up the issue.[37] Nor did the emphasis on the crucial role of women as spouses, mothers, and homemakers diminish. The feminism of Catholics, where it showed itself, was a social feminism of "complementarity," emphasizing the specificity of women's contribution while upholding an equality of basic rights, access to education and the professions, and equal pay for equal work. It was not an egalitarian feminism that was blind to any sense of gender-specific social roles or that tended toward competition rather than collaboration.

32. Black 1989, 161–204.
33. Bard 1995; Dutton 2002, 154.
34. Droulers 1981, 110–11 and 211; see Bard 1995, 273–80.
35. Droulers 1981, 225 and 217; see Corlieu 1970.
36. Sertillanges 1930, 337; see McMillan 1981, 369; Bard 1995.
37. Hause and Kenney 1981, 23–27; see Offen 2000, 199.

Some women's questions divided social Catholics. Some would still support, on an anti-individualist principle, a family vote, where the father of a family would cast multiple votes according to the size of the family, sometimes with women voting for themselves. Male unionists tended to favor measures that would discourage the employment of women, including low-paid work at home, as in the fashion industry. The UFCS fully endorsed the ideal of allowing mothers to stay home, but agitated for legislation that would improve the conditions of work at home, thus enabling women to earn some supplementary income. It also insisted with success within the councils of the CFTC that no policy be adopted that would advocate restrictions on the hiring of women, this in the face of widespread worry about the declining birthrate in France.[38] Part-time opportunities—for example, for postal workers—were also on the UFCS agenda. The theme of the *Semaine sociale de France* in 1927 (at Nancy) was "The Woman in Society," where no one disagreed that women's special contribution to society was through the family; apart from that there was a spectrum of opinions.

If Catholics were conflicted about feminism, however, anticlericals were at least equally so. Nelly Roussel was a champion of reproductive freedoms and hence shunned by Catholic feminists. As she wrote in 1906, the anticlerical liberals

> speak of letting us escape from the domination of the priests only to put us more firmly under the domination of our husbands, and they wonder why women are so religious? What have the free-thinkers done to break the bond? How dare you reproach women for seeking refuge in the shadow of the churches, when the door of the churches is the only door open to them?[39]

The senators who prevented women's suffrage from being enacted in 1920 were the Radicals who feared that women in their vast majority, not being sufficiently enlightened, would vote against the left. This same calculation was not lost on French Catholics, but it did not make them keener to push for the franchise.[40] There were plenty of other women's issues to debate, however. Butillard's UFCS pressed consistently for legislative remedies, some crowned with success in the 1930s: "family allowances (to assist women who leave the workforce), maternity leaves in state industries, and state aid to battered children."[41] The organization also backed several measures that went into effect for protecting girls in and after school. The UFCS supported coeducation, provided there were enough women teachers and enough staff to supervise playgrounds and washrooms. They may have tipped the scale on other practical issues favoring the mother in the home, censorship of movies, the family vote, and the sale of liquor.

38. Droulers 1981, 224; Chabot 1992, 323; P. Smith 1996, 185, 244.
39. Bard 1995, 280.   40. McMillan 1981, 367–70.
41. Black 1989, 195.

Belgium: An Auspicious Start, a Robust Development

The work of Marie-Louise Rochebillard was the initial impetus not only for Andrée Butillard in France, but also for two Belgian women in particular, Louise Van den Plas in Brussels and Victoire Cappe in Liège.[42] Both daughters of the bourgeoisie took a new line, not as ladies bountiful bestowing charity on their less fortunate sisters in the shops, but as champions of feminist self-help—for Cappe especially, incarnated in labor unions for, of, and by working women themselves. They insisted on the equality of men and women and on "reciprocal solidarity" between working-class and bourgeois women. The anti-socialist or Christian unions in the textile industry before World War I always had a large contingent of women workers, though not as leading officeholders.[43] Ceslas Rutten, OP, and René Debruyne were busy developing the Christian unions (as we have seen in chapter 5) to help workers and counter the threat from Catholic indifference and socialist unions of alienating the working class from the church. Rutten and a cohort of young priests formed by Mercier in the seminary in Louvain were alert to the importance that raising the consciousness of working-class Catholic women would have for the success of this mission.[44] After Victoire Cappe impressed the Mechlin (Malines) Catholic Congress of 1909 with the need for and possibilities of this approach, Rutten and Mercier lent their support to the establishment of a national office in Brussels to promote unions and services in aid of Catholic women of the working class.[45] This was the general secretariat of the Christian Women's Professional Unions, set up in 1912, modeled after Rutten's general secretariat of Christian Professional Unions from 1904.[46] These two national offices in Brussels, after World War I, merged into the coordinating umbrella organization that was Louis Colens' National League of Christian Workers, the ACW/LNTC.

The two women co-heading the working-class women's secretariat were Victoire Cappe (from Liège, 1886–1927) and Maria Baers (from Antwerp, 1883–1959), one primarily for French-speaking Wallonia and one for Dutch-speaking Flanders, but both national figures and participants or leaders in international organizations. Both, for instance, took part in the 1919 International Labor Conference in Washington, D.C., that dealt with working hours, maternity protection, and night work for women. At first they were the only two permanently employed staff of the women's labor organizations. A look into their backgrounds and connections with organized Catholicism furnishes insight into the nature and scope of religious social action, especially in Belgium.

Victoire Cappe was reared with her three younger sisters largely in her

---

42. De Decker, Ista, and Keymolen 1994, 2:333–39; see Hilden 1993, 296–302.
43. Strikwerda 1997, 302. 44. Gerard 1994b, 1:125.
45. Keymolen 2001, 89–105.
46. On the former, see Eaton 1955, 65–76; on the latter, Gerard 1994b, 1:128–32.

maternal grandmother's house, although until 1897 the Cappe family's residence in the same complex exhibited similar prosperous conditions, with servants for every need.[47] When she was eleven years old, however, the enormous debts of her father, a lawyer, led to a crisis. Fleeing Liège, he took his family to Brussels; the law soon found him there, as well. Until 1899 they managed there somehow, but then he took off for Greece, hardly to be heard from again, until he died in 1910. The girls' mother, too, left them with the grandmother in Liège; back in Brussels, she made do as a saleslady in a clothing store. Victoire and her sisters of school age attended a boarding school, Victoire at a teachers' training school run by a congregation of sisters, from 1901 to 1905. The beloved grandmother also saw to their baptism at this juncture, as the parents were not religious. Victoire decided not to marry on that occasion "because it was said to be more perfect, not to marry and to enter into religion."[48] An indifferent student in subjects other than reading, writing, speech, and especially religion, she took very seriously the advice of her religion teacher, Abbé Jean Paisse, to consider something in the social sphere. In the meantime she was able to take two more years of advanced normal school while living at her grandmother's home, graduating in 1907 at the age of twenty-one.

While teaching for a living, she found her way into the social legacy of Antoine Pottier, a controversial seminary professor of moral theology and a social activist in Wallonia.[49] Jean Paisse had been a student of Pottier; the new school of Christian democrats in the region came about under his influence, though Pottier (1849–1923) had been in Rome since 1902. Christian feminism (for instance, that of Louise Van den Plas) was another aspect of this new wave to which Paisse introduced Cappe. With his encouragement the young Victoire Cappe took the initiative of founding first, in 1907, a union for the needlecraft trade, women working at home or in a shop as so many did in those years.[50] The exploitation of these women became the object of considerable public attention, and Victoire Cappe's organizational progress was followed closely in the Liège Christian democratic newspaper. Victoire Cappe took an active part in the 1909 Malines Social Congress organized by Rutten at Cardinal Mercier's instigation.[51] Her lively presentation at one of the sections of the convention described the women's union she had spearheaded in Liège. It also constituted an eloquent plaidoyer for expanding similar initiatives throughout Belgium. She had informed herself well on the state of social Catholic thought and projects in other countries. Her career as leader of a campaign for the elevation of women at work and in the home was launched. In 1912 the general secretariat of the Christian Women's Professional

---

47. Keymolen 2001, 26–30.
48. Ibid., 35, citing Jacques Leclercq in the periodical *La Cité Chrètienne* of May 2, 1928.
49. Jadoulle 1991; Misner 1991, 222–26.   50. See Eaton 1955, 60 and 65–69.
51. Keymolen 2001, 83–100.

Unions could be set up in Brussels, with Cappe and Baers as the general secretaries, with the job of promoting and coordinating such unions throughout Walloon and Flemish Belgium. Until the outbreak of war, the work flourished. Victor Brants, the professor of social economy at the University of Louvain, became a valued advisor for Cappe until shortly before his death in 1917.[52]

Maria Baers's path to leading that campaign alongside Victoire Cappe was quite different. She was the daughter of a solid Catholic family in Antwerp, baptized soon after birth (1883) and destined for a much longer life and work (d. 1959). Her father was in the business of importing foodstuffs from the colonies. He took her along to the port often enough that she gained an idea of and an interest in the role and condition of labor in international trade. After schooling appropriate for her social class with the Notre Dame sisters, she took some courses offered by the Volksverein in Mönchengladbach, Germany, and some higher education in (scholastic) philosophy and the social sciences in Brussels and in Fribourg, Switzerland.[53] In 1911 she joined a social studies circle directed by Laurent Perquy, who was like Rutten a socially active Dominican priest. She gave presentations at study days so competently that Perquy persuaded her to join Victoire Cappe in creating a national movement for women at work, the general secretariat that was established in Brussels in 1912.

In that capacity, each in their respective areas of Belgium, both Baers and Cappe spurred the establishment of unions for women who worked in fields left mainly to women. The outbreak of war in 1914 and the occupation of Belgium brought much of that work to a standstill. The educational side continued, leading to the renaming of their secretariat from general secretariat of the Christian Women's Professional Unions to general secretariat of the Christian Social Works for Women, with many departments covering services, study circles, vocational training, and home economics coordinated by Baers and Cappe. Principal among the works were a permanent Social School, analogous to the ENS in Paris, and the Leagues of Christian Women Workers.[54]

In the changed circumstances after World War I, fewer women were employed in piecework at home or in small shops. A stronger emphasis on the role of wives as managing the home and family also served to diminish the push for women's unions such as Victoire Cappe organized. In addition, the Christian union federation under René Debruyne was anxious to add the women to their

---

52. Ibid, 111f; but see 103–5, 413f.   53. Keymolen 1985.

54. The École sociale and the Belgian women's leagues got their statutes in 1920. The latter went under the designation of Ligues ouvrières féminines chrètiennes (LOCF) and Kristelijke Arbeidersvrouwengilden (KAV; subsequently Kristelijke Arbeidersvrouwenbeweging). To be noted are the "O" and the "A" for workers or working-class. The "F" and the "V," of course, correspond to "women." There was also a more general Catholic women's organization, the FFCB; see Eaton 1955, 81–114 and 198–202; HMOCB 2:345–74 and 379.

membership rolls. With other factors, thus, the women's leagues, especially the KAV, became the most robust part of the organizations in the secretariat. By 1924, the women's unions all became affiliated with the ACV/CSC. As a result, the KAV leaders, such as Maria Baers, took part in federation affairs on an equal footing with their male colleagues. Baers became a vice president of the ACW/LNTC (the umbrella working-class *standsorganisatie* brought together by Colens) and member of the governing board of the ACV/CSC (the union federation) from 1923, while serving as Belgian senator from 1939 to 1954.[55] In these capacities, and with the strength of the forces mobilized behind her, she did more for the working class and Catholicism in Belgium and internationally than the labor priests Perquy and Rutten might have thought possible when they recruited her.

Thus in France and Belgium women came to play a distinct role in Catholic labor movements. In the mixed and male-dominated unions normal elsewhere, there was little opportunity for women's voices to be heard. The French (Lafeuille) and Belgian (Baers) female leaders took up the cause in the international confederation of Christian unions (the CISC; see chapter 3). Maria Baers was a member of the central commission of the CISC from its beginning. Before each of the four congresses of the CISC in the 1920s, culminating in the one in Munich in 1928, the women's unions met separately and then set forth their proposals at the general congress. This body then was their conduit to put women's issues before the International Labour Organization in Geneva. The ILO declined to carry out a multinational survey of married women working for wages, as proposed. At least, however, such questions were not ignored in the labor consciousness of the CISC organizations.[56]

Young Women in the JOC

When Joseph Cardijn arrived for his parish assignment in Brussels (Laeken), he was put in charge of the female patronages, as we have seen. Between the end of the war and 1925, while organizing the first JOC sections for males, he also kept his hand in the world of Catholic social concern for young women of the working class. It is not surprising that some of his Laeken charges turn up later as leaders of the JOCF, the Young Christian Workers for Women. Nelly Dutrieux of Laeken was the first secretary general of the JOCF.[57]

The JOC formula ran up against more resistance and gained adherents among parish leaders more slowly when proposed for girls than for boys. It is understandable that the women and clergy in charge of the patronages would

55. Gerard 1994a, 210.
56. See Pasture 1999, 112–16; Launay 1990, 87.
57. Vos 1994, 2:497; Bragard et al. 1990, 92–94 and 117–19.

think that their way of doing things was more appropriate for girls, many of whom worked in homes or small shops run by women. There was a certain initial reluctance even to use the "O-word" of JOC, *ouvrière*, as applied to girls, evidence perhaps of a refusal to look the problem of factory girls in the face. When such groups did get started, they were claimed not by one group, like the ACJB, as was the case with boys, but by three or four previously existing Catholic women's organizations. The most important of these was the predecessor of the Belgian Leagues of Working-Class Women (LOFC/KAV), which had started its own youth sections or auxiliaries.[58] While Cardijn was working to achieve working-class autonomy for the Belgian and French male counterparts, his influence was great enough to achieve a similar arrangement for the JOCF/VKAJ with the adult women's organization, the LOCF/KAV.[59]

Cardijn was in fact the official chaplain of all four branches of the Belgian JOC, separated by language and by sex: French-speaking and Dutch-speaking, male and female organizations, each with their own officers. Whereas such a quadripartite structure for the Belgian JOC was present to Cardijn's mind pretty much from the outset, in Guérin's case in Paris, it took a combination of unforeseen occurrences to get him to contemplate a female JOC, a JOCF.[60] First of all, he was not assigned to the patronages for girls in the parish. Then he was unused to dealing with women outside his family. In his schooling and working years, he interacted predominantly with men and boys. There were any number of patronage organizations and activities for young women; he may have thought, like so many, that their paramount need was to be "protected" and helped into a satisfactory marriage. At any rate, for some time after the formation of the JOCF, he would address its members as "mademoiselle" and shake hands with them only awkwardly.

All the same, there was the example of the JOCF in Belgium and even in the Nord of France that seemed to call for replication on a national level. In 1928 there were already twelve groups between Lille and Roubaix-Tourcoing, welcomed by the priests Palémon Glorieux and Louis Liagre. The latter laid out the rationale to Guérin for a coherent national movement in terms that could not fail to move him. No other group could do for young women in industry what a JOCF could do "*par elles, pour elles, entre elles.*" Only they themselves could transform the milieu in which they live. For this, a movement was needed that had at its disposition "an elite of well-trained leaders, capable of taking initiatives." How could such training be acquired, except by placing them in positions of responsibility, really turning over to them the job of leading their section? The existing organizations for young Catholic women might be aghast at such advice. Even Andrée Butil-

---

58. Eaton 1955, 222–32; Alaerts 2004, 69–91. 59. *HMOCB* 2:438–40; see *HMOCB* 2:368.
60. Pierrard 1997, 141–50.

lard's UFCS had its eyes primarily on married or adult women in terms of formation. And yet only a national organization with resources and a certain prestige would be able to undertake this project on a sufficiently broad scale.[61]

Concurrently, another force was storming Guérin's gates in the person of Jeanne Aubert, then eighteen years old and already a veteran of four different jobs in the previous three years, while also taking evening courses. She had met Georges Quiclet at work and heard him describe enthusiastically the JOC study week he attended in April 1927 in Belgium.[62] Of particular interest to her was the fact that young women also participated, wearing the same badge as the young men and conducting the same *enquêtes de milieu*. A visit to Guérin confirmed or even surpassed her expectations. Soon there was a section functioning under her leadership and that of Jean Guichard with the recognition of the Brussels JOCF. Jean Guichard, SJ, was Boulier's replacement at the Action populaire (Guichard would be chaplain of the JOCF in France for more than twenty years). As Pierrard explains, one hurried to "make it official," since the leaders of the Girl Guides and other Catholic organizations for girls and young women resented this independent rival in their recently staked-out territory.[63] The JOCF also incurred considerable resistance from priests and women engaged in the customary patronages. After all, these religious sisters and other (older, bourgeois) women were informed that they need not "assist" in the running of the sections. There were repeated attempts from this quarter in the first years to force Guérin, who authorized this policy, to resign from the movement.

As Liagre's memorandum had argued, a national headquarters and organization, with a staff and a paper of its own, would be needed. In the course of 1928 this also came to pass: Jeanne Aubert took the post offered her as secretary general, leaving the factory (but not the milieu) for good. The JOCF was well and truly launched in France as in Belgium.[64] In the years following, Georges Guérin traveled around France guiding the tempestuous spread of the male side of the movement. Charles Bordet was his alter ego as assistant chaplain of the national movement in Paris. And Jean Guichard assisted Jeanne Aubert in the training of generations of female militants in the JOCF.

Forming the KAV in the Netherlands

The construction of the female element of the working class in the Dutch Catholic pillarization process lagged somewhat behind the women's movements in neighboring countries. Perhaps the threat of the de-Christianization of the Catholic working class was not so severe there. All the same, the "red

61. Ibid., 145.
63. Pierrard 1997, 147.
62. Debès and Poulat 1986, 63.
64. See J. Aubert 1990; Whitney 2009, 109–14.

chaplains" in the dioceses and the major spokesmen of social Catholicism appreciated the importance of women's organization fairly early on.[65] Thus Henri Poels drew emphatic attention to the need for a women's organization in 1919, preceded by Catholic feminists at the turn of the century.[66] In the lay ranks, Adrianus Cornelis De Bruijn was also interested in promoting a female wing of the Catholic workers' movement that he headed.[67] But it was not until 1933 that an organizer hired by the RKWV could set up a Catholic women's labor *standsorganisatie* (Katholieke Arbeiders Vrouwenorganisatie [KAV]) in the diocese of Roermond (Dutch Limburg). This woman, Mia Schmitz, had done her research on the LOFC/KAV of Belgium, spending some time in Brussels. Back in the Netherlands she traveled from parish to parish and succeeded in establishing a growing movement. As in the other working-class movements, the emphasis was on connectedness, bringing the members out of their isolation, and on formation, imparting the knowledge and skills that enabled them to improve their family life and their social situation.[68]

A newer profession that was open to women was that of social work. Its practitioners were at first daughters of the middle class, but without adequate training and support (including, of course, income), it was not a rewarding lifetime occupation. In the framework again of the RKWV, a young woman from Amsterdam, Fé Haye, a university graduate in biology influenced by Alphons Ariëns, started the Catholic School for Social Work in 1921 with advice from Maria Baers in Brussels. This institution guided women of both bourgeois and working-class background to become skilled volunteers as well as professionals engaged in social work. It continued after World War II under the vigorous leadership of Willy Hillen, a longtime participant in social and political activities of Catholic women.[69]

During the enforced suspension of organizational activity during the German occupation, activists took refuge as well as they could under the wings of Catholic Action, the only alternative to the more autonomous social action to which they had been accustomed. Unofficial consultation and planning, of course, took place quietly. The main upshot of this conspiration in the present connection was the formation, from the end of 1944 on, of the future nationwide shape of the Dutch KAV. This took place within a coordinated effort of the Bishops' Commission for the Reconstruction of Catholic Organizational Life.[70] The women workers' organization had just reached a degree of maturity and influence in church life in the two southern dioceses of the five in the

65. Duffhues 1992, 176, 190.   66. Derks 1993.
67. See Derks and Huisman 2002, 41–62, here 50, citing an RKWV document from 1926.
68. Ibid., 59–61.
69. Derks, Halkes, and Van Heijst 1992, 217–25; Derks and Huisman 2002, 110–11.
70. Derks and Huisman 2002, 69–75.

Netherlands when the war came down upon them. It might well have been the case that a reconstruction under these conditions would have relegated them to a minor or marginal position within an overall design of pillarized mobilization. A key role in avoiding this pitfall was that of an aristocratic lady, Maria Van Nispen tot Sevenaer (1903–99), daughter of a prominent Catholic political leader.[71] She managed to gain the confidence not only of KAV leaders, who were indignant over the male leader's (De Bruijn's) notions of their place in the movement, but of De Bruijn himself and the influential clerical adviser to the bishops, Siegfried Stokman, OFM. They then persuaded the archbishop of Utrecht, Jan De Jong, to adopt a somewhat more centralized version of the vital prewar organizations, now standard across all five dioceses.[72] The new name of the RKWV became KAB (Katholieke Arbeidersbeweging). It was an umbrella organization of labor unions, *standsorganisaties*, and institutions for social work and culture. The policymaking board included five representatives, one for each of the diocesan *standsorganisaties* (working men, working women, young men, young women) and one for the unions. In addition, five paid officers served on the board, along with eight representatives of the various general KAB committees. Total membership increased from prewar levels to about 340,000 in 1954 (a turning point to be noted later on).

The emancipation process of women in the world and the social action of European Catholics spanned the twentieth century. Our look at its initial stages in various countries has revealed a pattern of cooperation and coordination between women and some men, notably some priests, educators, and labor leaders. The dawning realization that the customary feminine roles (maternity and rearing of children, homemaking, mutual support), though hallowed and enduring, were subject to change and reform made its way in fits and starts. The process in the field of women's work for pay is one we can follow to some extent also in the following chapters. Political and economic developments in the turbulent period of suspended war, depression, worse war, and recovery conditioned the ongoing quest for social justice and equity.

71. According to ibid., 72–74.
72. Ibid., 79–80, citing Peet 1987 and 1993.

CHAPTER 9

Christian Labor in Weimar Germany

When one turns to defeated Germany after World War I, one is struck by the prominence accorded by historians of Christian labor in this period to matters of party politics and government. Rapid adjustments had to be made to post-monarchical forms of government for which the Christian parties and labor movements were not prepared. Nevertheless, in the new republics, Christian unions and workers' leagues strove to wield political influence and had a significant measure of success. And indeed, the cause of democracy depended on them to the extent that they could do so. The failure of democracy to withstand its adversaries in the interwar period, then, raises the question of Christian labor's role in support of political democracy.[1] To what extent were these social Catholics committed democrats, and to what extent did, for example, an affinity with authoritarianism, undermine their resistance to totalitarian alternatives? After all, organized labor, Christian as well as socialist, was now in a position to make demands on political parties that depended on them for votes in the new, more democratic suffrage system. Labor clout in the Center Party was already more firmly institutionalized before the war than was the case in France or the Low Countries.

A Christian trade union personage such as Adam Stegerwald represents this rise in political status.[2] In the last months of the war he was a member of the Prussian upper house after having served on various wartime commissions. In 1921 he became Prussian state prime minister at the head of a coalition cabinet. At the same time he remained head of a non-socialist trade union federation that counted in its ranks nearly a fifth of all unionized German employees.[3]

1. See Mazower 1999, 3–40.   2. See Forster 2003.
3. See Schneider 1989, 127; for blue-collar workers, see Schneider 1982a, 452: Christian unions enrolled 11 or 12 percent of union totals in the blue-collar category.

The context for further developments from this initial situation may be briefly sketched. The short life of the Weimar Republic fell into three phases between 1918 and 1933.[4] The first went from the shaping of a new republican constitution at Weimar and the "Diktat" of Versailles by way of lagging reparations payments to horrendous inflation and the occupation of the Ruhr by French troops in 1923. From 1925 to 1928 or 1929 there followed a period of relative prosperity and recovery, buoyed by American investment. After that, recurrent tensions about reparations payments, the structural weaknesses of the new German state, and the Depression dominated political life until the seizure of power by Adolf Hitler and the National Socialist German Workers Party in 1933.[5]

In the first years after the defeat in World War I, German social Christians harbored cautious hopes that a new democratic political and economic order could be shaped out of the lessons of failed liberalism, but with liberal (parliamentary) as well as social elements.[6] Some spoke of "Christian socialism."[7] More typically Catholic laborites organized and made propaganda in the interests of workers, but with dire warnings *against* a socialist program that would touch property rights or secularize the schools. A constitutional assembly met at Weimar (February through July 1919), while chaotic conditions descended on many parts of the country. Nevertheless, a coalition of moderate ("majority") socialists, Center Party delegates, and democrats had a three-fourths majority in the assembly. They supported a number of compromises displeasing to the nationalist-authoritarian right and the radical left, as well as to some of their own partisans, and managed to pass a constitution. It provided for a republican and democratic form of government (a *Volksstaat* rather than an authoritarian state) that was quite a departure from previous regimes in many ways. The social Catholic element in the Center Party agreed with the majority socialists that provisions for the legal standing of works councils and even a national economic council comprising employer and employee representation were a promising development toward a more harmonious and just social order (articles 151–65 of the Weimar constitution). The Weimar constitution did make significant inroads in the prevailing liberal or individualistic jurisprudence by recognizing an unqualified right of association, which guaranteed the right to unionize (article 159).[8] Collective bargaining thus received a legal status on which labor could count. A priest from the Volksverein, Heinrich Brauns, serving as the long-lasting minister of labor in the Weimar Republic,

---

4. See Balderston 2002.
5. See McElligott 2014, especially 78–97.
6. Kolb 2010, 29; see Mazower 1999, 24.
7. Knapp 1975; Focke 1978, 71–114; Ludwig and Schroeder 1990.
8. See Stegmann 1974, 134–37.

favored the system of compulsory arbitration of labor disputes that became law in 1923.

The Weimar Republic rested on regrettably shaky economic and electoral footings. After 1920 the social democrats, the Center Party, and the bourgeois republicans never again formed a working majority in parliament. A combination of anti-socialist animus and social democratic internal differences made the social democrats hesitant to collaborate in governments dominated by representatives of other classes. The upshot was that the factually Catholic party was practically always in the government, whereas the social democrats only came out of the opposition from time to time.[9] This in turn meant that many of the natural allies of the labor wing of the Center were most often in the parliamentary opposition. Fortunately, partisan differences between Christian and socialist labor did not preclude all parliamentary cooperation. It did mean, however, that "difficult, painful decisions" such as suspending the limitation of the workday to eight hours, were the responsibility of a Catholic rather than a socialist minister.[10] Employers regained a good deal of their relative power and influence, starting with the stabilization of 1923.[11]

Leading Catholic Labor Lights in Weimar's Early Years

The new Weimar Republic struggled to find its footing. In hindsight, if not at the time, it is clear that the most serious threat to the infant democracy of the Weimar Republic came from the right of the political spectrum. Adam Stegerwald put together and headed a federation of non-socialist unions called the Deutscher Gewerkschaftsbund, the DGB.[12] This included his own GcG (the Gesamtverband der christlichen Gewerkschaften, the federation of Christian unions for miners and industrial workers) and a large office workers' union federation. The DGB unions were interconfessional or nonconfessional, with only the GcG component and Catholics in the other unions susceptible of voting for the Center Party. What is more, they included a substantial number of members of monarchist persuasion alongside those who willingly accepted the republican form of government. The Protestant membership would distribute their votes among parties of the right. Stegerwald's strategy was not to browbeat these workers or the parties they supported, but to win them over to a constitutional republican attitude. The DGB would encourage this by effectively

---

9. On the Catholic party, see Cary 1996, 103–24.
10. Evans 1999, 203.
11. Maier 1975, 13 and 510–15; see Kolb 2010, 130–36.
12. Schneider 1989, 156–57.

voicing their economic and social claims within the parliamentary framework. In other words, he tried to work with the dubiously democratic right, in view of its numerical and social strength, to democratize it and make it serviceable for the common good, also as seen from the worker's point of view.[13] In the world of labor, Adam Stegerwald and the DGB constituted a distinctly rightist element with a practical rather than an emphatic ideological stand in support of parliamentary democracy; the DGB styled itself "Christian-national."

Beside Christian unions, however, in Germany as elsewhere on the continent, there were important milieu organizations constituting a distinctively Catholic labor movement. To follow the story of Stegerwald's Christian unions (*Gewerkschaften*) in the Weimar Republic is certainly necessary to the history of social Catholicism, but one must pay heed also to the Arbeitervereine and their vigorous if rather didactic and austere publications.[14] The Volksverein and the Arbeitervereine did their real work at the local level with training courses and a press service for local Catholic newspapers, spreading the good word of solidarity and social responsibility through the ups and downs of the national economy. A weekly paper, the *Westdeutsche Arbeiter-Zeitung*, or *WAZ*, with analogous periodicals in southern Germany, served a membership of over 300,000.[15] Several of its leading figures, for example Johannes Giesberts (1865–1938), were repeatedly elected to the Reichstag and to state legislatures throughout the Weimar years. In the words of Helga Grebing, the Catholic workers' milieu organizations, as distinguished from the interconfessional trade unions, constituted the "leftmost column of the non-socialist labor movement" after World War I.[16]

---

13. Revising earlier interpretations of Stegerwald as himself dubiously democratic, recent studies by Cary (1996) and Patch (1998) in particular have influenced my description here. Cary, e.g., states (1996, 303–304; see also 163): "Stegerwald understood that a stable democratic order was impossible unless conservatives had a place in it.... [H]is agenda was not that of a fascist, but of a reform-minded conservative democrat." Patch notes the similar outlook of Stegerwald's aide in the DGB headquarters, Heinrich Brüning, the future chancellor of the Weimar Republic who had to cope with the Depression by means of emergency measures on the authority of the president, von Hindenburg. By 1938, strangely enough, Stegerwald seems, despite the harassment he experienced from the regime earlier, to have come to a certain appreciation of Hitler's achievements (Forster 2003, 612). Then he was arrested after the July 20, 1944, assassination attempt, with which he had nothing at all to do, and survived to help found a predecessor to the Christian Democratic party before dying on December 3, 1945, in Würzburg.

14. A close American counterpart of the Catholic workers' associations of Europe was the Association of Catholic Trade Unionists (ACTU) started by John Cort in the 1930s. In both cases, the members of the Catholic association, which was not a trade union, belonged to and were active in their respective unions. In the Dutch and Belgian cases, however, the unions themselves were Catholic (i.e., pillarized).

15. On the WAZ, see D. Müller 1996, 212; Aretz 1978, 25–29; for membership, see Klein, Ludwig, and Rivinius 1976, 27.

16. Grebing 1985, 195.

When one looks at the grass roots of the Catholic labor movement and specifically of the Catholic workers' associations, the career of Otto Müller (1870–1944) comes into high relief.[17] As a young priest of the archdiocese of Cologne he was assigned to a parish in Mönchengladbach and collaborated with the Volksverein. He was a principal in the founding of the *Westdeutsche Arbeiter-Zeitung* in 1899 and headed the Volksverein's department for the organization of Arbeitervereine from 1904 to 1917. He was also executive secretary of the organizationally distinct Arbeiterverein federation of Western Germany, headquartered in the same building in Mönchengladbach as the Volksverein. The death of Cardinal Fischer in 1912 and the accession of Felix Hartmann as archbishop of Cologne from 1912 to 1919 put a crimp in Müller's activities at the diocesan level. Hartmann aborted Müller's promising efforts to launch a parallel women's movement. Then, in August 1918, Cardinal Hartmann dismissed him from his post as diocesan moderator of the Catholic workers' association.[18] This was while the war was still on and a reform of Prussian suffrage was being debated. The Catholic workers' organizations were in favor of one man one vote; the *WAZ* took up their cause. Their statutes as church organizations prohibited electoral activity. The bishops took a firm stand against modifying the rather clericalist-paternalistic statutes; Müller's opposition led to his separation from the Cologne branches under Cardinal Hartmann. However, Karl Joseph Schulte, then still bishop of Paderborn, used his influence to let the supervisory board of the broader supra-diocesan Catholic worker federation of Western Germany, of which Müller had been executive secretary all along, elect him its *Präses* (presiding officer).

Soon, however, revolutionary events overtook this controversy about the political activity of the Arbeitervereine. With the republic proclaimed, all church people were anxious to line up as many votes as possible for Center candidates for the national assembly after November 1918. No one worried about politicizing the Catholic workers or their organizations. The inner-church struggle then turned to the role of the clerical moderators (*Präsides*) of the labor movement. Would they continue to run the organizations as before? Otto Müller wanted a lay co-moderator alongside a priest at every level of the organization in a framework of much greater lay participation and initiative. This became the practice. Even if the priests had been called spiritual advisors, as in the Netherlands, their role would no doubt have remained quite prominent, under the motto "Workers up front, with priestly leadership."[19] Unlike in Dutch Catholicism, the priest advisors or chaplains in German Catholic organizations of *white-collar* workers did not have a comparable role, as white-collar employees were treated differ-

17. See Aretz 1979, 3:191–203.
19. Haffert 1995, 67.
18. O. Müller 1976, 2:942, 951–60.

ently from skilled and unskilled labor. The diocesan moderators were placed in the sometimes difficult position of reconciling episcopal priorities with the claims of the working class. All the same, with the support of bishops (Schulte was now, since 1920, cardinal in Cologne), the Catholic labor movement revived in this format, despite the difficulties, and with a new democratic élan. It never quite regained its former relative strength, all the same.

The lay and worker element was strengthened by the institution of labor secretariats, operated jointly by the regional Arbeitervereine and the Volksverein.[20] These resembled the contemporary social secretariats of Belgium and France; they also often worked hand in glove with the locals of Christian labor unions. Staffed by a lay secretary trained through a Volksverein course, these secretariats offered help at negotiating the bureaucratic hurdles facing workers applying for unemployment or health benefits; they encouraged savings programs and initiated consumer co-ops. Not under the formal supervision of clergy, such secretaries could take part in and support specific labor struggles more freely than the Arbeitervereine in their official meetings. They were also an influential presence in the regional meetings of delegates from the small local associations.[21] The Center Party might even choose one to stand for a Landstag or Reichstag seat. Labor figures such as Otte, Kaiser, Elfes, and Joos came through one of the ten-week training courses directed by Heinrich Brauns in Mönchengladbach before World War I, then served as Volksverein stewards or labor secretaries back in their home towns.

Heinrich Brauns (1868–1939) was another leading figure.[22] He was well known from his earlier career as the Volksverein priest and labor educator who was present almost from the beginning of revived Christian unionism among the miners around Essen in 1894. He had the unusual distinction of serving as labor minister in all the varied cabinets of the Weimar Republic from 1920 to 1928. When the monarchy fell in November 1918, he had hurried to Berlin to urge the formation of a new party, more inclusive than the old Center and more democratic.[23] Though this was not to be, he entered politics for the first time, having spent the years since 1900 at Mönchengladbach training a generation of labor functionaries and other social Catholics in practical social policy. In this

---

20. In Bavaria these labor secretariats were set up under the aegis of the Verband Süddeutscher Katholischer Arbeitervereine led by Carl Walterbach (1870–1952) as *Präses* and Rudolf Schwarzer (1879–1964) as lay general secretary. This milieu organization had its own "Mönchengladbach" in Munich, the "Leohaus." It was developed with the aid of the entrepreneurial talents of Georg Ernst (1880–1953); see Denk 1980 and Krenn 1991; for the labor secretariats in particular, see Krenn 1991, 111–19.

21. Haffert 1995, 71.

22. Mockenhaupt 1973, 1:148–59.

23. Cary 1996, 52–53; Mockenhaupt 1977, 112–40.

capacity he had defended the interconfessional unions against their Catholic integralist critics who wished to deprive them of their autonomy. He was elected to the constitutional assembly and subsequently to the Reichstag, therefore, as a champion of worker self-determination and interconfessional cooperation. His political strategy insisted on the integration of the working classes in the government processes—not just as present by virtue of persons like himself from non-socialist parties, but definitely also by the socialist deputies and ministers elected by the larger part of the working class.

Adam Stegerwald's career made him another key figure.[24] He was a participant in the emergency negotiations to mediate the Stinnes-Legien agreement with leading industrialists on November 15, 1918, to form a joint consultative body, the ZAG (see chapter 2). This "Central Cooperating Partnership between Business and Labor" was a consultative body put together in the first place to assume responsibility for an orderly demobilization of industry, given the governmental vacuum. Under the leadership of Carl Legien, the socialist ("free") unions welcomed the support of the Christian unions against the attempts of revolutionary "Spartacists" to overthrow society as one knew it. The danger of a communist dictatorship was a real one as the emperor fled into exile. So the leader of Christian labor joined hands with the reform forces of German socialism to stave off a worse catastrophe than had already taken place. In that desperate hour even the captains of German industry were anxious to join forces with moderate labor union leaders. The *Zentralblatt* of the Christian unions reported a few days later, "Democracy has made its entrance into German heavy industry."[25] Unfortunately, most industrialists were not prepared to offer a permanent abode to their new guest. They were able to subvert the ZAG once it had served their transitional purposes.[26] They could not ignore unions any more, to be sure, though they reverted to their wary treatment of organized labor.

Although Stegerwald was glad to have a seat at the table for Christian labor, his reach went far beyond that. Alongside socialist labor and its party, he thought, there needed to be another labor movement that could include all those working people in a democratic state who were repulsed by the Marxist vision of a society shorn of patriotism, religion, and private-property rights.[27] To create such a movement, he organized the DGB (Deutscher Gewerkschaftsbund) in 1919, bringing the office and sales workers' unions that were of a distinctly nationalist cast under the same roof with the Christian union federation

---

24. See Forster 2003; Misner 1991, 273, 281–85.
25. Schneider 1989, 140; see the text of the agreement on 426–27.
26. Balderston 2002, 1; Kolb 2005, 14 and 179–80.
27. Morsey 1973, 1:210–12.

that he already headed (the GcG). The DGB was a decidedly more neutral body in worldview than the GcG. It included not just workers with religious loyalties, but persons and organizations for whom the church affiliation was of little interest. Stegerwald was always a politician as well as a labor leader. His federation of labor and employees' organizations provided a model, he thought, for the new party that the Weimar Republic needed, a more comprehensive (and hence less Catholic) party of the center. Stegerwald, supported in this by Heinrich Brauns, was convinced that the party system had to be reshaped, since the parties formed for the nondemocratic suffrage of imperial Germany no longer corresponded to the needs of political decision-making.[28]

Hence, in a controversial pronouncement he made at the tenth convention of the Christian Trade Unions (GcG) in Essen in November 1920, Stegerwald called for a realignment of political parties on nonconfessional lines, just as his GcG and DGB were open to anybody who respected religion.[29] The different proposals by Brauns and Stegerwald to form a new party out of all non-socialist but socially progressive forces, a center party that would abandon the name and the factual Catholic exclusivity of the Center, were ably turned aside by the leaders of the existing Center Party.[30] Brauns thought that the protection of confessional schools, the main point of contention between center and social democrats, was sufficiently guaranteed by the Weimar constitution. Now that the rights to associate and to vote were so broadly extended, the need was for a broad centrist party to mediate between the socialist labor left, with its revolutionary program, and the extreme right, with its reactionary tendencies.[31] The parliament's work would be immeasurably assisted by such an updated rearrangement of the political parties. Given the resistance of the parties as constituted, however, Brauns shifted his focus to working for labor justice within the political constellation in which he found himself. Stegerwald let his trial balloon drift in the political currents and maintained his active role in the Center Party. He even became the prime minister of Prussia in a minority coalition cabinet during some tense months in 1921—Matthias Erzberger's assassination happened in August.[32]

Christian Labor's Aims and Gains

The staff in the Berlin headquarters of the Christian unions (GcG) worked hard keeping the movement afloat through the years of inflation and building it up again thereafter. Stegerwald remained head of the GcG as well as the DGB, but

28. Morsey 2002, 35–36.
29. See Patch 1998, 27–29; see Patch 1985, 63–75; Forster 2003, 279–89; Schneider 1989, 157; Cary 1996, 74–99; Mommsen 1996, 64.
30. Cary 1996, 92.
31. Brauns 1976, 105–7.
32. Patch 1985, 70–72; Forster 2003, 290–319.

brought in Bernhard Otte of the textile workers' union to be general secretary of the Christian blue-collar Gesamtverband as he devoted himself more to the bigger political and labor picture (DGB). Otte, interestingly enough, acknowledged that the Christian tradition proposed no concrete pattern for an economic order or system, no Third Way. It differed all the same from liberalism and socialism by insisting on a further purpose for all economic activity beyond increasing wealth, purposes requiring justice and charity.[33] In 1924 GcG opened a training center, "Unser Haus," in Königswinter near Bonn. Theodor Brauer helped develop the ideological line of the federation and school its activists.[34]

On the DGB side, Stegerwald moved his new personal assistant, a young economist and future German chancellor, Heinrich Brüning, into the position of business manager or director in late 1920. The constituent Christian trade unions, of which the miners under Heinrich Imbusch and the metalworkers under Franz Wieber, along with Otte's textile workers, were the most important, retained their own structure and engaged in their own labor organizing, bargaining, and parliamentary exertions.[35] Less concerned than Stegerwald and Brüning about bringing nationalist-authoritarian elements into the Weimar fold, each functionary developed a characteristic talent. Otte was the organization man of the Christian unions, markedly adaptable to changing circumstances. Jakob Kaiser, at work in the Berlin union headquarters since 1921, was convinced of the legitimacy of the Weimar Republic: for him democracy was nonnegotiable. He was in charge of liaison with the regional offices of the Christian unions, with an eye toward placing union representatives on the Center Party's electoral lists. Brauer's chief concern was the solidarist and corporatist ideal of a vocational order and the role to be played in it by trade unions. What they all had in common that set them apart from the nonlabor contingents in the Center Party and at large was a particular concern for the interests and rights of workers in society.

That meant "economic democracy" in some form or another, preferably by employers accepting union representation of their employees and bargaining in good faith. The call for economic democracy echoed in both socialist and Christian labor venues. In the wake of the political democracy that came with the Weimar Republic, it was natural to think of some sort of democracy or say in the economic sphere for the working masses. The notion was obviously susceptible to different interpretations. In socialist usage it meant an eventual nationalization of productive capital. For Christian theorists and activists, however, it did not necessarily mean an overthrow of capitalist ownership of the means of production, but measures that would restore the priority of

33. Hömig 2003, 119.
35. See Patch 1985 and Schneider 1982a.

34. Rauscher 2004, 54.

human persons (owners, managers, white-collar and blue-collar wage earners) over things—that is, capital. In this solidarist outlook the separation of ownership and labor that characterized modern industry was not of itself reprehensible, but it was problematic in that persons (workers) became subject to the controlling laws of profit and return on investment in an unbalanced way. The advantages of competition in the commodities marketplace over a state-administered economy appealed to the solidarists with a background in economics. The ideal of the older generation of Catholic social ethicists seemed to be fulfilled in the ZAG, a working community with equal labor and capital representation, or even in the constitutional guarantee of the right of association. But as the ZAG failed to show results, others wished to go further. They wanted *Mitbestimmung* (codetermination) realized in works councils and worker participation in stock ownership.[36]

The eight-hour day (forty-eight-hour week) was one main point,[37] a concrete and burning demand that seemed within grasp. Before World War I the unions had achieved a ten-hour day, six days a week. The ZAG agreement of November 15, 1918 (in paragraph 9) stipulated the eight-hour day as mandatory, but the requirement did not hold up during the economic hardships of the ensuing years.[38] Nevertheless, it remained a principal demand of the unions. When the inflation crisis subsided, Brauns managed to reestablish the eight-hour day in certain industries, with exceptions permitted. He submitted legislative proposals to establish compulsory arbitration of labor disputes, to develop works councils and codetermination, to provide housing for workers and ease the lot of victims of war. He encouraged a sort of social partnership where the sometimes recalcitrant partners (labor unions and manufacturers' associations) would confer in a three-cornered dialogue with public officials. Thus his unbroken tenure in office enabled him bit by bit to build on the legal precedents and institutions of the Bismarck legislation in the 1880s. The outcome of World War I and the disastrous inflation that followed would be followed a few years later by the Depression and the Nazi takeover. The development of the social state of Germany in the Weimar Republic would be short-lived,[39] but it would be taken up again after World War II.

No doubt the signal achievement of Weimar social policy, a prime concern of Heinrich Brauns, was to confirm the principle of unemployment compensation as an insurance program, one regularly financed and administered by employers and employees in industry.[40] These laws passed only in 1927, after years of negotiations.[41] They aimed at a social state rather than a welfare

36. Stegmann 1974, 199–200; Klein, Ludwig, and Rivinius, 1976, 1067–69.
37. Mockenhaupt 1977, 197–201.   38. Schneider 1989, 426.
39. See Hong 1998.   40. Mockenhaupt 1977, 207–9.
41. Mommsen 1996, 226.

state, the difference being that the principle of prepaid insurance prevailed for the workers' lifetime needs in productive industries, reducing the ambit of the welfare safety net from general tax revenues to other cases of need. These achievements of the Weimar Republic in social legislation were the result not only of Brauns's patient cultivation of good relations and understanding with his colleagues in the Reichstag, both on the right and the left, but also of Stegerwald's strategy of seeding the German National Party on the right with his DGB colleagues. Remarkably, despite the resistance of industrialists in the Center and the other parties to reinforcing the eight-hour day in particular, the 1927 legislation finally made its way through, with the support of an unusual swath of parties from moderate left to right.[42]

The consistency and originality of the line Brauns followed often escaped observers. As minister of labor, Brauns was not one to propose vast programmatic or systemic changes. Nevertheless, he did keep a decidedly non-utopian ideal in mind, one he hoped to serve with all his varied proposals and initiatives in social policy. That ideal was the (timeless) solidarity of human persons in community and the (contemporary) dominance of industrial labor, with the need to assert the dignity of workers as human persons conscious of their worth and determined to play a responsible role in the world of work and of affairs. In 1922 he expressed himself as to this orientation in a way that showed his fundamental agreement with the Catholic solidarist school of Heinrich Pesch while addressing himself to a broad pluralistic public. "The unifying thought at the base of [Weimar's developing] labor code is a new idea of work and the place of the worker. All these laws no longer see labor as a commodity.... They pivot on the worker as a person and on that person's humane integration and role in the realms of rights and the economy."[43] This was not just a moral ideal, but had direct economic ramifications. Human capital, he was convinced (though he did not call it that), was the most important factor of productivity. In terms of legislative options, his solidarist perspective cashed out in insistence on social equity as justice and not just charity, and on participation (hence self-governing boards with employer and employee representation to administer the funds).[44] Employers, however, had had enough and were happy to see him leave his cabinet post in 1928.[45]

42. Ruppert 1992, 256.
43. Brauns 1976, 92–93, in Mockenhaupt's edition; the work was first published in 1922.
44. Christine Teusch (see Ballof 1975), one of the few women in the center's parliamentary delegation, reminded the Reichstag that the Center's former social policy expert and advocate, Franz Hitze, had insisted upon the principle of unemployment *insurance* rather than welfare a quarter-century earlier. It was also she who brought the unions' proposal to the floor to create industry-wide job registries in connection with the insurance administrations; Ruppert 1992, 252–56; from 1918 to 1920 she had been in charge of women's issues for the GcG.
45. Winkler 1994, 329.

Lively debates took place not only in the political arena of Weimar Germany, but among Catholics as to the proper updating of Catholic social theory in the modern industrial economy.

Controversies over Capitalism and Socialism

In the mid-1920s tensions between Catholic employers and their workers in the Rhineland presented a problem to the hierarchy.[46] The German bishops had considered various ways, even excommunication, to dissuade Catholic workers from joining socialist unions. At the same time, they tried to remain above the fray by not taking sides between the Christian unions and employers, as in the Ruhr mining fields after the French-Belgian occupation of 1923—an awkward balancing act for the parish clergy in the mining regions. In the months following April 1925, Cardinal Schulte of Cologne, at the request of Catholic industrialists, invited labor leaders and social economists (Goetz Briefs, Theodor Brauer) to an exchange of views on the legitimacy of capitalism. The release of his so-called *Kölner Richtlinien*, the "Position of Catholics in Regard to the Present Economic and Social Order," was delayed until January 1927. It made use of the term *mammonism* for the abuses of capitalism, but both industrialists and trade unionists viewed it as having come down on the side of the status quo. It defined capitalism broadly—so broadly that it would apply to any economic system in which capital was indispensable—and thus offered little guidance for reform.[47]

A related series of conflicts involved the lay representatives of Catholic labor, Joseph Joos (1878–1965) and Wilhelm Elfes (1884–1969). Joos was identified with the confessionally Catholic labor movement as editor of the *WAZ*.[48] Joos himself, though a worker denied secondary education, never belonged to a union. He became a Center Party deputy in the Weimar Assembly in the democratic breakthrough of 1919 and remained in the Reichstag until its dissolution in 1933. Wilhelm Elfes replaced Joos as chief editor of the major labor weekly in

---

46. See Haffert 1995, 122–37. This was contemporaneous with the Austrian bishops' statement on social questions in Advent of 1925 and the consolidation of Catholic workers' organizations in Belgium and the Netherlands.

47. See Stegmann 1974, 165–67, and Nell-Breuning 1972c, 99–115, here 106–9. The text can be found in a booklet with a characteristic title, *The Catholic Church's War on Two Fronts against Capitalism and Socialism* (*Der Zweifrontenkrieg der katholischen Kirche gegen Kapitalismus und Sozialismus*, in Briemle 1928, 1–9), together with the Austrian bishops' statement of 1925 (ibid. 10–38). The editor, one Theodosius Briemle, then printed bishops' warnings against socialism from the revolutionary days of 1918–19, the 1925 Heidelberg Program of German Social Democracy (58–66), a section (66–74) dwelling on the prominence of Jews not just in moneyed circles but among socialists, and finally a selection of choice quotes showing how antireligious the socialist movement was.

48. Wachtling 1973, 1:236–50.

1919, but Joos continued to write prominent articles and gradually became the main spokesperson for the Arbeiterverein movement. In this capacity with *WAZ* and hence with the Arbeitervereine, he was, as Stegerwald would acidly note, "an employee of a church organization."[49] Notably, he and the Arbeitervereine supported the left wing of the Center Party and thus did not share Stegerwald's preoccupation with his unionists in the nationalist parties.

In 1926 an episode involving the editorial line of the *WAZ* had repercussions that brought a new generation of leaders to the direction of the Catholic workers' movement in Weimar Germany. It illustrates the role that the mutual prejudices of Catholics and socialists played in their inability to pull together in time to prevent the loss of democracy. At the center of the dispute was one Wilhelm Elfes. Elfes was a laborite since his youth, when, shortly after being orphaned at the age of thirteen, he learned the smith's trade. He was working in the railway shops in Krefeld as a mechanic in 1904 when he found what he was looking for: in the pages of the *WAZ* he was introduced to an authentic workers' paper and movement that was not marred by anti-religious declamations. This brought him to a local Arbeiterverein and thence to a full exposure to Heinrich Brauns's Volksverein course in 1908. It cost him his job, but after some months of seeking and finding other work, the Arbeiterverein in Krefeld decided to hire him as second secretary. Then, in February 1911, Otto Müller brought him to Mönchengladbach to be assistant editor of the *WAZ*. In 1919 Elfes succeeded Joos as editor of the labor weekly.[50] In regard to the socialist unions, like so many of his Christian unionist colleagues, he regretted the strident and coarse anticlericalism of socialist propaganda. He criticized the dominant unions for neglecting sound trade-union goals that could better the workers' lot and instead devoting their resources to "silly partisan agitation."[51] In 1919 he expressly blamed the unfortunate split between Christian and socialist unions on the latter.

In 1926, however, Elfes detected some indications that the free unions were not as irresponsible in their training and publicity as before. Closer to home, he picked up the mood of disgust that was growing in Christian labor grassroots over the complete indifference or stubborn refusal of employers to pay any heed to the human dignity of their workers. Industry's abandonment of the November 1918 ZAG agreement rankled. Just at this time, Otto Müller and Joos were meeting with Catholic industrialists under the patronage of Cardinal Schulte to try to defuse tense labor-management relations in a time when unemployment remained high and employers maintained their rejection of the eight-hour day. Elfes gave voice to the workers' mood in the pages of the *WAZ*, beginning with the issue of February 27, 1926.[52] Certainly, he wrote, it is good

49. Wachtling 1974, 132.
51. Ibid., 79.

50. Esser 1990, 26–43.
52. Ibid., 82.

to see efforts at reviving a ZAG-like arrangement between employers and employees; nevertheless one must realize "how unpopular this idea has become across the whole labor spectrum. Instead, what the most alert minds of those working in factories and shops are thinking of is a [horizontal] 'working arrangement' among all union organizations." There was little or no sign in his view that "the ruthless force and lack of comprehension" of the bosses was about to fade. Therefore unionists will be forced, whether they like it or not, to cease their internecine struggles. Instead, communist, socialist, and Christian workers will "have to employ all their efforts in closest contact with each other for our economic struggle for life, respecting every sincere worldview and political conviction" in a unified movement.[53] Elfes thus underlined the need for a unitary labor union confederation on the basis of religious and political pluralism, so as to concentrate on economic issues. Qua labor organizations, they should keep at arm's length of overtly partisan politics.

The ideal of a unitary labor union movement effectively dedicated to the social and economic emancipation of the working class was not at all new in social Catholicism. Expressing it in these terms, however, was to criticize the existing ties in Catholicism between labor and the Center Party as well as between the DGB and other non-socialist parties. Was there not also an implication that the claims of the working class possessed a practical priority before the claims of religion? This disturbed a person like Joseph Joos, but also challenged the efforts of Müller and Brauns patiently to continue work on a long-term process of interclass harmonization. Not only that, but Elfes challenged the bishops' line on expropriation of the princes, a referendum question on which they had issued a pastoral letter. And the *Gesamtverband* of Christian unions found their anti-socialist raison d'être put in question, as did the Center Party. Theodor Brauer published more essays on the incompatibility of Christian and socialist social ideals. Stegerwald paid a visit to Mönchengladbach and demanded that Otto Müller add a trade unionist to the editorial staff of the *WAZ*.[54] The upshot was that the Joos and Müller "recommended" Elfes for a suitable position in the civil service without telling him. The socialist Prussian minister of the interior offered him the post of police president in Krefeld. Upon realizing with pangs of regret that his senior colleagues wanted him out, he accepted that office and stayed until removed by the Nazis in early 1933.

53. Ibid., 77.
54. Ibid., 80–83.

Struggles and Setbacks

There were other strains in the Catholic bloc, as well. After World War I, Müller and Brauns, who had been so involved with the Volksverein in Mönchengladbach, found it less and less relevant to their practical interests.[55] On the one hand, the unions and Catholic workers' associations more and more took over the training of Catholic labor functionaries by themselves. The large Catholic Women's League also declared its autonomy from the Volksverein. On the other hand, August Pieper and Anton Heinen of the Volksverein self-consciously took up a new direction. These two now saw their mission as promoting adult education of all classes with a view to inculcating a communitarian outlook.[56] This was to go to the roots of the social problem, they thought, implicitly dismissing the pragmatic approach taken by Brauns and Müller as superficial.[57] The practical problem raised by this switch in programs was the lack of a sufficient public for their recast course offerings. Since they were no longer geared to the civic action and practical skills that worker secretaries or union functionaries needed, they attracted only volunteers in church work of various kinds who mostly lacked the stipends that would increase enrollments. The formation work of the Volksverein would receive occasional subsidies for its adult education from the Weimar ministries of labor and agriculture. Still, the disgust of the practice-oriented leaders was unmistakable. In 1921 Otto Müller referred to the new line taken by Pieper and Heinen as "sentimental" "rubbish about community." Gustav Gundlach, SJ, was an academic critic.[58] Looking back in 1955, Paul Jostock concluded "that A. Pieper and A. Heinen, two principle pillars of the Gladbach central office, dug the grave of the Volksverein despite themselves."[59]

Even though this ill-defined romantic exaltation of organic community was popular in the burgeoning youth movements of the time, the Volksverein struck postwar youth as an old-hat organization that did not appeal to them. The principal audience that the Volksverein still attracted seems to have been farmers and teachers. Cardinal Schulte made a gesture to bring the Volksverein some episcopal support and strengthening, but Fr. Pieper wanted independence. A bit like Stegerwald in this, he was something of an anticlerical when it came to episcopal oversight. The dire financial straits of the Volksverein started to become clear in 1928.[60] At this point the bishops did reluctantly take charge,

---

55. Misner 1994e.
56. *Gemeinschaft* as opposed to *Gesellschaft*; see Baumgartner 1977, 87–117.
57. Hürten 1992, 121.
58. See Baumgartner 1977, 9 and 117. Stegerwald too, in 1928, rejected the romantic but "obfuscatory politics of a folk-community ideology." However, this was under the immediate impact of his failed bid to be elected the Center Party leader; Ruppert 1992, 344.
59. Klein, Ludwig, and Rivinius 1996, 2:152–56; see D. Müller 1996, 122–23.
60. Around the same time, the counterpart of the Volksverein-cum-workers-organization

accepted the resignation of the feckless business manager, and integrated the Volksverein into official Catholic Action. Its troubles were not over, however. The Nazis administered the coup de grace in 1933; after the Second World War, despite its glorious pre-1918 history, it did not rise again.[61]

Stegerwald, for his part, remained focused on achieving a better synergy of the non-socialist labor movement with parliamentary and party politics. He was acutely conscious that the labor constituency was not just inevitably split by the threatening collectivist theses of socialism and attitudes toward democracy but also, unnecessarily, by religious loyalties and antipathies that spilled over into electoral politics. He also had to remind his Center Party colleagues from time to time that he was head of a union federation many of whose members belonged to other political parties. In the Christian blue-collar part of his union federation (at the eleventh congress of the Christian unions in Dortmund in 1926),[62] he prevented an unambiguous expression of support for the much-assailed parliamentary democracy of the Weimar Republic. He did this at least partly so as not to offend the non-democrats in the employees' unions of the DGB. His argument alluded to the alternative of monarchy: hence it recalled Leo XIII's famous teaching on the relative indifference as to "forms of government" (classically monarchy, aristocracy, democracy). Such "Leonine accidentalism" was still normative in Catholic thought at that time and suited Stegerwald's tactical needs in wooing the nationalist wing of labor.[63] It also weakened his defense of the Weimar Republic.

The failure of Center and SPD voters to elect Wilhelm Marx as second president of the Weimar Republic in 1925 seems ominous in the light of later developments—Field Marshal Paul von Hindenburg was elected. In the 1928 elections the social democrats gained ground and headed a coalition. In the negotiations to form a broad enough cabinet to govern, Hermann Müller (SPD) wanted Brauns to remain as minister of labor, but he finally fell victim to the crosswinds of complicated partisan maneuverings.[64] Brauns left his post after eight strenuous and eventful years. His successor was prodigal in praise for what he had accomplished. While remaining in the Reichstag, Brauns also had to step in as interim director of the Volksverein in 1928 and 1929 to keep it afloat. Subsequently, just before the crucial Reichstag elections of March 1933, a decision of the Center Party removed his name from its list of candidates.[65]

---

in Bavaria, the Leohaus, got into financial deep water and even fraud (Krenn 1991, 108), leading to Georg Ernst's resignation in 1933. Fascinated by the potential of the cinema, he put the Leohaus into debt trying to develop a capability for making films.

61. Klein, Ludwig, and Rivinius 1996, 2:297–410.
62. See Schneider 1989, 185.
63. Cary 1996, 22.
64. Mockenhaupt 1977, 244–51.
65. Ibid., 1977, 157–60.

Even in retirement, however, Heinrich Brauns was not spared harassment at the hands of the Nazi regime.

Along with adverse economic winds, other political machinations and challenges also hampered the effectiveness of the Center Party in the final years of the Weimar Republic.[66] In 1928 illness forced Wilhelm Marx (who was also Reich chancellor several times between 1924 and 1928 and longtime chairman of the board of the Volksverein) to step down as leader of the Center Party. Stegerwald was in a strong position to be his successor, having served as Marx's deputy. Joseph Joos was put forward by party and Arbeiterverein members for various reasons having to do with reservations about Stegerwald. Some feared Stegerwald's well-known inclinations for coalitions with rightist parties, particularly the German National People's Party, where his Protestant labor allies had some seats. Government employees and agrarians in the party resented the Christian unions' well-publicized opposition to their own special interests. Would Stegerwald give up his posts in the union federations to become party leader? Yes, he said, but only if he were also head of the Center caucus of Reichstag deputies, which in practice he already was. This demand made him seem unduly power-hungry to some.

Joos had one quality recognized even by his critics that made him attractive as a candidate for leader of a party that was increasingly divided by interest groups. He was a conciliator. Though clearly aligned with workers and the left wing of the Center in the early years of the republic, he had always been open to compromise. A word portrait by a colleague catches his image in party circles:

Joos was a typical Alsatian, adroit, never offensive, possessing pronounced abilities for mediation and for expressing the finest nuances in a writing style that he had honed over the years as editor of the *WAZ*. When the debate went to such extremes that no ordinary human being could detect a common element, that was when he shone. Holding a slip of paper with a couple of notes, he would formulate his resolution and the reasons for it. Each side got a bit of credit and had to retreat a bit, but the weary controversialists also perceived the welcome possibility of bringing the debate to a satisfactory close. Thus, among the initiates, Joos bore the honorific title of "resolutionary."[67]

The other side of the coin, however, was that he had difficulty taking a stand and seeing it through against the inevitable complaints from one side or another. Stegerwald, for his part, was seen as determined and able—he was certainly qualified by much more leadership experience than Joos—but also stubborn, uncultivated, and unsympathetic to the status aspirations of the aca-

66. See Cary 1996, 135–41.
67. Cited in Wachtling 1974, 94.

demically qualified bureaucrats in the civil service, by now heavily represented in the party ranks. Added to this was Stegerwald's view that the ties to the world of Catholic associations and clergy were a hindrance to a political party's effectiveness. Joos and many others saw the Center's ability to appeal to a common religiocultural identity as still the Center's most powerful means to overcome the divergent interest politics that threatened to pull it apart.

The upshot was that the two Catholic labor leaders blocked each other's candidacy to succeed Wilhelm Marx as head of the party. At the last minute the party convention in December 1928 chose the canon lawyer Msgr. Ludwig Kaas, a little-known Reichstag deputy, with Joos coming in a distant second and Stegerwald a still more distant third.[68] Kaas, after a year or so, became more and more of an absentee party leader, unable to exercise the leadership that the times demanded.[69] Stegerwald came to terms with his defeat at the party convention and accepted the position of Reichstag caucus chairperson. He gave up his labor posts in the course of 1929 to devote himself full-time to politics, as he had intended to do in a higher capacity. He joined the socialist-led coalition cabinet in 1929 as minister. In 1930, under his one-time assistant, Brüning, he became minister of labor. It was a thankless task as "the triple burden of social welfare, taxation, and reparations" issued in financial breakdown during the Depression.[70] His and Brüning's governmental responsibilities ended with the appointment of Franz von Papen, whose policies they opposed, as chancellor in May 1932. Joos, still trying to hold the party factions together, picked up a good deal of the organizational work that Kaas neglected. Brüning shaped the public image of the Center Party as much as or more than anyone. The fact that the party remained intact in its final years had more to do with external circumstances than with the quality of the party leadership. The Nazi threat in particular brought a certain cohesion into its ranks for its short remaining life.

Catholic Labor with Brüning and against Hitler

The dismissal of Elfes from the *Westdeutsche Arbeiter-Zeitung* turned out to be something of a boon for the Catholic workers' movement in that two young trade union functionaries and Arbeiterverein members moved into positions of influence. Nikolaus Gross, originally a miner and then a regional secretary for the GcG in various places, became editor of the *WAZ* in succession to Elfes.[71] Heinrich Imbusch had brought him to Otto Müller's attention. At the

---

68. Lönne 1996, 162–65; see Morsey 2002, 37–39; and Kolb 2005, 79.
69. Ruppert 1992, 355–57.
70. McElligott 2009, 4.
71. Nikolaus Gross (1898–1945) was beatified by Pope John Paul II in 2001.

same time, Müller brought Bernhard Letterhaus to the central office as secretary of the West German federation of Arbeitervereine. In 1928 the Arbeiterverein moved its headquarters from Mönchengladbach to Cologne. In its new building, the Ketteler-Haus, with the connected apartment for the Letterhaus family, they would face the rise of Nazism and its supremacy, carrying on even after the liquidation of 1938.[72] They realized, despite all the talk of winning over workers en masse to their Christian ideal of labor, that their movement was engaged in a holding action, retaining its mostly older members.

Nevertheless, the new and more dangerous political threat from Nazism called forth a vigorous response. As one of the largest Catholic associations and the only one representing workers, the Arbeiterverein consolidated its membership, put itself behind Brüning's emergency plans, and proved to be quite immune to the Nazi siren song. It was also supposed to be able to carry on under Hitler by terms of the 1933 concordat with the Vatican, since it was not a labor union but a church organization. It actually did so in the first years of the regime. The editorials in the weekly regularly decried the religious repression in Soviet Russia, choosing incidents that bore an uncanny resemblance to Nazi moves. Letterhaus organized large demonstrative "pilgrimages" of workers to traditional Rhineland sites between 1933 and 1935. But the Hitler regime put a stop to that, concordat or no concordat. The two leaders were under surveillance for resistance activities and were executed as Allied forces closed in, Letterhaus on November 14, 1944, and Gross on January 23, 1945.[73] This was tragically in keeping with their dedication to an independent democratic labor movement that had marked their lives in the remaining years of the Weimar Republic.

Bernhard Letterhaus (1894–1944) was another Catholic labor activist, like many of the JOC leaders in other countries, who was intensely aware of what a hindrance his all too brief schooling was for him and for his like in the working class. Like Cardijn, he wanted to be a priest. Though his parents were as staunch Catholics as Cardijn's, they could not see their way clear to let him have a ninth and a tenth year of education. With exceptional intelligence and drive, he educated himself, especially after his military experience during World War I. Having worked in the textile industry before the war, he became an employee first for the Center Party, then, in 1920, for the Christian textile workers' union at its Düsseldorf headquarters. Maintaining a union stance in its negotiations with firms and politicians was urgent and consumed his days. He regretted that he was not able to devote more time to disseminating his hard-won knowl-

---

72. Aretz 1978; see also Aretz 1975, 2:11–24.
73. Aretz 1980b, 4:170.

edge and insights more broadly to Catholic workers whose situation he knew so well. Thus, when the new position was offered him at the Arbeitervereine, whose principal mission was formation, he eagerly accepted the challenge.[74] He personally trained the labor secretaries, traveled about giving lectures and stimulating local groups, wrote for the *WAZ*, and entered politics in the train of Joos and others as deputy in the Prussian and Rheinland legislative bodies.

In 1928, having just arrived in Cologne with the rest of the Arbeiterverein staff, Letterhaus gave a major address to the first congress of the Catholic Worker International (see chapter 3). He acquitted himself of the assignment masterfully and with verve. He spoke of the situation of the wage-earner in capitalist countries and assessed it from the perspective of Catholic social ideals.[75] He acknowledged that industrial capitalism had provided an unparalleled standard of living for millions of workers. This level of material security, still insufficient in many cases, would not have come about except for the restraints on laissez-faire achieved by other societal forces, notably labor unions. This improvement in meeting the material needs of the majority of Europeans was not therefore the result of the individualistic ideology most capitalists swore by. Nor, as doctrinaire Marxists would have it, was such progress merely illusory—it was real enough, though precarious.

There were, however, he emphasized, psychic and social needs of the human person, the fulfillment of which was still denied to wage earners in general. It was not humane to spend a working life in a shop carrying out assignments with no opportunity to contribute one's ideas to improve production and working conditions. To exclude the workforce of an enterprise or industry from all knowledge as to what was going on there, when their livelihoods were most at stake, was unworthy of a human being. Letterhaus's personal emphasis on the need for education of workers and for transparency of management came to the fore here.[76] Letterhaus hoped, given a greater communicativeness and less secrecy on the part of management and manufacturers' associations, to narrow the gap between capital and labor and enhance productivity at the same time. Workers who were treated as partners rather than tools, he argued, would see their human dignity respected and would respond in kind.

---

74. Aretz 1975, 2:13.

75. Klein, Ludwig, and Rivinius 1976, 2:1042–79. To judge by the 1928 statutes of Germany as well as the international Catholic labor movement (Hömig 2003, 130–33), the reservations or nuances about Third-Way thinking that we noted in chap. 3 for the theorists did not come through very well to the activists. The "main aim" of the movement is described as "to construct a new economic and social order out of the principles of Christianity." They also described themselves as the movement of and for a *Stand*, despite Gundlach's observation that they in fact belonged to an economic *class* and wanted justice and equality for that class.

76. Klein, Ludwig, and Rivinius 1976, 2:1059–63.

The times were inauspicious for further stages on the path toward a social state. Heinrich Brüning was chancellor from April 1930 to May 1932.[77] Letterhaus and others in the Christian labor movement supported his austerity measures to get the Reich's financial house in order. Despite the way this affected workers, Letterhaus trusted Brüning's economic competence and sense of social fairness in an increasingly desperate situation. Brüning could not get a majority in parliament to support his budget, however, and had to rule without parliament by the emergency powers of the president, von Hindenburg. A most unreliable source of authority! Von Hindenburg replaced him with Franz von Papen and Kurt von Schleicher, neither of whom could round up support in the new parliament with a Nazi plurality. Another election, another majority of extremists: somewhat fewer Nazis, but more communist deputies. Rule by emergency presidential authority continued. Von Hindenburg appointed Adolf Hitler as chancellor on January 30, 1933, and the last Reichstag election, with plenty of Nazi terror, took place on March 5.

Center Party votes were needed to pass the enabling act of March 23, 1933, and they were forthcoming. It handed dictatorial powers to the government under the chancellorship of Hitler by a "democratic" parliamentary abdication. The alternative, Center Party deputies were convinced, would be a civil war or violent coup d'état. Some persuaded themselves to vote for a suspension of civil rights (ostensibly until 1937) only to prevent a bloodbath of the socialist and trade union supporters. Apart from the socialists, Catholic labor circles remained the firmest opponents of the takeover. In the caucus before the decisive vote, Heinrich Brüning, Friedrich Dessauer, Heinrich Fahrenbrach, Heinrich Imbusch, Joseph Joos, Jakob Kaiser, Adam Stegerwald, and Joseph Wirth were among the fourteen of the seventy-four Center deputies who were prepared to vote no. In the end, again out of well-grounded fear of bringing down retaliation against anything or anybody connected with the Center Party, most of the fourteen joined the rest of the party in voting for the Enabling Act.[78]

The case of one of the Reichstag members, Heinrich Imbusch (1878–1945), heir to the proud traditions of miners who had owned a home and garden, is emblematic of the trajectory of organized labor in the Weimar Republic. He was the leader of one of the most important Christian trade unions in the GcG and DGB, the miners' union. In the Ruhr, it held its own with the socialist union

77. Kolb 2005, 120–22; see Balderston 2002, 88–98.
78. Patch 1998, 289–99. A controversy has raged among historians as to whether Cardinal Pacelli influenced Msgr. Kaas, the head of the Center Party, to accede to the Nazi seizure of power. The motive would have been to smooth the path for the concordat between the Vatican and Germany that was in fact concluded only four months later. Hubert Wolf (2010, 126–78, especially 170–78) argues convincingly, however, that the Center Party parliamentarians acted on their own under pressure without knowledge of any Nazi proposal for a concordat.

and even overtook it in membership, partly because of Imbusch's dynamic leadership. At no time did he forget that he was a union man first and foremost. His attitude hardened at the time of the 1923 occupation of the Ruhr by French and Belgian troops, when the mine owners took advantage of the country's desperate need for export income.[79] They embarked on a course of rolling back the legal gains that labor had made during and after the war: participation in policy decisions through the ZAG, the eight-hour day (for miners, seven hours per shift actually down in the bowels of the earth), and, of course, wages. In response, the collaboration of socialists *and* the labor deputies in the parliamentary delegations of three non-socialist parties that led to the legislation of 1927 was the high-water mark of that strategy of Stegerwald and Brauns. The industrialists fought back and garnered the support of civil servants and other bourgeois factions in these parties to neutralize union influence. In the case of the Center Party, Stegerwald's third place in the election for party leader to succeed Wilhelm Marx was one probable effect of this lobbying.

Imbusch took the measure of the reaction against the foundations of labor peace enshrined in the Weimar constitution from the tenor of the mine owners' stands in collective bargaining and arbitration. His visceral dislike for these capitalists lent a passion to his defense of workers' rights that often excluded any willingness to parlay with them beyond assailing their positions and arguments. In 1932, having taken the place of Stegerwald at the head of the DGB while retaining his base in the miners' union, he called for a nationalization of the mines.[80] In general, his positions were close to those of pragmatic socialist union leaders, more so than most of his colleagues in the Christian unions. He went into exile in the Saar when his union was disbanded in 1933. The arc of his career before then describes the overall fortunes of the working class in Weimar Germany: breakthrough in the November 1918 ZAG agreement and in the Weimar constitution, resistance against the setbacks of 1923, political influence despite the reluctance of other classes in the few years of relative prosperity, followed by enormous difficulties, economic and political, from which Hitler emerged to force the independent labor movements underground and into the resistance.

The rise to power of Hitler in 1933 meant the dissolution of labor unions or, in Nazi-speak, their "coordination" with the newly established German Labor Front. Jakob Kaiser regretted his vote for the enabling act and declined to sign the document that put an end to the Weimar trade unions and replaced them with the German Labor Front.[81] Although jailed for a time as an "enemy of the

---

79. Fischer 2003, 214 and 233–43; see also 63.
80. Schäfer 1990, 229 and 237–38.
81. See Patch 2005, 185–87. There were also those who tried to accommodate social Catholicism

Reich," he managed somehow to carry on in Berlin as an unofficial advocate for the small army of trade union functionaries deprived of their positions and their pensions. He would gather their documentation and then visit government offices and even the office of vice-chancellor von Papen to plead their cases. Under cover of this activity, already risky in itself, he entered the resistance even before Letterhaus. He worked especially with other former labor leaders, especially with Max Habermann of the white-collar side of the DGB and Wilhelm Leuschner, the noted social democratic resistance figure.[82] Kaiser was one who survived the Nazi regime, despite his centrality to the July 20, 1944, plotting.[83]

The travails of democracy were particularly stark in Germany, and the Christian labor movement underwent them in dramatic fashion. What was learned from these experiences can only be seen from the later post–World War II story of the successor generation in a profoundly changing culture.

---

to the new regime for a while. Theodor Brauer, the labor intellectual, even celebrated the end of the unions in May 1933, as clearing the ground for the establishment of an "organic vocational order" à la *Quadragesimo Anno* (Hürten 1992, 225; see Schneider 1982a, 759–62; Patch 1985, 224). Brauer was no Nazi sympathizer, all the same. He was arrested in July and eventually was able to emigrate to the United States. Among leaders of the Catholic Arbeitervereine, by contrast, no such cases of even temporary accommodation are to be found; Aretz 1982, 2:186.

82. Hoffmann 1996, 355–70.
83. Kosthorst 1975, 2:151; see Mommsen 2003, index.

CHAPTER 10

Italy and Austria

CHRISTIAN LABOR AT GRIPS WITH AUTHORITARIAN RULE

The defeat and disintegration of the Austrian Empire led to the Treaty of St. Germain with the victorious powers in 1919 Paris. Italy having joined the latter, it incorporated the formerly Austrian territories of the Trentino, South Tyrol, Trieste, and Istria. This chapter traces the history of Christian labor movements in both Catholic countries, focusing on developments roughly from the Versailles peace conference to the Depression. Again, democracy was at stake. How did the anti-democratic reaction affect workers? How did Catholic workers' organizations cope with this trend while bending their efforts to improve the position of the working class in a capitalist economy?

Catholic Labor Unions and the Italian Popular Party

The formation and alliance of the Christian workers' federation in Italy, the CIL, and the newly formed Christian democratic party, the PPI, is recounted in chapter 2.[1] In the century before, the Papal States had reluctantly succumbed to the unification of Italy, leaving the pope a "prisoner in the Vatican," surrounded by anticlerical (liberal) forces in the prevailing Catholic perspective. The Roman Question was the name given to the situation sealed in 1870, when the unifying Italian state took over Rome and surrounding provinces from papal rule and the popes refused to accept the Law of Guarantees passed unilaterally by the Kingdom of Italy. Rather than accept a settlement of claims for compensation as if the Papal States were simply a principality now merged into united Italy,

---

1. See Sergio Zaninelli 1981a; Vecchio 1981.

popes Pius IX and Leo XIII insisted on recognition as a sovereign power quite independent of the Kingdom of Italy.[2]

Meanwhile, social Catholicism made great progress in some parts of the country, notably in the North (Lombardy, with Liguria, Piedmont, and the Veneto). The problems of the South, the *Mezzogiorno*, were also high on the concerns of Luigi Sturzo, whom Pope Benedict XV appointed to be secretary of the Popular Union, the guiding institution at the national level of Italian social Catholicism.[3] The social changes and expectations induced by the war from 1914 to 1918—the government promised to spread the fruits of victory democratically—called imperiously for the creation of a national labor federation and a political party for those mass elements that remained averse to socialism—which is to say, for those Catholics of Italy, who found the undemocratic ruling class of prewar years as repugnant as socialist candidates. What alienated so many Catholics about the socialist and the liberal parties, besides their respective class-based antagonisms and deficient political programs, was the anticlerical (Masonic) bias both had in common.

The existing labor unions led by Catholics got together in March 1918 for the founding congress of the CIL (the Confederazione italiana dei lavoratori) and provisionally named Giovanni Battista Valente as its general secretary.[4] This was followed by Sturzo's success in founding a political party, the Popular Party (PPI, Partito popolare italiano) by the end of the year. It will be noticed that both bodies appealed explicitly to Christian principles while at the same time declaring their autonomy with respect to the church hierarchy. Neither claimed to speak for the church, or for all Catholics, or only for Catholics. Both wanted to relieve the hierarchy and the papacy of responsibility for initiatives or political choices that they, as nonconfessional organizations, might make. Knowing that other options would rightly always be open for Catholics, they requested no express backing or permission from the official church. Accordingly, they expected church authorities to abstain from anything like an exercise of veto power.

Without wishing to unfold the meteoric history of the PPI from 1919 to 1926, this issue of autonomy is one of several factors that connect the newborn party's fate to that of the Catholic labor movement.[5] (Another, noted in chapter 3, would be the international ties that both the political and the labor organizations cultivated systematically.) The rise and fall of the two bodies was not merely simultaneous but interdependent in terms of constituency, leading personnel, and overall democratic aims. The democratic turn, enabled or even

2. Wolff 1987.
3. See Misner 1991, 240–61.
4. See Robbiato 1984, 935; Canavero 2003.
5. For the PPI during this period, see Molony 1977 or Pollard 1996, 77–82.

forced by the war, required the political organization of previously nonvoting masses as well as the union organization of the working masses for the pursuit of their legitimate economic and social interests. Both required an independence or autonomy in relation to the official church that would respect the distinction between the proper mission of the church as community of faith and the legitimate pluralistic political and economic interests pursued by Catholics and others in society. Further complicating the relationship of the two newly organized branches of the Catholic movement in Italy was the issue of the autonomy of the labor movement from the political party.[6] Yet another complication would soon become apparent: both new foundations depended upon the social and operational support of the web of existing Catholic organizations. If the attitude of the official church turned frosty, that would spell trouble, no matter what.

The necessity of autonomy vis-à-vis the hierarchy was nevertheless clear to Luigi Sturzo and Giovanni Battista Valente and to many other social Catholics, though not to all, and certainly not to many conservative Catholics untouched by a social Catholic outlook and prone to authoritarian solutions. The conviction of Christian democrats was that social justice in the modern world could only be achieved through democratic processes. No one who shared the ideals of social justice and democracy was to be kept out of these two parallel movements. Hence the appeals to "all the strong and free," as the PPI manifesto of January 18, 1919, stated—not calls for obedience to papal or episcopal directives or appeals to denominational loyalties.[7] The programmatic maturity of both the PPI and the CIL at this time is impressive, ahead of analogous platforms of the 1920s. Valente, of course, benefitted from his time in Germany with Stegerwald's Gesamtverband of Christian unions.[8]

The other labor leaders who came together in the CIL would have their differences but were at one on the program points of 1918.[9] First and foremost was the burning question of the hour—putting a system of social insurance in place that would move relief of insurable misfortunes of the worker from the realm of spotty charity and the dole to that of covered risks: old age, accidents, sickness, unemployment. This would require the nation to adopt the policy of mandatory contributions rather than voluntary adherence. The Catholic unions specified the principle of three-way funding from contributions of the wage-earner, the employer, and the state. Longer-term goals included the participation by workers in a firm's ownership and management so as to put an end to their status as proletarians. This may seem quite advanced,

6. Canavero 2003, 231.
8. Saba 1983.
9. Tramontin 1980, 3:361–65; see Zaninelli 1982, 491–95.

7. Malgeri 1980, 3:327.

especially for Italy, where the rift between Catholicism and the legal country was recent and deep. One might expect cries of state socialism, but patriotic wartime dreams of national rebirth, together with the increased civic importance of industrial workers, had so changed the face of European politics that such demands could no longer be simply dismissed. (Nor could they be realized in the few years remaining of parliamentary rule.)

It is true that the socialist unions had made some of the same proposals—for instance, the eight-hour day—and brought them to the attention of the government before 1918. The red unions had a head start on the white ones, which in most areas played catch-up. Due to a 1904 provision of the Giolitti government, socialist unions alone could appoint representatives to government boards such as the High Council of Labor.[10] Hence they alone were in a position to put such items on the study agenda of official bodies. Their rivalry with the Christian-led unions during the immediate postwar period went so far as to perpetrate daily assaults on CIL members.[11] Still, after a while, PPI and PSI (socialist) deputies in parliament could and to some extent did vote together to press such issues. The Catholic unions, which had protested their exclusion from the beginning, made a big push for rights of participation in these consultative bodies at all levels. Despite the presence in the cabinet in the years 1920–22 of a PPI deputy as undersecretary of labor (Giovanni Maria Longinotti, the fatherly friend of the later Pope Paul VI, Giambattista Montini), such recognition was not forthcoming.[12]

Giolitti's obstructionism at this late date perhaps had much to do with his liberal resentment toward Luigi Sturzo, whom, as a political priest, he was unable to treat *sine ira et studio*. Sturzo rightly regarded nonconfessionality, or autonomy with regard to the church hierarchy, as a necessary condition of participation in the democratic process. It made no impression, unfortunately, on his political rivals (or on political cartoonists, needless to say). In regard to Catholic labor organizations, however, Sturzo wanted them to submit to party discipline in the interest of a united interclass front. Sturzo had Valente replaced as general secretary of the CIL for that reason;[13] the young Giovanni Gronchi took his place in 1920, while Valente became editor of the CIL newspaper.

Giolitti's animosity toward white unions and grudging favoritism with regard to the red ones offended Valente deeply—after all, the CIL, unlike the socialist CGL, was in principle committed to the common good and hence willing to consider the welfare of other classes as well as that of the industrial proletariat.[14] The white labor movement was committed to the Christian ideal

10. Pollard 1997, 173.
11. Canavero 1982.
12. Malgeri 1980, 3:98–99.
13. Malgeri 1983.
14. Valente 1978.

of interclass solidarity. In practice, however, interclass solidarity had meant paternalism or at least initial domination of labor organizations "by wealthy Catholic notables and by the clergy."[15]

All the same, by early 1919, the CIL had a million members. This comeback took place on the basis of a network of Catholic institutions for and of workers, concentrated in white parts of the country in the North. Comparative success in labor organizing was more notable in agriculture than in urban industry, apart from the textile union that Achille Grandi headed from the Milan area beginning in 1916. As for agriculture,

> Catholic trade union membership was chiefly found among sharecroppers, small tenant farmers, and even small landowners, but there were significant pockets of support among the *braccianti* and other labourers in Cremona, the stronghold of the Catholic deputy and peasant leader Guido Miglioli, and in other provinces in the Lombard plain. The particular strength of the Catholic organisations in the agricultural sector may be attributed to a number of factors: the appeal of the Catholic ideal of the small peasant landowner to marginalised groups (as opposed to the Socialist aim of collectivisation); the idea of the "co-management" of large farms adopted by Miglioli, and, possibly, the feeling that the Socialists were not fundamentally interested in the agrarian question.[16]

Miglioli, highly educated, dedicated himself to the workers in the Po Valley dairy farms around Cremona.[17] He could make common cause with neither the landowning plutocracy of anticlerical and anti-democratic liberalism nor the Marxist vision of a dictatorship of the proletariat. Miglioli worked against paternalism in the unions he organized by first dropping any religious qualification for joining except respect for one another's religious beliefs and loyalties. Second, he carried out aggressive labor actions when they had a chance of improving conditions, whether his own bourgeois kind would approve or not. He was in fact a pioneer of a fairly radical kind of *Mitbestimmung* calling for worker participation in (or even control of) the management of the large local dairy operations for years before 1914. In the course of World War I, as parliamentary deputy, he wholeheartedly supported advanced causes such as the eight-hour day even for agricultural workers. He took up the slogan of peasant soldiers, "*la terra ai contadini*." After two decades of grassroots pressure, he brought the Cremona movement to an arbitration success in 1921, the "Lodo Bianchi."[18] It provided for a fundamental change in the relationship of employer and worker in this grain and dairy region.[19] Up until then, of course, the landowner or

15. Pollard 1997, 171.
16. Ibid., 174.
17. Fappani 1982.
18. Ibid., 381; Foot 1997, 423. The deal thus agreed upon was named after the professor, Antonio Bianchi, who worked out the draft.
19. Tramontin 1980, 3:272–74.

leaseholder ran the farm, paid wages, provided housing, and so forth, all on the basis of contracts that he could change almost at will. Now the farm would be transformed into a cooperative of production, 30 percent of the profits of which would go to the owner to indemnify him for his loss of control and as return on his investment. He might also receive a salary for his management services. The workers and laborers, for their part, would receive a minimum wage and participate in the overseeing of the operation and its profitability through representatives, while sharing among themselves 70 percent of the return. They would also have the opportunity to buy into the capital of the enterprise, becoming partners with—or eventually buying out—the agrarian capitalists.

This pact was signed in August 1921 by representatives of the landowners and the workers after Miglioli's white leagues carried out repeated strikes and occupations. The unhappy farm owners only signed under coercion, in that the workers had already taken over effective control of the farms. They discovered, however, that they could nullify their concessions by hiring fascist squads to destroy union headquarters and the cooperatives, thus reestablishing their own control. Cremona rapidly became the fief of Roberto Farinacci, the most brutal and anticlerical of fascists. Under him, Blackshirts took over municipal government and banished Miglioli himself from the area after giving him a beating and burning his house down. The agreement never went into effect, therefore. Similar if less radical plans were, however, implemented elsewhere, thanks to the Catholic farm unions, during the *biennio rosso* (red years) of 1919–20.[20] The ultimate aim of many Catholic agrarian activists was the peasants' own ideal of broadly distributed small ownership of farm land (a family farm ideal repudiated by the red farm workers' movement). That aim, however, did not stand in the way of immediate practical steps that would improve the lot of the rural worker, whether they were hired hands, sharecroppers, or tenant farmers. Thus one pressed for longer contracts, with protections against evictions and cancellations, "seeking to assure that the farm worker did not feel exploited by the bosses, but at least to some degree could feel he shared in the fruit of the land that he worked."[21] One leading authority goes so far as to claim that the brief white union burst of activity after World War I, together with socialist organizing, actually started a new trend that continued after the white and red unions were put out of action: to wit, a gradual transfer of farm ownership from investors to the farmers themselves.[22] It was a bad business, after all, for investors, in that it could only remain profitable for them if the exploitation of farm labor continued unabated.

20. For details on these white peasant leagues, one can usefully consult the biographies and bibliographies in *DSMCI*, vol. 2 (1982) of figures named in this chapter.
21. Tramontin 1980, 3:274.
22. Zaninelli 1981b, 348–50.

As the fascist violence grew, the white and red rural unions reluctantly sought each other's help in 1921 and 1922, but it was too little, too late.[23] As was the case in urban unionism, the Christian unions came to exemplify the Italian proverb of the earthen vase caught between the stone jug and the iron barrel. Before the red labor organizations and the allied socialist party leaders could see the white leagues and their representatives in the PPI as necessary partners rather than rivals for the allegiance of the masses, the Blackshirts and their "unions" had detached much of the higher clergy and moneyed elements in Catholic Italy from any ties to democratic social Catholicism. Then too, Achille Grandi, now (1922–26) head of the CIL, could not see his way clear to an actual merger with (and domination by) the socialist union confederation.[24]

Although Miglioli and Sturzo both concentrated on farm labor, not fully appreciating the key role of industrial labor, the northerner and the southerner did not see eye to eye on the way forward. Miglioli wanted to take the interclass PPI to the left and make it the party of "the Christian [rural] proletariat."[25] Sturzo, with the development of the South at heart, saw the natural market for the North of Italy to be central Europe, while southern Italy would find its economic health in trade with the Mediterranean basin—to put it anachronistically, in agribusiness. He opposed all radicalism. Though he had worked with Miglioli over the years and congratulated the dairy workers for their breakthrough, he certainly did not see the Lodo Bianchi as a model with wide applicability. In his words to the Cremonese, he struck his typical notes of interclass solidarity (no dictatorship of one class over the others) and urged them most of all to increase productivity.[26] Moreover, he was head of a party that was on the whole so anti-socialist that parts of it welcomed the new fascist movement once it showed it was anti-socialist, too. Not that the reds were ready for pluralistic cooperation in labor policy, either: they were on the whole so anticlerical that they could not bring themselves to acknowledge the good faith of Catholics, not even of a Miglioli.[27]

The autonomy from clerical authority claimed and exercised by the white unions could be more or less emphasized, but it was practiced seriously on the union end; it was a necessity, a condition of any possible effectiveness in their struggle for social justice. The authorities of the waning liberal government and the representatives of the secular left, unfortunately, would not acknowl-

---

23. Foot 1997, 429.
24. Grandi (1883–1946; see Robbiati 1998) started work as a linotypist at age eleven in 1894 and was employed as a Catholic labor propagandist in Lombardy starting in 1907.
25. De Rosa 1982, 619.
26. Foot 1997, 424.
27. Antonio Gramsci was a partial exception to this state of affairs; see, e.g., Foot 1997, 431.

edge that the clerical leading-strings had been cut. To admit it would have been to make a proportionate place for the CIL at the labor-management negotiation table. Hence the issue of labor pluralism (as opposed to a socialist, later a fascist monopoly) became a life-or-death issue for the white unions and all too soon for any free union movement at all.[28] The unions, red and white, suffered massive hemorrhages of membership in 1923–24 with the rise of the fascist movement. Benito Mussolini finally took power after the March on Rome in late 1922. With the coincident election in February of 1922 of the Milanese Achille Ratti as Pope Pius XI, it soon became apparent that the autonomy and the freedom of unions to organize and bargain would no longer be possible. If any components of the Catholic labor movement in Italy were to be saved (for instance, cooperatives, credit unions, study circles), it would have to be under the shelter of the institutional church by way of "Catholic Action."

Catholic Action and Catholic Labor
The Antecedents of Catholic Action before Pius XI

The organizations of Catholics formed in nineteenth-century Italy had observed the *non expedit* policy and hence concentrated on local elections while abstaining from national politics. What was most significant was the network of self-help institutions, centered on the parishes and stimulated and federated in the Opera dei Congressi. This was a predominantly lay organization, somewhat on the lines of the German Catholic associations that gathered once a year for a *Katholikentag*.[29] The term Catholic Action (Azione cattolica) was applied loosely to the whole phenomenon of organized lay undertakings on behalf of religion. Pope Pius X dissolved the Opera dei Congressi in 1904, when its internal tensions between democrats and paternalists broke out into the open. He then appointed lay leaders whom he could trust over its reorganized parts, establishing papal and, at the local level, episcopal control over its activities. Besides the sections for propagating the Catholic social vision (the Unione popolare, then under Giuseppe Toniolo) and for social and economic action such as credit unions and labor organizations (the Unione economico-sociale, or UES), Pius X set up an electoral union to guide partial Catholic participation in elections, case by case. The days of the *non expedit* were fading. Other national Catholic lay organizations recognized as part of Catholic Action were the Gioventù cattolica (young men) and the Federazione universitaria cattolica italiana (FUCI) founded in 1896 for university students.[30] The Union among Catholic

---

28. Zaninelli 1981b, 354.
29. Misner 1994c; Tramontin 1981; Misner 1991, 240–56.
30. Giuntella 1981.

Women, which Pius X approved separately and directly, rather than tolerating a lay intermediary between women's organizations and the hierarchy, was viewed as something of a women's auxiliary of Catholic Action.[31]

Benedict XV created a central office for all these organizations in December 1915. The president of the Unione popolare since 1912, the young Giuseppe Dalla Torre, was named president also of the overall organization. The pope charged the Unione popolare with devising a programmatic action plan for all the components of Catholic Action. These would henceforth be affiliates or subgroups under a joint board of directors, with the Unione popolare as its brain trust. Luigi Sturzo was its secretary, thus becoming a stable presence at the national level of the Italian church. Pope Benedict XV gave Christian unionists a space in the UES (Unione economico-sociale) in which to develop and then let them go their way independently. During the red biennium in March 1920, he reproved the self-styled extremist tactics of the extremely militant Ufficio del lavoro in Catholic Bergamo under the short-lived leadership of Romano Cocchi, but let the clergy cooperate with the rest of the lay leadership of Catholic labor.[32] In 1918 Armida Barelli (1882–1952) founded the national feminine youth organization that was still lacking. Since 1915 she had had remarkable success in Milan, organizing women's groups into a branch of Catholic Action. The war brought about a sharp upward reevaluation in the minds of many churchmen of the need for articulate and engaged Catholic women in Italian society.

The Stamp of Pius XI

Achille Ratti was elected pope as Pius XI in early 1922 and wielded power at the apogee of papal prestige in Catholicism until 1939.[33] He wanted Catholic Action to be the prime instrument in making the church more influential and effective in modern Italy—and succeeded to a considerable extent.[34] As the creaky mechanisms of the liberal state gave way to the strong-man rule of Mussolini, Pius XI issued new statutes for Catholic Action.[35] They would transform it into a mass-mobilizing force that was headed for an uneasy coexistence with the rival pretensions of the Fascist state to mobilize Italian society for its own purposes. The electoral union had become redundant with the formation of the PPI and even more so with the coups of the coming dictatorship. The Economic-Social Union and the Unione popolare similarly faded. The labor unions it had fostered were now autonomous economic associations, not religious ones, though

31. Dau Novelli 1998, 114.
33. Chiron 2004.
35. Durand 1990, 362–63.

32. Foot 1997, 425; *AAS* 1920.
34. Casella 1992; 1996; Misner 2004a, 655–58.

obviously a product of Catholicism. They fit in poorly with the religious and clericalized focus now being emphasized in Catholic Action. Count Dalla Torre welcomed these developments from his position as editor of the *Osservatore Romano*, to which he had moved in 1920. Luigi Colombo, the lawyer-activist who preceded Grandi as the first president of the SIT (the largest Catholic industrial union, for textile workers), became head of Italian Catholic Action (ACI). The pope knew Colombo from the latter's similar position in the huge Milanese archdiocese.[36] He could rely on him and Ida (Armida) Barelli to execute the new policy firmly and energetically.

We had a look at the Italian model of Catholic Action from one perspective earlier, in chapter 4. Another look is now in order to place it more fully in its Italian context and development, together with labor issues. The Italian Azione cattolica that emerged from its 1923 statutes would remain in force until 1946. It approximated the stark simplicity of a fourfold organization of the faithful: one national association for the parish circles of each of the "natural" groupings: adult men, adult women, young men, young women. The actual four associations at that point were those of Catholic men (in process of formation), of (male) youth, of university students (male: FUCI), and of women. The women's association was subdivided into university women (a somewhat suspect group), adult women, and the dynamic feminine Catholic youth organization. They were joined (only) at the top by a Giunta centrale that brought their presidents together with a few other members (clerical assistants), all appointed by the pope.[37] Pius XI made no attempt to palliate the top-down character of his Catholic Action approach. Although autonomy-minded members of the PPI and CIL did not find it congenial, there were plenty of Catholics who did. For them as for the pope, democracy and autonomy were weak reeds on which to lean. Authoritarian leadership was deemed necessary. Nevertheless, until fascist oppression made it impossible to engage in any other open organized activity, the membership of the Catholic organizations grouped together in Catholic Action slumped. The men's organization did not reach 100,000 until well after the Lateran Pacts of 1929.

The attitudes of Catholics toward Fascism and its leader, Benito Mussolini, ran the gamut from wholehearted welcome to uncompromising rejection, but most were somewhere between these two poles and subject to change.[38] Many preferred to regard the Fascist regime as a tolerable status quo, different from the conservative liberalism of the recent past but not necessarily worse on the whole. Those taking a stance now dubbed *afascismo* could regard it as a passing

36. Traniello 1995, 263.
37. Durand 1990, 363; Moro 1981a, 119.
38. Campanini 1998; Pollard 1994, 381–88; Durand 1990, 385–90.

phenomenon. They could dedicate themselves to nurturing the seeds of a future Christian order through Catholic Action, within the shell of Fascist Italy.[39] A number of the Christian democrats (in particular, Luigi Sturzo, Francesco Luigi Ferrari, and Giuseppe Donati) immediately and unwaveringly opposed the fascist phenomenon as completely unacceptable. During the red biennium just after the war, Mussolini's movement looked like socialists, so most Catholics had regarded them as a threat. Then, when he turned his squads on socialist agitators, people took another look but were largely in the dark as to the anti-social alliances that Mussolini was forming. Soon enough he eschewed his anticlerical positions and promised a return to normalcy, law, and order. At this point Pius XI became pope and retained Cardinal Gasparri as secretary of state. Both were attentive to the possibility of coming to terms with the strong man, to the benefit of the papacy and church. Such an understanding had eluded Pius XI's predecessors. After all, the liberal politicians in charge were not interested in any arrangement that might enhance the ability of the Vatican to wield its influence. In fact, it came about that Pius XI and Mussolini could arrive at a settlement of the Roman Question, hanging fire since 1870, in the famous Lateran Accords of 1929.[40] During the years (1926–29) that secret talks were in progress between the Vatican and Fascist Italy, Pius XI was willing to show Mussolini that the church would stay out of or withdraw from party politics.[41] The PPI, for all its vaunted nonconfessional character, labored under the unfortunate birth defect of being led by a priest, Luigi Sturzo. The Vatican insisted that he quit his political post in early 1924 and go into exile in London in October.[42]

Catholic Action was to be strictly religious, but by no means merely a "private affair" (as Lenin would have it). The short formula used by Pius XI to describe Catholic Action was the laity's "participation in the apostolate of the hierarchy."[43] That meant that its mass organizations could not be political parties or labor unions, since neither politics nor economic activities were the apostolic responsibility of the hierarchy. Instead of withdrawing into the spiritual realm, though, the lay participants in the hierarchically directed movement were to permeate the structures of society. Thus they would prepare the moral and spiritual groundwork for nothing less than the conquest or re-Christianization of

39. Moro 1981a, 232–33.
40. Coppa 1999, 87–96.
41. See D'Agostino 2004, 164–75.
42. See Pollard 1996, 79–82.
43. See Fouilloux 1990a; Chiron 2004, 199. Equivalent formulations can be found in Pius XI's first encyclical, *Ubi arcano*, par. 58 (in Carlen, 3:225–38, and in his 1925 encyclical *Quas primas* and several other papal letters and messages. The "classic reference" (Barral 1996, 594) is from 1934 (August 28 letter to Cardinal Schuster): "Catholic Action, which by definition is the collaboration of the laity with the hierarchical apostolate ... is an aid to the sacred hierarchy, to which it is subordinate, patterning itself according to its structure and organization."

society, including the political and economic sectors as well as public culture.[44] One must be clear that this integralist goal of Catholic Action was as yet untouched by pluralism. That is, neither the conservatives nor the progressives in Catholic circles, neither the authoritarians nor many of the democrats, recognized religious or cultural pluralism as legitimate, much less desirable, except as a lesser evil. Moreover, Pius XI may have supposed that the secular state of nineteenth-century liberalism was on its last legs—hence his lack of appreciation for Sturzo's attempt to integrate into it the Catholic element. From the papal perspective it was the moment for the Roman Catholic Church to step forward with its claims to provide the guidance society needed in a state that would recognize its supreme authority in the moral sphere. When he spoke of the kingship of Christ, as he often did, he included a prominent role for the Vicar of Christ in its temporal realization.[45]

The ramifications of the papal approach were many, positive and negative. Certainly, in the context of Italy and other authoritarian or even totalitarian states, if the hierarchy were able to preserve a zone of freedom for Catholics to pursue their own cultural life and the formation of youth in particular, this could and did in fact serve as a nursery of forces capable of advancing human rights. In democratic states to be, the Catholic Action emphasis on spiritual formation and training of zealous elites reaped a harvest of articulate lay activists who provided indispensable leadership, including also for political and economic values, when civil society reconstituted itself. Admittedly this did not take place in a new Christendom as Pius XI projected, but in a more broadly democratic social state. In the end it was shortsighted to suppose that in a modern society the plurality of basic worldviews could be reduced to one reigning Christian set of values without trampling on the personal dignity of human beings, itself a primary value of Catholic social teaching.

Pius XI's insistence on determining the scope of Catholic Action in terms of the apostolate of the hierarchy also posed a challenge to dominant forms of social Catholicism as they had developed since the nineteenth century. Henry Poels's subtle distinction between a Catholic and a churchly or ecclesiastical *standsorganisatie* reflected the reality of a labor movement for Catholics only (and hence not itself a labor union) dedicated to the spiritual *and* secular (vocational, civic) formation of its members, with lay people increasingly setting the policy and directions of the movement on their own responsibility. As we have seen, the relative autonomy of such organizations from the hierarchy also ran athwart of the Catholic Action approach of Pius XI. The Vatican declined to

44. Moro 1981a, 101–4.
45. Traniello 1995, 264–68 with 277.

acknowledge the Catholic Worker International (see chapter 3). Joseph Cardijn, in contrast (chapter 7), deftly negotiated the tensions between hierarchical clericalism, bourgeois paternalism, and lay initiative, making a convert of Pius XI to the Jocist way of specialized Catholic Action.

Christian Labor and Catholic Action in Italy

Achille Grandi, proponent as head of the CIL of a moderately militant trade unionism, worked collaboratively with the diocesan labor offices and was also a PPI member of parliament. As union numbers sank in 1923–24 and Catholic cooperatives in the countryside were exposed to the demolitions of the large landowners and their fascist paramilitaries, the white unions found ecclesiastical support more and more conditioned upon a separation from party—that is, elective—politics and upon a diminution of their autonomy—that is, their freedom of action to engage in job actions in the interests of workers. A pincer was closing in on the CIL unions from two sides. On the governmental side, Mussolini made no secret of his desire to eliminate the socialist and all other independent unions from the Italian scene. Step by step, as he consolidated his power, anti-union measures were taken. The agreement of October 2, 1924, between Confindustria (the national manufacturers' association) and the Fascist labor confederations, known as the Palazzo Vidoni pact, stipulated that they would bargain only with each other, thus effectively excluding the red and white unions from any meaningful role in labor negotiations. The Rocco law on trade unions, debated and passed in the first months of 1926, outlawed strikes in favor of compulsory arbitration.[46] The mere existence of unions (outside of the Fascist corporatist bodies), though without any freedom of action, was expressly permitted as de facto associations.

While this was going on the papal policy of gathering all lay Catholic organizations into the embrace of Catholic Action posed the question from the ecclesiastical side. Was continuation of the CIL unions under the aegis of Pius XI's Catholic Action a realistic alternative? After all, they could hardly survive without the financial support from dioceses and from Catholic Action in its previous form. Could some relative autonomy be agreed upon that would permit them to act like unions? This was still not altogether precluded until Mussolini's dictatorship was fully established in 1926. The Social Week of 1924, held in Turin under the sponsorship of the reorganized Catholic Action, around the theme of Social Authority in Catholic Teaching, was not promising.[47] The announcement of the theme quoted from Pius XI's inaugural encyclical *Ubi arcano*:

46. Pollard 1985, 33.
47. Duchini 1990, 63–64; Moro 1981a, 129.

Many believe in, or claim that they believe in and hold fast to, Catholic doctrine on such questions as social authority, the right of owning private property, on the relations between capital and labor, on the rights of the laboring man, on the relations between Church and State, religion and country, on the relations between the different social classes, on international relations, on the rights of the Holy See and the prerogatives of the Roman Pontiff and the Episcopate, on the social rights of Jesus Christ, Who is the Creator, Redeemer, and Lord not only of individuals but of nations. In spite of these protestations, they speak, write, and, what is more, act as if it were not necessary any longer to follow ... the teachings and solemn pronouncements which may be found in so many documents of the Holy See, and particularly those written by Leo XIII, Pius X, and Benedict XV.

There is a species of moral, legal, and social modernism which We condemn, no less decidedly than We condemn theological modernism.[48]

"Modernism"! No more damning label could be applied to Catholic activists, soon after the modernist crisis in the church.—Curiously enough, contrary to previous custom, no discussion after the speakers' preapproved presentations was allowed.

Over the winter Grandi and Giovanni Gronchi and no doubt other white union leaders had many a talk with their erstwhile colleague, Luigi Colombo, now with Catholic Action. In the interval between the Palazzo Vidoni pact and the Rocco law, they tried to find a way to save what could be saved of the white labor movement.[49] Meanwhile, in deepest secrecy, moves were under way to open talks between the Vatican and the Italian state to resolve the Roman Question, this time seriously. The end result for social Catholics was meager, the setting up of a sort of research office and coordinating headquarters for all the Catholic cooperatives and credit unions that remained. This was called ICAS, the Istituto cattolico di attività sociali, headed by a priest, Giovanni Balduzzi, and directly subordinated to (and protected by) the central office of Catholic Action in Rome.[50] The main function of its studies section was to prepare the annual Social Week of Italian Catholics. In this sense it carried on, within the framework of reorganized Catholic Action, one of the functions of the defunct Unione popolare.[51] Lodovico Montini, the brother of Giambattista Montini (the future Pope Paul VI), served in this capacity.

The nails were driven into the coffin of the CIL as of the PPI in the waning months of 1925. In September those who attended the Social Week in Naples heard Dalla Torre denounce the very idea of autonomy in political or economic positions for any body of organized Catholics. As individual citizens they retained their freedom of choice, but all Catholic group undertakings had to be

---

48. Par. 60–61, in Carlen, 3:236–37.   49. Tramontin 1980, 3:285.
50. Moro 1981a, 166–68; Brunori 1981.   51. Albertazzi 1984, 3:941–48.

regimented under Catholic Action. Catholic Action, for its part, had to remain "apart from and above the political parties." Dissensions within Catholic Action, rife with regard to the proper attitude to be assumed in regard to the Fascist regime, had to cease, so as to arrive at the "supreme purpose of Christian restoration of society and state."[52] Then in the following months the central office of Catholic Action issued directives, in the tenuous hope of being able to work within the system for the better, that in effect gave up any resistance to joining the Fascist labor corporations.[53] Finally, the Christian labor leaders drew the consequences and shuttered their operation. Grandi's lamentation in a letter to a friend is understandable: "Catholic Action is taking on a great responsibility not only as to Catholic workers but all Italian workers. History will be the judge."[54]

The Concordat with Italy

What stance would the pope take with respect to Mussolini's regime? Pius XI's pontificate was rich and varied—one must not forget his condemnation of the Action française in 1926 and the letter to Bishop Liénart in 1928.[55] His closest collaborators often could not tell how he would respond to a given situation until he did. Nevertheless, for our present context, Pollard's focus hardly overstates the case:

In the 1920s and 1930s, under the guidance of Pius XI and Cardinal Gasparri, the policy of the Holy See towards secular governments and secular society in general could be summed up as "Concordats and Catholic Action." Vatican diplomacy in the reign of Pius XII was directed towards securing cast-iron, juridical agreements—concordats—as a means of regulating relations between the Church and national governments.[56]

With a view, of course, to re-Christianizing society under papal guidance.[57] In hindsight, it is apparent that Pius XI, at least until 1937, harbored illusions about how the Fascist regime might ultimately be subverted to serve the church's purposes.[58] True enough, he never thought that Mussolini had the interests of Christianity or the Catholic Church at heart. He hoped, however, that he might lay the groundwork for a future Christian society by taking advantage of Mussolini's suppression of Masonry, anticlericalism, and socialism. Catholics could then step into the breach and build up a sounder alternative through Catholic Action, protected through a concordat as "religious, not political."[59]

52. Moro 1981a, 137–38.
53. Ibid., 159–66; see also Webster 1960, 102–5.
54. Maraviglia 1994, 70.
55. Chiron 2004, 261–68, 211.
56. Pollard 1985, 4–5.
57. Chiron 2004, 196.
58. See Fattorini 2007 or 2011.
59. That this illusory strategy was itself too "political" in a reactionary sense is easy to conclude

Cardinal Gasparri was able to negotiate a treaty that created the Vatican City State and moreover declared in its first article that Roman Catholicism was "the only State religion" of Italy. The treaty was accompanied by a concordat (the second of the three "Lateran Pacts" of 1929) guaranteeing the church the freedom to carry out its religious mission. Given such concessions, the pope must have thought it was worth the sacrifices that the Catholic movement had made to achieve this result. Of particular note was Article 43, which would become a flashpoint of a major dispute in the very year of *Quadragesimo anno*, 1931. According to Article 43 of the concordat, Catholic Action was to be kept apolitical in the sense that all its organizations "maintain their activity wholly apart from every political party and under the direct control of the hierarchy of the Church for the diffusion and practice of Catholic principles." Clergy were reminded to stay clear of political parties. In return, "the Italian State recognizes the organizations forming part of the Italian Catholic Action" thus constituted.[60] By virtue of Article 1 of both the treaty and the concordat, Italy guaranteed "the free exercise of the spiritual power" to the Catholic Church. By Article 43, the mass organizations sponsored by the church were included under the guarantee of freedom. These pacts were signed by Mussolini and Gasparri on February 11, 1929, and then had to be ratified.

A one-choice plebiscite in March was the occasion of more or less favorable winks and nods in church circles, particularly on the part of Luigi Colombo (who would soon resign from the Catholic Action board). The reprisals to be expected in districts with a low turnout had their effect in advance. Mussolini reverted to his earlier anti-church rhetoric in defending the Lateran Pacts before his handpicked legislative assembly, indicating he had no intention of allowing any real freedom to the church in Italy; totalitarian claims to shape all of Italian society were upheld. The pope protested vigorously just before the ratification of the pacts in June, insisting on the centrality of the concordat and the autonomy of the church in the religious realm, the limits of which it would decide for itself. Mussolini went ahead with the ratification all the same. There followed a period of growth and renewal in Catholic Action cadres, closely

---

today. The connection between the dignity of the human person and certain human rights such as religious freedom for all and participation in government through democratic processes was not yet made in magisterial declarations. Catholics in positions of authority still tended to assume that there was a peculiarly Christian economic and political system that was necessary for the health of society. Democracy was a possible trait, but not a necessary one, of this restored Christendom. The state should be a confessional state, and any real societal pluralism of worldviews and religious convictions could at most be tolerated on its fringes. Paradoxically, however, the concordat strategy did succeed in providing a setting in which truly democratic and Christian future leaders were formed (Moro 1979). Catholic Action, with all its compromises, remained an independent or non-fascist mass organization, the only one that survived in Fascist Italy; see Coppa 1999b, 108–19.

60. Text in Pollard 1985, 214, and in Coppa 1999a, 204.

tracked by the police. Mussolini had evidently not reckoned with this revival and cracked down on the Catholic press (much reduced already), on parish centers, and on Catholic Action groups that showed too much vigor or where ex–Popular Party members were active.[61]

The crisis between the two signatories to the Lateran Pacts came over the education of children and youth. Who would get to influence the coming generations? The church considered this the right of the parents and then of the church itself. The Fascist position exalted "the ethical state" and claimed totalitarian control of the education of youth as a top priority. Regardless of what the provisions of the concordat in this regard (Articles 35–37) might say, Mussolini could not let the Catholics train successors with another worldview "and present them to the masses as such. If he let them do it, he would open a breach in his own ranks."[62] Labor issues also played a catalytic role in the crisis, as Pollard notes.[63] The central committee of Italian Catholic Action was planning a manifestation of Catholic social thought in the form of an international congress in Rome to celebrate the fortieth anniversary of *Rerum novarum*. Attacks in fascist newspapers on such meddling of the church in labor affairs led to skirmishes from March 1931 on the part of "unauthorized" fascist toughs. The Catholics nevertheless forged ahead with their plans, coordinated with the expected issuance of another papal statement on the reorganization of society in its economic dimensions (*Quadragesimo anno*).

The fascist press restrained itself as long as the 10,000 foreign Catholics were in Rome for the celebrations (May 15, 16, 17) and then broke out with denunciations of the unpatriotic complaints that the Italian local leaders were voicing to the Catholic Action heads about their life under Fascism. (The political police always had full details of these supposedly closed meetings.) Mussolini abruptly switched the campaign against Catholic Action to the governmental level at the end of May.[64] All over Italy police raided and shut down all the Catholic youth clubs. In Rome on May 30, 1931, the future pope, Msgr. Montini, was present at the FUCI offices when the police descended, searched the premises, and carted away boxes of papers.[65] All these Catholic organizations remained closed until September.[66]

61. Pollard 1985, 124–27; Moro 1981a, 191–211.
62. Comment of Palmiro Togliatti, the Communist leader, in 1931, as quoted by Moro 1981a, 234.
63. Pollard 1985, 134–45, 164, 173; D'Agostino 2004, 223–28.
64. Misner 2004a; Chiron 2004, 242–46.
65. Hebblethwaite 1993, 109–110.
66. A clandestine group of young Milanese Catholics, dubbed the "Movimento Guelfo," distributed thousands of flyers to the visitors in Rome celebrating the fortieth anniversary of *Rerum novarum*. The text denounced the political repression in Italy. They carried on such avowedly anti-fascist activity entirely apart from Catholic Action structures. The police did not catch up with them until later; see Moro 1981a, 247–54.

In his June encyclical, *Non abbiamo bisogno*,[67] Pius XI vigorously condemned the attacks on Catholic Action while holding out an olive branch to the government. Although Mussolini could not afford to let a Catholic Action in any way politicized to pass unchallenged, he was also interested in an accord that would quiet the choleric pope and integrate Catholicism into the Fascist state. The pope, for his part, was willing to apply the brakes to the remaining democrats in Catholic Action if the work of spiritual formation and influence on youth under the guidance of the hierarchy could continue or even, as he hoped not without reason, be extended.[68] Thus, in the *Osservatore Romano* of September 2, 1931, an official accord between the government of Italy and the Holy See was published. Its three points offered apparent further concessions to Mussolini: no politics, no labor union activity or training, no team sports for the young, just "occupations of a recreational or educational nature with a religious purpose."[69] The lay element was brought more firmly under hierarchical responsibility by the provision that the critical level of control was to be diocesan—the local bishop was to appoint, and be responsible for, all its leaders. Purging Catholic Action of old PPI activists was of the highest priority for Mussolini. By making the bishops responsible for Catholic Action, he would get tighter control.

The outcome of the 1931 September Accords is variously judged. In practice, the national offices went on as before, except that new people gradually replaced the directors who took seriously Pius XI's protestations that the church had a duty to teach about the moral and religious elements also in issues of labor and statecraft. The limitation of the youth clubs' activities did not stunt their growth. Many authors think that Clause 2 forbidding trade union activities put the quietus on the *sezioni professionali* that ICAS had set up to foment Catholic influence within the regime's corporatist unions. Pollard, however, notes the rapid emergence in post-fascist Italy of the ACLI (a Catholic labor milieu organization).[70] He argues that Clause 2 actually preserved the principle of a Catholic labor movement and provided a cramped organizational home for Catholic unionists to bridge the long hiatus between 1924 and 1944. *Il Lavoro Fascista* led the charge against Catholic Action in March 1931 because it claimed to have a role in judging economic institutions through its *sezioni professionali*. Here is the text of the second clause—Pollard makes a good case that Mussolini yielded to Pius XI's intransigence on this point:

67. Rendered by Hebblethwaite 1993, 110, as "We do not need this."
68. Pollard 1985, 157–61.
69. Text in Pollard 1985, 216, and Coppa 1999, 111.
70. Pollard 1985, 183.

The Azione Cattolica does not include in its program the constitution of professional associations and trade unions; consequently it does not set before itself any tasks of a trade union order. Its internal professional sections, already now existing and governed by the law of April 3, 1926 [the Rocco law], are formed for exclusively religious and spiritual purposes and *they propose further to contribute to the result that the trade unions juridically recognized* [the fascist ones] *may respond ever better to the principle of collaboration between the classes and to the social and national ends which, in a Catholic country, the State with its existing organizations proposes to attain.*[71]

All the same, there would be hardly any room for social issues to be discussed in Catholic Action forums. Mussolini's blow of the end of May, shutting down all the youth organizations until September, had effectively muffled the reception of *Quadragesimo anno* in Italy. (Chapter 11, following, delves into the encyclical itself and some of its consequences.) Paradoxically, in the very year when Pius XI celebrated papal social teaching and elevated it into a tradition for the church at large, it was overshadowed by *Non abbiamo bisogno* and soft-pedaled in the concordatary church of Italy.[72] No Social Weeks were held in Italy in 1930, 1931, or 1932. Studium, FUCI's independently chartered cooperative publishing house, which did not seem to be harried by the police, did put out an edition of the encyclical for study circles.[73]

Austria: Democratic Labor or Authoritarian Dead End?

The outcomes of World War I and the Paris Peace Conference were especially severe in regard to Austria (Treaty of St. Germain, September 10, 1919). The new nations that had taken shape from the remnants of the former Austrian Empire were recognized: Hungary, Czechoslovakia, Poland, and Yugoslavia. Other territory was lost as well, as in northern Italy. The "little Austria" that was left (with a population of some seven million, of whom two million were in "red Vienna") was subjected to unrealistic reparations that had to be modified subsequently. Many Austrians, for economic and nationalistic reasons, wanted to become part of Germany. The Peace Conference prohibited any such move unless the League of Nations approved, which was out of the question. Austria had very little space for maneuvering or setting its own course, given the political and economic constraints.

In the new, reduced, solely Germanic Republic of Austria, upper-crust liberals lost power to two mass parties: the Austro-Marxist Social Democrats (SDAP: Social Democratic Labor Party) and the conservative Christian Socials

---

71. Ibid., 1985, 216; see also 164. Emphasis mine.
72. Agostino 1991, 501.
73. Giuntella 1981, 299.

(CSP: Christian Social Party). The political parties contributed to the consolidation of the cultural camps dominating the nation, Catholic vs. socialist. The official church no longer had the Habsburg monarchy to lean on and turned to the Christian Social Party qua partner in government.[74] The Christian Socials embraced predominantly agrarian and middle-class interests. The Christian labor organizations were very much a minority in their own party and even more so in the labor movement as a whole. Christian (Catholic) labor unions did gain strength over the course of the 1920s, but never constituted much of a presence in heavy industry. As things turned out, prospects of a democratic alternation of power or power-sharing between the two evenly matched camps dimmed and eventually went down to authoritarian defeat in the wake of Hitler's rise to power in neighboring Germany.

Pre-War Legacies

The corporatist tradition that Baron Karl von Vogelsang had fostered so emphatically in Vienna did not remain unchanged or unchallenged after *Rerum novarum*.[75] Franz Schindler (1847–1922), a moral theologian and political adviser, trained some of the upcoming generation of priests in social ethics, stressing the need to study social conditions critically with the aid of serious economics and sociology. By 1905 he had departed quite clearly from the blanket rejection of capitalist industrialism that characterized Vogelsang's thought and that continued to characterize some of the Catholic "Wiener Richtungen" between the wars. In particular, Schindler's new brand of social consciousness would temper the approach of the Christian Social Party through the activity of his student (and successor as professor of moral theology in Vienna), Ignaz Seipel, and that of the young lay director of the Austrian Volksbund, Richard Schmitz.

Schmitz worked at the Volksbund starting in 1911.[76] In that year it made a splash by inviting Heinrich Brauns, himself enmeshed in the Catholic dispute over the interconfessional trade unions in Germany, to address a "social week" in Vienna. The Volksbund, after all, was to be the Danube's version of the Rhineland's Volksverein. It wanted to become the training ground for a new kind of Christian Social Party activist as the Volksverein was for the Center Party. The Christian Social Party had not made meaningful inroads into the industrial working class as such, but catered to the independent craftsmen

---

74. See Boyer 2005, 6–35 for the whole period; here 10; Boyer 1994; Diamant 1960, 7–78; Staudinger 1983, 1:253–56, and Van Duin and Poláčková 2005, 127–43.
75. Misner 1991, 169–88.
76. Boyer 1995, 307–11; Weinzierl 1983, 448.

and small shopkeepers of Vienna. By delineating a clearer social Catholic line, a positive Christian democratic orientation, the Volksbund aimed to change this state of affairs and enable the CSP to enter the new age of mass parties.[77] This meant it would distinguish itself, on the one hand, from liberalism and the anticlerical liberals (who in Austria were also largely Catholics) with their defense of the privilege of property and the status it brings. On the other hand, at the levels of ideas and political mobilization, it would resolutely oppose socialist or social democracy with its opposition to Christianity, its Marxist attack on private ownership of productive resources, and its ideal of a dictatorship of the proletariat. The Volksbund founders and leaders saw themselves frankly as embarking on an effort to hold the Austrian fort for a self-conscious kind of Catholicism against the socialist labor rivals who had such a head start.

A forerunner but right-wing example of this combative Catholicism was Anton Orel, who considered the Volksbund approach itself much too tame. Orel was the founder of the first Catholic workers' youth movement in German-speaking countries, around 1905. When he issued a "Manifesto to the working youth of Austria" at Easter 1907, the fierce anti-capitalist and anti-Semitic character of his program for the betterment of working conditions for apprentices did indeed become "manifest."[78] The charismatic traits he had in common with Marc Sangnier in France, who inspired him, gave his youth movement a certain élan, in tandem with a reactionary strain that would bedevil Austrian social Catholicism. He held himself and his movement to be the authentic social Catholics, the true heirs of Vogelsang. (In comparison with Orel's youth movement, the adaptability to modern conditions that characterized Sangnier's and Cardijn's approaches stands out in bold relief.)

For a while Leopold Kunschak, the leading Catholic voice of labor, folded the youth auxiliaries of his Christian workers' associations (Arbeitervereine) into Orel's movement. He shared his economic and cultural anti-Semitism with Orel, having picked it up independently from the Vogelsangian line.[79] This does not mean that he ever incited his audience to violence against Jews. What he favored was a policy that could be described as "separate but equal" (with the inequalities in practice that inevitably follow from such a public policy). The anti-Semitism common among Central European Catholics of the time was especially pronounced in the Austrian Catholic labor ranks. Poor nonassimilated Jews were one thing; prominent communists who were Jewish were quite another. "Social Catholics" did not shrink from fomenting a visceral distaste for Jewish influence in Austrian society. They regarded secularized,

77. But see Wohnout 2004, 172–74.
78. *Dokumente* 1980, 194; Pelinka 1972, 231.
79. Pauley 1992, 38–44 and 158–62; Weinzierl 1983, 470.

liberal, moneyed Jews as enemies of traditional Catholic culture as well as oppressors of the Catholic working masses. They harbored the common fantasies about Jewish plots to achieve complete control of the economy and politics.[80] Some prominent Catholics framed "the Jewish question" in outright racist categories.[81]

Kunschak, a former saddle maker's apprentice, led the initially quite small labor wing of the Christian Social Party in Vienna by virtue of having founded the Christian Arbeiterverein in 1892, just after *Rerum novarum*, when he was only twenty-one. The Arbeiterverein gave rise gradually to Christian unions. With the additional support of the Volksbund, Kunschak was active in politics before World War I and continued thereafter, representing the anti-socialist labor movement.

The Christian Social Party and Labor

The Christian union organizations had to start over from practically nothing after the defeat in 1918, as the socialist labor movement mobilized thousands, indeed one million by 1921 (a huge figure for such a small country, not sustainable at that level). The socialist unions also aimed at being the sole federation to represent workers in collective bargaining and, through the SDAP, in politics, as well. Nevertheless, the Christian union federations from before the war picked up the pieces. Favored by Christian Socials when in power, they grew from a starting figure of only about 25,000. Their members were often harassed in the workplace by socialist coworkers until, in 1928, the Heimwehr became active against both socialist and Christian unions, which by this time counted 100,000 members. The attacks by the Austro-fascist Heimwehr, financed by industrialists, on the Christian labor organizations began to persuade socialist union members to redirect their hostility against the enemies of democracy.[82]

Through this period Kunschak and Franz Spalowsky, the head of the Christian union central commission, battled within the Catholic camp in vindication of workers' rights while carrying on a campaign against the socialist unions for the right to form and belong to Christian unions unhindered by violence or other discriminatory moves. In October 1919 they prevailed upon the socialist prime minister, Karl Renner (later president of the republic, 1946–50), to disapprove of any such infringements of the right of association. After 1920 and especially from 1922 to 1932, the socialists were excluded from the coalition governments of Christian Socials and German nationalists. The socialist

80. Kertzer 2001, 272–75. 81. Connelly 2007.
82. Blenk 1975, 125, 139, and 153.

leader and ideator of Austro-Marxism, Otto Bauer, was opposed in principle to participating in the cabinets of bourgeois governments. Even so, some cooperation between the two camps, CSP and SDAP, took place, notably in the matter of legislation on social insurance.[83]

The Austrian Christian labor movement adopted its only platform or mission statement at Linz in 1923.[84] The Linzer Programm, as it was called, owed more to the Vogelsang tradition of *Sozialreform* (calling for a radical reshaping of society and political economy) than to the incremental and meliorist *Sozialpolitik* of Schindler and the Volksbund direction. It envisaged a corporative system that would organize society according to vocational groups (branches of industry). These would be largely self-administering, hence relieving the state of much of the need to regulate the economy. In each *Berufsstand* or corporative body there would be a place for the wage-earners of the industry as well as the holders of property interests in economic enterprises (the employers). Employers and employees would form subgroupings with equal rights in the corporative, regulative structure (not in the individual firms). The platform also advocated some level of codetermination (*Mitbestimmung*) and profit-sharing. The attitude toward social democracy and its free unions was one of clear opposition. The Marxist aims set forth in socialist declarations were in stark opposition to the Christian democratic and corporatist vision that the Catholic labor theorists put together from Catholic social thought in Vogelsang and *Rerum novarum*. Anti-Semitism expressed itself here in decrying Jews' roles in both capitalism and Marxism.[85]

The rivalry or rather bitter hostility between the small Christian labor movement and the well-developed Austrian proletarian socialist movement was just another facet of the relations between the two camps led respectively by Seipel and Bauer.[86] It was certainly part of the context for the Austrian bishops' statement of Advent 1925, "Teachings and Instructions on Contemporary Social Questions."[87] This pronouncement was conceived by Bishop Sigismund Waitz of Innsbruck with the encouragement of Cardinal Gustav Piffl of Vienna and the concurrence of the other bishops. Both of these prelates were inclined toward the solidarist school of Catholic social ethics rather than to the anti-modern, anti-capitalist trend of the Wiener Richtungen. It is no surprise to see the typical design of the statement, first critical of economic liberalism, then of socialism, so as finally to lay out what Christianity counseled in the economic situation of the 1920s. What may surprise and what caused a stir was the vehement *tone* of

---

83. Klose 1983, 336.

84. See Lugmayer 1924.

85. See Patch 2005, 187–193, here 188, for this whole section in greater detail; see Pelinka 1972, 213–16; Pauley 1992, 158–61.

86. Weinzierl 1987.

87. In *Dokumente* 1980, 206–21.

the condemnation of "mammonistic capitalism." Economic liberalism's ideal of laissez-faire, the bishops declared, has become "capitalism in the worst sense, rule by force of possession."[88] In the next paragraph, they stated that there was nothing wrong in principle with capitalist ownership of industry, commercial finance by credit, or employment for wages, all targets of the Orelians. But they denounced the commodification of workers' labor and the plutocracy, the like of which "has only been seen in the worst of pagan times."

Such rhetoric was supposed to show that the church was not in the pocket of the capitalists as the socialists charged; it may also have been intended to show that the passion of the anti-capitalist Catholics was justified and could be shared even by those who did not reject modern economic reality root and branch as immoral. But it lent itself easily to equivocation. Thus Orel, who rejected private property rights as "pagan" (from Roman law) and the charging of interest on loans as usury, was able to fasten on the denunciation of "mammonistic capitalism" as a description of the essence of capitalism, whereas the solidarists behind the document (such as the young Johannes Messner) condemned the "mammonistic" abuses but not the employment of private capital itself for gain. The question would not be settled until after *Quadragesimo anno* appeared, when the bishops took further action to assure greater uniformity of views among Catholics.

The greater concern of the bishops was with the attraction that socialist notions held for working-class Catholics. In the second part of the instruction, social democracy with its Austro-Marxism was linked to communism and Bolshevism, but (the bishops stated) it was the inhumane conditions forced upon the working masses by no-holds-barred capitalism that provoked the revolutionary desperation in the first place.[89] Socialism's wrong answers (attacks on property, marriage, social order) were to be distinguished from some of its other ideas, such as unionization. These are good, but only if divorced from a project of class war. The bishops appealed to Christian workers to avoid socialist associations and newspapers, since they were anti-religious and thus subversive of all good order.[90] What Christianity had to offer (in the third part of the pastoral letter) was the conviction of the personal dignity of the human being, employer and worker alike. In the path indicated by *Rerum novarum*, this grounded a respect for one another's rights—for instance, a fair wage and property rights for workers within a solidary community. A justice that can only be approximated in the present time will be perfected at the end of time in the justice of the kingdom of God.

88. Ibid., 207.
89. Ibid., 211.
90. The leading socialist daily, the *Arbeiter-Zeitung*, had a circulation of 112,000, compared to the Christian Social paper's 50,000 (the *Reichspost*; Pauley 1992, 153).

Dialogue vs. Civil Strife

There were outliers in the Catholic camp in Austria between the wars. One was Michael Pfliegler, a priest who would become well-known in the field of pastoral theology after World War II.[91] In contrast to the normative conduct not only of priests but of all adherents of the Catholic camp, Pfliegler sought contact with workers who were socialists.[92] He did not think it was incumbent upon him to change their political loyalties; he regarded the alliance of Catholicism and a political party to be an undeniable pastoral liability, not an asset. With August Schaurhofer, a clerical inspirer of the Volksbund, Pfliegler was open to every opportunity to address a crowd of workers.[93] Such opportunities were not often offered, but a young Catholic worker provided some occasions between 1927 and 1931. His name, oddly enough, was Otto Bauer (known as the "little Bauer" to distinguish him from the socialist leader mentioned earlier).

This Otto Bauer came out of Anton Orel's youth movement.[94] He also fell in with the younger German Catholic socialist, Heinrich Mertens, whom Orel attracted to Vienna for a time.[95] Of particular significance was his study of the writings of Wilhelm Hohoff, a German priest who worked out a synthesis of Thomistic economic notions and Marx's critique of capitalism. During or after World War I, in his early twenties, Bauer found his vocation to "enter into the proletariat." He had been a commercial employee and now became an unskilled metalworker; he joined a socialist union. Mertens and a local music teacher circulated a short-lived periodical that attracted a nucleus of workers and others to discussions in 1925. By the end of 1926, Bauer decided to start the Bund religiöser Sozialisten (League of Religious Socialists), which put out a little journal and held meetings. The thesis, rejected by most in the two camps, was that biblical religion and socialism were compatible after all and could even be mutually supportive. The association placed itself firmly in the socialist camp, since that was where the workers were.

Its very existence and its publicity drew attention to itself, because it was so contrary to the common sense of the two opposing camps. Its strategy was, however, in official conformity with the social democratic platform, which proclaimed tolerance for a pluralism of worldviews among its members while ruling out any division in the action of the labor movement. The religious socialists, under Bauer's leadership, asked for and received that toleration. Addressing the churches, they called for an end to discrimination against socialists. Though the association was nonconfessional, Bauer and others of its

---

91. *KSL*, 2110–12.
92. Aussermair 1979, 126–32; Schulmeister 1966, 1:225.
93. On Schaurhofer, see Bosmans 1978.   94. Aussermair 1979, 124.
95. Knapp 1975, 391.

members were Catholics; this posed the question "Can a Catholic be a Socialist?"[96] In the pages of a new journal for priests, *Der Seelsorger* (January 1927), Michael Pfliegler had caused a stir with a call for a ministry to workers that would build on their socialist commitments rather than condemn them or attempt to make them Christian Social Party voters. Hence Bauer asked Pfliegler to address a public "Meeting for Christianity and Socialism" on a Saturday evening on the subject. Pfliegler did so, concluding that, no, a Catholic could not join the socialist party, given its anticlerical policies—for instance, its active encouragement of workers to take their families' names formally off church rolls. Nevertheless, he took pains to offer a sympathetic interpretation of what validity divisive slogans such as "class struggle" might have. A class struggle in the sense of a struggle for the liberation of the proletariat was an undeniable necessity, provided only that it be conducted with moral means and not be taken over in the interests of a campaign against Christianity.

Despite this nuanced "no," Pfliegler remained a friend of the Bund religiöser Sozialisten, publicly supporting their efforts (until *Quadragesimo anno* came out in 1931) in his talks before clergy in the liturgical movement and youth groups. His Advent Sunday addresses to workers in 1930 formed a high point in this bridge-building activity. A thousand workers turned out each Sunday evening to hear Christianity interpreted so as to make sense in lives shaped by industrial labor and the socialist response. Naturally this did not make him popular with bishops, but his own bishop, Theodor Innitzer (who succeeded Piffl in Vienna in 1932) urged him to do a second doctorate to qualify for university teaching, which he did. Bishop Waitz inspired articles that argued the incompatibility of what the religious socialists were attempting with faithfulness to Catholicism, but his assistant on the 1925 bishops' statement, Johannes Messner, found words of acknowledgment while making it clear that he could no more agree with some of their views than Michael Pfliegler could. Fairly early on, nevertheless, the comparatively down-to-earth Cardinal Piffl had received Otto Bauer and one or two other Catholic members of the Social Democratic Party.[97] The cardinal seemed to admit the existence of differing economic ideologies within the Catholic body and hence the legitimacy of his visitors' double allegiance. When it came to cultural-religious policy, though, as in regard to socialist efforts to keep children religiously untainted, opposition was indicated. When Piffl asked what the church could do, the delegation suggested "worker priests."[98]

96. Aussermair 1979, 46–50.
97. Ibid., 1979, 40–41.
98. Just what "worker priests" meant to them in 1928 is not documented. Ernst Michel, in an address given October 27, 1929 to the religious socialists' second public meeting in Vienna, spoke of

The third camp in Austrian society was the German-nationalist one. It was not organized in a large political party, but constituted a reservoir of dissatisfied voters with a potential attraction to Nazism. In 1927 some nationalists in an armed organization killed two socialists in Burgenland. The local jury found the murderers not guilty on July 14, and on the next day, the 15th, red Vienna exploded in riots, setting the Palace of Justice on fire. The socialist labor movement called for a general strike for the day after that. The Christian labor movement's organs responded with condemnations of the (socialist) murderers and arsonists of July 15, without so much as a mention of the violence against socialists outside Vienna. They also applauded the executions that followed. The camps armed themselves, with the Christian labor movement creating a militia called the Freiheitsbund. Without a commitment to pluralism and the rights of social democrats as well as themselves, the Christian labor bloc was unable to form an alliance with them in defense of democracy.[99]

Like Kunschak's movement as a whole, the Freiheitsbund had a double identity.[100] It pursued social reforms that would raise workers' standard of living and status. This grounded its anti-capitalistic identity as part of the world of labor. It did so, however, within the Catholic-conservative camp—hence its anti-Marxist identity, as part of the Catholic subculture, felt to be the only legitimate culture. In Pelinka's diagnosis, the ties to the Catholic camp were unconditional and in cases of conflict always won out. Though the labor leaders in the Christian Social Party always tried to defend democracy and social equity, at least behind the scenes, they were unable to set the course of the Christian Social Party as a whole and fell in with the decisions taken against labor interests, deeming religious unity to be of transcendent value. Here is where a significant difference between the Austrian situation in the First Republic and that of the pillarized societies of Belgium and the Netherlands can be seen.[101] Whereas in the Lowlands a pragmatic consensus prevailed that each pillar's existence would be respected or at least tolerated, the Austrian camps envisaged a nonpluralist solution to society's problems by depriving the church, or the Jews, or the socialists, of any role in determining public policy.

On the Catholic side this became clear at several points in the last years of the First Austrian Republic (1918–38) as the will to repress the socialist opposition became ever stronger in the tactics of the ruling Christian Social Party.

---

another theme that one connects more usually with French Catholicism, of the proletariat as analogous to a "mission country"; Aussermair 1979, 67. He regretted the prohibition against Catholics joining the socialist movement for this reason: how could workers hear the Christian message if it comes in a foreign tongue (non-indigenized garb)?

99. Patch 2005, 187–93; see Diamant 1960, 80 and 286.
100. Pelinka 1972, 30–34.
101. See Pasture 2004, 43–44.

It led Seipel and party leaders, among other things, to accept the nationalistic Heimwehr into the Catholic camp, despite its sometimes violent opposition to the Christian labor movement and support of company ("yellow") unions. Othmar Spann's ideas of an authoritarian corporatist order became the ideology of the movement and gave it a pseudo-traditional image. The struggles of Engelbert Dollfuss to make Austria safe, if not for democracy, at least from Bolshevism and Nazism, followed. He was able to co-opt *Quadragesimo anno* in his desperate dictatorial efforts and thus contributed to the reactionary aura that surrounded the 1931 encyclical. How this unfolded is treated in the next chapter.

The social, economic, and political developments of the interwar period left the Christian labor movements in Italy and Austria as well as Germany battered and suppressed. Aggravated by the Depression, forces adverse to social justice and human rights even took the encyclical *Quadragesimo anno* hostage. From this low point in the "dark continent," was there to be any revival?[102]

102. Mazower 1999.

CHAPTER 11

Quadragesimo Anno, 1931

ITS CONTROVERSIAL RECEPTION

Among Pope Pius XI's many pronouncements, none roiled the world of labor more than his encyclical "On Reconstructing the Social Order and Perfecting It Conformably to the Precepts of the Gospel": *Quadragesimo anno*.[1]

Pope Pius XI issued this encyclical "forty years" after *Rerum novarum* (1891) and thus created the tradition of papal social encyclicals. It was a time of much distress and tension in Italian society, just before Mussolini let loose his crackdown on Catholic Action. In Europe at large, poverty and indebtedness surged, especially, it seemed, in republics with a democratic constitution. When *Quadragesimo anno* appeared on May 15, 1931, many who read it scrutinized it first of all for what the pope had to say about a corporatist social order. When they got to paragraph 81, in the section on the "Reconstruction of the Social Order," they found a topic sentence with a thesis to be developed: "First and foremost, the State and every good citizen ought to look to and strive toward this end: that the conflict between the hostile classes be abolished and the harmonious cooperation of the Industries and Professions be encouraged and promoted."[2]

This was a sentence lifted from a speech given by Eugenio Pacelli to the German Katholikentag of 1929, when he was still nuncio to Berlin. In fact, the initial drafter of the text for the encyclical was a German Jesuit, Oswald von Nell-Breuning, who revealed

---

1. The text in quotation marks is part of the introductory heading of the encyclical (http://www.vatican.va/holy_father/pius_xi/encyclicals/documents/hf_p-xi_enc_19310515_quadragesimo-anno_lt.html); also in Carlen, 3:415–443. See Christine Firer Hinze's 2005 comprehensive commentary on the 1931 encyclical for its treatment of *Rerum novarum* and other specific topics.

2. Carlen, 3:427f.

his part in the genesis of *Quadragesimo anno* four decades later.[3] This clue leads us to the Königswinter Circle, a group of German social Catholic thinkers that shaped Pius XI's formulations.

The Rise and Decline of Corporatist Outlooks in Catholic Social Teaching

The solidarism of Heinrich Pesch (chapter 4) was the theoretical soil in which *Quadragesimo anno* was planted. The encyclical's central call for a corporatist "vocational order" (*berufsständische Ordnung*) reflects much of the thinking we have already seen, especially in Dutch, Belgian, and German Catholicism. The German contribution, particularly that of Gustav Gundlach, SJ, came largely through the meetings of the Königswinter Circle of Catholic social ethicists that met as the encyclical was being drafted.[4] Outside the participants in this limited study group, *Quadragesimo anno* found many observers quite unsure as to what the terms, rendered here in English as "the Industries and Professions," were actually supposed to mean in Catholic social teaching. Even apart from the controversy over Fascist corporatism, which Christian labor rejected, there were divergent notions abroad in the Catholic world as to corporatism and class consciousness. If by corporatism one meant bringing workers and employers in an industry together, then unionists such as Imbusch could see in it a welcome revival of the earlier idea of socialization in industry—namely, positive relations on a basis of equal standing to discuss concerns between industry representatives and trade unions. The ZAG agreement of November 15, 1918, as a precursor of social partnership, would be an instance. It would include *Mitbestimmung* or regular consultations at the level of the industrial sector.[5]

On the other hand, if one were partial to the romantic *Lebensgemeinschaft* ideal of organic "life community," one might see in vocational order an imperative for "small is beautiful" in the sense of encouraging artisanal industry or bringing workers in a plant together with clerical staff and managers in a religious bonding. This orientation itself could be either along lines of economic status, an *Arbeiterstand* distinct from and parallel to the *Stand* of entrepreneurs or investors, but also from farmers or merchants or specialists in a cadre, or it

---

3. See Nell-Breuning 1971, 289–96, trans. in Curran and McCormick 1986, 60–68. Starting in 1968, Nell-Breuning, the main drafter of *Quadragesimo anno*, finally revealed his role and that of the Volksverein's "Königswinterer Kreis" of Rhenish Catholic scholars in the preparation of the encyclical; see Droulers 1981, 152–57; Misner 2004a, 664–68, and 2005, 116; Patch 2005, 182–86; and Hinze 2005, 162–72.

4. See Nell-Breuning, 1972c, 99–103. For details provided by one of its participants, see Mueller 1963, 116–17, or 1984.

5. Stegmann 1974, 167–72; see Schäfer 1990, 253.

could prioritize the vertical connections across class lines of those who work in the same field. In any case, it ignored the advancing differentiation of modern secular society. These longstanding variations of vocational-order thinking rendered the reception of *Quadragesimo anno* problematical.

Added to them, however, was a newer theoretical attempt on the part of Gustav Gundlach to clear up the rampant ambiguities in social Catholic discourse on corporatism. As a leading solidarist thinker after Heinrich Pesch, the Jesuit was also definitely a progressive thinker within the Catholic social thought of the period. He did not deny the validity of Marx's analysis of two *classes* formed under capitalist conditions, one in possession of the means of production and the other not. Even in the twentieth century this view corresponded to the realities of society more accurately than the passé idea of estates. Gundlach urged nostalgic forces in the Catholic labor movement to wake up to this reality. Moderated conflict between capital and labor was necessary and healthy if carried out with due regard to the common good. Decades of declamations against class struggle were, to say the least, too undifferentiated. Attempts of one class to subjugate and exploit the other (industrialist exploitation, Marxist class warfare), to be sure, were incompatible with the higher common good. All the same, modern society was divided into *classes* with conflicting interests. Justice would not be served by denying this reality.[6]

Did the notion of *Arbeiterstand* have any usefulness in this era? Yes, Gundlach thought, it could refer to the rightful place of workers in an industrial economy and permit a way of thinking open to the emancipation of the working class. A problem with this was that the Catholic workers' movement had its time-honored usage according to which class was a purely materialistic notion of workers' role necessarily bound up with class struggle in a winner-take-all sense. In this view, only *vocational group* (*Berufsstand*) was compatible with a Christian idea of a good society. While retaining the rhetoric of vocational groupings, however, what they were really thinking of were classes. Part of this confusion of language carried over into a connected notion. The Catholic labor

---

6. Gundlach 1929a, 1929b, 1929c; this emphasis did not prevent Gundlach from championing an ideal of vocational order; see Schwarte 1975, 32–33, 494–527, especially 502. See 36–43 for his indirect but determinative role by way of the Königswinterer Kreis in the preparation of *Quadragesimo anno*.

Gundlach was a disciple of Heinrich Pesch, SJ, and of Werner Sombart, professor of economics at Berlin. Gundlach created a stir in Catholic workers' organizations by acknowledging and receiving into Catholic social thought as valid some basic content of Marx's idea of class. This was a necessary contribution to sociology in Catholic circles, according to Nell-Breuning 1972c, 109–11. This understanding of class legitimated a (democratic, nonviolent) class struggle in the prevailing class society; Nell-Breuning presupposed it in the drafting of *Quadragesimo anno*. Many readers, however, would take *QA* no. 81 about moving from the confrontation of hostile classes to a harmonious cooperation of the professions as disavowing all forms of class conflict (see, however, *QA* no. 114).

movement aspired to a *Lebensgemeinschaft* of workers that combined economic, cultural, political, and religious elements. Gundlach's subtle attempts to modernize the idea of a vocational order aimed only at *Leistungsgemeinschaften* or communities of economic endeavor organized around a product or a service. These would be something like trade associations, in which the enterprise that included both employers and employed would be the common denominator alongside the other distinction of social class. When *Quadragesimo anno* came out, the cognoscenti could interpret the terms *class* and *profession* in this solidarist sense, but there was no longer an opportunity to work this through to a new standpoint.[7] Because of the confusion caused by undemocratic corporatist regimes in Austria and Portugal claiming to implement *Quadragesimo anno*, even Gundlach and Nell-Breuning abandoned the never-realized project of a vocationally ordered society. It was not resurrected after World War II, but the project of social partnership took its place.[8]

What then were these "Industries and Professions?" In the official Latin of the encyclical they were called *ordines*; in Italian, *le varie professioni*; in French *des "ordres" ou des "professions,"*—alternatively, *groupements corporatifs*; in Dutch and German, *standen* and *Stände*.[9] They were organizations of those engaged in "the same industry or profession," irrespective of their position in the labor market as employers or employees (*QA* no. 83). Paragraphs 91–96 followed shortly thereafter; they constitute Pius XI's very own comments on the Italian system of corporatism instituted by the Fascist regime.[10] It was natural to take these paragraphs on the Fascist system of corporativist labor relations as consonant with the encyclical's call for a "harmonious cooperation of Industries and Professions."

When one reads the pope's paragraphs (91–96) today, knowing how fascism turned out, it is quite disconcerting. It seems inconsistent with the teaching on social justice that pervades the rest of the encyclical.[11] For here Papa Ratti first gives credit to Fascist state corporatism for what he considered were obvious advantages (*QA* no. 95): "The various classes work together peacefully, socialist organizations and their activities are repressed, and a special magistracy exercises a governing authority." He was "compelled," however, as he hastened to say, to lodge an objection, though muted in tone. "The State . . . is substituting itself for free activity." The new order seems overly regimented from above. Might it not be designed to serve particular (viz. Fascist Party) ends,

---

7. Aretz 1978, 38–41.
8. Stegmann 1982, 123–25.
9. See Nell-Breuning 1932, 148.
10. These paragraphs came from Pius XI himself, as we know from Nell-Breuning's accounts: 1972b, 119; originally in Nell-Breuning 1971, 289–96; trans. Curran and McCormick 1986, 60–68.
11. Hehir 1995b, 1204; Kettern, 1998.

rather than leading to the reconstruction and promotion of a better social order? Mussolini did not take kindly to this paternal observation. It was perhaps the straw that broke the concordat camel's back and led to the suppression of all Catholic Action youth groups from the end of May until September, as we have seen.

Mussolini did not misunderstand the intended message. The "Professions" or *ordines* of which *Quadragesimo anno* spoke were not an arm of the state, but something irreconcilable with Fascist aims. The social order envisioned was to be a paradigm of the Christian anthropology of solidarism. Gustav Gundlach, SJ, provided the grounding for this or any reconstruction of the social order with his elaboration of the principle of subsidiarity, the axiom that responsibilities should not be shifted from smaller to larger social units without necessity.[12] The idea was not new, but Gundlach gave it its own name. Only in the second half of the twentieth century did it become more widely recognized and appealed to. It undergirds the whole section consisting of paragraphs 76–90, directly preceding the pope's paragraphs commenting on Italian corporatism. Its definition comes in a discussion of the prevailing individualism of modern society that, in principle, seems to recognize no intermediate bodies between the individual and the state, thus running the risk also of statolatry, "étatisme." Now it is true (the defining no. 79 goes on), "as history proves," that simply resurrecting the small associations of former times would not be equal to current demands. However, that does not invalidate "that most weighty principle" of "social philosophy":

> Just as it is gravely wrong to take from individuals what they can accomplish by their own initiative and industry and give it to the community, so also it is an injustice and at the same time a grave evil and disturbance of right order to assign to a greater and higher organization what lesser and subordinate organizations can do. For every social activity ought of its very nature to furnish help to the members of the body social, and never destroy and absorb them.

The familiar topos of a solidarist third way between or beyond liberalism and socialism received here a most noteworthy elaboration.[13] One who holds fast to Aristotle's insight that human beings are social animals sees that individualistic liberalism grievously underestimated the social component of personhood. Materialistic socialism's flaw, on the other hand, was not to recognize the dignity of the human *person* as the raison d'être of social phenomena. Hence the socialist worldview subordinated the individual to the collectivity.

---

12. The principal of subsidiarity, Gundlach's signal contribution to social philosophy, and its intrinsic relation to the Peschian principle of solidarity are discussed in Schwarte 1975, 373–82.

13. Giblin 1994b, 808; Misner 2003; Misner 2004a, 667.

Solidarism rightly sees in the human person the intrinsic interrelationship of both aspects. The cognate principle of subsidiarity (from "furnish help" to, *subsidium*; *QA* no. 80) extends this insight into the area of norms governing the associative life of human beings in all its phases and aspects.

The principle of subsidiarity survived the fascist shipwreck in which *Quadragesimo anno* was willy-nilly involved.[14] Now it can be seen that in *Quadragesimo anno*, the pope's mild critique of fascist corporatism is embedded in and follows from a presentation of the most anti-fascist, anti-totalitarian premises of social philosophy. However, it was the use made of Pius XI's encyclical, and his own authoritarian mindset, that paradoxically undercut the contribution that this teaching of his might have made in its own time. In the form of acknowledging the importance of intermediary bodies between the individual person and the central government of a state, the principle of subsidiarity has found certain positive applications in the 1930s and more so since. It is a principle that underlies the existence of civil society as now understood and promoted.

Besides the issue of corporatism, which attracted so much attention until World War II—and the at-first less prominent teaching on subsidiarity as a requirement of social justice—*Quadragesimo anno* treated many other important issues.[15] Nell-Breuning has noted how gravely misunderstood were the observations on capitalism (paragraphs 101–10) and how doctrinaire were the paragraphs on socialism (110–23). The treatment of capitalism makes sense if one acknowledges the distinction between capitalism as an economic system and capitalism as a social order pitting finance and management against labor. In the first case a capitalist economic system simply utilizes accumulated investment to increase productivity. The encyclical regards this as a given, in itself morally neutral, capable of functioning for good or ill, depending on its role in society as a whole. Capitalistic society or capitalism as a *social* order, on the other hand—that is, as a political economy resulting in a society where class interests and antagonisms are dominant—comes under criticism. The former, however, is not held directly responsible for the latter. This rather sharp distinction between a mode of economic organization and how society manages it, however clearly expressed in the encyclical (*QA* no. 101), either escapes many readers or appears illusory.[16] Its target was the fairly widespread tendency of the time to view capitalism in root and branch, however defined, as incompatible with Catholic social teaching. At the same time, *Quadragesimo anno* scored the deformations, the monopolistic cartels, and harmful financial speculations

---

14. See Nell-Breuning 1972a, 134–35.
15. See Nell-Breuning 1936; Giblin 1994b, 802–12; Hinze 2005.
16. Giblin 1994b, 809.

that marked industrial economies of the 1920s as making a mockery of the free market and sound competitive practices.

As for socialism, Gundlach's bent led him to postulate an irreducible incompatibility between it and Christianity. The sentence in the encyclical (no. 117) expressing this most succinctly comes with an escape clause, all the same. "Socialism, *if it remains truly socialism*, . . . cannot be reconciled with the teachings of the Catholic Church because its concept of society itself is utterly foreign to Christian truth." The definition of "its concept of society" follows in paragraphs 118 and 119 and sees materialism as essential to socialism; Nell-Breuning fully shared that view in 1931, but intensive contact later with social democratic intellectuals disabused him, as he admitted.[17] The appeal of communism and socialism was of course the main threat that churchmen saw to the vitality of Christianity in the working class. The hopes bound up with the encyclical were to show that there was a better way to improve the lot of workers than a winner-take-all class struggle.

In the course of 1931 church-state relations in Italy were patched up and entered a period of consensus. There were some Catholic economists and political economists (for instance, Amintore Fanfani, at the Catholic University in Milan), who took the corporatist state for a more promising (and at any rate actually existing) starting point for a reconstructed social order than, say, Anglo-American liberalism. Pius XI and much of the Vatican looked about and saw the outlines of a Latin bloc of Catholic authoritarian states (Italy, Portugal, Spain, but also corporatist Austria with Dollfuss and Hungary with Miklós Horthy). This seemed to them the direction to encourage.[18] After all, one could hardly expect anti-clericals, or democratic socialists or Protestants, much less Nazi Germany and Soviet Russia, to attend to the guidance that only the church (the pope) could provide to society. Perhaps the Catholic states would be amenable to the Catholic solution of the Depression-era social question. Thus the (societal) corporatism of *Quadragesimo anno* became mistakenly identified with the policies of fascist and authoritarian states in the minds of many observers.[19]

Nell-Breuning's self-critical reflections forty years later reflect the fortune of *Quadragesimo anno* in Germany, Austria, and Italy and in subsequent papal teaching. (In his view, its real contributions were mostly overlooked except in Gundlach's work as ghostwriter for Pius XII.) Perhaps, as Droulers comments,

---

17. Nell-Breuning 1972b, 80–82; he welcomed the less deductivist approach of *Mater et magistra* on this topic in 1961.

18. Moro 1979, 503–8; Agostino 1991, 547; Traniello 1995, 295; Chiron 2004, 214.

19. E.g. John La Farge, SJ, in the United States, until 1938; see D'Agostino 2004, 220–21; see Corrin 2002, 188–97.

this has resulted in an unduly pessimistic view of the encyclical's reception.[20] One thing it did accomplish was to make it plain that Leo XIII's foray into social-justice issues with *Rerum novarum* was not to be a one-time effort on the part of the papacy. Although the next two ten-year marks would not bring forth a major social encyclical, the celebration of *Rerum novarum* in *Quadragesimo anno* meant that not just the minoritarian Catholic labor movements but the official church would regard these statements on behalf of social justice to be a prominent feature of twentieth-century Catholicism. It became a tradition to look to specifically papal (and Vatican II) documents to represent official "Catholic Social Teaching." This is obvious in the usage of now standard works on the subject.[21]

In the absence of any express preference for democracy as a framework for human rights and social justice, *Quadragesimo anno* was read differently in countries under dictatorship than in the free world, where social Catholics continued by and large to be democrats and to support democratic policies. Here the more astute filled in the picture with the missing political rights. They prized the encyclical as an expression of important principles, not as a blueprint of or even a call for *the* Christian social order. In the optic of Pius XI himself, it was designed mainly for the only kind of society he considered fully viable, one in which the Roman Catholic Church had a recognized position as the only representative of the true religion (see the encyclical *Mortalium animos* of 1928). He valued an activated laity in the form of Catholic Action, including the forms it took in the Belgian and French Young Christian Workers movement (JOC). The reconquest of the modern world for Christ the King and Christ's church—that is, the Roman Catholic Church under the pope—was the explicit aim of his pontificate. To the extent possible, and with the adaptations necessary, he saw to it that the Catholic Action model was extended to all countries and all apostolates. This definitely included the different categories of those who work for a living in the world (*QA* no. 141).

Quadragesimo anno, for all its drawbacks and for all the hindrances it encountered that stunted its fruitful reception, did speak to the issues of the time. Threats as great or greater than fascism loomed in the 1930s: the Depression, the rise of Nazism, the promised world revolution of communism, and the travails of democracy. Under such pressures, social Catholicism in Italy, without its stiff defense by the pope, would certainly have come close to extinction.

---

20. Droulers 1981, 155.
21. As in *StL* 3:349, *NDCST* 1994, or Himes et al. 2005, 3–5.

Catholic Action Youth Groups, FUCI, and the Formation of a Christian Democratic Elite

In any case, little was left of the pre-Fascist social Catholic organizations in Mussolini's Italy by 1931. Christian democrats were out of action and silent. The same went for activists in the CIL unions. Only a few PPI exiles kept the flame burning, but it could not be seen or felt in Italy. Some quasi-exiles harbored in the Vatican (Alcide De Gasperi, Guido Gonella) could occasionally reach Catholics in Italy through the columns of the *Osservatore Romano* or the *Illustrazione Vaticana* (1933–38). Ex-popolari were more numerous in the ranks of Italian Catholic Action than the pope thought, but they went along with the consensus that prevailed in that same period from 1933 to 1938.[22] There was one Italian Catholic who could command an audience: the pope. But Pius XI (and after February 1939, Pius XII) saw no alternative to dealing with the Fascist regime, which by now was firmly in charge of Italy and which after all did not set out to render Catholicism altogether impotent, as Nazi Germany and Soviet Russia were intent on doing. Religious education was an exception to the Fascist educational monopoly that Mussolini conceded—reluctantly—to the Catholic Church of Italy in the Concordat of 1929. Pius XI would make great counter-concessions to preserve and if possible increase the chances of influencing the youth of Fascist Italy.

The student organization, FUCI, in the first years of Fascism harbored a critical tendency open to the thinking of progressive French Catholics. In 1933, however, as a consequence of the September accord of 1931 on the permissible limits of the freedom of Catholic Action organizations, Msgr. Montini was replaced by a priest with no sympathy for the modernizing line.[23] FUCI's lay leader, Igino Righetti, had to shift to another position in Catholic Action in 1934, but even before he did, the pages of the *Azione fucina* were opened to new clerical writers who evinced a markedly friendly tone to the regime and its kind of corporatism.[24] Before considering the further influence of the Montinian line in Italian Catholicism, however, the much more widespread action of the Catholic Youth (*Gioventù*) demands our attention. This is not because of any social justice preoccupations, but to account for the strength and some distinctive characteristics of Italian social Catholicism in the post-Fascist era.

---

22. Pollard 1985, 158–63.
23. Wolff 1990, 114 and 167–68; Hebblethwaite 1993, 112–17; Moro 1981a, 265–68.
24. Wolff 1990, 146.

Luigi Gedda's Catholic Youth Organization

One effect of the post-concordat troubles between the regime and Catholic Action was to cause the latter to emphasize growth above all else. The top cleric of Catholic Action, Giuseppe Pizzardo, for one, realized that the regime would respect nothing less than a mass-membership organization. The illusions of 1929 and 1930—namely, that the Lateran Pacts would be the first stage of a process that would bring Mussolini's regime around to become a truly Catholic state—grew dim. One adjusted one's sights to a longer march through the institutions. An imposing but strictly legal constituency (no politics) would create the most favorable conditions, one thought, for the eventual success of the project of re-Christianizing society. Although, as we are now in a position to observe, civil society did not come back under the dominating influence of the church, the stress on membership numbers and mass appeal did lead to unprecedented success. It was instrumental in creating a large movement that played an important role in Fascist and post-Fascist Italy.

This took place under the leadership of Luigi Gedda. He was named lay head of the Catholic Action Youth (GIAC) in 1934. After the signing of the Lateran Pacts, one started to create specialized subgroups by categories for different social settings like the groups specialized by milieus (workers, students, professionals) of Cardijn's JOC model in France and Belgium. Such an ambitious project became impossible after the dissolution of the groups from May through September 1931.[25] Gedda had to confine his organization's activities to religious formation and exercises only. He was neither pro-regime nor anti-, but simply pro-church and Catholic Action. In the years (1933–38) of "consensus" between regime and broad elements of the Italian populace, including active Catholics, Gedda developed the movement with flair. An occasional public manifestation of faith brought forth protests from the authorities, but for the most part the movement did its work quietly in the parishes of the countryside, preventing a total identification of a million boys and young men with the Fascist regime. A whole array of attractive mass periodicals bolstered the effort. As Renato Moro comments, this amounted to a distinct modernization of Christian socialization of the young, with particular attention to the cinema (movies shown in parish halls).[26] And as Durand notes, by its very existence such a movement would in given circumstances nourish anti-fascism.[27] In the religious revival that attended World War II, the movement flourished even more. Soon after the fall of Mussolini in 1943, Gedda wrote to Marshal Badoglio: the Catholic Youth, he stated, with its now 2,500,000 members, might serve as a basis for a new, more Christian regime.[28]

25. Osbat 1981, 94.
27. Durand 1990, 389.
26. Moro 1981a, 273.
28. Moro 1981a, 371.

There were some philo-fascists prominent in Catholic Action, part of the clerico-fascisti who abandoned the PPI for Mussolini in 1923–24. Agostino Gemelli was the founding president of the Catholic University of the Sacred Heart in Milan and founder of the important *Vita e Pensiero* publishing house.[29] While opposing the quasi-Hegelian philosophy favored by fascists, he and the academic and church circles he influenced took a political line best summarized under three heads:

(1) wholehearted acceptance of the Fascist corporative system as a real application of Catholic social principles, (2) participation in Fascist "imperial" programs, with their doctrines of living space and geopolitics, (3) justification of the Fascist racial campaign [1938–39] on the ground of Catholic tradition.[30]

They saw the Fascist attempts at reorganization of society as potentially in line with the Third Way that social Catholics so ardently desired, beyond the one-sided individualism of laissez-faire capitalistic liberalism and the collectivism of communist socialism. "The Fascist conception of the State, as the Nation organized, [has] led to corporativism.... The new doctrine and the new system rest, more than might appear at first sight, upon a conception of the world particularly dear to us, and true, according to our way of seeing things: the primacy of the spiritual."[31] Fascist propagandists did not accept this thesis, and with reason. Gemelli, however, was a power in Catholicism and was treated with the respect due to useful, if not particularly keen-sighted, allies.

Pius XI kept juggling supporters and critics of the regime. He appreciated old friends like Gemelli and the clerico-fascisti. Through most of the two Fascist decades, they could project the Catholic presence publicly in the intellectual and financial sectors, and gradually also in the bureaucracy of the state and in the IRI (Institute for Industrial Reconstruction).[32] He encouraged the apolitical, devotional, and moralizing successes of the Catholic Youth as a mass organization. Not only the pope, but broad ecclesiastical fronts looked with favor on these developments and contrasted them with the struggle of Catholics under an incomparably more hostile regime in Nazi Germany. It is also a fact that Pius XI protected and encouraged the Montini-Righetti line of Catholic Action after it had been equivalently disavowed by the accord of September 1931. To quote Webster's early but excellent study once more: "Given the totalitarian

---

29. For other facets of the modernizing antimodernist Agostino Gemelli, OFM, one can start with the short biographical entry in *DSMCI* 1982, 2:225–30, by Gustavo Bontadini. See also Bocci 1999, especially 287–326, on Gemelli's rethink dating from the 1942 Christmas Message of Pope Pius XII touching on democracy.

30. Webster 1960, 156.

31. See ibid, 158, citing a 1933 statement by Gemelli.

32. See Zamagni 1993, 300.

conditions of Italy in the 1930s, lay autonomy was out of the question. Indeed, Righetti and Montini succeeded in rearing a new generation of Catholic political leaders only because they had the backing of Pius XI himself."[33]

FUCI and the Laureati Movement

The Montinian approach diverges clearly from the Gemellian as well as from the Geddian line. Being limited to an elite, university students and graduates, FUCI obviously had a different audience than did general Catholic Action and Gedda's mass movement. One difference between the Fucini and those behind the Catholic University in Milan was obvious: Righetti and the FUCI, with Montini's support, did not favor the rise of Fascism, while Gemelli found it on the whole advantageous. Other differences are important, as well, however. Gemelli, an adult convert and anti-modernist, fell in with the clerico-moderate, then clerico-fascist set in Milan, whereas Montini belonged by family tradition and inclination to the democratic wing of Italian Catholicism. Righetti and Montini looked for a reciprocal influence of modern culture and Catholicism;[34] Gemelli wanted to utilize modern science and scholarship to reorient modern culture along a one-way track to an organically unified Catholic society. Gemelli, though no philosopher, swore by the neo-Thomism of the nineteenth-century Thomistic revival; Montini was attracted to the new departures in Thomism taking place in French Catholic circles and particularly to Jacques Maritain.

Igino Righetti had seen the need for a specialized organization for university-trained professionals and intellectuals beyond their student years, a sort of a FUCI alumni association to carry on the Montinian agenda. Despite the post-1931 restrictions on Catholic Action, he and Montini secured Pius XI's approval for a Movimento laureati, as it was called, with practical autonomy from the officials of the men's section of Catholic Action. The pope gave his blessing in September 1932, while Montini and Righetti were still the national leaders of the FUCI.[35] It would be inaccurate to see the Laureati as a hotbed of anti-Fascism, for it was not. Many of the younger graduates who joined accepted the Fascist Italy they had grown up in as normal. In the period of consensus in the 1930s, they could pursue careers as Catholics and Italians without undue tension or discrimination. All the same, the Movimento laureati definitely aimed to develop Christian, not fascist, cultural and professional leadership. The high points at the national level were at first the Social Weeks.[36] From 1935

33. Webster 1960, 138.
35. Wolff 1990, 165.
34. Moro 1979, 262.
36. Duchini 1990, 79.

on, these were again suspended; the Laureati managed to hold their own modest national congresses, like the FUCI of which they were the offshoot. Despite police surveillance and their rather autonomous relationship with Catholic Action, the movement could carry on its work of serious study and reflection during the remainder of the Fascist regime.[37]

Righetti, as lay head of the FUCI, was part of the leadership of Catholic Action at the national level. Even before handing the FUCI over to Giovanni Ambrosetti in the autumn of 1934, he was asked to pull together the Social Weeks of 1933 and 1934 while he was laying the organizational groundwork for the Movimento laureati. (ICAS was in crisis, and its staff had departed.) Righetti then used the Social Weeks of 1933 and 1934 to continue the organizational work while turning the review, *Studium*, into the organ of the Laureati.[38] Righetti saw the new task as tailor-made for the Laureati in a long-term campaign he sketched out for a thorough renewal of Catholic Action in the direction of social-justice themes.[39] A start was made in 1934, when the Social Week convened in Padua with the not-too-alarming theme of "professional morality." He continued as appointed leader of the Movimento laureati to plan the 1935 Social Week on "labor." This controversial theme created enormous difficulties; first delayed, the Social Week was then called off in the run-up to the Italian invasion of Ethiopia, which set imperialist Italians, including Catholics, against much of the rest of the world and was an embarrassment to the Vatican. Whereas ICAS did not resume the Social Weeks again until 1945, FUCI and the Laureati did resume their own meetings, the Laureati for the first time in January 1936. Adriano Bernareggi, soon to be bishop of Bergamo, provided sympathetic and knowledgeable support of a Montinian sort to the Laureati from 1934 to 1953.

The attempt to bridge the gap between the church and modern social issues by starting with the Social Weeks was thus thwarted. Other ambitions that were to be instrumental toward this end were likewise frustrated. The intellectual elite wanted to break out of their isolation and address those involved in the world of organized labor. They hoped to begin the reorientation of Catholic Action to the social issues that it had eschewed. Now they were thrown back into their narrow space. At least they had this space within Catholic Action at the national and diocesan levels. Worse was yet to come in 1938, when Catholics and the pope did not welcome the alliance between Mussolini and Hitler and the period of church-state consensus gave way to a trend of cautious detachment from the regime on the part of Catholics. The Movimento laureati managed to hold a congress that year again in September, in Florence. Bishop

37. Moro 1981a, 280–84.
39. Moro 1979, 330–33.

38. I.e., Ph.D.s; Wolff 1990, 178–80.

Bernareggi, however, was instructed to stay away. The program was reduced to addresses by clergy, with no discussion, so that the regime would have no cause to object to anti-Fascist utterances.[40] The October decree that imposed legal disabilities on Italian Jews after the Nazi example brought forth a timid response from churchmen. Only the provision forbidding marriage between "Arians" and Jews was rejected strongly as an infringement on the religious freedom guaranteed to the Roman Catholic Church by the concordat.[41]

The Social Weeks collapsed under the combined weight of governmental suspicions and ecclesiastical restrictions. Righetti had another card up his sleeve, however, to avoid the total silencing of dialogue on contemporary issues in the Italian Catholic Church. From 1936 on he organized within the framework of Catholic Action, hence for the laity, an annual "week of religious culture" held at a retreat in the hill town of Camaldoli. These were really weeks for the dialogue of theology (represented by clerical speakers) and modern culture (represented by lay presenters from FUCI and the Laureati). Thanks to Montini's assistance, the clergy present were among the most biblically and historically oriented to be found in Italy.[42] Even Righetti's and Pius XI's deaths in early 1939, though, did not signal further onerous restrictions on the intellectual movements of Catholic Action—as just noted, Mussolini's embrace of Hitler started a process of distancing from the regime in the Italian church circles.

These were the years when Aldo Moro and Giulio Andreotti, future leaders of Italy, were presidents of the FUCI. The particular significance of the Camaldoli weeks in the present connection lies in the week held in 1943 with the help of a reactivated ICAS. Sergio Paronetto and other Laureati, looking beyond fascism, conceived and carried through the project of producing a successor to the Mechlin (Malines) Social Code of 1927. This was the so-called Camaldoli Code of 1943; the Studium publishing house put it out in 1945 under the title *Per la comunità cristiana*.[43] Social Catholicism and Christian democracy were again stirring and preparing for the responsibilities that faced them in postwar Italy.

Catholic Party Authoritarian Rule in Austria, 1933–38

In Austria *Quadragesimo anno* also became a topic of politics. Ignaz Seipel left the chancellor's office in 1929, as he was becoming disillusioned with parliamentary government ("formal democracy," as it was called by its critics). In

---

40. Moro 1981a, 344. 41. Ibid., 334.
42. Moro 1979, 538–43.
43. Paronetto et al 1945. Text reprinted in Gatti and Allara 1993, 43–164; see also Casella 1981, 96–97.

the provincial elections of April 1932, the newfound strength of a fascist party unnerved his successors and led them to seek ways of avoiding parliamentary elections. They feared being put in the position of having to make concessions to the socialist camp so as to fend off the nationalist German and equally anti-religious threat from the right.[44] In May of 1932 Engelbert Dollfuss, short of physical stature and of years of age (forty), but a committed Catholic and a risk-taker in the face of Nazism, became chancellor. He took advantage of a breakdown of procedures in the parliament in March of 1933 to shut it down and govern by decree, deeming this the best choice to thread a way between the two dangers he saw in socialism and Nazism—this was, after all, the month of Hitler's takeover in Germany, with designs on Austria, as well. In this attempt he garnered the support of Mussolini, as well as the latter's insistence on crushing social-democratic organizations along the lines of the Italian corporative state.[45] While in Rome Dollfuss resumed stalled negotiations for a concordat with the Vatican and urged them on to their conclusion.[46]

After suspending the Austrian parliament and taking emergency control of the government, Dollfuss addressed the Katholikentag held in Vienna in September 1933 with a programmatic speech that articulated his vision of a *Ständestaat*, a state to be organized by vocational groupings. "We want a social, Christian-German state on corporative bases with a strong authoritarian leadership."[47] Occasionally he referred to this design as a *Quadragesimo-Anno-Staat*. Of the three camps in interwar Austria, he could rely only on the Catholics (and the church could rely only on the Christian Socials and their successors). The concept of a vocationally ordered state had its attractions. In place of the partisan wrangling of the camps in electoral and parliamentary politics, there would be a series of boards that were to offer objective advice from the perspective of economic actors for the common good. Instead of a disruptive labor-management tug-of-war, both would have equal status anchored in the corporative bodies. In practice, however, Dollfuss was to be the only decision-maker, a dictator—and the economic crisis was to be mastered by favoring industrialists.[48] The picture that he repeatedly conjured up—a peasant at table with his farmhands after a hard day's work, eating from the same serving dish—hardly had much relevance to the realities of Austria's industrial economy or divided populace.

From March 1933 through the bloody suppression of Viennese socialists in February 1934 and continuing past the adoption of a new authoritarian consti-

44. Patch 2005, 191; Staudinger 1983, 258–73; Evans 1999, 190.
45. Mazower 1999, 30, 67.
46. Weinzierl 1983, 482–87.
47. Weinzierl 1995, 31; Evans 1999, 194; see Boyer 2005, especially 12–16.
48. Hanisch 1994, 315–17.

tution for the Austrian *Ständestaat* in May of 1934, Austrian social Catholics in government circles were engaged with others in lobbying and debating about the shape of this new corporative state.[49] The failed Nazi Putsch of July cost Dollfuss his life, but gave his fiction of a corporative state almost four more years for his successor, Kurt Schuschnigg, to try to fend off the Nazis within Austria and across the border. In the new state, the political parties, including the Christian Social Party, were abolished and replaced by a single legal party, the Vaterländische Front. In parallel fashion, all the union federations were suppressed and a single *Gewerkschaftsbund* was created. The members of Dollfuss's old party and the leaders of the Christian unions reappeared in analogous positions in the new formations, along with more or less acceptable allies in the new regime. Johann Staud went from the position of general secretary of the Christian unions to that of leader of the unitary *Gewerkschaftsbund*.[50] He would die in 1939 in a Nazi concentration camp. There was a parallel (employers') trade association federation with similar continuities of personnel in relation to predecessor organizations of the 1920s.

The bishops, with Theodor Innitzer (archbishop of Vienna from 1932 to 1955) in the lead, were for some time quite supportive of the Dollfuss authoritarian program. They did not mourn the demise of the parliamentary Catholic party or the independent trade unions. They were cognizant of the need to raise the level of pastoral care and looked to the pope's program of Catholic Action as a model.[51] Innitzer even sent a trusted aide to Italy to see what synergies there might be between a fascist state and Catholic Action. Very likely they told themselves that there would be no severe crises with Dollfuss such as Mussolini's crackdown on church youth organizations in Italy in 1931.

The dictatorship draped itself in the banners of papal social doctrine after the manner of *Quadragesimo anno* (1931).[52] Some, like the president of the national assembly, invoked the encyclical in the same breath with fascism: democracy and Marxism, he said, had been thrown overboard, "so as to build a solid new house on the foundations of true Christian conviction according to the guidelines of the encyclical *Quadragesimo anno* and after the great example of Fascist organization of the state."[53] For its part, the episcopate supported the new regime qua authoritarian, but drew the line against totalitarian claims in

49. On the suppression of the socialists, see Maderthaner 2002; Kitchen 1980. On the new constitution, see Binder 2002, 74–75; Bischof et al. 2003.
50. Blenk 1975, 106–13.
51. Klostermann 1967, 77.
52. See Gulick 1948, 1423–27, for an early and insightful analysis of the inconsistencies, even invalidity, of such a claim. However, Seipel's interpretation was regarded as authoritative, according to Wohnout 2003, 153–54; Wohnout 2004, 182: by this time, for "Seipel, a rebuilding of society and organizing of the professions went hand in hand with the undoing of the democratic state."
53. Hanisch 1994, 317.

the indoctrination of youth: "There are grounds to suspect certain dangers of the adoption [here in Austria] of imitations of the Italian practice along Fascist lines.... In our circumstances there is no place for Fascism as an import, indeed it must be decisively rejected in its basic character as an absolutistic totalitarian state."[54] This was in 1933. Later on, as Schuschnigg tried to reinforce "patriotic education," the bishops on their part took the Catholic youth organizations officially under the wing of Catholic Action, protected as it was supposed to be by the Concordat of 1934.[55] The authoritarian state in Austria, unlike German Nazism, did not want to weaken Catholicism, only make it more serviceable to its own ends. The strains between the two institutions, devoted in common, it would seem, to a harmonious social order, cast an ironic light on the project of "a social, Christian-German state on corporative bases with a strong authoritarian leadership."

On the trade-union front, Catholics accepted the dictatorial regime and positions in its new *Gewerkschaftsbund*.[56] Only reluctantly did they go along with the policies of economic stabilization by reducing social expenditures as necessary steps to a sound vocational order. As objects of the Heimwehr's assaults, meant to force their members into a company union mentality, they responded with a new self-consciousness of their identity as workers, as part of the working class having interests at odds with those of their employers. In fact, as Pelinka has noted, they in effect gave up the notion of *Berufsstand* that they enshrined in their Linz Program of 1923.[57] Their talk of *Stand* no longer referred to the earlier corporatist notion, as including all engaged in a given branch of work, employers and wage workers, but was now equivalent to class without the socialist overtones, an *Arbeiterstand*. From the ranks of Catholic Action, where they could take cover as nonpolitical, they managed to slow the dismantling of social insurance programs.[58] Signs of mutual cooperation between the Christian laborites and the illegal socialist trade-unionists began to emerge. (When it came to the crunch, however—after the pattern Pelinka highlights—the Catholic identity and milieu of the Christian Socials who remained faithful to the party always won out over a working-class identity.)

Even apart from tactical adjustments to altered power relationships, there were precedents and valid reasons for this shift on the part of Christian labor. The Dutch notion of *stand/standen* as evolved by Poels was openly class-specific. The specialized Catholic Action pioneered by Cardijn in the JOC was class- and age-specific (although the French had the term *milieu* to use instead

54. Ibid., 314.
55. See Gellott 1987, 175–250; Gellott 1988, 581–83.
56. Patch 2005, 190–93.
57. Pelinka 1972, 242.
58. Hanisch 1994, 316.

of *class*). Gundlach urged the German Catholic Arbeitervereine to acknowledge that they were perforce class organizations. Moreover, as the Austrian Catholic labor leaders pointed out persistently (and correctly), the encyclical *Quadragesimo anno* nowhere advocated the end of autonomous labor unions. Nor did it approve of the state-imposed labor organizations of Mussolini's Italy. Dollfuss, however, did not see it that way. At least in the emergency situation in which he saw Austria, he assumed or convinced himself that what Mussolini was insisting on was a responsible realization of the corporative order espoused by *Quadragesimo anno*.[59] After all, Pius XI never defended democracy as necessary for human dignity and justice.

Nevertheless, Dollfuss had to be concerned with the hostility of the social democratic working people whose organizations he was suppressing and whose leaders were going underground or into exile in Czechoslovakia. Even an authoritarian state needed the consent of the governed in some degree. He asked Ernst Karl Winter to become vice mayor of Vienna with the mission of reconciling the working class to the new regime. Winter was a Catholic "social monarchist" of a Vogelsangian background, but a critic of the authoritarian regime. He was also definitely opposed to any merger into Germany, even a "good" Germany of the future. He accepted the task with great misgivings so as somehow to affect the situation positively or at least limit the negative consequences. He realized that without a reconciliation between industrial workers and the emphatically Catholic regime, Austria was doomed. With his appreciation for Marxism as a response to the plight of the working class, he was able to make positive contacts with Otto Bauer, the leading figure on the socialist side, until the latter fled Austria. Although Winter had the (hardly unconditional) support of Dollfuss, this was not enough to counter the opposition of other Catholic politicians and labor leaders. The "Aktion Winter" was crippled almost at birth first by the slaughter of socialist workers in February and then by the Nazi assassination of Dollfuss in July 1934.[60]

The general picture is that the social contingent of the Austrian Catholic camp went along with the *Ständestaat*, even though the latter reduced the rights and interests of working people and excluded the democratic structures that they valued.[61] Social democrats tended reluctantly to the same conclusion: to work with the authoritarian regime as the lesser evil compared with a Nazi takeover.[62] It was the same for Winter. The choice was rendered less painful for him by the sincere Catholicism of Engelbert Dollfuss (and Kurt Schuschnigg,

59. Weinzierl 1995, 41.
60. Jagschitz 1983, 511.
61. As Pelinka 1972, 242, has persuasively argued; see also Weinzierl 1983, 484–85.
62. Kitchen 1980, 5.

his successor). Some social Catholics were taken in by the appeal to *Quadragesimo anno*, as indeed the pope himself seems to have been. Of the social democratic organizations that were suppressed, the Bund religiöser Sozialisten of the Catholic Otto Bauer was among the first to go. (This Bauer was under arrest for some time, but left Austria before the *Anschluss* and spent the war years in the United States, as did Winter and others.)

The anti-capitalists among the social Catholics were certainly not satisfied with the result. The democrats and moderates of the social-policy orientation went along and tried to make the best of it, as evidenced by the service of Richard Schmitz, installed as mayor of Vienna, and Josef Dobretsberger in the Dollfuss-Schuschnigg cabinet. The solidarist moral theologian, Johannes Messner, as seen earlier, tried to clarify the nebulous use of the expression "vocational order."[63] This involved defending a solidarist conception against the utopian demands of the Wiener Richtungen, for one thing, as *Quadragesimo anno* had done. Also in the line of the encyclical, he declared that the prevailing authoritarian mode of the corporative state could only be a transitional stage to a more organic form of society. This would have to do a relatively better job of promoting personal freedom as well as the authentic common good. Sadly, however, the reservations expressed by Austrian social Catholics, Dobretsberger and Messner and Pfliegler, Kunschak and Spalowsky and Staud, Schmitz and Winter, did not prevent them from being co-opted in the suppression of democracy and respect for human rights in Austrian public life.

The end of the corporatist experiment came with the German military takeover of Austria, the *Anschluss* of March 12, 1939. Hitler made his grand comeback to Vienna. He was the answer to German nationalists' prayers and courted the favor of the other two camps, as well. To the socialist workers, repressed under the previous authoritarian regime, he promised jobs and acceptance. He met with the especially gullible or overawed Cardinal Theodor Innitzer on March 15 and promised the church a "religious Spring."[64] As to the Jews, not in favor in any of the camps, Hitler's murderous intentions soon became apparent.

63. Messner 1936.
64. Pelinka 1998, 173–83, here 181.

CHAPTER 12

France, Belgium, the Netherlands

CHRISTIAN LABOR IN THE DEPRESSION YEARS

In Western Europe the Christian labor movements and unions continued to unfold their activities and even solidify their gains in the 1930s. In this period they struggled under economic hardship followed by harsh wartime repression. It was also a time when the Christian laborites staked out positions and accumulated experience with which they could then contribute to the reconstruction of Europe after World War II.

For the Christian unions in all three of the Western European countries in view here, the 1930s were a time when they finally achieved a certain recognition of their role in society at large alongside socialist unions. The shape that this recognition took, however, differed in each case.

The Dutch Catholic unions found their niche as a trade union federation early on, in the 1920s, thanks in part to the leading political roles that patrons such as Aalberse and Nolens played. It was their autonomy and clout within the Catholic Party that had to be vindicated in the face of corporatist advocates, notably J. A. Veraart. By 1929, however, Catholic union leaders A. C. De Bruijn and Jos Serrarens were both ensconced in the upper house of parliament, and their labor unions were routinely involved in negotiations and tripartite consultations (in Dutch, *overleg*).[1]

In France, with its lesser degree of unionization of the work force, the CFTC was predominantly white-collar and marginal until the Popular Front legislation of 1936. Though not directly

---

1. Van Meeuwen 1999, 399–404.

involved in the Matignon Agreement that led to this legislation, the Christian unions found its provisions quite positive and were able to take advantage of them. Their delegates procured a seat at the tables where hundreds of collective agreements were worked out.[2]

In Belgium the political upheaval of 1936 affected the strong Christian labor movement in a different fashion.[3] The old man of the socialist party in Belgium, Emile Vandervelde, even welcomed its participation in the 1936 wave of strikes that took place after the French example.[4] The Christian unions came out of the political demobilization of the Catholic Workers League strengthened rather than weakened. They forged a relationship with the Belgian Catholic Bloc (party) that left them freer to concentrate on properly trade union issues while maintaining a representation in parliament.

In different ways and to varying degrees, the Christian unions in these three countries had arrived by the end of the 1930s. They would arise again after the occupation during World War II.

France

Following World War I there was a veritable explosion of literary and intellectual Catholicism in France, the likes of which had not been seen since well before the separation of church and state. It may suffice just to recall the names of writers such as Georges Bernanos, Paul Claudel, and François Mauriac or other prominent Catholic opinion leaders like Jacques Maritain, Emmanuel Mounier, Georges Bidault, Étienne Borne, the Dominicans of Le Saulchoir and the Editions du Cerf, and the Jesuits of Lyon (Fourvière)—for instance, Henri de Lubac, author in 1938 of *Catholicisme: Les aspects sociaux du dogme*.[5] From the 1930s to the 1950s the intellectual productions coming out of modern Catholicism in France outshone analogous efforts in the rest of the world. Authors such as Marie-Dominique Chenu and Jacques Maritain would lend their weight to democratic forces and progressive social activism while contending with bourgeois conservatism and Marxist thought.[6]

In the working-class world French Catholicism could not boast of organizations comparable to those of the Workers' League and unions of Belgium or the Catholic labor movement of the Netherlands (or of pre-1933 Germany). But the small textile unions in the Nord had held their own and even received unusually firm backing from the Vatican, as we have seen (chapter 6). And

---

2. Launay 1986, 41–45.   3. Gerard 2004b, 108.
4. Polasky 1995, 234.
5. For introductions to this intellectual flowering, see Rémond 1996 or 1979; Fouilloux 1998; Komonchak 1999; Schloesser 2005, 2010.
6. See Chenu 1955; Mayeur 1988, 25–34; Poulat 1993; and Horn and Gerard 2001, 25–30.

the rest of the CFTC, with its predominance of office workers, grew at a modest pace, as well. The Christian unions enjoyed the continued support of the Jesuits' Action populaire and the *Semaines sociales* contingent in French Catholicism. The rather marginal Popular Democratic Party, a "party of Christian democratic inspiration," could be counted on to support social legislation congenial to the CFTC.[7] Gaston Tessier, secretary general of the CFTC, was engaged in all these directions. When Francisque Gay started a daily newspaper in 1932, *L'Aube*, Tessier joined him as cofounder. Unlike most other French political parties, the PDP had no daily. It was not the only party for Christian democrats, however, and Gay did not want his paper to be limited to or monopolized by the PDP. He actually aimed for a new political formation that would unite broader socially conscious elements around a Christian democratic core. Between the socialist left and the ultra-conservative right in France there was no major moderate party that could gather enough votes to govern. This broader project did not come to fruition at the time. Like several other new Catholic periodicals founded around this time (*La Vie Intellectuelle*, *Esprit*, *Sept*, *Terre Nouvelle*), however, *L'Aube* served to sensitize its readers to the societal ideals of the Catholic tradition.[8]

Tessier contributed much-noticed articles to *L'Aube*. For a while he had a regular column, until the governing board of the CFTC asked him to give it up. His criticism of conservative Catholic attitudes and organizations made some union leaders uncomfortable. Organizationally, though, formation in the principles of Catholic labor unionism was always a prime concern of the trade unions in the CFTC. Sustained effort went into the workshops and other training sessions of union activists so that they would be able to present well-founded grievances to management. They represented their fellow employees on committees and boards having to do with working conditions more often than their numerical weakness would warrant. Such militants would be among the most avid readers of *L'Aube*, which discussed current developments with democratic readings of Catholic social teaching. In the process it chipped away at the conviction nourished among many Catholics by a much larger daily, *L'Echo de Paris*, that a Catholic's political home could only be on the right among the conservatives. The campaigns and programs of the JOC had a parallel orientation among young workers, which eventually was of substantial import for the CFTC unions. The JOC was the most dynamic organization of French Catholic Action.

All this came to a head quite abruptly in June 1936. Following the election victory of the leftist Popular Front, a wave of sit-down strikes crashed across

7. Delbreil 2004; McMillan 1996b.
8. E. Weber 1994, 182–206, puts all this nicely in perspective; see Cadiot 2006.

Paris and then other industrial regions of France.[9] Since the French Communist Party was behind the Popular Front, though not one of the Front parties itself, the JOC and the CFTC initially took a very reserved stance, to say the least. Soon, however, they found that the labor solidarity that resulted was to their advantage and actually brought them recognition and a role that the Christian unions did not have up until then. In large part their growth came because the patient work of education and formation of potential leaders in the preceding years had prepared them for the challenges of 1936, when the hour of labor struck.

In the first half of the 1930s the emphasis on leadership training in the CFTC began to affect more factory workers, not just office employees.[10] Also in 1935, the still rare factory-worker representative on the CFTC central committee, Jean Pérès, took charge of the training courses that had always been important in the life of the confederation. He brought in Paul Vignaux, an academic historian of medieval philosophy and founder of a CFTC union of the teaching staff at state universities, to add heft to the curriculum. Previously the courses concentrated heavily on Catholic social teaching and religious formation, basics badly needed among the militants, at least until JOC members, with their milieu-based religious formation, joined the union in numbers. Now social history and ideas, even socialist ones, became more prominent in the training courses conducted by Vignaux and his associates. At the headquarters level, work on a basic position paper was going forward, published in January 1936 as *Le Plan de la CFTC*. Such plans or maps of the shape of the society to be constructed were all the rage; the Plan of Labor by the revisionist socialist in Belgium, Hendrik De Man, along with the Plan of the CGT (the socialist-communist Confédération générale du travail in France), calling for national economic planning to foster growth, were the most notable. Zirnheld, Tessier, and the CFTC, building on the platform put forward in 1920, summed up their contribution to the good society—enjoying social peace with justice in an industrial age—in the slogan "*the free union in the organized profession.*"

Corporatism and the Autonomy of Christian Labor

Freedom of association, particularly the freedom to form a real labor union with a claim to be heard in labor negotiations alongside other unions (CGT) and to work with them, but only on mutually agreeable terms, was of course a necessary plank for a minority union like the CFTC. But it was also a matter of

---

9. Jackson 1988, 85–104.
10. Launay 1986, 267–74; 1984, 37–40.

principle that would only become more urgent under Vichy after the defeat of France.[11] Working men and women too were persons with rights and responsibilities, which they could not simply discharge to an organization that brought them under one political and ideological banner. The other part of the maxim, "in the organized profession," requires a bit more explanation. The "profession" (or "occupation") here is, first of all, the branch of industry one worked in. Industrial organization, in the view of *Le Plan de la CFTC*, was sorely needed. Workers, as contributors to the common good, needed to be represented by organizations with a recognized status in society. Again, a third way was sought beside the competitive free-for-all of economic liberalism and the regimentation of fascism as well as Soviet communism. The *Plan* espoused the challenging view that values both of freedom and of social justice are best served by negotiated collective agreements. The CFTC *Plan* saw the way forward from where France was in the 1930s in a twofold series of freely formed institutions, all with business and labor participation, culminating in two national consultative bodies.[12]

The first or economic series would start with a process in which every employee of a firm or a plant, from loading dock to executive offices, would have a vote for representatives on a works council, representing the human capital of the enterprise.[13] At the regional level an economic council of industries would have equal representation of employees and owners or shareholders. The National Economic Council (Conseil national economique, CNE) would be directly elected by economic producers and would have advisory duties concerning regulations, credit, currency, and foreign economic relations. It would also work out legislative proposals to bring before the parliament. The idea was to secure a broad consideration of interests that would, in this rather idealistic way, settle many matters by agreement and, where appropriate, propose well-thought-out legislation to parliamentarians not intimately familiar with many facets of the national economy.

The second set of institutions (the professional or social body) had as its local basis the purely voluntary membership organizations that were the labor unions (*syndicats*). The other types of employees (salaried professionals, managers, officers of the firm) would form their own free *syndicats*. They would also be represented proportionally at the regional and national levels. Regional labor councils and a High Commission of Labor (Conseil supérieur du travail) would register and ratify the collective bargaining agreements that were

11. Vignaux 1943, 45–57.
12. For this, see Launay 1986, 306–13, and *Plan de la CFTC* 1936, 9–22; see especially Patch 2005, 194–99.
13. For the centrality of works councils in French labor law and hence in industrial relations in practice, as context for this element in the CFTC *Plan*, see Le Crom 2003 and Didry 2007, 97–101.

worked out on each level. In all of this the right to strike would be preserved as a last resort. The idea of codetermination or even co-management at plant or firm level was suggested by the emphasis on work as the motor of production.[14] The labor councils would be formed by agreement among the various unions of the labor force (for instance, CGT and CFTC member unions).

Of course, this was a variety of the pervasive 1930s "corporatism" or corporatist modeling of a reformed political economy. Like some other Catholic attempts, it was rather detailed as to ordering the relations of employers and employees (the social side), while leaving mechanisms for solving the economic crisis (the economic side) to be worked out in consultation. Certainly it was a sketch of the principle of subsidiarity at work. The *Plan*, however, avoided the terminology of "corporatism," "corporatist," or even "*organisation corporative.*" For the CFTC these terms already were victims of guilt by association with the state corporatisms of Italy, Germany, and Austria. One of their failures was in supposing that capital was the essential factor in production, rather than labor (human capital). This was the besetting confusion of liberal and moderate socialist plans, as well. In the state corporatisms this was compounded by the plague of unfreedom, of fascist or Soviet dictatorships.[15] The remedy proposed corresponds to this diagnosis. Why two parallel bodies? Because the properly economic order, dealing with production of things, had to be counterbalanced by and even subordinated to the social or professional order, concerned with persons.

Hence the proposal to institutionalize a public economic body (for economic planning or *concertation*) called for a parallel and independent series of institutions that would make up the professional body. Engagement in this second social body was completely voluntary (among those who by reason of their jobs would ipso facto belong to the economic body) and was based on freely formed *syndicats*, unions. In this way the priority of human values and human free initiative might be preserved in the face of the economic pressures of modern society. Only thus could the workers organize as they wished and have an independent say in how they would make their living.

In that era of corporatist proposals, the CFTC did not shrink from suggesting that the prevailing jurisprudence gave too absolute a status to the property rights of industrialists. For instance, the *Plan* questioned the right of heirs to take over a firm as their own property. The need for the restructuring of the national and international political economy was acknowledged for the sake of the common good. But what was clearly nonnegotiable in any set of possible reforms was the need for free labor unions, *syndicats libres*: voluntary

14. Launay 1984, 40.
15. Launay 1986, 306–10; Droulers 1981, 169.

organizations, recognized but not controlled by the state. The particular emphasis in the French situation was on the plurality of labor confederations: union pluralism. The CGT did not have the right to arrogate to itself the monopoly of labor representation, as happened at the Matignon. Workers, professionals, and commercial employees, even government employees, must be free to form their own unions and federations.

There were those Catholics who considered such proposals to be socialistic, to be sure. But even among Catholics of conservative bent who were active in defending Catholic education against anticlerical threats, the corporatist tradition of René de La Tour du Pin was iconic.[16] It would so emphasize the values of social harmony as to bring the employers and the workers into one corporation where the propertied classes would maintain the upper hand. Any criticism of private property rights brought on an allergic reaction, but a free labor union willing to sit down peaceably with employers was welcomed, at least in theory. The difference between the two socially conscious Catholic outlooks generally corresponded to whether one was attached to democratic institutions or saw mainly their flaws and failings in operation and feared populist tendencies.

Vignaux refers to the two social Catholic stances that faced each other in high tension during these years as traditionalists and syndicalists (unionists).[17] The former, ably and respectably represented at the academic level by François Perroux (1937), sought to tame capitalism by an obligatory work community of all those involved in a given sector or industry (*communauté de travail*; compare *Leistungsgemeinschaft* in Gundlach's German; compare, too, the Dutch *bedrijfsorganisatie*). The latter, the syndicalists, went along with this to the extent of proposing an economic body of all engaged in production, but insisted on a distinct social or professional body to be organized on the basis of free labor unions. Membership in these latter would not be a matter of obligation. Hence the unions would remain free to organize workers on their own and negotiate agreements with employers and society as a whole in their members' interest and in the interest of justice and the common good. A network of such collective bargaining agreements (*conventions collectives*), pursued long and consistently enough, would give rise to a freer and more humane equivalent of the communitarian regime sought by the traditionalists.

The syndicalists were thus part of a more left-leaning Catholic orientation referred to at this period as democratic Catholics. Their political allies included members of the small Christian democratic parties, the Jeune république and the more moderate PDP. The latter's domestic platform overlapped

16. Bonafoux-Verrax 2004, 193–212.
17. Vignaux 1943.

remarkably with the program and inspiration of the CFTC.[18] Numbered among the journalistic organs of this trend were *L'Aube* and certain publications launched by the Dominicans of Editions du Cerf. Père Marie-Vincent Bernadot provided a sounding board for such progressives in *La Vie Intellectuelle* and *Sept*, journals he created with the blessing of Pope Pius XI to oppose the attraction of the reactionary Action française in Catholic circles.[19] These small but influential journals, including Emmanuel Mounier's *Esprit*, founded around the same time, refused to align Catholics with the conservative Fédération nationale catholique and in general loosened the association of Catholicism with conventional rightist politics.[20]

Every year the *Semaines sociales de France* would gather speakers and audiences from the various socially involved currents of French Catholicism for a week of focusing on one or another problem area. Leaders of this institution were Eugène Duthoit of the Institut catholique of Lille and the team of the *Chronique Sociale* of Lyon, especially Marius Gonin (until his death in 1937).[21] Along with other figures from the CFTC, the clergy of the social secretariats and academia, Jules Zirnheld participated regularly, speaking on the role of labor unions in a well-ordered economy (twenty-seventh *Semaine sociale de France*, Angers 1935), as he had in Mulhouse in 1931. These summer meetings contributed substantially to solidifying Catholic support for social justice in the interwar years.

The Popular Front and Communism

Meanwhile, politics became ever more heated.[22] In France itself, disgust with politicians' ineffectiveness and scandals enabled right-wing leagues to stir up an assault on the parliament itself in February 1934. It looked momentarily as if an Austrian shutdown of democracy was about to take place. Feeling the pressure of the Nazi regime in Germany, Soviet Russia resolved to seek allies in the democratic West. The Communist line in France and elsewhere abruptly became one of partnership with all anti-Nazi forces in the defense of the laboring masses. That meant that the Communist Party, with *L'Humanité* as its mouthpiece, stopped attacking socialists and went all out for a common front with the socialist parties and any other radicals or moderates that could be persuaded to join.[23] It worked to the extent that a rapidly formed Popular Front

18. Delbreil 2004, 123–26. 19. Laudouze 1989, 143–52.
20. Rémond 1996, 139–70.
21. Intellectual activists such as Joseph Folliet and Joseph Vialatoux also formed part of this center in Lyon; see Comte 1992; Durand 2006; Lécrivain 1990; Ponson 1991).
22. Halls 1995, 15–28, is a fine overview of these developments and the Catholic role therein.
23. Murphy 1989, 7–14.

won a solid majority in the parliamentary elections of May 3, 1936. The leader of the Socialist Party, Léon Blum, formed a government in June with Socialist and Radical Socialist politicians taking seats in the cabinet. The Communist Party (and a couple of democratic Catholics) supported the government in parliament. The PDP, in opposition, was fairly restrained. Even the ostensibly apolitical Fédération nationale catholique held its fire.[24] The Popular Front was not professedly anticlerical, after all, and did not constitute an immediate threat to, say, the Catholic schools.

However, given the hostility between Catholics and communists everywhere, this election disturbed Catholic France as a whole. The "outstretched hand" (*main tendue*) that Maurice Thorez ostentatiously extended to workers of all persuasions and particularly to democratic Catholics seemed a dishonest ploy.[25] Catholic fears were stoked by events in Spain, where a parallel *Frente popular* had beaten rightist parties in the election of February 16. In July Generalissimo Francisco Franco revolted, and the Spanish Civil War broke out. Catholics in France and elsewhere heard about the support that Russia was lending the Spanish government, but even more about the atrocities committed against priests and nuns, supposed clients of the defeated parties.

In June of 1936, however, events unfolded on a different plane. Having made their political choices, workers now voted, not with their feet, but at work. Beginning in factories around Paris (Renault among others) and sweeping across the country, workers laid down their tools, turned off their machines, and took over their factories. Led or channeled by the local CGT militants in most cases, these sit-down strikes expressed their impatience for a new deal, a new order. Far from trashing the premises, however, they generally took care of the machines and the goods, feeling at home in the place where they spent so much time and wandering about to acquaint themselves with other parts of "their" shop and with their coworkers. In the face of the solidarity of the industrial masses, the government could not have put down the resistance if it had wanted to.[26] Nor could the employers take the loss of production indefinitely, especially with a government in power elected with the votes of the working class.

The strikes put social Catholics in a delicate position. While the Jesuits of Action populaire debated among themselves what kind of a statement to put out to their advisees, Cardinal Verdier responded quickly.[27] Known as he was to be sympathetic to the Christian unions and to the labor cause in general, he did not condemn the strikes with a single word. Rather, he had an appeal read in the churches on Sunday, June 7, and published in *La Croix* the evening

24. Bonafoux-Verrax 2004, 302–31.
25. Jackson 1988, 259–64.
26. Ibid., 86–92; Christophe 1986, 81–117.
27. Murphy 1989, 34–36.

before. It called upon all French citizens to work together to find solutions.[28] His words gave pause to those who could only think of the violation of property rights involved in the sit-down strikes; they encouraged those who were well-disposed to deal constructively with the Popular Front and the unions. Under Desbuquois's leadership, the Action populaire issued a statement in *La Croix* on Friday, June 12.[29] It welcomed the attention being given to workers' legitimate grievances in its first lines, but then made the point that the occupations of the factories were illegal under existing law and dangerous, given the supposed communist plotting behind them. Desbuquois was apparently more concerned about the growing Christian employers' movement making a sharp right turn than about the Christian unions falling prey to the communist left.[30] He crafted the statement to calm the waters and to keep wavering employers on board with professional organization according to *Quadragesimo anno*. As he explained to Tessier, he was also thinking of warding off a possible Vatican reaction against some suggestions of the CFTC *Plan*, those having to do with the primacy of labor in business and new notions of shared property rights over a firm.

At any rate, some leading employers (not in the Catholic movement) called upon Léon Blum to convoke a summit conference of labor leaders (CGT only!) and employers' organizations. This led quickly to the Matignon Agreement of June 7, 1936, the same day that Cardinal Verdier made his appeal, in which the employers agreed to far-reaching reforms. The obligation to enter into collective labor contracts with immediate wage increases was the big concession of the employers' delegation.[31] The labor representatives undertook to bring the sit-down strikes to an end. On the side, employers agreed not to oppose legislation making negotiations over wages and working conditions mandatory at the request of either side, and to arbitration if negotiations did not lead to agreement.[32] Other bills led quickly to the forty-hour week and (another spectacular breakthrough) paid vacation time, as soon as August!

The CFTC, very much a minority in this setting, was swept along by the tide. Though not approving of the illegal occupation of factories, as it was generally referred to, the union officers responded positively to the grassroots leaders, often JOC adherents, who took initiatives as CFTC union members.[33] They saw

---

28. Christophe 1986, 266–67.   29. Droulers 1981, 186–90.
30. On the Christian employers' movement, see Gremillion 1961, 23.
31. Lorwin 1954, 73–77, 313–15; see Fine 1969, 121–28.
32. See Le Crom 2003, 22–26.

33. In the provinces, things seemed a bit more chaotic than around Paris. A novelistic treatment of a sit-down strike in a Roubaix textile factory, as experienced by a fictional JOC/CFTC protagonist, is worth reading for the flavor of the time: Maxence van der Meersch, *Fishers of Men* (van der Meersch 1947), originally published in 1938; see Whitney 2009, esp. 216–30.

at once that the *conventions collectives* of the Matignon Agreement were what they had been proposing all along, even if it was achieved without their participation.[34] The same was true of the legislation that followed, instituting the forty-hour work-week and minimum wages. The rush on the part of workers to join a union spilled over to the CFTC. After temporary joiners dropped out again, CFTC had still doubled its membership to about 380,000. This sufficiently increased the proportion of factory hands, including metalworkers, to affect the complexion of the confederation, which was weighted toward office and sales workers. The separate women's unions in the confederation came under pressure to merge with the corresponding men's unions, threatening the prominence of female union leadership. Probably the most positive result of the Popular Front reforms for the CFTC was the strong participation of its representatives on bargaining committees for the numerous *conventions collectives* that had to be arrived at. The dominant CGT had to recognize, though begrudgingly, the laborist good faith and standing of the Christian unionists from this time on. The years-long emphasis on schooling its militants stood the CFTC in good stead when they became negotiators. The presence and self-confidence of Catholic labor movements became evident to a broader public in the course of 1937, when both the CFTC and the JOC held large gatherings in Paris in celebration of their fiftieth (CFTC) and tenth year (JOC) since their founding.[35] By this time both were widely recognized in public opinion as social actors. The critical years of 1936–37 marked a distinct breakthrough for the Catholic labor organizations.

The Vatican and Catholic public opinion generally were much preoccupied with signs that communism was gaining ground in the West during the Depression. In the wake of Spain and Thorez's "outstretched hand," this attitude only hardened.[36] In an interview that *Sept* accorded Léon Blum, the prime minister declared that collaboration was possible between Catholics and his Front populaire government.[37] *Sept* commented, "Why not?" without endorsing the platform of the Socialist Party, to say nothing of the communists. An outcry followed nevertheless, leading eventually to the Vatican closing down *Sept* in August 1937 by forbidding the Dominicans to publish it any longer. An independent lay weekly, *Temps Présent*, then took up the cudgels with editors Stanislas Fumet and Joseph Folliet and the collaboration of Jacques Maritain.

In the midst of all this upheaval in 1936, Maritain's most famous book, *Integral Humanism: Temporal and Spiritual Problems of a New Christendom*, appeared.

---

34. See *Plan de la CFTC 1936*, 14; Zirnheld 1937, 266.
35. Launay 1986, 377–79; Pierrard 1997, 187–90; Whitney, 2009, 209–42.
36. In Cardinal Liénart's case, for instance; see Masson 2001, 202.
37. Feb. 19, 1937; see Coutrot 1982, 215–24.

It elaborated on an unconventional proposal that Charles Journet had made in 1931—that the notion of Christendom (*chrétienté*) should be applied to the shapes that Christianity assumes in different eras. The times now seemed to be calling for a new set of relationships with society ("the world"), a "new" Christendom. This would have to be a humanism, a new humanism, under Christian inspiration but pluralistic, anti-totalitarian, and recognizing the lay and autonomous character of the state. Whereas the Christendom of medieval times had "a Christian *sacral* conception of the temporal" world, this new historical ideal "would entail a Christian *secular* conception."[38] The autonomy from a commission granted or withheld by the ecclesiastical hierarchy that was thus accorded to lay members of the church corresponded well with a long-felt need of Christian labor. It also implied, albeit with subtle distinctions, a new slant on Pius XI's model of Catholic Action.[39] The central message was that Christians had the chance and hence the obligation to rescue the modern world from worshiping political power or economic success as the ultimate goods. There was to be no retreat from exerting their influence in a pluralistic manner as citizens of the cultural, civil, and public realms.[40] Key would be the role of the working masses in ushering in a more humane postmodern world.[41]

Maritain did not propose this as a utopian scheme nor yet as a political party platform, but as a sketch of a polity that would be thoroughly consonant with Christian doctrine and at the same time enhance the freedom and dignity of the human person. Christian democratic politicians in the postwar era in France, Italy, and Latin America made it their shared *vade mecum*. In 1930s France it put Maritain firmly on the side of those who opposed totalitarian regimes, left and right, and in the camp of democratically committed Catholic labor advocates such as Tessier and Vignaux.[42] In the judgment of Chenu, one knew by then that the "prophetic" pages of chapter 6 of *Humanisme intégral* (dating from 1934) "nourished the Christian generation of 1936, of 1940, and of 1945."[43]

---

38. Maritain 1996, 255–84, esp. 273–75. 39. Ibid., 322, 339–41.
40. Chenaux 2006a, 33–34, 52–62.
41. Maritain 1996, 315; again, see Horn and Gerard 2001, 29–30.
42. Greeting a pilgrimage of the French CFTC in Rome on September 18, 1938 (in Pius XI 1985, 810–16), Pius XI praised these Catholic unionists for their programmatic positions and recent growth. He then briefly critiqued the extremes of collectivism and individualism. Mutual charity is missing from both deviations and is needed to cure their practices. Turning to Catholic Action, he first redefines it as simply "the life of the Church," noting that the activists of the CFTC need no admonition to coordinate their activities with Catholic Action. While stressing the interior life of grace, he states that Catholic Action is not out to displace any good works. They are all precious contributions to Catholic Action, here described with his customary definition as "the participation of the laity in the hierarchical apostolate." Did Gaston Tessier, in the audience, compare this to his own implicit claim of autonomous action on the part of unionists? Did he think of Maritain's thesis of the "secular conception of the temporal" and of lay Christian action in the public realm?
43. Chenu 1955, 36.

In March 1937 Pius XI published two encyclicals, *Mit brennender Sorge* against Nazism and *Divini redemptoris* against communism. Given the damage wrought by the advance of communism, especially in Spain, the Vatican cooled to the campaign against the Action française that Pius XI had committed to Bernadot. In the view of Vatican circles, Maurras's movement went from propounding a heresy ("*politique d'abord*") to representing a disciplinary issue. This would be cleared up by a profession of contrition by Catholics in the Action française and by the lifting of church sanctions against them by the new pope, Pius XII, in early 1939.[44]

By the end of 1937, all the same, Cardinal Verdier let on in his Christmas message that Pope Pius XI was inclined to grasp a hand extended to the church even by communists.[45] This could not be done in such a way as to become "fellow travelers," but in the spirit of Mt 11:28–30: "Come to me, all who labor." The church had resources to offer that communist doctrine lacked. In the *Aube* of December 28 Gaston Tessier noted that the CFTC had been in touch with "the communists" on policy matters for some time. It also may be that the suppression of *Sept* and the increased sympathy for Maurras did not reflect the pope's more urgent priorities.[46] By the late 1930s it was no longer communism but Hitler's Germany that was his most urgent international preoccupation.

After the Popular Front

The same shift in focus was if anything more clear in the case of the Christian unionists. Zirnheld was now the president of the much reduced International Federation of Christian Trade Unions as well as of the CFTC. If that old prisoner of the German army needed any alerts to the danger from that quarter, Jos Serrarens, the CISC secretary general, was ready with firm stands against any "New Order" under Nazi domination. Soon, however, the backlash against labor rights on the part of industrialists, combined with the urgent need for greater rearmament, resulted in the abandonment of the forty-hour week policy. A general strike in November 1938 in protest against this move was quickly put down. Labor clout dissipated again.[47]

The international situation clearly spelled hostilities with a resurgent

---

44. See Prévotat 2001 for all this; see Laudouze 1989, 160–75.

45. Murphy 1989, 102–7.

46. The depth of the pope's shift in perspective in 1937 is suggested in notes taken by Secretary of State Pacelli from private meetings with Pius XI. (Access to these documents was opened to researchers in 2006.) Fattorini 2011, esp. 76–85, gives ample citations and commentary on what it is perhaps not too drastic to call a change of heart. For French communist commentary, see Murphy 1989, 105. Chenaux (2009, 112–15) sums up the rather startled reaction to the papal reflection; see Ventresca 2013, 114–25.

47. Magraw 1992, 279–96.

Germany. When Hitler in March 1939 went far beyond the Munich agreement of the previous September by taking over what remained of Czechoslovakia and made demands of the Polish government that were clearly unacceptable, the French and their British ally responded by promising aid to Poland in the event of an invasion. The Germans did attack Poland on September 1, and France and Britain accordingly declared war on Germany. The hope was that Hitler was too occupied in Central and Eastern Europe to invade the West just yet and that defenses could be strengthened in time to turn back eventual attacks. Poland was divided between German and Russian armies. The Germans attacked Finland and Norway during the winter. Finally, on May 10, 1940, the invasion of the Netherlands, Belgium, and France took place. Terrifying Stuka raids and tank battalions turned the attack into a rout. Marshal Pétain sued for terms in mid-June.[48] In its defeat France was divided into zones, with two-fifths of the country, in the South and the East, under the administration of the French Vichy government. France was now an ally of Germany, not Britain. The other zones to the West and North were occupied by German forces. The industrial area around Lille (the Nord) was cut off from the neighboring areas of France and administered out of Brussels.

The Pétain government at Vichy swore by "Work, Family, Fatherland" rather than the Republic's "Liberty, Equality, Fraternity." It was unabashedly authoritarian, aiming to be a paragon of state corporatism. Some moderate union leaders, like other democratically inclined citizens, hoped to resurrect some form of the *politique de présence* that they had resorted to in earlier hostile circumstances. The confusion cleared up for the CFTC and many others after November 9, 1940, when the government issued a decree suppressing all the union federations and analogous employer associations at the national level. They were to be replaced by unitary corporatist organizations under state oversight, a solution that to some laborites seemed to hold promise. By November 15, however, ex-CGT and ex-CFTC officers produced a document in Paris that became known as the *Manifeste des Douze* because it was signed by twelve unionists, nine from the CGT and three from the CFTC. These were Jules Zirnheld, who would die before the end of the *annus horribilis* that was 1940, Gaston Tessier, the general secretary, and Maurice Bouladoux, the federation's deputy secretary.

This text of the *Manifeste des Douze* is of course remarkable not only for its content and its courageous stand against the new order, but also simply because it was jointly signed by leaders of the Christian as well as the socialist trade unions.[49] In 1936 the CGT had not acknowledged that the CFTC unions

---

48. See Jackson 2003.

49. See Halls 1995, 249; Saudejaud 1999, 30–41, describes how this surprising joint declaration came about and (42–92) its mixed reception in the ranks of the CFTC.

were a legitimate part of the labor movement. Now some CGT leaders, minus the former communist adherents, invited their CFTC colleagues to join them in issuing the manifesto. The result was agreement on six "Principles of French Unionism" (the original title of the manifesto) in opposition to the Vichy version of corporatism that loomed ahead. The signers took their stand against the domination of capital and in the defense of the "general interest" (Catholics would understand "common good"). They proposed "the formula of the future: the free trade union in the organized profession and in the sovereign state." They contended that the only way to end class struggle ("which has up to now been more a fact than a principle") is by full acceptance of collective bargaining. The fourth principle they enunciated was "respect of the human person" without invidious discrimination because of race (specifically anti-Semitism), religion, opinions, or wealth. Then follow "liberty" (including freedom of choice of a union to join or not to join) and international collaboration. With that the national union officers turned to save what could be saved of unionism at the local level or effectively went underground until a later day.

Belgium

The exceptional growth and vitality of the Christian labor movement in Belgium (into the 1980s and beyond) calls for a closer look at developments in the 1930s.[50] On the political side a restructuring and modernization of the Catholic Party finally took place. It reduced the virtual political autonomy of the labor movement in the shape of the ACW/LNTC, but gave it a worthwhile place in the party's internal deliberations. On the economic side, the troubled 1930s saw a successful consolidation of the Christian trade unions (ACV/CSC), so much so that by 1938 they were becoming the equal of the socialist ones. The initial trends, to be sure, did not look promising for labor or democracy. The Christian democrats shared the ideal of re-Christianizing society ("building the Christian city," in the parlance of a notable review of the period),[51] but not at the sacrifice of their political autonomy and not by authoritarian means. The latter did appeal to many in the coming generation. Among the Catholics who enjoyed the advantages of education beyond the age of fourteen, a pronounced disgust with parliaments and political parties often came to prevail. The compromises and frustrations that came with partisan politics increasingly became the target of criticism. This was particularly the case in the Francophone youth organization, the ACJB. Its working-class sister, the JOC, following the Catholic Action pattern of Italy in this respect, also abstained from party politics and

50. See Pasture 1992.
51. See Conway 1990 and Sauvage 1987.

took its cues from the bishops rather than from the lay-led ACW. A yearning for real democracy was nonetheless basic to its work of formation and training of leaders. The bishops, for their part, had not given up on the Catholic Party. In Belgium, since the First World War, universal suffrage and parliamentary democracy were in place, though not without considerable dissatisfaction being manifested among rightist Catholics.

For the ACW/LNTC, the Catholic workers' league or *standsorganisatie*, and for the ACV/CSC, the Catholic trade union federation, interest-group politics in a democratic arena was inseparable from their mission to improve the life of the working class. From their solid base in the Flemish part of the country, the ACW/LNTC acted much like a political party, putting up their own candidates and electing them until the 1936 refounding of the Catholic Party. Of course, the movement's empire of savings banks, cooperatives, women's organizations, and the allied trade union and JOC forces helped bind their members to the Catholic pillar, as did the parallel institutions of the Catholic Farmers' League.[52]

Taken all in all, nevertheless, these were critical times for political Catholicism in Belgium.[53] Its constituencies went in different directions in trying to cope with the Depression. A good number of voters abandoned the Catholic Party in 1936 for two splinter groups, one authoritarian and one Flemish nationalist. The Nazi takeover in Germany and the Spanish Civil War brought home the possibility of major change in the absence of sensible reforms. However, the authoritarian movement called "Rex" (recalling its origin in the 1920s in the "Christ the King" theme of Pius XI) eventually overreached itself, provoking a virtual condemnation by Cardinal Van Roey and suffering an electoral collapse in a Brussels by-election in 1937.[54] In the meantime the Catholic Party re-formed itself into the Belgian "Catholic Bloc" with two fairly autonomous wings, Flemish and Walloon, distinguished in the first place by language. Both still retained the adjective "Catholic" in their names—it would be replaced by "Christian" only in 1945.

The reorganized party, with its two regional and linguistic wings, was now constituted by its individual members instead of by its organized constituencies or *standen* (that is, the Farmers' League, which had been hit by the failure of its big bank, the ACW Workers' League, the bourgeois Fédération des cercles, and the less well-organized small business association). It set up a fairly standard political party organization. The Farmers' and Workers' Leagues continued independently as milieu organizations. According to the party statutes,

52. Evans 1999, 174–75; Craeybeckx 2000, 114.
53. Gerard 2004b, 103–8 for the subsequent text.
54. Craeybeckx 2000, 147.

they participated as such in the selection of candidates and the drafting of platforms, "but they accepted the creation of a streamlined party structure and a political leadership that could decide party policy."[55] On Catholic confessional interests such as schools, they continued to vote with the other Catholic deputies; in labor and social issues, they acted as a pressure group within the party and the parliament for their own constituency.

An interesting note has to do with personalism, a perspective that the newly reorganized party adopted and that would become increasingly dominant in the political thinking of European Catholics. Jacques Maritain addressed the 1937 Paris conference of the CISC on the subject.[56] Putting forth the dignity and rights of the human person qua social as the guiding values of the party simultaneously shifted it from being a party primarily concerned with defending the rights and interests of the Catholic Church to one having a properly political program while drawing on Catholic thought.

The ACW thus continued to exercise a strong role within Belgian political Catholicism, even as it weathered the Depression and increased its strength in the world of labor and industry. Its own component parts became more autonomous with the greater differentiation of tasks taken up in the realms of insurance, cooperatives, and health. As Emmanuel Gerard maintains, Louis Colens's ambition to create a many-sided labor movement to rival that of the socialists had come to fruition.[57] The Christian trade unions (ACV) entered a new stage, as well. In a striking variation from the experience of their French labor counterparts in the pivotal year of 1936, the socialist unions abjured Marxism and accepted a certain measure of collaboration with the strong Christian unions.[58] By 1938 the ACV unions had attained full recognition on the part of their socialist counterparts, the employers in industry, and the government. Their theorist, Joseph Arendt, could well say that they had reached a new stage in their development.[59] What led up to the turning points of 1935–36 that constituted the breakthrough?

Like the socialist unions, the Catholic ones in Belgium were not laid low by the Depression, inasmuch as they continued to serve as the conduits for unemployment subsidies under the Ghent system.[60] This was an effective inducement for workers to join or not to abandon their unions in hard times; the percentage of organized workers continued to rise.[61] As part of the ACW, the ACV unions could wield political clout. The longtime president of the ACW and

55. Gerard 2004b, 108.
56. See Pasture 1999, 194–99.
57. Gerard 1994a, 195–97.
58. Strikwerda 2003; see Lamberts 2006, 366–67.
59. Mampuys 1994, 215.
60. Vanthemsche 1990; Craeybeckx 2000, 122–23.
61. Mampuys 1994, 170.

former president of the ACV, Hendrik Heyman (1879–1958), held the cabinet post of Industry, Labor, and Social Welfare from 1927 to 1932 and did what he could for the workers' cause. One result was making the practice of extra pay for each child in a worker's family more broadly obligatory.[62] Meanwhile, the central government grew more disposed to deal with labor, of course at the national level. The role of organized labor was still further enhanced under the government program set up in 1935 to deal with mass unemployment; it was administered through the national (Catholic and socialist) trade union confederations.

The next generation of leadership was to a great extent already in place: Henri Pauwels (1890–1946) as head of the ACV/CSC confederation and, from 1932 on, August Cool (1903–83) as its secretary general.[63] Emiel Verheeke (1881–1963) headed the Flemish textile union. If in the mid-1920s the individual unions (such as Verheeke's for the textile industry, or others for metallurgy) were more prominent in the lives of their members than the confederation, the need for a more powerful union movement led to a centralized strike fund (built up out of members' dues) at the level of the ACV.

In terms of political allegiances, the socialist Belgian Workers Party and the Catholic political party remained the dominant parties and hence rivals in seeking the electoral support of their respective labor movements. A remarkable convergence nevertheless occurred in the 1930s. The way one historian puts it is striking: "The Socialist Party and its union forsook the practice of class struggle and joined the Christian labor movement in seeking reconciliation between capital and labor."[64] The shift in the socialist stance emerged most clearly in the "Plan of De Man"—that is, Hendrik De Man, who followed Emile Vandervelde as leader of the socialist movement.[65] The government had tried to cope with the Depression by deflationary policies, keeping prices of exports low by keeping wages low. But still there was slumping demand. Strikes broke out, but to not much avail, as companies were going bankrupt. In this situation De Man put forth his labor plan. Contemporary with Franklin D. Roosevelt's New Deal and Hitler's interventions in the economy to boost employment, it called for nationalization of the energy and banking sector so that the state could stimulate the economy. It involved a kind of corporatism "based on

---

62. Gerard 1994b, 165.

63. On the women's side, too, new leaders emerged; De Decker, Ista, and Keymolen, 1994, 378. Philippine Vande Putte (1903–63) assisted Maria Baers in her para-union working-class womens' organization, as did Maria Nagels (also born in 1903). Baers herself was also a member of the ACV's governing board and became a senator in 1936, while serving on international commissions, as, for instance, in the ILO.

64. Craeybeckx 2000, 135; see Pirotte and Zelis 2003, 238–40.

65. Polasky 1995.

negotiations, including joint committees" of labor and management.[66] This overlapped to a great extent with what the Christian unions already backed, under the term *overleg* (consultation).

One long-term result of all this was that the Belgian Christian unions, while retaining a place in the ranks of the Catholic Party, could not be viewed as falling under the category of Catholic Action. There was an amicable parting of the lines of responsibility between the bishops and the lay persons who ran the unions. This was a deconfessionalization of the unions that occurred so quietly and naturally that no one called it such. Or, as Jan De Maeyer has suggested, the pragmatic strain of the Belgian Christian unions had been so strong that they simply took their Catholic identity into the service of the cause of labor.[67]

This was the solid internal situation of Christian labor when the Germans invaded in May 1940 and set up a military occupying authority.[68] Previously, in September 1938, the union leadership had issued confidential instructions to the effect that in case of an occupation by German forces, all (official) union activity was to cease. Henri Pauwels, for his part, responded as the elected Belgian government did by refusing to work under an administration imposed by foreign military might. ACV/CSC leaders, including Pauwels, the president, and August Cool, the secretary general, departed for France as the German forces took over. Some members of the governing council remained in Belgium, however. In June, after consultation with the union chaplains Rutten and Belpaire, these men decided to pick up where they had left off in May. Soon there was no place in France for those who were trying to maintain an exile organization there. Pauwels and Cool returned to Belgium with their families by July 15—Pauwels decidedly anti-collaborationist, Cool less so.

For the Flemish majority in the union confederation, however, as for King Leopold III, who remained in occupied Belgium, the German force majeure posed more involved issues. During the strange summer of 1940, it appeared to many as if German supremacy in Europe would be permanent. It seemed incumbent upon the Flemish leaders to make the best of the situation if a "New Order" was really taking shape.[69] A *politique de présence* seemed appropriate. While Pauwels and Cool were still in France, the leaders who stayed put decided to drop the name of their organization and set up in its place a committee to guide the fortunes of Christian professional organizations. For months discussions took place within the Catholic unions (including a reluctant Pauwels) and political circles (for instance, Flemish nationalists) and with employers

---

66. Craeybeckx 2000, 142.
67. De Maeyer 2003, 119.
68. Mampuys 1994, 216–24.
69. See Craeybeckx 2000, 158–60, with background (146–54) on right-wing and Flemish nationalist movements in a divided Catholic pillar.

and socialist union leaders to create a successor organization along corporatist lines. Soon, however, in November, the military administration put a clamp on these efforts. Determined to strangle any independent organizational life of the preexisting labor unions, the German labor commissar in Brussels created the Union of Manual and Clerical Workers (UTMI) and proceeded to regulate labor-management relations. "This form of state corporatism, forced upon the Belgians by the Germans, would have very little influence on postwar socioeconomic developments."[70]

The Christian unions actually agreed to this "reform" in November 1940 (though Pauwels refused to go along with the majority). This was the end of the ACV/CSC for the duration, although August Cool and Jules Roscam, a longtime activist for the diamond workers, were invited to join the eight-person provisional executive committee of the new body to represent the Christian professional organizations. It took them until March 1941 to withdraw their collaboration, by then convinced that the undue German influence undercut any true representation of the interests of Belgian labor. The final step in the dissolution of the Christian unions came in August 1941. Some components of the ACV/CSC decided to merge into the now thoroughly controlled UTMI: among them was the most prominent collaborator in the textile unions, Emiel Verheeke, and members of the Christian unions of the clerical, rail, and trade school employees.

In the ensuing years under occupation, Henri Pauwels repaired his relations with Gus Cool, overly compromised in the view of the Walloons, at the urgent request of, among others, Cardinal Van Roey. As the latter counseled the deposed duo in late 1942, leaving postwar labor organization to the socialists and communists was not an outcome for which Christian labor leaders on either side of the linguistic divide would wish to be responsible.

The Netherlands

By the time the Depression hit, the Catholic labor movement in the Netherlands was also well organized and active, as we have seen (chapter 5). It was one of the more highly mobilized segments of the Catholic pillar. It even boasted members of parliament and a couple of senators from the Catholic labor movement. The Dutch openness to a role for government in industrial relations has already been noted, especially in the form of tripartite consultation, the much-cited *overleg*. When unemployment assumed Depression dimensions, an evolving "culture of consultation and cooperation" was where one turned in

---

70. Notes Lamberts 2006, 370.

the quest for remedial measures.[71] In the Catholic pillar the encyclical *Quadragesimo anno* naturally lent further credence to this approach. On the socialist side the Marxist-flavored official ideology gave way to a more cooperative, persuasion-oriented kind of socialism, influenced by the Belgian socialist leader Hendrik De Man and his *Plan van de Arbeid*. In 1937 the Dutch socialist party and its associated unions officially adopted a similar *Plan van de Arbeid*, thus tacitly drawing closer to the Protestant and Catholic labor movements.[72]

Within this framework Catholic labor organizations continued to develop. The Young Christian Workers (JOC or KAJ, referred to as "*Kajotters*") did not come to the Netherlands until the 1940s, but since 1920 a similar milieu organization took root in the more Catholic South of the country (dioceses of Breda, 's-Hertogenbosch, and Roermond): *De Jonge Werkman*.[73] Henricus Poels stood behind it as propagator of the Catholic milieu organizations we have met under the denomination of *standsorganisaties*. This one, as it name suggests, was for young workers seventeen and older. It got started a few years before Joseph Cardijn inspired the Belgian JOC/KAJ and its feminine counterpart. In 1931, in imitation of the Belgian example, diocesan organizations of the *Jonge Werkman* merged at the national level with that of the archdiocese of Utrecht. From its ranks rose future Catholic labor leaders such as P. J. J. (Jan) Mertens (1916–2000), years later head of the Catholic union federation (Nederlands Katholieke Vakverbond) until he became minister of social affairs (1973–77). The milieu organization afforded the young typesetter without even secondary education a chance to learn and sharpen his skills as its local leader in the diocese of Breda since 1937. When the organization was dissolved in 1940 with the occupation, he could continue under the banner of Catholic Action, ready to rebuild the adult organization after 1945. Such a future was possible for working-class youth only because of the robust development of the Catholic labor movement in the 1930s.

Catholic labor union membership increased from 21 percent of organized labor in 1930 to over 23 percent in 1940, the second-largest confederation after the socialist NVV, which held steady at 40 percent.[74] In this period the labor federations resorted to dealing with counterparts in the High Council of Labor more intensively than before. They found parliament and the political parties with which they were allied less able to act effectively. (A Keynesian countercyclical approach was still foreign to the statesmen of the early Depression; destitution was widespread.) A. C. De Bruijn skillfully handled the tensions between the two wings of the Catholic labor movement (the *stands-*

---

71. Hein Wiedijk, in *HJS* 243; Windmuller 1969, 66.
72. *HJS* 373–87. 73. Peet 1987, 19.
74. Roes 1985b, 42; see *HJS* 781–86.

organisatie and the union federation). A related set of tensions existed between the RKWV as a whole and the Catholic Party. The comparatively favorable situation of Catholic labor must not be exaggerated: its parliamentary contingent was a minority within a minority party in a government that operated under emergency rules because of the economic crisis and later because of the Nazi threat. Whether the general outcome for workers was a case of "suffering from unity," as Jos van Meeuwen highlights, or cooperation for the common good, as John Windmuller emphasizes, is a matter of phase and perspective.[75] De Bruijn would occasionally wield the threat to take the labor contingent out of the party to form its own coalition.

The High Council, meanwhile, became a forum where top employer, labor, and government representatives met with one another on a regular basis and on a politically neutral ground.[76] By preparing drafts of legislation that were then presented to parliament, the members of the High Council promoted a series of framework laws on collective bargaining, social insurance, and various other openings for government intervention in the sense desired by the (not yet so-called) social partners. An industry boards law went into effect in 1933; a law governing collective agreements in industry was passed in 1937 with the backing of Christian and socialist unions. It gave certain such agreements binding force across an industry. On their own, in 1938, business and labor organizations instituted a joint commission for organized consultation (*overleg*).[77] There was thus a bipartite consultation mechanism alongside the tripartite High Council of Labor. This level of consensus on labor-management relations was unique in the countries along the Rhine in 1939.

By 1933 the RKWV provided a broad spectrum of services, not just unemployment aid and job services, to its members. Its daily newspaper, *De Volkskrant*, was well established. A sanatorium for tuberculosis sufferers was created; there were housing and health insurance programs operating; a banking system helped finance such projects and encourage worker savings.[78] Youth and family programs were intensified, with a school or formation center founded principally to impart higher skills to the young jobless. Starting in 1938 a major propaganda campaign for measures to implement *Quadragesimo anno* was launched by the RKWV, aimed at all the other milieu organizations in the Catholic fold. A paragon of mobilization, indeed!

Given the vitality and mature development of these *standsorganisaties* in the effectively pillarized Netherlands, the alternative model of lay activity, Catholic Action, made little headway.[79] Diocesan structures were set up, especially

75. Van Meeuwen 1998, 404; Windmuller 1969, 131.
76. Windmuller 1969, 63–78.
77. Roes 1985a, 51; Windmuller 1969, 85.
78. See Somerville 1933, 95–104.
79. De Haan 1994, 327–33.

after Pius XI issued urgent instructions in 1936, but the bishops already had sufficient influence over and confidence in existing Catholic organizations, including political and labor organizations, to refrain from bringing them officially under a Catholic Action mandate. Perhaps Pius XI had some appreciation for the Dutch accomplishments in this regard. In his noted encyclical against communism, *Divini redemptoris* of March 19, 1937, he expanded upon *Quadragesimo anno* in certain passages.[80] In paragraphs 46–54 the encyclical laid out most distinctly the character of social justice and its relation to Christian charity, concluding (again with *QA*) that harmonious labor-management relationships "can only be achieved by a body of professional and interprofessional organizations ... working together to effect, under forms adapted to different places and circumstances, what has been called the Corporation." In an earlier passage commenting on *QA* (no. 32), he stated that a "sane corporative system" directed toward the common good would "respect the proper hierarchic structure of society." It seems unavoidable to see here a reference, disguised by paradoxical wording ("hierarchic"), to the principle of subsidiarity.

In concluding, after appealing to the clergy to "win back the laboring masses to Christ and to His Church" (62), the pope turned to the laity and Catholic Action (64–66). He noted as well the Catholic groups that did not fall under "Catholic Action" as such (67). These he was happy to call "its auxiliary forces." He included within this category what we are calling milieu organizations in the spirit of Cardijn and Poels. His description fit them perfectly (68): "associations of workmen, farmers, technicians, doctors, employers, students and others of like character, groups of men and women who live in the same cultural atmosphere and share the same way of life." Even though these associations on the Poels model had received a frosty reception at the Vatican in 1929 in the form of the Catholic Worker International, the pope now commended the flourishing *standsorganisaties* of Dutch and Flemish Catholicism. They would need only to be supplemented with the more official cadres of Catholic Action proper.

When the war came on May 10, 1940, there was comparatively little collaboration with the occupying power, little interest in a "New Order" under the circumstances.[81] Someone suggested that it would be prudent for Cardinal De Jong to issue a conciliatory letter, to which he replied, "What? And become a second Innitzer?"[82] By August 1941 a joint pastoral letter of the Dutch bishops, read from the pulpits, protested above all the Nazi takeover of the RKWV and

---

80. Droulers 1981 notes the influence of Gustave Desbuquois, SJ, on these passages.

81. Heerma van Voss 1995, 54.

82. Damberg 1997, 551. Pius XI had reprimanded Innitzer over his obsequious reception of Hitler in Vienna at the Anschluss; see Liebmann 1987.

instructed its members to resign from the successor organization as its leaders had done:

> We cannot say how profoundly we regret the end of the RKWV. It was especially precious to us because it included in its two hundred thousand members a great part of the good and loyal Catholic people; because for a half century our most exemplary men, priests and laity, beginning with Schaepman and Ariëns, have devoted their best efforts to it; [and] because the Roman Catholic Association of Working People has done such enormous good for society and religion.[83]

At the end of the 1930s the Catholic labor movement of Western Europe faced the same threats and defeats as other democratic institutions. In Italy, Germany, and Austria it was suppressed. In France, Belgium, and the Netherlands, however, it had gained new strength and stature. New possibilities for fruitful common action with the larger labor organizations on behalf of the working class had emerged. The cauldron of World War II would test the ideas and the resolve of all parties. The postwar opportunities would reveal what they had learned and how capable they were of realizing their goals in freedom and respectful rivalry.

83. *HJS* 436–40.

CHAPTER 13

Labor and Catholicism under the Impact of World War II

During World War II, with independent labor organizations suppressed, activists shifted their focus to planning for the postwar future while maintaining or even increasing like-minded contacts to the extent possible. Participation in various levels and kinds of resistance to the wartime occupations proceeded in tandem with laying the groundwork for life after liberation. With the final victory of the Allied forces over Nazi domination, the challenge became urgent to build democratic structures and to undertake the beginnings of reconstruction with whatever resources were available. Then, from about 1947 on, there quickly followed the new situation of the Cold War. Western European countries, with the Atlantic allies, faced off against another totalitarian power imposed in the name of communism. Organized labor, with its communist, social democratic, and Christian democratic contingents, had to come to terms with this situation. It also had to take up again the central efforts to press the workers' demands for fair wages and working conditions. How would Catholic labor contribute to this struggle? How would this affect the modern Catholic social tradition on the appropriate means to further economic justice and humanize the world of work? Lessons learned from the past helped to bring about a favorable outcome in the economic revival of the 1950s.

There were early signs that labor's role in the postwar restructuring of European society would be considerable. Perhaps the first notable event to signal the possible shape of labor organization in the postwar period occurred in Belgium. Catholic and socialist unions had agreed to a system of *overleg* (that is, consultation between management and labor with government participation) in

1939. They continued the practice underground during the occupation, now, of course, hidden from the government. In the course of 1943 labor and industry representatives stepped up the pace of such clandestine consultations.[1] The two economic partners hastened to cement this development even before Brussels was liberated in September 1944 and before the London-based government in exile could have much input. This led to the conclusion of a Social Pact in Belgium in April 1944.[2] It contained far-reaching concessions in the direction of labor co-management. These labor advantages were whittled down in the subsequent years, but the voice for labor remained strong in the industrial economy of *concertation*, or social capitalism.[3]

In Italy it was the heirs of the divided labor movements who made contact with each other and concluded their own pact on the day before Allied troops took possession of the city of Rome on June 4, 1944. Mussolini had been overthrown and placed under arrest in July 1943. When the successor regime accepted surrender to the Anglo-American invaders on September 8, the campaign for military control of the peninsula continued between Allied and German forces at enormous cost in human lives until April 1945.

Urgent negotiations occurred among Italian labor leaders and culminated in the Pact of Rome of June 3, 1944. The signers of this document were Giuseppe Di Vittorio (for the communist wing of the unitary union that they were announcing), Emilio Canevari (for the socialists), and Achille Grandi (for the Christian democrats). It was a declaration of the founding of the CGIL, the Italian General Confederation of Labor.[4] The declaration foresaw strict autonomy from political parties, mutual respect and equal representation of the three currents of organized labor in the new confederation, and the reorganization of associated trade unions on parallel democratic principles. It had the at least provisional support of the leaders of the renascent political parties representing the three wings of organized labor.[5] It of course excluded fascist elements, except for staking a claim on the assets of formerly fascist labor organizations. The cohabitation of communists and Catholics in the same house of labor, however, would not last many years.

In France, while the war was going on, the defeated nation coped with the

---

1. See Gerard 1994d, 109. Consultations between leaders of the former rival labor organizations *without* employers' representatives took place everywhere they were possible. For the Netherlands, see *HJS* 448, and the overview by Jan Peet, in *HJS* 415–22.

2. Luyten and Vanthemsche 1995; see Pasture 1993 for a study in English.

3. For the category, "social capitalism," see Van Kersbergen 1995, 186–91.

4. See Saba 1994 for text, prehistory, and documents; see also Vecchio, Saresella, and Trionfini 1999, 79–80: Bruno Buozzi would have signed for the socialists, but he was arrested by the Nazis. They lined him up with a dozen other prisoners and gunned them all down, the same night that the labor conspirators' Patto was finalized, June 3, 1944.

5. Fontana 1981, 217–18.

peculiar combination of the German military occupation in the North and West two-thirds of the country, while the Vichy regime of Marshal Pétain in the South worked in alliance with the conqueror. Hopes for enhancing the role of Christianity in this new order diminished over the following years, when the tide of war turned palpably against Hitler's sway. Resistance grew among disparate patriotic groups (bourgeois, socialist, Christian, communist) and in various forms (underground propaganda, intelligence, armed force). In the end General de Gaulle managed to pull it together under one banner from London. The episcopate, however, suffered a diminution of authority among Catholics, given its loyalty to Pétain. It was also in France, however, that the church embarked upon the most radical new and bold approach to the problem of broad de-Christianized swaths of the population: the Mission de France.

Diverse Responses in French Catholicism

Before and after the declaration of war against Germany on the part of Britain and France (September 3, 1939), the French government was mobilizing its forces for defense. When the German armies actually launched their invasion (May 10, 1940), they nevertheless quickly overwhelmed defenders in Belgium and northern France. In June, after surrounding a large part of the French army in northwest France, they took 1,850,000 French soldiers captive and transported 1,600,000 of them to prison camps in Germany. There they were to remain until peace was declared, according to the armistice signed already on June 22, 1940. Many prisoners were released or escaped in the next two years, but there were still about a million in the camps at the end of the war. The impact of this captivity was enormous, not only on the prisoners and their families back in France, but on the workforce and their unions.

Other provisions of the armistice allowed a French government to operate under conditions of allegiance to Nazi Germany. A hero of the First World War, Marshal Philippe Pétain, took charge of the new government that the French set up at (unoccupied) Vichy and called for a national revolution with conservative values. This did not seem so ludicrous then as it does in hindsight—quite the contrary, since the Vichy regime seemed to many to have a promising and influential role in the new Europe, the new order that would follow the expected German military conquest. In the meantime, German forces occupied the strategically sensitive parts of the country, though the Southeast of France, the "free zone," remained unoccupied until November 11, 1942. Even in the areas under military occupation, the Vichy regime still administered civilian affairs.

Labor Issues

In the immediate aftermath of the defeat and the armistice, Jules Zirnheld, the ailing founder of the Christian labor unions and veteran of German imprisonment in World War I, wrote a heartfelt letter to Marshal Pétain.[6] This was on July 8, 1940, two days before the French parliament handed over all legislative powers to the marshal. In the letter Zirnheld expressed the wish that the progressive 1936 social legislation of the Third Republic be maintained in force. Of course, he asserted the right to freely form labor unions. He received a respectful response. At the same time Gaston Tessier continued and intensified his contacts with representatives of the socialist CGT.

One of the early edicts of the Pétain government, though, hit the unions hard. A law of August 16, 1940, created a "provisional organization of industrial production" in preparation for a new system to be laid out in a *Charte du travail*. In the meantime it dissolved existing labor union national confederations (CGT and CFTC), though not union locals, regional offices, or trade federations. National associations of employers were also dissolved in view of the coming reordering of labor relations and industrial affairs. This was followed by the decree of November 9, 1940, which put the law into effect. Thereupon twelve now former trade union leaders, socialist and Christian, responded with the unique joint Manifesto of November 15 (see chapter 12). The *Charte du travail* or government plan for labor relations came out in October 1941, still to be worked out in detail. For the years from June 1940 to June 1943, the implications of the *Charte du travail* dominated the planning of the Christian and other labor forces in wartime France.[7]

The staunch position set forth in the *Manifest des Douze* of November 15, 1940, by the twelve labor leaders, in favor of autonomous labor-union freedom and pluralism, upheld the principle of free unions, not controlled by the state, but able to strike, if necessary, and to conclude agreements by collective bargaining. The manifesto found a mixed reception in labor circles.[8] Given the military defeat of France, collaboration with the new arrangement between the German overlords and Marshal Pétain seemed to offer certain relative advantages to the working class. A prominent CGT official, René Belin, joined the Vichy regime ("the national revolution") in July 1940 as minister of industrial production and labor, seeing the opportunity to apply his

---

6. In Launay 1982, 191.

7. See Saudejaud 1999; Launay 1984, 51; Launay 1982; Montclos et al. 1982; Adam 1964, 47–53; see Le Crom 1995, 187–94. Other recent works touching on Tessier or the ex-CFTC in context during the war years include Halls 1995, esp. 51 and 247–56; Cointet 1998; Comte 1998; Moore 2000; and Wieviorka 2013. For references to Catholic resisters in Axis countries, see W. Kaiser 2007, 119f.

8. Saudejaud 1999, 37–46.

corporatist ideas in that capacity.⁹ In the circumstances, the preponderance of opinion in the CFTC as elsewhere found this an appropriate attitude, even if Tessier, Zirnheld, Bouladoux, and others to be mentioned did not. Belin's anticipation that a state-corporatist *Charte du travail* was coming stirred further interest. A labor policy seemed to be in the works that Belin could help shape as an improvement over the chaotic situation after the fading of the Popular Front. Pétain, with his rightist ties and his prescription of "Work, Family, and Fatherland," appeared to many French Catholics and indeed to the generality of the French as incorporating the hope for an orderly existence under German hegemony. Some saw a chance to lay the moral foundations for a real new order of a post-capitalist, socially harmonious society. The bishops of France declared a stance of "loyalty without enthrallment," cautiously designating the Vichy regime as the "established order" to be supported as having a "legitimate authority."¹⁰

Of course, even so, the good Catholic union man, if informed by the persistent though quiet efforts of a Tessier and by the Christian democratic ideas propagated by *L'Aube* and *Sept* in the prewar years, would interpret the corporatist plans for the *Charte du travail* differently. Would it not turn out to be like the fascist state corporatism of Italy or Hitler's national-socialist labor organization? The *Manifest des Douze*, though, did not become known at all in some regions, even within the ex-CFTC. The censored press of course gave it no publicity. The channels of discreet communication that soon took shape in labor as in other circles did not penetrate the prohibited zone of the Nord at this point. Thus the robust Christian union movement around Charlemagne Broutin and Jules Catoire, and hence Lille's Cardinal Liénart, as well, were left out of the loop. Nevertheless, the official news of the law of August 1940 gave rise to varying responses. Broutin (in step with Liénart) voiced an initial willingness to participate conditionally in the shaping of the Vichyite initiative, whereas Catoire's miners in Pas-de-Calais vowed no participation in the new organizations at all.¹¹

The main occupied zone was another case, partly because of the key role of organizations headquartered in Paris. The offices of the unions' trade organizations (of office workers, metal workers, and so forth), remained in operation

---

9. Chélini 2000, 69.
10. Jackson 2001, 268–71; see also Halls, 1995, 45–67. Note the special case of Cardinal Liénart; see Masson 2001, 238; Bourdais 1995, 113. Liénart hoped for the best from Pétain, but his part of France in the Nord was not in the southern territory under the administration of Vichy. Like Paris and two-thirds of France, it was occupied directly by German forces throughout the war. Unlike Paris, it was attached to the German command in Brussels, making communications with the rest of the French church still more difficult. On the young cardinal in Lyon, Pierre-Marie Gerlier, see Cointet 1998, 24–27.
11. Saudejaud 1999, 46–57; also 130–32, on joining the mine strikes of May 1941.

there. (These were the federations, which were members of the confederation, the CFTC; only the overall confederations [CFTC and CGT] were dissolved at this point). A strong push to take part in the establishment of the bodies foreseen in the *Charte du travail* took root among these Parisian unionists, spearheaded by Jean Pérès, the national secretary of the Christian metalworkers' federation. In fact, the labor ministry in Vichy regarded him, with his rich labor background, as the representative of the CFTC in its panels, and he enjoyed free passage between the zones.[12] From his headquarters in the occupied zone, he openly recommended working with the government to his fellow union members.

In the Southern "free" zone, however, Christian unionists were active in consulting with each other and with new arrivals from the Paris metropolis, from annexed Alsace, and from others who could make it through the checkpoints to the relative freedom of Lyon.[13] Colleagues from the occupied zones also found their way there and played a continuing role in stimulating opposition to the *Charte du travail*. At one point, in March 1941, they succeeded in blocking the appointment of Jean Pérès as representative of the ex-CFTC to the panel created by the government to comment on drafts of the not-yet promulgated Charte. They argued that Pérès did not have the confidence of their unions; their envoy proposed instead Marcel Poimboeuf, who was appointed. The understanding was that he would resign as soon as a decision in favor of a sole government-approved labor union confederation was finalized. In Toulouse Archbishop Jules-Géraud Saliège was an especially strong critic of certain measures taken by Vichy. He refused to concede that the battle for France was over.[14]

Of all the objectionable things in the government's design of a state corporatism to regulate industry, the single labor union (*syndicat unique*) was the most unacceptable to opponents from the ranks of the CFTC, because it would lead not only to the submersion or total elimination of Christian labor, as in Italy and Germany, but to the loss of liberty in labor relations. As an alternative they pointed to the practice of inter-union commissions (*commissions intersyndicales*). When it was a question of consulting or dealing with organized labor as a whole, such a commission, sometimes formed with a ratio of five CGT and two CFTC members, could handle the task. Thus the other parties to the talks (employers, state officials) would have the benefit of the pluralism of labor worldviews incorporated in the separate confederations.[15] Otherwise, given the circumstances, a significant positive element of the labor world would simply be suppressed.

As it was, wartime difficulties, such as internal borders, censorship, and

---

12. Ibid., 64–71.   13. See Comte et al. 1998, 1–58.
14. See Duquesne 1986, 160, for his encouragement of Jean Brodier.
15. Saudejaud 1999, 312–13.

shortages of paper, hampered efforts to get the message out to union members and form an organized opposition. Tessier, of course, had no office or staff, and had to take a job with the CFTC federation of insurance workers. He worked patiently and behind the scenes to maintain contacts and an esprit de corps. Some mail and travel was possible, especially to the Southern free zone, and it was there that the most consistent nuclei of convinced abstentionists (with regard to *Charte* organizations) took root. Some members took leadership roles in organizing the underground resistance—for example, Jean Brodier, André Etcheverlepo, Louis Naillod, Marcel Poimboeuf, Marcel Vanhove, and Paul Vignaux. A major mode of spiritual resistance was that of distributing underground literature, especially the famous *Cahiers du Témoignage chrétien* and other printed matter, to counter Nazi propaganda.[16]

A special case was that of Yvon Morandat, a soldier with a background in the CFTC and JOC. He found himself evacuated to London after the defeat and joined the Free French forces of de Gaulle there. Brodier and Vanhove were among his reception committee when he landed by parachute one night in November 1941 in the countryside near Toulouse. They introduced him to their trusted acquaintances. He wasted no time assembling a network for intelligence and eventual sabotage and uprisings in aid of de Gaulle's campaign of liberation. Morandat himself departed after twelve months.[17] During the same period Tessier and Paul Verneyras in the occupied zones to the North aided the underground—for example, by gathering and passing on information about troop movements from rail workers.

The consultations within the ex-CFTC in regard to the *Charte du travail* fall into three phases. From the first announcement of the planned reform in August 1940, the division between pro and con deepened as to taking part in the preliminary measures that were under way; many local unions and union leaders took a wait-and-see attitude. Some participated in governmental consultations so as to shape the outcome in an acceptable way: a *politique de présence*. In the course of the next two years, the opponents of state regimentation of unions concluded that only a united front of all ex-CFTC units would have a chance of warding off an unacceptable form of the *Charte*. Then in early September 1942 the first decrees of the implementation of the *Charte* were officially published; it was clear that the authorities had disregarded the modifications that CFTC elements had proposed to date. Representatives from all departments in the occupied zone met in Paris on Sunday, September 13, 1942, to decide on a course of action.[18] After both sides had made their case, the votes on the mo-

16. On the *Cahiers du Témoignage chrétien*, see Bédarida 1977.
17. Saudejaud, 1999, 222–35; see Comte 1998, 94–97; see also Comte et al. 1998, 27f.
18. Saudejaud, 1999, 190–96.

tions showed a gaping lack of consensus. Tessier and his fellow opponents of the *Charte* still had broad swathes of the ex-CFTC to persuade: the undecided and the Pétainists. The debate dragged on through the political convulsions of the Vichy government and the fortunes of war into 1943. Eight months of further persuasion, combined with the labor requisitions, the German occupation of the free zone in November 1942, and the abandonment of the crossing guards at the edge of the prohibited zone to the North, made possible a broader and more representative gathering of Christian unionists in Paris on June 27, 1943.[19] This time the result was far different. The advocates of participation in the implementation of the *Charte* had dwindled to a small minority and saw their position rejected by a determined majority.[20]

Gaston Tessier's participation in the Résistance continued. At its founding on May 27, 1943, the Conseil national de la résistance (CNR), brought together by the persistence of Jean Moulin, named Tessier to be the representative of the CFTC as one of the sixteen constituent bodies of the Gaullist movement of liberation. The CGT was the other labor confederation in the CNR. Georges Bidault represented the Christian democratic political tendency and assumed the presidency when Jean Moulin was arrested.[21] Tessier was in charge of the committee for planning relief supplies and provisions. Immediately following the liberation of Paris, on August 30, 1944, Tessier was able to reclaim the central office of the CFTC.

The French Episcopate and Other Catholic Organizations: The Mission de France

From the beginning of the German military occupation (or in the South, "alliance"), Catholic Action and other Catholic organizations had to deal with an unexpected and confusing situation.[22] The German forces were under initial orders to treat the French as allies—unlike the Polish, whom they had violently and indiscriminately subjugated the year before. The bishops urged cooperation with the "legitimate authority" of Vichy and continued to do so even after its servile status with respect to the German occupiers became more and more evident. Parish-based organizations such as the venerable St. Vincent de Paul Society gave much-needed aid to families in wartime penury. Breadwinners were often prisoners of war or, later, *réfractaires*—that is, those who were

---

19. Ibid., 259–302.
20. Launay 1982, 205–9.
21. Muracciolo 2000, 199.
22. On the Mission de France in the war years, see Cointet 1998, 276–99; Cavalin and Viet-Depaule 2007; brief exposé in Roucou 2001, 100–114; Vinatier 1983, 221–52.

evading forced deportation for labor in Germany.[23] Milieu organizations such as the Young Christian Workers organization (JOC) and its parallel Catholic Action groups (especially the JAC in farming and the JEC among university students) were under more pressure from the formation of a *Jeunesse unique* like the *Syndicat unique* after the pattern of Italian Fascist and German Nazi youth organizations. The bishops rose to the defense of the Catholic youth organizations and succeeded in avoiding their suppression (or *Gleichschaltung*, to use the German term).[24]

The newer LOC (Ligue ouvrière chrétienne) for Jocist alumni changed its name to Mouvement populaire des familles (MPF) in August 1941 for apostolic reasons. They did not want to highlight the Christian aspect of their approach, with its overtones of bourgeois paternalism, and thus put off their working-class fellows before they could convince them of their good faith and solidarity. The objective in view was nothing less than "a great People's Movement of Families that will lead the working class as a whole to Christianity."[25] To this end they provided services so much needed in the war years. They set up food pantries, arranged summertime respites in the country for children, plotted vegetable gardens in the neighborhoods, ran family centers and programs for wives of prisoners, and delivered packages to their husbands and other prisoners. All this grassroots activity was consciously separate from the Secours national, the government agency headed by the very Catholic Robert Garric. The agency did provide financial subsidies in some cases.

At another level, that of the institutional church, the concern felt by social Catholics over the de-Christianized proletariat also haunted chief pastors of the church in France. Before and during World War II there was considerable ferment and activity in French Catholicism as to the "de-Christianization of the masses." *Essor ou déclin de l'Église?* (1947), the pastoral letter of Emmanuel Cardinal Suhard, archbishop of Paris, would focus international attention on this concern.[26] Already during the occupation, the archbishop launched two remarkable initiatives, the *Mission de France* and the *Mission de Paris*.

Suhard might not have seemed the man to take on this challenge. Suhard (1874–1949) grew up in a solid Christian environment and then taught in a seminary for twenty-nine years before being named bishop of Bayeux and Lisieux, another predominantly practicing Catholic part of France. By 1935 he was archbishop and cardinal of Reims and turned his attention to the problem

23. See Drapac 1998, esp. 124–30 and 200–36.
24. See Bourdais 1995.
25. Duriez et al. 2005, 71; Duriez 2001, 220–22; Fouilloux 1990c, 484–88; and Drapac 1998, 235.
26. English translation: *Growth or Decline? The Church Today*; see Suhard 1948, 52–54. Wattebled 1990, 114–16, puts the magisterial document in the context of the French church of the time in regard to workers; see also Fouilloux 1997 and 1998.

of regions in France with a glaring shortage of priests. Here he began casting about for new ways to evangelize those who had little or no contact with the Christian tradition, especially the broad masses of the working class that for generations may have been baptized as infants, but with little or no follow-up. As a member of the national conference of cardinals and archbishops (the ACA, Assemblée des cardinaux et archevêques), he tried to overcome the reluctance of bishops to share priestly personnel with dioceses needing to staff unserved parishes. In Paris his predecessor, Cardinal Jean Verdier, had dealt with large blocks of working-class population where a parish had never been established. Verdier succeeded in building and staffing churches in many of these areas in and around Paris. All the same, when Suhard became archbishop of Paris in 1940, just as the Blitzkrieg was descending upon France, the issue continued to be a top priority for him.

By July 1941, as head of the ACA, Suhard persuaded the other archbishops to authorize the creation of a seminary to train priests for a new organization, the Mission de France. He engaged Louis Augros, a Sulpician, to head the Mission and its new seminary at Lisieux. It would consist of diocesan priests, working in teams, to be sent to areas of France not currently served by priests, there to revive Catholic Christianity. The first seminarians who had applied for the novel program, some thirty of them, arrived to start their theological and pastoral training in October 1942 with Augros and four professors. Augros saw to it that teamwork was emphasized in their studies. They would also do a few weeks of farm or other manual labor as they prepared for their assignments. Moreover, Augros brought in other theologians and pastoral experts to conduct short courses and stimulate discussions.

Abbé Henri Godin was one such invitee. Godin was a fervent but restless young priest of the people who was not content with the strides the JOC had made. Nor did his experience with it satisfy his apostolic aspirations when he became chaplain of two JOC federations in Paris by 1937.[27] In April 1942, when he was thirty-six, he met a kindred soul, the JOC chaplain Yvan Daniel, thirty-three, at an intensive week-long workshop for JOC lay leaders. They quickly found themselves in agreement that the Young Christian Workers' groups, at least in Paris, were too parochialized, which hampered the movement's potential.[28] Louis Augros came upon the Godin's writings for the young workers and invited him to share his thoughts for the Lisieux community, as well. Here paths crossed that would lead to mighty upheavals in the French church. Augros suggested that Godin ask for a meeting with Cardinal Suhard, which was promptly set up for August 28, 1942.

27. See Poulat 1999, 74–94; Arnal 1984, 53–58.
28. Poulat 1999, 89.

When Godin and Daniel met with Suhard, the archbishop, perhaps as a way of breaking the ice, asked what men thought of him on the factory floor. Godin burst out, "They think you are a dirty capitalist!" The cardinal, taken aback, was silent for a moment, then ventured that at least the JOC was quite a success. Godin replied with a comparison to leaky barrels: all the effort poured into flourishing JOC groups "comes to naught in the parishes. The JOC is more or less impeded from going as far as it is meant to go."[29] Godin had come to the conclusion that the parishes, with their mindset, were simply incapable of making the workers feel in their element. Hence they left the parish to which the JOC may have brought them. The (adult) members of parishes, from the parish priest on down, were all products of or aspirants to a "bourgeois" culture. Godin by contrast was taken with the idea that one had to shape and create a sort of Catholicism imbedded in the working-class world, apart from the usual middle-class culture of the parishes. Had not Suhard called for a mission in France, analogous to the foreign missions with their challenge of indigenization?

Suhard asked the JOC chaplains Daniel and Godin to draw up a written report with the cooperation of Augros and the Mission de France. By Easter 1943 the two priests had submitted their report. On Easter Monday the cardinal told his priest secretary, "I did not sleep all night. I am overcome. I knew quite a bit, but I did not know that things had come to this pass." He had copies sent to several leading clerics; soon he came to the decision to found the Mission de Paris for the workers in the red belt of the outskirts. These decisions drew the attention of a national and (when the war was over) international spotlight. The book resulting from the report, *La France, pays de mission?*, was published in July 1943 and reprinted over and over.[30] The Mission de Paris got off to a start in the same month when the cardinal persuaded a curate in his forties to take on the job of superior.[31] A dozen young priests of the archdiocese, volunteers, went on retreat at the seminary in Lisieux from December 19, 1943, to

---

29. Cointet 1998, 284.

30. Godin and Daniel 1943; see Ward 1949 for a translated and edited version with biographical and other supplementary material. Cointet (1998, 285), from a greater critical distance, observes as to the work of 1943: "The tone is given [already in its preface by George Guérin, the national chaplain of the French JOC]: disenchantment of the young chaplains of the JOC, who draw from their experience ... a pessimistic diagnosis of French Catholicism. The meeting with an aged cardinal, at heart a teacher and not much of an intellectual, along with the permissiveness of a clergy who have nothing left to offer beyond hiding the weaknesses of the institution, gave rise to the diffusion of *La France, pays de mission?* The slim volume sold 100,000 copies in a few years because of its simplistic and authoritative tone plus a readiness to credit sociological findings ... and because of its vision of the missions in colonial lands, not well known, and viewed through the rose-colored glasses of utopians." For more background and detail, see Poulat 1999, especially 159–66. Cole-Arnal 2001, 121, dates the appearance of the book to September rather than July of 1943.

31. Margotti 2000.

January 16, 1944, under the patronage of St. Theresa of Lisieux and with the guidance of the Mission de France. There they had further assistance and encouragement from the Jesuits of the Action populaire (including Père Desbuquois) and the Dominican Marie-Dominique Chenu, along with the diocesan priests Georges Michonneau and Abbé Guérin. The Mission de Paris was not meant to be anti-parish, but rather to try out ways of penetrating the worker milieu in innovative ways, apart from the conventional parish. Nor was it at odds with the Mission de France, a project of the whole episcopate of France and conceived for both rural and urban mission territories. It was, however, the initiative of Cardinal Suhard for his archdiocese only.

A dramatic turn, which only heightened the élan of this new mission to the urban proletariat, took place the day after the participants returned to Paris from Lisieux. On the morning of January 17, 1944, Abbé Godin was found dead in his bed. A faulty coal stove in his small apartment was not properly vented; the fumes had asphyxiated him as he slept.[32]

Forced Labor in Germany and Worker-Priests

As we turn to the celebrated experiment of the worker-priests, it must be noted that neither the Godin-Daniel book nor the retreat at Lisieux had advocated a specific solution to penetrate the barrier between parishes and the proletarian neighborhood. No one focused on the few cases of priests taking employment like an ordinary worker as a solution to the problem of the vast gulf separating the proletariat from Christianity.[33] The dominant approach toward that end was rather an analogy with the missionary approach in Africa. A relatively few priests there were able to catechize and convert large numbers through the ministrations of many native catechists.[34] These lay leaders and families worked as "the leaven in the dough" of existing natural communities.

Two factors at work in wartime France converged in the worker-priest movement of 1943 to 1954. One consisted of the ecclesial developments just outlined that led to the innovative Mission de France and Mission de Paris. Their priests formed small teams determined not to live apart from working people. The second factor making the situation all the more acute and urgent in occupied France was the requisition of workers to provide forced labor in Germany. At first the Vichy government had tried to satisfy the demands of the occupiers by a voluntary system: for every three workers volunteering for work

---

32. Ward 1949, 60–62; Poulat 1999, 112–13.
33. Arnal 1986, 61, 68; see Cole-Arnal 2001 for the unfolding of the whole movement in brief; Poulat 1999, in detail.
34. Godin and Daniel 1943, 134–35; in Ward 1949, 173–74.

in Germany, one prisoner of war would be released and repatriated. But this scheme provided only a small portion of the 250,000 workers demanded in the first year for the German war effort. So a compulsory labor service (Service du travail obligatoire, or STO) was instituted in February 1943.[35] Some 640,000 were deported for forced labor by July 1944. Any young man born in 1920, 1921, or 1922 was liable for requisition. Many took what measures they could to evade being picked up, even joining the *maquis* (the underground military resistance). As Wilfred Halls emphasizes, these decrees from Vichy occasioned the first major break in the Catholic episcopate from its policy of preaching obedience to "legitimate authority."[36] Especially significant in this connection were the statements of Cardinal Liénart, a champion of Christian labor and the JOC from the beginning of his episcopate.[37] Though overshadowed among the atrocities of the time by the tragedy of the deportation of Jews to the death camps, these workforce deportations and camps were the worst wound inflicted on the French since the 1940 defeat.

Among the prisoners of war already in Germany were hundreds of priests.[38] At least a few of them could help the STO deportees in Germany find their footing as members of the body of Christ in their strange surroundings. These included a number of Jocists and a number of seminarians. Some had voluntarily chosen not to evade the requisitions so as to share and strengthen the faith of their fellow countrymen under duress.[39] They thus perforce shared a life with proletarians for months and years on end—and came face to face with the absence of religion in the experience of so many of their countrymen. The JOC leadership and the bishops counseled their young men that they need not obey this unjust law, but on the other hand they could report and do good apostolic work in the emergency situation. Ill-prepared as the youth were for what faced them, the risk of capitulation was great. As Émile Poulat has laid out in detail, priests too volunteered to be taken to Germany as laborers or artisans with false papers (and at the same time as clandestine chaplains), with the approval of the hierarchy.[40] "By the end of the war, 3,200 seminarians and 275 priests had provided religious support.... The JOC had formed a thousand cells."[41]

35. Harbulot 2000, 645–46; Cointet 1998, 287–99; Duquesne 1986, 273–307.
36. Halls 1995, 311–14; see Arnal 1986, 58–61.
37. Masson 2001, 291–99; see Cointet 1998, 289–93.
38. Poulat 1999, 209–33.
39. Paul Beschet (2012, originally published in 1947), furnishes an unusual first-person account of the STO experience: his own and that of other Jesuit seminarians in Germany among the STO and POW forced laborers, including a number of Jocistes; see Arnaud 2010, index of the labor conscripts (*requis*), including Beschet, noted.
40. Poulat 1999, 263; see Arnaud 2010, 394–97.
41. Cointet 1998, 293.

One upshot of all this activity and tense negotiations between church and occupation authorities was a crackdown on the JOC.[42] The Gestapo shut down its national headquarters in Paris and arrested Abbé Guérin on August 3, 1943 (he was held until Christmas). The Germans were of course suspicious of Suhard's influence; the Gestapo had searched his offices previously. Now, when the cardinal protested the suspension of JOC activities and Guérin's jailing, the commandant of the German armies in France informed him that the bishops' stance was impeding the implementation of the labor requisitions.[43] Hence retaliatory measures could be expected.

The priest-prisoners and deportees brought back with them after liberation an experience of contact with the life of the working man that left a deep impression. In some cases they were determined (problematical as that would be) to continue their vocation in a factory side by side with other workers.[44] Eventually, in the postwar years in France, about a hundred priests went into full-time factory or construction work. From Arnal's perspective the original focus on incorporating and spreading the Christian message in the working-class milieu ("leaven in the dough") shifted to a more outright liberationist emphasis on revolutionizing economic structures.[45] At first the typical "PO" (*prêtre-ouvrier*, worker-priest) kept a low profile at work, but freely divulged his identity in conversations with coworkers. By 1949 and the early 1950s, however, quite a few of them felt called upon to take a more active part in the workers' struggles. Engagement imposed itself as their Christian duty. Since the communist-oriented CGT was the union federation that had the loyalty of most of their companions at work, many joined up (the CFTC was virtually absent from their workplaces). Even those who did not become union members took part in work actions and strikes. A few became somewhat notorious by 1949, at the same time as the Cold War divided Europe and the political world. Pope Pius XII's anti-communist focus resulted in the decree of the Holy Office dated July 1, 1949, that prohibited all collaboration of Catholics with communists.[46]

The inner-Catholic tensions continued to increase from that point, culminating in the decision to shut down the "experiment" (*expérience*) of the worker-priests' ministry. This became public at the latest in early 1954, after the cardinals Feltin, Gerlier, and Liénart received from Pius XII the nonnegotiable word to that effect in November 1953.[47] The bishops who had worker-priests in

42. See Bourdais 1995, 165–74.
43. Cointet 1998, 292; Bourdais 1995, 187–88; Gueŕend 2011, 209–31.
44. Arnal 1986, 58–61 and 75–111; Cole-Arnal 2001.
45. Arnal 1986, 52, 111.
46. See Suaud and Viet-Depaule 2005, 443; Cole-Arnal 2001, 135–39.
47. Leprieur 1989, 710–16, provides a schematic chronology of the unrolling of relevant events in 1953 and 1954.

their dioceses wrote to each of them on January 19, 1954, informing them that they were "to devote only a limited time to manual labour, in order to safeguard their readiness to answer to all the demands of the sacerdotal state."[48] The priest-workers had to inform their superiors of their response by the deadline of March 1, 1954.[49] Some priests complied, some did not. The reactions in the church and public at large were seismic, with repercussions extending notably to the Vatican censures of leading theologians (Chenu, Congar, Féret).[50]

The connection of some worker-priests with the Lisieux seminary of the Mission de France led to difficulties for the latter, as well. After 1949, when Cardinal Suhard died, Cardinal Liénart was the prelate in charge of the Mission de France. Having been in relative isolation during the wartime years when it took shape, he relied largely on secondhand knowledge. Despite his labor credentials and closeness in spirit to Suhard, Liénart acceded to the criticisms of the seminary and Vatican pressures. Père Augros had to leave in 1952;[51] for a time the seminary was closed, then moved to Limoges. Amid continued difficulties, an expedient in the form of a *praelatura nullius* (a sort of a diocese without territorial boundaries) was settled on eventually (1954), with the headquarters and the seminary reestablished at a different site, Pontigny.[52]

Social Catholicism in the Postwar Reconfiguration of Labor Relations

The immediate postwar years could not relieve the devastations of wartime. As signs of hesitant recovery showed themselves, the aid and influence of the Anglo-American victors obviously was a key factor. A few years later, when the "economic miracle" took shape, they continued to play an essential role, while local and national forces were also decisive. We have already observed some instances of socialist and Christian labor coming together. It was the

---

48. Petrie 1956, 173; see Viet-Depaule 2001, 117–31.

49. The letter goes on to state that the priests are actually required to resign from their employment altogether and "from all temporal responsibilities to which the trust of your comrades may have called you." They must let all union memberships lapse as well as participation in labor "committees [and] other organisations proper to the working class or of wider scope.... As we address you thus, we realise how severe must be the wrench you feel to the depths of your being, not with any selfish regard for yourselves, but because of the love you bear to your worker brethren"; Petrie 1956, 173. They insist that the priests comply, nevertheless, and they offer assistance in finding a community of priests in whose company they can resume their vocation in more conventional circumstances. For the similar letters of the French Dominican provincials to their worker-priests, see Leprieur 1989, 62–64.

50. See Leprieur's 1989 study of Dominicans and worker-priests, esp. 212 35.

51. Vinatier 1991, 62.

52. Roucou 2001, 105–7; Cavalin and Viet-Depaule 2007, 133–81.

work of economists more in tune with Anglo-American economic thought of the period, however, that set the main lines of postwar economic recovery. The Catholic social tradition had tended quite generally to regard market economics rather coolly, and vice versa. Just after World War II, all the same, in some places and circles, in Benelux and Germany and Italy in particular, the standing of the Catholic Church and its social teaching had never been more respected. Some market-oriented economists had become sensitive on their part to the requirements of equity and justice in economic policy, while Catholic ethicists acknowledged the advantages of markets. In retrospect it may seem that the fact that both Catholics and socialists largely came around to find the economists' approach acceptable and even congenial was another economic miracle.[53] But that is getting ahead of ourselves.

Along with or beside the paramount influence of Allied occupying forces and aid (most notably the Marshall Plan), social Catholic, social democratic, and classic bourgeois capitalist ideas for an economic future vied with each other in the nascent democracies. In Italy the leader of the new Christian Democratic Party, Alcide De Gasperi, chose a leading liberal economist as his minister of finance: Luigi Einaudi. In Germany, similarly and to much greater effect, Konrad Adenauer, head of the Christian Democratic Union, went for the neo-liberal economic proposals of Ludwig Erhard after the reform of the currency in 1948.[54]

The emergence of the Cold War exacerbated the tensions between Western European movements of Marxist inspiration and democratic ones. On the Western side of this postwar conflict, the Marshall Plan had its beneficial effects in the reconstruction of ruined economies. The European Coal and Steel Community (ECSC, founded 1951) signaled French-German cooperation. It too was the brainchild of an economist, Jean Monnet, but encouraged by Georges Bidault and Robert Schuman. Such new designs of political economy, variations of a social market economy, or social capitalism conducive to social justice shaped postwar society in the formerly belligerent countries.[55]

Catholic Nonunion Workers' Organizations

Before these developments could take place, in 1944, the old men of the pre-fascist Christian unions, Achille Grandi and Giovanni Gronchi, though they were

---

53. See Glossner 2010, 1–7, which unfortunately came to my attention too late to utilize more fully.
54. Van Hook 2004, 292.
55. See Piketty 2014, 237–70, 350. For "social market economy," see Van Hook 2004; for "social capitalism," Van Kersbergen 1995.

cautious about it, understood the reasons for a unified labor confederation and felt that it was right to sign on.[56] At the same time, however, they arranged, in concert with Vatican officials and others, for the establishment of a nonunion organization for Catholic workers, the Associazioni cattoliche lavoratori italiani (ACLI), something like the para-union milieu organizations of Catholic workers (KAB) that we have seen in 1920s Germany and the Low Countries. A first sign of the changing situation in Italy is that the AC in ACLI does not stand for "Catholic Action," but for "Catholic Associations" of Italian workers—that is, all the organizations and programs set up and run for and by workers under Catholic auspices. Unlike Henri Poels's idea within the Catholic pillar of the Dutch, however, these were definitely churchly organizations under the authority of the hierarchy (including in Italy the Vatican), at least until they declined clerical assistance around 1971, after the Second Vatican Council.[57]

Other organizations, originally formed in the Catholic labor subculture or milieu, met wartime needs and in the process shed their exclusive attachment to the church. This was part of what can be clearly seen in retrospect as a shift from a goal of re-Christianizing society to the more modest or evangelical aspiration of bearing Christian witness and offering service to their fellows across the pluralistic spectrum. Notable in France, for instance, was the evolution of the MPF (Mouvement populaire des familles) in terms of its place within official Catholic Action. The predecessor organization of the MPF was formed in 1935 by Jocist alumni who married and started families.[58] Like the JOC itself, it remained firmly ensconced in the framework of Catholic Action as one of the specialized or milieu organizations. It renamed itself the MPF ("people's family movement") in August 1941 in the process of offering a whole array of services under wartime conditions to hard-pressed families. Its volunteers continued their yeoman work into the postwar years and on into the Cold War period. At this point the MPF felt called upon to promote controversial leftist political stands, and the bishops realized that they could no longer back the organization as an official part of Catholic Action. At the same time, the official church wanted to make clear its dedication to the working class.

In 1949, therefore, the ACA decided to call into being a Catholic Action organization of lay labor activists (ACO), the bulk of them former Jocists. Catholic Action in the realm of (adult) labor was reconceived as a "spiritual organization that leaves to its members the responsibility for their temporal commitments"—one application, it may be, of Maritain's distinction of sacral and profane Christendoms in his *Integral Humanism*.[59] The chaplains of ACO

---

56. Saba 1994, 149.
57. See Pasini 1982, 170–75, and Formigoni 1997, 165–69.
58. Belouet 2001, 92; Duriez 2001, 218.   59. Poulat 1999, 614.

(Action catholique ouvrière), like those of the JOC, devoted themselves to the ongoing formation of the committed laity (as well as urging their clerical brethren to support the effort on the spiritual plane). The distinction between the spiritual engagement of lay participants in the mission of the church and their temporal engagements (party, union, journal) enabled the bishops to encourage and aid the lay apostles in carrying out their Christian commitment in secular society. The insistence on the special mandate or commission from the bishops, however, was not a satisfactory linchpin for the relationship.[60]

Hence the deconfessionalization or maturation of the originally church-affiliated labor unions did not mean that labor involvement of Catholic organizations ceased.[61] An organization such as the ACO had as its raison d'être the dedication and continuing formation of its adherents so that they would be better equipped to take economic and social measures for the common good in the social and political arenas. A reorientation of such groups and *standsorganisaties* was necessary to function more effectively in an increasingly pluralistic and differentiated social context. "Secularized society" need not mean that religion becomes passé or entirely private. It might mean that Christians find their field of public action by democratic means in a pluralistic civil society while preparing the ground for (or even relinquishing the idea of) a "new Christendom."[62] The degree of mobilization under clerical auspices obviously was in decline.[63]

The French case is distinctive. On the one hand, the international echo of French Catholic intellectual life in this period attests to Gallic influence abroad. Elsewhere, however, the legacy of the Rhenish pattern of mobilizing Catholic workers apart from the Christian unions was more powerful. In France there was, of course, the JOC and its offshoots as part of Catholic Action, but no KAB or Catholic Workers' Movement as in German and Dutch-speaking regions. These movements were organizations of Catholics but, à la Poels, not churchly until they were brought under the protective wing of Catholic Action temporarily during the Third Reich. After the war they resumed their former autonomy

---

60. See Debès 1982 for the basic study of ACO; also Wattebled 1990, 198–203; Horn and Gerard 2001, 37–40; Duriez 2001; Duriez 2001 et al., 227; Duriez 2003, 212–14. For an insightful exposition of the mandate issue, see Tranvouez 2011b, esp. 71ff; he concludes thus, on 84: "The positive outcome of Catholic Action [in France] can be read as an undoubted success based on unsettled footings: the historical good luck of a misapprehension."

61. Misner 2005, 117–22.

62. See Casanova 1994, 61–65; Delors 2004, 9–17.

63. For further aspects and context of the history of Catholic labor and World War II, one can compare Horn and Gerard 2001; Horn 2008, 175–224 and 232. See also Duriez 2003 for the interaction of the contexts of Catholic Action, labor movement, Vichy, and Libération, with references to significant recent bibliography, 206; and Chenaux 1990 for the involvement of social Catholics in the early stages of European integration.

and unfolded a broad range of activities. Sometimes they also formed caucuses within the union federations and political parties open to their influence.[64]

The Postwar Economy and the Question of Unitary Labor Unions

How did the prewar Christian unions respond in this new context? The ones we have examined can be arranged into two groups.[65] Those of France, Belgium, and the Netherlands were suppressed for four or five years during the Nazi occupation. The Christian labor movements of the formerly fascistic states (Italy, Germany, and Austria), on the other hand, had ceased to exist for longer periods of time. The leading personnel of both sets took shelter underground or under church auspices as best as they could, but obviously the continuity of the labor movement in the Axis countries suffered more greatly. (Switzerland as neutral does not fit under either category, and Vichy France was, of course, a special case.) Added to the time factor and the concomitantly more thorough generational break was the factor of totalitarianism in Axis countries. There resistance had to contend with the fact that the oppressive regime was homegrown. In the occupied countries, smarting from defeat by a foreign power, the forces of resistance could more readily call upon feelings of nationalism or patriotism for support.

The reborn labor unions of the two sets of countries, as it happened, took two different paths.[66] In the Netherlands, Belgium, and France, the prewar unions did not combine in a unitary union. In Germany and Austria (also in Italy, until the communist element set the tone in the confederation), strong new unified labor federations of shared socialist and Christian heritage came into being. A major reason for this was a keen sense of past failure in respect to labor solidarity. A common democratic labor front, if the socialist and Christian worker forces had been able to bring it off in the 1920s or 1930s, could

---

64. Accounts of their activities can be consulted in authoritative national histories or reference works: for the Netherlands, see Roes 1985a and Peet 1993, as well as *HJS*; for Belgium, *HMOCB* 1994; for Germany, Rauscher 1981–82; for Austria, *KSL* 1980; and for Italy, the monumental *DSMCI* edited by Traniello and Campanini. Their present successors form a network of some fifty national or regional organizations affiliated with the Mouvement mondial des travailleurs chrétiens, or World Movement of Christian Workers, with a website at http://www.mmtc-infor.com/m/en.html; see Pasture 2001.

65. On these developments, see several contributions in *Between Cross and Class* (Heerma van Voss, Pasture, and De Maeyer 2005) by Ciampani and Valente, Misner, Patch, and Strikwerda, as well as Pasture 2007 (here 1:309) and 2004; see also Hiepel and Ruff 2003. See also earlier works: Pasture (1999, 209 52; 1994c; and 2001), Duriez et al. 2001, 183–257; Ciampani 1990 and 1991; Bedani 1995; and J. Kaiser 1996.

66. Pasture 2005b, 20–21.

have stood up better against the totalitarian takeovers by Mussolini and Hitler. Democratic labor, they were now convinced, must not be divided by political ideologies and partisan struggles. Labor could stand together for its common interests as long as the commitment to democracy was strong and the mainly socialist majority abstained from simply co-opting the trade unions for their allied political parties. Christian labor was concerned, in addition, to enable its interclass approaches to the common good to bear fruit in the framework of the comprehensive labor movement—a hope that was by no means utopian. So they joined in the new DGB (German Labor Federation) and the ÖGB (Austrian Trade Union Congress) and the CGIL (Italian General Confederation of Labor).

That reasoning resonated with many of the union leaders in the occupied countries who were planning for a future in liberated Europe. The history of Christian labor, as we have seen, was dotted with attempts to overcome the unfortunate need for divided Christian and socialist or Catholic and Protestant union organizations.[67] In the abstract, at least, labor unions that could concentrate on working conditions and negotiations with employers, independently of religious, ideological, or partisan-political divisions, seemed to be the ideal. Yet another model was an actual labor *party* as in Britain, where one's religious and democratic convictions were respected while joining together in a political party on a platform of welfare-state reforms. Christian democrats in Belgium actually took steps to form such a new party with hopes of drawing voters from the left of the Catholic interclass party as well as from the socialist base.[68] The plans for this Union démocratique belge (UDB) aborted, though it found an interest in 1944 from such as Henri Pauwels of the Christian unions. On the strictly labor union side, a merger with the socialist union federation was not seriously considered. Here as in the Netherlands, pillarization of the subcultures was so solidly rooted that such an across-the-board reorganization of trade union structures and membership was deemed neither practical nor desirable at the time.[69]

Thus, in Belgium and the Netherlands, the Christian labor organizations reestablished themselves in the same basic configuration that served them well before the war. They had their own unions and an independent confederation, which cooperated as seemed appropriate with the other confederations, such as the large social democratic one. In France the CFTC was even more clearly set off from the communist-dominated CGT. In the longer term, to be sure, the Belgian ACV-CSC was the only major instance of one of these Christian union federations remaining unmerged and indeed becoming the largest confedera-

67. Strikwerda 2005, 342.
68. See W. Kaiser 2007 for this and analogous moves in other countries.
69. See Conway 2001, 271f and 278.

tion in the country.[70] In the process it became more and more autonomous and independent of the ecclesiastical leading strings of the 1920s.

In the Netherlands, as well, the pillars eventually became porous.[71] The Catholic and socialist trade union confederations federated in 1976 and merged in 1981. But in the early 1940s planning during the occupation for the postwar situation, employer and labor representatives came together in secret and, not unlike their Belgian counterparts, agreed on a plan for a joint consultative body. A "Foundation of Labor" (*Stichting van de Arbeid*) was announced immediately upon liberation on May 6, 1945. The interest groups participating included "industry, labor, small business, and agriculture.... The key concession came from the labor side which publicly renounced, at least for the time being, any claim to active worker participation in management in return for 'ample representation' on official economic advisory bodies to the government."[72]

In the other category, the Italian CGIL split in 1948 in the climate of the Cold War. Giulio Pastore traveled to London in 1947 to take part in the initial conference heralding the European Recovery Program, also known as the Marshall Plan, despite majority opposition to it in the CGIL. American funds supported the noncommunist elements in CGIL. The three currents of the CGIL could hardly keep neutral during the hard-fought political campaign before the crucial election of April 18, 1948, which led to the victory of De Gasperi's Christian Democrats. Then in July, the Communist Party leader, Palmiro Togliatti, was the object of an assassination attempt. Unprecedented left-wing demonstrations erupted, especially in the industrial triangle of Turin, Genoa, and Milan. All this agitation led to splits in the CGIL, with the Catholic ACLI declaring CGIL defunct by July. The Confederazione italiana sindacati lavoratori (CISL) took shape by stages under Catholic leadership (led by Giulio Pastore and Mario Romani) until its official founding in 1950.[73] Note that the "C" does not stand for "Christian" or "Catholic," though the prime movers were all dedicated Catholics.[74] CISL would become the second-largest labor confederation in Italy after CGIL.

In France the CFTC had its own transformation.[75] A left-wing group in the confederation around Paul Vignaux, called "Reconstruction" after its periodical, stirred discussion about the future direction of the CFTC for several years. Finally a majority of the CFTC decided in 1964 to drop the denomination "Christian" from its name and become the Confédération française et

---

70. Pasture 1992; 2003; Strikwerda 2003.   71. See Coleman 1978.
72. Windmuller 1969, 107; see Peet 1993, 128–31.
73. Vecchio, Saresella, and Trionfini 1999, 238–45.
74. See Saba 1996, 357–66.   75. Georgi 1995; Vignaux 1980.

démocratique du travail (CFDT). As a Christian union leader in St. Étienne told an American observer, "We do not want to be, and we are no longer, merely foot soldiers occupying the terrain after it has been made safe by a bombardment of papal encyclicals."[76] Actual adherence to the Catholic Church on the part of its members or leaders was no longer considered a sine qua non of its mission. But they saw a need for an alternative to the red CGT and a greater capability to press the cause of workers in the overall context of the Western alliance, rather than upholding the Soviet cause. (The reader may recall that in the early 1950s the priest-worker movement saw several of its members joining and becoming local leaders of the CGT, since it was the only labor organization where they worked that could count on the support of the other workers.)[77] The CFDT has maintained its place in the French labor scene to the present as the second-most-influential union confederation after the CGT.

Germany, up until 1989, presented the special problem of its division into West Germany and East Germany. The several zones of occupation shaped its first years after World War II. When the Russians in the eastern zone including Berlin proved recalcitrant, the Americans, British, and French moved ahead to bring their respective zones under Western influence. What did and did not shape the future of Germany was expressed in words addressed to the new Christian Democratic Party in November 1947 by Jakob Kaiser. This former Christian union organizer from Berlin still hoped that the occupying powers would allow the German populace as a whole to work out its future, which was not to be. "Germany will not get well by setting up a liberal system" in the West in opposition to "the Marxist threat" in the eastern zone and then by erecting "a wall between the two."[78] What happened next, within three weeks, was that the Soviet occupation authorities deposed Kaiser from his position as zonal president of his party, the Christian Democratic Union, reducing it to a shadow existence in Eastern Germany. In 1949 the Federal Republic of (West) Germany and the Democratic Republic of (East) Germany came into being. In 1955 the West German Federal Republic gained sovereign status and joined the North Atlantic Treaty Organization (NATO). The Berlin Wall followed in 1961, not to come down until 1989.

Through 1947 the vision of a Christian socialist economic program of reform and recovery was quite prominent.[79] The Ahlen Program of the CDU (Christian Democratic Union) in the British Zone of February 1947 rejected a capitalistic system as vigorously as did the unitary trade union (DGB) of Hans

---

76. Lorwin 1954, 298.
77. See Cole-Arnal 2001, 132–35; Poulat 1999, 549.
78. Cited in Kosthorst 1975, 143.
79. See Langner 1980, 41–61; Van Hook 2004, 143–49.

Böckler. It also took up the longtime Catholic labor demand of codetermination (*Mitbestimmung*), hoping thus to incorporate unprecedented labor influence in the oversight of industry. Here Christian laborites and other Christian political democrats found provisional agreement, although the phrase "Christian socialism" was no longer to be found. The idea of a broad working-class party after the British Labour Party example also had its advocates for a while, but as in Belgium it soon fell by the wayside in favor of a Christian Democratic Party (CDU) in rivalry with the Social Democratic Party of Germany (SPD).[80] Sagely, Adenauer worked consistently to cement the interconfessional character of the CDU, unlike the Catholic pre-Nazi Center Party, which Protestants avoided. In Christian labor circles, which were already interconfessional in Adam Stegerwald's time, a fairly general consensus had long since developed that only unitary unions (such as the new DGB in formation) could play an effective role on the national stage. Adenauer welcomed the Christian DGB members and constituents in the CDU, along with its *bürgerlich* majority, as one forceful component in the interclass party.

Advocates of an industrial market economy, meanwhile, were active, though not prominent among Catholic social thinkers. Alfred Müller-Armack led a band of Protestant economists alive to the shortcomings of laissez-faire capitalism but convinced of the necessity of a competitive market for a thriving economy. He was inspired to dub his conception the "social market economy," thus depriving the Social Democrats of an attractive slogan for their alternative.[81] Konrad Adenauer took up the proposals of Ludwig Erhard with alacrity in 1948, when he first heard of them.[82] Erhard became the economics minister in Adenauer's first cabinet in 1949 and thereby the architect of the "social market economy" that abetted West Germany's move to general prosperity in the 1950s.

Where was social Catholicism in all this? There was, to be sure, much controversy and argument in German social Catholicism of the era. In 1949 a *Katholikentag* convened in Bochum. This traditional gathering of German laity, the seventy-third in a series going back to 1848, attracted enormous throngs to its festivities and deliberations to discuss the topic "Justice makes for Peace." The particular issue that attracted the most attention was *Mitbestimmung*, the participation of workers in employers' decision-making (that is, codetermination by labor representatives on boards of directors and management of industrial firms).[83] The *Katholikentag* participants endorsed the labor unions'

---

80. Lienkamp 2001, 202.

81. With greater stress on the first word; see the incisive critique of Müller-Armack's conception by Nell-Breuning 1990, 222–38.

82. Langner 1980, 60; for the following, see 55–102.

83. See Oelinger 1980, 157–61.

quest in a text declaring, "Codetermination of all workers in social, personnel, and economic questions is a right of natural law in God's order which corresponds to the needs for mutual responsibility. We favor its legal grounding." A month later, on September 29, 1949, by coincidence, Adenauer addressed the first postwar Bundestag, noting that "the social and societal recognition of the workers makes necessary a new order of the ownership question [that is, codetermination] in heavy industry."[84] Subsequently, industrialists resisted the union claims. Compromises were reached over the next few years, but a real measure of codetermination remains on the books and in the practice of Germany to a degree unique in industrialized countries. In Catholic social ethics the claim that *Mitbestimmung* is "a right in natural law" was soon regarded as an overstatement. In June 1950 Pope Pius XII adverted clearly to the issue in an address to participants at an International Congress of Social Studies. There he took a cautious position on the advisability of large-scale codetermination itself.[85]

The codetermination issue played a role in another important milestone in economic policy, the establishment of the European Coal and Steel Community (ECSC). To break the stranglehold of the powerful cartels controlling the coal resources of the Ruhr, the Allies proposed separating ownership of coal-mining firms from manufacturers of steel, or even, in the British view, proceeding to the nationalization of both. However, this left the problem of trade across national borders unsolved, with deleterious effects on industrial revival in Germany and bordering countries and hence the prospect of nationalistic antagonisms flaring up again. In particular, French manufacturing needed a reliable and competitively priced supply of Ruhr coal. Konrad Adenauer welcomed the French proposal for a supranational authority in charge of a common market in coal and steel for those countries that would sign on. In fact, six nations (France, Germany, Italy, the Netherlands, Belgium, and Luxembourg) signed a treaty creating the ECSC on April 18, 1951. It was a tough sell all around, but a major step toward European peace and economic union. The strong support among the Christian labor representatives in Adenauer's governing party for codetermination, a feature added to Monnet's Schuman plan, helped Adenauer overcome the resistance to the radical step of ceding sovereignty in a sensitive matter of economic policy.[86]

84. Van Hook 2004, 258.
85. Pius XII 1950, 485–88; also available as http://www.vatican.va/holy_father/pius_xii/speeches/1950/documents/hf_p-xii_spe_19500603_studi-sociali_fr.html. It may be noted that on this issue of *Mitbestimmung*, the two leading Jesuit social Catholic scholars, Nell-Breuning and Gundlach, parted ways; see Schwarte 1975, 559–74, with references also to other papal utterances on the topic; see also Gundlach 1964.
86. Wells 2007, 8–18. Reviewing Isabel Warner's *Steel and Sovereignty* (Warner 1996) in the

As Germany constructed an economic order that could take advantage of the Marshall Plan and trade in the context of the Western (Anglo-American) economic dominance, did the path taken by Erhard and the CDU endanger social-ethical principles? A sympathetic and authoritative observer, Oswald von Nell-Breuning, SJ, concluded by 1954 that social market economics was more consistent than previous systems with the principle of solidarity. Indeed, the solidarism of his mentor, Heinrich Pesch, furnished the true theoretical basis on which the social market economy rested. This no longer required the notion of a more or less stable vocational order so prominent in social Catholicism up until that time.[87] What Catholic social thought always insisted upon, according to Nell-Breuning, was the dignity of the human person and our need for mutual support in social structures. From this it follows that a market economy may not treat the labor market as if it were like other markets—simply a market of things to be traded.[88] For the social Catholic outlook, that approach to the labor market always raised an alarm. But it was offset by the design of a free competitive order in a strong state with institutions protective of persons, also as wage earners and property owners.

In terms of ecclesial developments, an overall trend toward deconfessionalization continued, with the wartime experiences of Christian labor accelerating the changing relationships between Catholic bishops and organizations, as we see in many cases. What this meant was not in itself a turning away from Christian dedication to social justice efforts so much as the withdrawal of the clergy and hierarchy from their active direction. Lay leaders took over more than ever, sometimes gently or not so gently nudging the institutional church out of the way. Consider, for instance, Leo Joseph Suenens, famous for his contributions to Vatican II. When he became archbishop of Malines (Mechlin, Mechelen) in 1961, of course, preparations for the Second Vatican Council were preoccupying the church circles. But unlike his predecessor, Cardinal Van Roey, Suenens, right through to 1979 when he retired, never had occasion to oversee the Belgian Confederation of Christian Unions in any particulars or be consulted by its leaders.[89] The same was true of the CFTC in France on its way to renaming itself the CDTF. Another case to the same point is the already mentioned MPF, the French working families' movement led by former Jocistes. Their party-political alliances, along with other factors, led eventu-

---

Journal of Modern History 71 (1999) 249–50, Harold James notes that Adenauer forged "a domestic political consensus in particular, convincing the trade unions that worker representation on a company's board was a more effective route to worker empowerment than nationalization. The unions, in turn, pressed the socialist party to accept the combination of private ownership with codetermination."

87. Langner 1980, 102–7.
89. See Pasture 2003.

88. R. Marx 2008, esp. 122 and 183.

ally to the restructuring of Workers' Catholic Action (ACO) by the French bishops in 1949 to 1951. All these developments and many more may be seen as manifestations of a broadly conceived secularizing process in European society at large. They are also instances of adaptations in Catholicism to a changing world[90]—to a "secular age," in Charles Taylor's sense. They form a pattern of ever greater differentiation and autonomy in relations between the labor activists and the institutional church.

90. See Damberg and Pasture 2010, esp. 70.

CHAPTER 14

Working within Secular Pluralism

To take a longer view: in the eighteenth century, Christianity suffered marked losses with the Enlightenment and the French Revolution. In the nineteenth century, concomitant with the rise of industrial society, a process of Christian revival and gathering strength began in many parts of Europe. One modernizing phenomenon of the period is precisely the sort of Christian labor movements that we have been treating here. Charles Taylor, in his impressive study *A Secular Age*, has dubbed this period, roughly from 1800 to the 1950s, "the Age of Mobilization."[1] Summing up, he writes that the aim of all this mobilization was "to penetrate more deeply the lives of the followers, to bond them more closely together, and to minimize contact with outsiders.... But these tightly organized churches ... with their strongly puritanical codes, their inherent links, of whatever sort, to political identities, and their claims to ground civilizational order, were perfectly set up for a precipitate fall in the next age which was beginning to dawn at mid-century."

Opening the Dikes

Examples of what Taylor means dot the history of Catholic working-class organizations in the mid-twentieth century. Perhaps the most striking illustrative case is the fate of the 1954 *Mandement* of the Dutch bishops.[2] To place it in context: in September 1944, Allied forces had liberated a mostly Catholic portion in the southern Netherlands, while the German hold on the rest of the country was

---

1. Taylor 2007, 423–72; quotation 472.
2. As recounted by Jan Roes (1990).

not finally eliminated until May 1945. Though there was much sentiment for a breakthrough that would facilitate contact between the pillarized segments of the population, the sturdy Dutch pillars—of Catholics, Protestants, socialists, liberals—reconstituted themselves. Neither clerical nor lay Catholic political leaders wanted to see their organizations submerged. The bishops had earned the added respect of the people by their firm attitude toward the German occupiers, and they intervened energetically in the liberated region. After the complete liberation, the Northern bishops joined their Southern colleagues in urging Catholics to band together as before. Within organized labor the Catholic and socialist labor union leaders made a practice of mutual consultations—but not about merging their respective federations.

By the early 1950s it became more obvious that some were chafing at the "closed Catholicism" that others prized so highly; they favored an "open Catholicism." Influential priests and lay people of this persuasion took the initiative to submit a draft of a pastoral letter in accord with this thinking. The five bishops of the Netherlands decided to commission their own text, which resulted in a *Mandement* (or joint mandatory letter) on "The Catholic in Public Life at the Present Time." Of its three parts, the first warned against a "false spirituality" that would have the devout abstain completely from involvement in public affairs and issues. But Catholics were to carry out their social and political engagement from within the Catholic social framework. "Therefore we give you the important directive: Unity in an organization of one's own and, from that base, collaboration with others, while maintaining one's own independence."[3] A detailed second section dealt with public issues where Catholics could make a particular contribution. Most pertinent was "vocational order," an arch-Catholic item of papal teaching in *Quadragesimo anno*, as we have seen (and in a version called "*publiekrechtlijke bedrijfsorganisatie*," or PBO, a proposal for industrial policy in the postwar Netherlands). It was the third section, though, that set off a blowback.[4] Here the bishops reinculcated and sharpened the sanctions they had issued in the 1930s. Catholics who joined a socialist labor union were not to receive the sacraments or a Catholic burial service. They were forbidden to read socialist newspapers or listen to such radio stations. At the last minute the prohibition against joining or voting for the socialist Labor Party was stricken from the text, thus avoiding the worst political explosion.

The response in the media, all the same, was vigorous and went on for months. The Catholic radio network (RKO) preferred to pass it over in silence, but that was not altogether possible. People in all camps voiced their wonderment and opinions. The bishops evidently had hoped that silent obedience

3. Roes 1990, 123.
4. "Het bisschoppelijk mandement en zijn gevolgen (1954)," in *HJS* 534–38.

would carry the day and that disciplined uniformity in such public and personal options would continue to hold sway, but they were mistaken. They wanted to hold together a combination of aims that no longer prevailed: maintaining both influence in the pluralistic world of postwar Netherlands *and* a tight inner cohesiveness of the Catholic pillar. The organizations of the Catholic pillar did not immediately crumble, but the notion of church authority invoked did undergo a change, even at the level of the hierarchy. The "mandatory letter" of 1954 still conceived its authority as strictly top-down, as in a Catholic Action framework from Pius XI's time, whereas by 1959 a Lenten pastoral letter indicated a differentiated view of hierarchical authority. In 1965, in fact, "the Dutch bishops publicly rescinded all the negative sanctions applied to Catholic membership in socialist or other non-Catholic organizations in 1954."[5]

In the sphere of organized labor in the Netherlands, the socialist union confederation suspended its consultations with the Catholic unions for a time. Catholic members of the (socialist) Labor Party refused to leave the party as directed, a sign of things to come. The first Catholic president of the Labor Party later remarked that "the bishops' Mandement did our party a lot of good."[6] As noted in the previous chapter along with similar cases in some other nations, the Catholic and secular unions merged over the period 1976–81 into the Dutch Labor Federation, or FNV.

The Dutch experience was perhaps the most striking example of Charles Taylor's generalization, but other Catholicisms underwent analogous transformations in the 1950s and 1960s. Of special interest because of the importance of the German unitary trade union federation, the DGB, are the mid-1950s controversies in and around its Catholic contingent. After Hans Böckler, the head of the DGB who favored a comprehensive big-tent approach to united labor, died in 1951, and after the policies of social capitalism favored by Chancellor Adenauer achieved the upper hand politically, the DGB became more and more ideologically aligned with the opposition Social Democratic Party. This left its Catholic members, who were attached politically to the Christian Democratic Party, struggling for influence with the labor confederation. They formed two groupings, one that advocated continued work within the DGB to have their social-Catholic point of view acknowledged, and the other that planned to revive or create a rival confederation of Christian labor unions.

The first, pro-DGB contingent had the strong support of none other than Oswald von Nell-Breuning, SJ.[7] The other group harked back to the KAB (Katholische Arbeiterbewegung Westdeutschlands), with its venerated prewar legacy of leading clergy and laymen, Otto Müller, Bernhard Letterhaus, and

---

5. See Coleman 1978, 84–92, here 91. 6. Roes 1990, 124.
7. See Schroeder 1992, 171 and passim, esp. 349–62.

Nikolaus Gross. From 1952 to 1957 the leadership of the KAB looked for ways to get a Christian union federation off the ground.[8] Moral and financial support came by way of the CISC (the International Federation of Christian Trade Unions), led by August Vanistendael as successor to Jos Serrarens. The Catholics who occupied prominent positions in DGB unions looked askance at the idea, even though their own efforts to moderate the DGB's political stances had a minimum of success. (However, the left-wing ideologue of the DGB, Viktor Agartz, was in fact relieved of his duties some months after giving the polemical principal address at the Frankfurt congress of the DGB in 1954.) Along with Michael Keller, the bishop of Münster, the archbishop of Cologne, Cardinal Joseph Frings, was the chief ecclesiastical patron of the KAB. Frings, in 1950, urged by Nell-Breuning, also supported Catholics joining the unitary union, but regretted its leftward course. In 1953 he acceded to the proposal of founding a separate Christian union federation as a last resort if reform efforts to bring the DGB back to a focus on workers' rights, with party-political and ideological neutrality, got nowhere.

The advocates of a Christian union announced the founding of the Christliche Gewerkschaften Deutschlands (CGD) at the end of October 1955. The Catholic bishops of West Germany indicated their support for the idea, most formally in early 1957. Protestant church bodies did not follow suit, despite the adherence of the Evangelische Arbeiterbewegung to the new foundation. The KAB leaders took the lead in organizing the new unions, but their own members left in thousands in protest. The much greater number of Catholic workers stayed unperturbed in the DGB unions. This brouhaha never reached the proportions of the contemporaneous *Mandement* affair across the border in the Netherlands. It was another sign, though, that the Age of Mobilization in Catholic subcultures was fading.

The DGB remained allied with the SPD, the Social-Democratic Party, while the latter, in its pivotal 1959 "Godesberg Program," declared itself to be an interclass party, a *Volkspartei*, and not just a party of the working class. At the same time, it embraced the social market economy that had proved so successful. Tony Judt puts it this way:

The new Party Program adopted there baldly stated that "Democratic socialism, which in Europe is rooted in Christian ethics, in humanism, and in classical philosophy, has no intention of proclaiming absolute truths." The state, it was asserted, should "restrict itself mainly to indirect methods of influencing the economy." The free market in goods and employment was vital: "The totalitarian directed economy destroys freedom."[9]

8. Ibid., 314–17; Aretz 1982, 205–10; Pasture 1999, 254–61.
9. Judt 2005, 370.

With such pronouncements from the SPD, the door was open for Christian workers and the middle class in Germany to join the party in a reformist, rather than revolutionary, movement. Nell-Breuning, for his part, quipped that the Godesberg Program contained a "compendium of Catholic social teaching."[10] This was but part of a general and historically significant convergence of many in all camps around what has been called "social capitalism."[11]

Aggiornamento

On the Catholic side, not only did the idioms of vocational order pass into desuetude, but the language of the social, indeed of a welcome increased socialization, took a prominent turn in the teaching of Pope John XXIII in his *Mater et magistra*.[12] This 1961 encyclical did not attract as wide attention as did Pope John's next one, *Pacem in terris*, in the context of the Cuban missile crisis. It could be dismissed as the pope's bow to the seventieth anniversary of *Rerum novarum*, treated at length in its first pages. The new direction was also somewhat obscured by the wording of the Latin version of the encyclical, on which several translations were based. In English as in Latin, the key notion came out as follows:

Certainly one of the principal characteristics which seem to be typical of our age is *an increase in social relationships*, in those mutual ties, that is, which grow daily more numerous and which have led to the introduction of many and varied forms of associations in the lives and activities of citizens, and to their acceptance within our legal framework.[13]

In the Italian, from which the Latin was translated, the italicized phrase is simply *socialization*.[14] John XXIII took socialization as a phenomenon of modern life, with its mobility and change, in response to the specter of individual isolation and economic subjugation, whether in the urban agglomerations or in the countryside. Socialization then, in his usage, comprised the multiplication of organizational ties at many levels, including government. He saw the welfare

---

10. Hengsbach 1990, 55.
11. Van Kersbergen 1995; Hill 2010; it is perhaps more often referred to as the social market economy or, from different angles, societal neo-corporatism or *concertation* or a "consultation economy"; see Judt 2008, 9–11, 2005, 360–89; see also Stjernø 2004.
12. Dorr 1991, 50–51; 1992, 132–38.
13. *MM*, no. 59 (italics mine).
14. This passage, *MM*, no. 59, 5:59–90, is at *MM* 45 in the Italian version: http://www.vatican.va/holy_father/john_xxiii/encyclicals/documents/hf_j-xxiii_enc_15051961_mater_it.html. See Dorr (1986, 95–97) and Mich (2005, 207–9) for the broader context. It may be noted that Vatican II, in *Gaudium et spes* 25, renders the notion as "socialization" in both Latin and English, with a reference to *MM*. It does not mean the nationalization of industries, at least for the most part.

state in Western Europe as on the whole such an appropriate development. As is clear from a number of particular applications mentioned in the encyclical, this constituted, in the history of papal social teaching, "a decisive move away from the right."[15] Marie-Dominique Chenu saw it as discarding the use of "the social doctrine of the Church" as a conservative anti-socialist "ideology."[16]

The drafters took care to cite the doctrine of preceding popes without allowing the previous polemic against socialism to obstruct reforms that may need the aid of proper legislation. The new encyclical appealed to the principle of subsidiarity (*QA* 80) to support this "move away from the right." Indeed, the paragraphs *MM* 53–58 leading up to the introduction of the treatment of socialization recalled and rebalanced the principle of subsidiarity. It does not serve only as a warning against over-intrusion on the part of government, but also as a reminder of the responsibility of "public authority" to provide, for example, "effective measures to prevent the recurrence of mass unemployment" (*MM* 54). Another example (*MM* 117): the common good in contemporary circumstances requires increased state and public ownership of property, but not to the detriment of private ownership, which itself is not an absolute. Both must be balanced in light of the common good. The same approach is taken with the question of private enterprise, state authority, and the principle of solidarity (*MM* 151ff). The encyclical repeated (*MM* 34) the condemnation of communism by Pius XI in *QA*; included therewith was materialistic socialism, as distinguished from various forms of socialization. It also took up another issue from the earlier encyclical (*QA* 65), that of some kind of worker participation in shaping the policies of their firm and nation. In the postwar context of the codetermination authorized by the 1951 treaty establishing the European Coal and Steel Community, *MM* 32 in effect endorsed the practice.[17]

Thus, while social democrats were discarding shibboleths of the left, Catholic magisterial texts were leaving behind pre-democratic corporatist watchwords such as "vocational order." Episcopal conferences were shifting away from the defensive and separatist elements of ultra-mobilization. It was in this atmosphere of "moving away from the right" that Pope John XXIII called for a council of all the bishops of the Catholic world. The European homelands of Catholicity still constituted the center of gravity in the worldwide church, so such trends were of considerable moment. *Mater et magistra* was one of the measures Pope John took to encourage new thinking without setting an authoritative line of his own for the council to follow. The 1961 encyclical served in effect as a harbinger of the remarkable and undeniable changes in the stance

15. Dorr 1986, 103.
16. Chenu 1979, 60–63; see Himes et al. 2005, 4.
17. See *MM* 92–93 and 97; Mich 2005, 199 and 208.

of the Catholic Church toward the modern world to be ratified by the Second Vatican Council.[18]

Labor issues did not constitute the flashpoints of the key debates or the final texts approved by the Council. In the preparatory work and in the determination of the basic pastoral thrust that the Council took, however, such issues were an ingredient in the tensions surrounding the direction the Council was to take.[19] The pope's chosen advisers, such as Pietro Pavan (who was also drafting the pope's *Mater et magistra* at this time), tried to influence the preparations for the Council in the direction of an analogous updating of the church's approach to the modern world. The preparatory commissions, however, were confided to Vatican offices under the influence of Cardinal Ottaviani and leading theologian Sebastian Tromp, SJ. The latter were not receptive. They conceived the proper work of an ecumenical council to be doctrinal, having to do with timeless truths that needed reinculcation, rather than with the pastoral challenges of the modern era. Theirs was not to be the approach that prevailed in the end, although it took strenuous and persistent efforts to overcome tenacious curial opposition.

Labor causes and issues were in fact involved at least as background in setting the course of the Council. Longtime champions of the cause of Christian labor, such as the bishop of Lille, Achille Cardinal Liénart, would not let the tradition of *Rerum novarum* fade but would reshape it in light of the signs of the times. Liénart was very prominent at Vatican II as one of the ten members of the Council of Presidents. On the second day of the Council, October 13, 1962, he took the unforeseen initiative of submitting a motion to delay a vote that was on the schedule. The vote was to assign bishops to the conciliar committees ("commissions") that would vet drafts ("schemata" or schemas) of declarations of the Council.[20] Seconded by Cardinal Frings, this has gone down in history as the crucial move in getting the Council started on the right foot, in accord with the intentions of Pope John XXIII. The immediate outcome of this intervention was that the majority of the bishops, with the pope's help, rejected the drafts distributed to them. In the Council's first period (October–November 1962), they deliberated on the one acceptable schema—that on liturgical reform—while they set about informing themselves and creating acceptable proposals in committees and informal collaborations with the help of experts.

Whether the Second Vatican Council would be well-advised and capable of addressing questions of worldly import such as economic inequities was a challenge that troubled the bishops and their advisers through the preparatory

18. O'Malley 2008; Schloesser 2007; Tanner 2005, 75–84; E. E. Y. Hales 1965.
19. See Komonchak 1995, 196–200, 260–62.
20. On the commissions, see Riccardi 1997, 27–32.

period (1960–62) and the sessions of the Council itself (1962–65). It required three years of concentrated effort on the part of the Council fathers and experts to work out and approve a more adequate message to the church and the attentive public. The reset began with proposals such as that of Cardinal Suenens to take the time necessary to draft two kinds of documents, one on the church's mission to the world (*ad extra*) and another on fitting the church to accomplish this mission more efficaciously (*ad intra*). Within this focus on reform of the church, many questions of detailed application would have to be devolved to future, often regional or local, decisions.

Concomitantly Liénart kept up contacts with former worker-priests, those who obeyed the prohibition against full-time wage labor for priests, in the hope of seeing the prohibition lifted. This finally happened at the tail end of the Council in December 1965 with the promulgation of the Decree on the Ministry and Life of Priests, *Presbyterorum ordinis* (no. 8). But before this could take place (almost without notice amidst the issuing of *Gaudium et spes* and the Declaration on Religious Liberty at the same time), the Council fathers from France had to wage a patient campaign behind the scenes.[21] Soon after Pope John XXIII made public in January 1959 his intention to call a Council, Cardinal Feltin of Paris sent him a proposal to relax the prohibition. The pope referred the matter to the Holy Office, which had issued the 1954 decision. Cardinal Pizzardo, the former head cleric of Catholic Action in Italy, was now secretary of the "supreme congregation," as the Holy Office was called. His official response to Feltin and Liénart in July was totally negative, to their profound consternation.[22] Passing over all the reasons Feltin's proposal had given, it portrayed the idea of priests in wage labor side by side with other workers as inimical to the mission of the clergy. The bishops must see to it that all the priests in even part-time employment of this kind be quietly reassigned. The mission to workers had to carry on without this type of involvement in the life of the working class. Before word of the ruling leaked out, Liénart replied to Pizzardo personally on August 31 with deeply felt and detailed objections to the stance taken by the Holy Office. In it he wrote, "When the Church sends missionaries" to pagan lands, "she does not tell them to stay on the ship that brought them" and only let some laypersons go on shore.[23]

This letter remained private. But Pizzardo's note of July was leaked and published in *Le Monde* of September 15, 1959, causing great embarrassment. Liénart was a pillar of the church: he exhibited solidarity with his priests, while nevertheless implementing the decree. At the same time he was personally

---

21. See Suaud and Viet-Depaule 2005, 465–88; Masson 2001, 444–49; Vinatier 1985, 175–227.
22. Vinatier 1985, 176–78.
23. Ibid., 183.

committed to undoing a ruling he considered perverse—as he had tried to do in 1954. His key chance came in 1963, when he could submit a report requested by Pope Paul VI on the issues involved, particularly the need for bishops' conferences and not Vatican offices to set the policy on such pastoral questions.[24] It was a powerful motive for the Council's position on the collegiality of bishops. As to wage labor for priests, in the end the Council stated the following (as alluded to previously) in *Presbyterorum ordinis* (no. 8):

All priests are sent as co-workers in the same apostolate, whether they engage in parochial or extra-parochial ministry. This is true whether they devote their efforts to scientific research or teaching, or whether by manual labor they share in the lot of the workers themselves—if there is need for this and competent authority approves—or finally whether they fulfill some other apostolic tasks or labor designed for the apostolate.[25]

Against the background of concern for the common good in the promotion of the human dignity of all, labor matters came up in conciliar discussions about several documents, but most focally in the preparation of the seminal Pastoral Constitution on the Church in the Modern World, *Gaudium et spes*.[26] Its preparation took place entirely during the period of the Council, not before. A document of this kind, though in line with the *aggiornamento* that John XXIII had in mind for the Council, was not anything the Vatican organizers of the preparatory commissions were able to conceive. And as it took shape in stages in conciliar commissions and subcommissions and a "mixed commission" (with members from the Theological Commission and from the Commission on the Lay Apostolate), it gave rise to continued puzzlement. How should an ecumenical council address so vast and unusual topic: the church and the world of the present time?[27] Should they be content to issue a letter to the listening world, perhaps even an encyclical letter from the bishops of the global church?[28] Most wanted in one way or another to attempt what could only be the beginning of a dialogue with the secular world of the twentieth century—dialogue was a theme of Pope

24. Ibid., 208–15; Masson 2001, 680–86, 582–84; for more background, see Turbanti 2006, 5–6.
25. See in Flannery 1996, 331, or http://www.vatican.va/archive/hist_councils/ii_vatican_council/documents/vat-ii_decree_19651207_presbyterorum-ordinis_en.html.
26. See Hollenbach 2005.
27. See Grootaers 1997, 412–28. For the whole arduous path to the completion of *Gaudium et spes*, I have relied upon Turbanti's painstaking investigation (2000). As to format, the original idea was to separate treatments of particular areas into appendices. Many bishops, however, wanted this or that topic taken up in the constitution itself. The end result was a pastoral constitution containing, after an introduction, two main parts: Part 1, "The Church and the Human Vocation" (nos. 11–45); and Part 2, "Some More Urgent Problems" (nos. 46–93). Part 2, chapter 3, "Economic and Social Life" (nos. 63–72), focused on economic development, inequalities, right to work, and participation in economic enterprises and ownership.
28. Turbanti 2000, 625; see Congar 2012, 714.

Paul VI's first encyclical in 1964, *Ecclesiam suam*. Many bishops were keenly aware that in the time remaining to draft such a message, they could hardly work out satisfactorily the many issues to be touched upon. Nevertheless, at the end they approved and issued not a letter but a long constitution. It was qualified as a pastoral rather than dogmatic constitution (see the important note 1 of the final text), but it was still the most solemn kind of pronouncement that a council could make. As a beginning of a new approach of the Catholic body to secular problems of the age, *Gaudium et spes*, for all its limitations and flaws, set a postconciliar agenda and pointed it in a challenging direction.[29] One can even see an adaptation of the JOC's "See—Judge—Act" method in the structure of the pastoral constitution, as Hans-Joachim Sander has pointed out.[30] The conscious approach from reading "the signs of the times" (*GS* no. 4) to offering the light of the Word of God in guiding the church's response to the needs of the world was without precedent in the teaching of ecumenical councils.

What positions did the Pastoral Constitution take as regards issues particularly close to labor movements? The autonomy of Christian labor unions from hierarchical authority was taken for granted. Even the appropriateness of an episcopal mandate to a parallel Catholic lay apostolate (as in the French ACO) hardly surfaced in the final texts.[31] In part this could have been a case of leaving organizational adaptations to the local hierarchies, but more generally it was the recognition that Catholic activists had their own baptismal commission to work for social justice, including the participation of workers in shaping their labor and the conditions in which it took place.[32] It was certainly not a question of abandoning the world of work, labor unions, and economic policies to a

---

29. Thus Hünermann 2006, 426–27; Alberigo 2006, 637–38. Some bishops and "periti" of the majority harbored serious reservations about the pastoral constitution; see Turbanti 2006, 41–42, and Routhier 2006, 144 and 168–69. Even Congar had his qualms (Congar 2012, 772–73); but the recently named Cardinal Joseph Cardijn came to the defense of its (and his) inductive approach. In a celebrated, even decisive, lecture on September 22, 1965, at the DO-C, the Dutch Documentation Center in Rome, the eloquent Dominican scholar Marie-Dominique Chenu persuasively put the effort in a most positive theological light (Routhier 2006, 130; Turbanti 2000, 643–51; Sander 2005, 655–63).

30. Sander 2005, 715–19.

31. Such issues came up in the drafting process without surviving into the eventual conciliar text. See Komonchak 1995, 196–200, à propos of the preconciliar work on a future treatment of the apostolate of the laity (see the Council's Decree on the Apostolate of Lay People, *Apostolicam actuositatem*, of November 18, 1965; also Turbanti 2000, 80, with n. 107). August Vanistendael, head of the CISC, was already being consulted as to what the Council might eventually say about labor unions in *Gaudium et spes* 67–72. Questions like this resurfaced as the final revisions were being made in committee in November 1965, and some members again asked Vanistendael to inform them on practices of codetermination and other specifics that they considered crucial. A majority insisted, however, that the constitution could not go into such detail; Turbanti 2000, 763.

32. See *GS* 68; of course, the new perspective of Vatican II on the People of God as in the Constitution on the Church (*Lumen Gentium*, chap. 2) was determinative here.

purely worldly realm where the Gospel would have nothing to say (*GS* 72). The most explosive issues of the schema were in other chapters: birth control (*GS* 51 with note) and the arms race and nuclear deterrence (*GS* 80). The consternation aroused by these controversies in the Council's final weeks threatened to scuttle the pastoral constitution with negative votes. The tempest passed, however, and when the initial votes were cast, 1,656 out of 2,227 bishops approved even of the war and peace chapter. On December 4, similarly, there were just 483 no votes. On the Constitution as a whole, the yes voters numbered 2,111 (on December 6); and on December 7, 1965, 2,309 of 2,391 fathers approved its solemn promulgation.

Prior to these votes, two or three declarations of the preparatory Schema XIII (in chapter 3, on socioeconomic life) had been the object, once again, of serious questioning in the mixed commission. The phenomenon of globalization (without the word as yet) was dawning on the European and North American churches, especially in the setting of the whole world's bishops gathered in council. Land reform, a hot issue particularly in Latin America, was addressed in *GS* 71 on ownership and private property (after an initial allusion in no. 65). Naturally the wording of the text was subject to close scrutiny. With a proper set of conditions, expropriation of latifundia could be needful: "insufficiently cultivated estates should be distributed to those who can make these lands fruitful."

The rights of workers and organized labor (*GS* 68) as well as owners and management were also firmly if broadly set forth. "Growth," according to *GS* 65, is not the result simply of the economic activity of individuals, "nor must it be entrusted solely to the authority of government." (There were no condemnations by name of the "isms": capitalism, communism, socialism—a contentious omission with regard to communism.) Economic development must be seen in light of the personal dignity of human beings created in the image of God. *GS* 68 stated one outcome of relating these two values to each other: "The active participation of everyone in the running of an enterprise should be promoted" (*GS* 68). This bland statement betrays little of the questions that arose over a contemporary issue in economic policy.[33] To Bishop Franz Hengsbach of Essen, it referred very concretely to the practice of *Mitbestimmung* (codetermination) in postwar Germany. He had sought enlightenment from management and labor circles as to what they expected from Schema XIII.[34] One practice

---

33. See the version of no. 68 on the Vatican website, http://www.vatican.va/archive/hist_councils/ii_vatican_council/documents/vat-ii_const_19651207_gaudium-et-spes_en.html: "In economic enterprises it is persons who are joined together, that is, free and independent human beings created to the image of God. Therefore, with attention to the functions of each—owners or employers, management or labor—and without doing harm to the necessary unity of management, the active sharing of all in the administration and profits of these enterprises in ways to be properly determined is to be promoted."

34. Turbanti 2000, 713.

they underscored was the establishment of works councils. These consist of elected representatives of wage and salary workers. A works council must be consulted on job cuts and have a right to weigh in on policies that affect working conditions. They do not negotiate wages—the unions do that, typically on an industry-wide basis. But works councils are important links in labor relations where they exist. In addition, in larger companies labor representatives have a voice in supervisory boards that choose the chief executive and approve major decisions. The bishops in the Council could not go into so much detail, but the social Catholic tradition of the Rhenish lands made its contribution in this and other ways. For the most part the labor gains in those countries in the twentieth century were simply welcomed as appropriate. Determining the "communal purpose of earthly goods" (GS 69)—the distribution of resources—remained a value prone to controversy according to circumstances.[35]

Out of "the barely organised shambles" that some participants perceived in the schema as late as the spring of 1965, one hoped for "a work that holds together."[36] Schema XIII became *Gaudium et spes* by the end of that year. Since then it has proved its worth as a stimulus for peace and social justice in places as distant from each other as the Poland of Solidarity and the Latin America of liberation theology and base communities. One may appropriately see it as the Council's repositioning of the church in "a secular age" as interpreted by Taylor's work, following upon "the age of mobilization."[37]

Certainly the magisterium then and since has not disavowed labor mobilization or support for labor organizations and workers' "participation in the running of an enterprise." Quite the contrary: What it no longer promotes is the need for Catholic workers to organize by themselves. In a secular age one should make room for a pluralism of religious commitments.

---

35. See Sobrino 2012, 75: "The 'Church of the Poor' did not prosper at Vatican II. It was only when Medellín adopted it that essential elements in the Council became historical fact." The influence of Louis-Joseph Lebret, OP (1897–1966), at Vatican II was known only in restricted circles until after the publication of Paul VI's encyclical *Populorum progressio* in 1967, which Lebret helped draft; see Deck 2005, 296–98, and Pelletier 1996. He was an expert on and an advocate for solutions to problems of underdevelopment in the Third World.

36. Congar 2012, 726; see Turbanti 2000, 570–94.

37. Taylor 2007.

Conclusion

I would like here to limn a broad view of some developments in the Catholic world of Western Europe in the age of industrialization, and of what I might call the classical age of social Catholicism, coinciding with Taylor's "Age of Mobilization," circa 1820 to the 1950s.

The effects of British industrialization were felt first in Belgium and France in the aftermath of the French Revolution. French and German Catholic thinkers responded to the signs of social disintegration by calling for the reforging of the social bonds in ways looking backward or forward.[1] Associations, charitable and social in inspiration, constituted the most practical and permissible form of mobilization to attempt to cope with the proletarianization of the masses. Political mobilization along religious or class lines started to develop. By the late nineteenth century there existed in Austria, Switzerland, and the Netherlands, as well as in Belgium and Germany, political Catholic mobilizations like the Center Party with social Catholic components of varying consistency and strength.[2] France and Italy, with their strong "liberal" or anticlerical regimes, permitted Catholic agencies such as social secretariats, rural cooperatives, and credit unions to form in some regions, but hardly anything like a national political party as yet.

It was at this juncture that Pope Leo XIII began to encourage such militant Catholicism in response to socioeconomic life in the modern world.[3] Along with some other dramatic interventions, also on the international level, the pope issued the famous encyclical "On the Condition of Labor," *Rerum novarum* (1891). Adopting modern language, he stated (in *RN* 2), "It is no easy matter to define the relative rights and mutual duties of the rich and of the poor, of capital and of labor."

The extent of the influence that the encyclical would have was

---

1. See Misner 1991, 35–55, for these first pioneers, and subsequent chapters for what follows.
2. Evans 1999.
3. Lamberts 2002.

not immediately apparent. But Catholic labor activists appealed to it with success in many countries, especially when they encountered opposition within Catholicism to their radical-sounding declarations and undertakings. They laid initial foundations for the growth of Christian labor organizations and movements in subsequent decades, but not without controversy.

Before and especially after World War I, labor leaders worked at establishing transnational links. This resulted in 1920 in the formation of the CISC (or in English the IFCTU, International Federation of Christian Trade Unions). From its central office in the Netherlands it worked to reconcile the Christian labor movements of warring nations and establish their presence in the work of the International Labour Organisation in Geneva. Crippled by the rise of totalitarianism in the 1930s, the IFCTU rose again after World War II in difficult circumstances and even branched out from its European home. Under the leadership of August Vanistendael, affiliates took root in Latin America, Africa, and Asia.[4] Given the interreligious and pluralistic character of its global constituents, it dropped the reference to Christianity in its name and became the World Confederation of Labour (WCL) in 1968.[5]

The organizations of European Christian workers matured and proved their mettle during "the economic consequences of the peace" after World War I and, in a different way and in vastly altered conditions, after World War II.[6] Activists took new initiatives, perhaps most notably and effectively that of the Young Christian Workers movement (JOC). "Catholic Action" became the watchword of the epoch for many groups, following the directives of Pope Pius XI. Intellectual support and research for social justice among Catholics was making its way out of exile.

In the meantime, though, the antipathies and separation between the Christian and socialist mobilizations of workers manifested their weaknesses in the face of Italian Fascist, German Nazi, and Soviet Communist regimes. Chastened from this experience and encouraged by the encounters with other laborites under oppressive conditions during World War II, Christian and democratic socialist workers sought strength in union. In the 1950s a process of deconfessionalization of the Catholic labor movements set in across the board, though with strikingly different modalities and timetables from country to country. Varieties of social capitalism or social market economy took hold,

---

4. See Pasture 1994b, 85–95; Pasture 1999.

5. For the founding "Declaration of Principles" of the WCL in 1968, see Pasture 1994b, 165–74; 1999, 404–12. Finally, in 2006, the WCL merged with the larger International Confederation of Free Trade Unions to form the ITUC, the International Trade Union Confederation, with central offices in Brussels; see http://www.ituc-csi.org/congress2006. A global network of Catholic milieu organizations of workers is the World Movement of Christian Workers; see http://www.mmtc.info/en/.

6. Keynes 1920.

accompanied by a prosperity shared across the social classes to an unprecedented degree. The time was ripe in European Catholicism for Pope John's bold initiative of calling an ecumenical council, Vatican II. The Eurocentrism of the Roman Catholic communion was also due for a look abroad at the signs of the times not only in Europe and America but in the Second and Third Worlds.

Charles Taylor applies the perspective he has gained from his historical reflection in a pointed observation: "Church authority required mobilizing Catholics, and this mobilization ultimately fostered Christian democracy. Vatican II was the moment when the long rejection of liberal society was ultimately abandoned."[7] This paradox applies also to the Catholic labor mobilizations in our European focus area and time period. While making use of and even testing the limits of contemporary possibilities of nineteenth-century liberalism by forming voluntary workingmen's associations, social Catholics were engaged in a campaign to make society "Christian again," not liberal or socialist. What eventually came about was a tamed and pluralistic liberalism, respecting religious and social freedom and justice. The Second Vatican Council signaled its acceptance of this development in its "Pastoral Constitution on the Church in [not "and"] the Modern World," *Gaudium et spes*.

This of course is not to say that all the features or dominant overtones of the word "liberal" are exempt from criticism in Catholic thought. The liberalism now found to be of positive value defends human rights, pluralism, democratic forms of government. Its Catholic form may be called "communitarian liberalism," which brings out what it has in common with certain varieties of socialist thought, according to John Coleman.[8]

With reference to economic systems, the adoption of a social market economy in postwar Western Europe was the historic outcome of a convergence between Smithian market economics, social democratic traditions, and the Christian socioeconomic trends we have noted. Reinhard Marx (since 2010 cardinal and archbishop of Munich) has restated and updated the social Catholic contribution in a remarkable book. It is titled *Das Kapital* after the work of his namesake, Karl, but subtitled "A Plea for Humanity." In the second chapter on markets and ethics, Marx notes Amartya Sen's parallel arguments and goes into some detail on the convergent thinking of influential theoreticians in postwar Germany that favored this outcome.[9] In subsequent chapters he brings out the potentialities of such approaches in the contemporary crisis and makes the case for a global social market economy. Most recently, from the perspective of economic history and analysis, Thomas Piketty warns that rapid worldwide growth cannot be sustained at the level of the postwar recovery of 1945–75.[10]

7. Taylor 2011, 265.
9. Marx 2008, esp. 92–96.
8. Coleman 2000; 2005, 527.
10. Piketty 2014.

There is a need to balance the increasing share of capital wealth by redistribution of some returns to those who earn their living by labor. How such new challenges resonate in the economic ethics of contemporary Catholics is not for this book to treat.[11] The contours of theoretical and practical Catholic approaches in the nineteenth and twentieth centuries, however, are becoming clearer with hindsight. This is a precondition for future fruitful labors.

The participation of organized Catholic workers in the struggles to humanize the arena where most adult persons spend the bulk of their lives (namely, at work) enriched those lives. The labor activists and their mentors and pastors who have learned from them have created a legacy of gospel inspiration for their successors. It constitutes a notable part of the story of modern worker emancipation in general and of Christian service to economic justice in particular.

11. See Finn 2013 for an American perspective.

REFERENCES

AAS (*Acta Apostolicae Sedis*). 1909–. Rome: Typis Polyglottis Vaticanis.
Acerbi, Antonio. 1988. *Chiesa cultura società: Momenti e figure dal Vaticano I a Paolo VI.* Milan: Vita e Pensiero.
———. 1995. "La fortuna della 'Rerum novarum' nell'insegnamento sociale della Chiesa (1891–1931)." In *La "Rerum novarum" e il movimento cattolico italiano*, by Giuseppe Camadini et al., 153–70. Brescia: Morcelliana.
Achille Ratti, pape Pie XI: Actes du colloque, Rome, 15–18 mars 1989. 1996. Rome: École française de Rome.
Adam, Gérard. 1964. *La C.F.T.C., 1940–1958: Histoire politique et idéologique.* Paris: Armand Colin.
Adam, Karl. 1929. *The Spirit of Catholicism.* New York: Macmillan.
Agostino, Marc. 1991. *Le Pape Pie XI et l'opinion (1922–1939).* Rome: École française de Rome.
Alaerts, Leen. 2004. *Door eigen werk sterk: Geschiedenis van de kajotters en kajotsters in Vlaanderen 1924–1967.* Leuven: Leuven University Press.
Alber, Jens. 1982. *Vom Armenhaus zum Wohlfahrtsstaat: Analysen zur Entwicklung der Sozialversicherung in Westeuropa.* Frankfurt and New York: Campus Verlag.
Alberigo, Giuseppe. 2006. "Transition to a New Age." In Alberigo and Komonchak, *History of Vatican II*, 5:573–644.
Alberigo, Giuseppe, and Joseph A. Komonchak, eds. 1995–2006. *The History of Vatican II, 1959–1965.* 5 vols. Maryknoll, N.Y.: Orbis; Leuven: Peeters.
Albertazzi, Alessandro. 1984. "Settimane sociali." In *DSMCI* 3:941–53.
Alexander, Edgar. 1953. "Social and Political Movements and Ideas in Germany and Austrian Catholicism (1789–1950)." In Moody, *Church and Society*, 325–583.
Allard, Jean-Louis et al. 1988. *L'humanisme intégral de Jacques Maritain: Colloque de Paris et trois textes de Jacques Maritain.* Paris: Éditions Saint-Paul.
Altermatt, Urs, ed. 1994. *Schweizer Katholizismus zwischen den Weltkriegen, 1920–1940.* Fribourg: University Press.
Altermatt, Urs, and Franziska Metzger. 2003. "Katholische Arbeiter und Milieuidentität in der Schweiz 1850–1950." In Hiepel and Ruff, *Christliche Arbeiterbewegung*, 159–75.
Année sociale internationale 1913–1914. 1914. Reims: Action populaire.
Antoine, Charles. 1908. *Cours d'économie sociale.* 4th ed. Paris: Félix Alcan.
Aretin, Karl Otmar von. 1970. *The Papacy and the Modern World.* New York: McGraw-Hill.
Aretz, Jürgen. 1975. "Bernhard Letterhaus (1894–1944)." In *ZGiLB* 2:11–24.
———. 1978. *Katholische Arbeiterbewegung und Nationalsozialismus: Der Verband Katholischer Arbeiter- und Knappenvereine Westdeutschlands, 1923–1945.* Mainz: Grünewald.
———. 1979. "Otto Müller (1870–1944)." In *ZGiLB* 3:191–203.
———. 1980a. "Einheitsgewerkschaft und christlich-soziale Tradition." In Langner, *Katholizismus*, 205–28.
———. 1980b. "Nikolaus Groß (1898–1945)." In *ZGiLB* 4:159–71.
———. 1982. "Katholische Arbeiterbewegung und christliche Gewerkschaften: Zur

Geschichte der christlich-sozialen Bewegung." In Rauscher, *90 Jahre Rerum novarum*, 2:159–214.

Arnal, Oscar L. 1986. *Priests in Working-Class Blue: The History of the Worker-Priests (1943–1954)*. New York: Paulist.

——. 1987. "Toward a Lay Apostolate of the Workers: Three Decades of Conflict for the French Jeunesse ouvrière chrétienne (1927–1956)." *Catholic Historical Review* 73: 211–27.

Arnaud, Patrice. 2010. *Les STO: Histoire des français requis en Allemagne nazie, 1942–1945*. Paris: CNRS éditions.

ASS (Acta Sanctae Sedis). 1865–1908. Rome: Typographia Polyglotta.

Atkin, Nicholas, and Frank Tallett. 2003. *Priests, Prelates, and People: A History of European Catholicism since 1750*. New York: Oxford University Press.

Aubert, Jeanne. 1990. *J.O.C., Qu'as-tu fait de nos vies? La jeunesse ouvrière féminine, sa vie, son action, 1928–1945*. Paris: Editions ouvrières.

Aubert, Roger, et al, eds. 1978. *The Church in a Secularised Society*. Christian Centuries 5. New York: Paulist; London: Darton, Longman, and Todd.

——. 2003. *Catholic Social Teaching: An Historical Perspective*. Edited by David A. Boileau. Milwaukee: Marquette University Press.

Aussermair, Josef. 1979. *Kirche und Sozialdemokratie: Der Bund der religiösen Sozialisten 1926–1934*. Vienna: Europaverlag.

Baadte, Günther. 1979. "Elisabeth Gnauck-Kühne (1850–1917)." In *ZGiLB* 3:106–22.

——. 1985. "Katholischer Universalismus und nationale Katholizismen im Ersten Weltkrieg." In *Katholizismus, nationaler Gedanke und Europa seit 1800*, edited by Albrecht Langner, 89–109. Paderborn: Schöningh.

Bachem, Julius. 1906. "Wir müssen aus dem Turm heraus." *Historisch-politische Blätter* 137.

Bachem-Rehm, Michaela. 2003. "Katholische Arbeitervereine im Ruhrgebiet 1870–1914." In Hiepel and Ruff, *Christliche Arbeiterbewegung*, 20–41.

Baechler, Christian. 1982. *Le parti catholique alsacien 1890–1939: Du Reichsland à la république jacobine*. Paris: Ophrys.

Balderston, Theo. 2002. *Economics and Politics in the Weimar Republic*. Cambridge and New York: Cambridge University Press.

Ballof, J. Dominica. 1975. "Christine Teusch (1888–1968)." In *ZGiLB* 2:202–13.

Bank, Jan. 1981. "Verzuiling: A Confessional Road to Secularization, Emancipation and the Decline of Political Catholicism, 1920–1970." In *Britain and the Netherlands*, vol. 7, *Church and State since the Reformation*, edited by Alistair Duke and C. A. Tamse, 207–30. The Hague: Martinus Nijhoff.

Bard, Christine. 1993. "L'apôtre sociale et l'ange du foyer les femmes et la C.F.T.C. à travers *Le Nord-social* (1920–1936)." *Mouvement social* 165: 23–41.

——. 1995. *Les filles de Marianne: Histoire des féminismes 1914–1940*. Paris: Fayard.

Barral, Pierre. 1996. "Le magistère de Pie XI sur l'Action catholique." In *Achille Ratti*, 591–603.

Barry, Gearóid. 2012. *The Disarmament of Hatred: Marc Sangnier, French Catholicism and the Legacy of the First World War, 1914–45*. Houndmills, Basingstoke, Hampshire, and New York: Palgrave Macmillan.

Barthélemy-Madaule, Madeleine. 1973. *Marc Sangnier 1873–1950*. Paris: Seuil.

Bartolini, Stefano. 2000. *The Political Mobilization of the European Left, 1860–1980: The Class Cleavage*. Cambridge and New York: Cambridge University Press.

BASMSCI (*Bolletino dell'Archivio per la storia del movimento sociale cattolico in Italia*). 1966–. Milan: Vita e Pensiero.

Baumgartner, Alois. 1977. *Sehnsucht nach Gemeinschaft: Ideen und Strömungen im Sozialkatholizismus der Weimarer Republik*. Paderborn: Schöningh.

Becker, Winfried, and Rudolf Morsey, eds. 1988. *Christliche Demokratie in Europa: Grundlagen und Entwicklungen seit dem neunzehnten Jahrhundert*. Cologne: Böhlau.

Bedani, Gino. 1995. *Politics and Ideology in the Italian Workers' Movement: Union Development and the Changing Role of the Catholic and Communist Subcultures in Postwar Italy*. Oxford and Providence: Berg.

Bédarida, Renée. 1977. *Les armes de l'esprit: Témoignage chrétien (1941–1944)*. Paris: Editions ouvrières.

———. 1998. *Les Catholiques dans la guerre 1939–1945: Entre Vichy et la résistance*. Paris: Hachette.

Belouet, Éric. 2001. "Le couple jociste." In Duriez et al., *Chrétiens et ouvriers*, 86–99.

Bendiner, Burton. 1987. *International Labour Affairs: The World Trade Unions and the Multinational Companies*. Oxford: Clarendon Press.

Benedict XV. 1917. "Dès le début." *AAS* 9: 417–20.

Berger, Stefan, and Hugh Compston, eds. 2002. *Policy Concertation and Social Partnership in Western Europe: Lessons for the 21st Century*. New York: Berghahn.

Berlin, Isaiah. 1990. *The Crooked Timber of Humanity: Chapters in the History of Ideas*. London: John Murray.

Bernardi, Peter J. 2009. *Maurice Blondel, Social Catholicism, and Action Française: The Clash over the Church's Role in Society during the Modernist Era*. Washington, D.C.: The Catholic University of America Press.

Beschet, Paul. 2012. *Mission in Thuringia in the Time of Nazism* [*Mission en Thuringe au temps du Nazisme*]. Milwaukee: Marquette University Press.

Binder, Dieter. 2002. "The Christian Corporatist State: Austria from 1934 to 1938." In *Austria in the Twentieth Century*, edited by Rolf Steininger, Günter Bischof, and Michael Gehler, 72–84. New Brunswick, N.J.: Transaction.

Bischof, Günter, Anton Pelinka, and Alexander Lassner, eds. 2003. *The Dollfuss/Schuschnigg Era In Austria: A Reassessment*. New Brunswick, N.J.: Transaction.

Black, Naomi. 1989. *Social Feminism*. Ithaca, N.Y.: Cornell University Press.

Bled, Jean-Paul. 2004. "Mgr Seipel et le christianisme social." In Sorrel, *L'engagement social*, 235–41.

Blenk, Gustav. 1975. "1918–1934." In Größl, *Christlichen Gewerkschaften*, 79–232.

Blom, J. C. H., and Emiel Lamberts, eds. 2006. *History of the Low Countries*. New York: Berghahn.

Bocci, Maria. 1999. *Oltre lo stato liberale: Ipotesi su politica e società nel dibattito cattolico tra fascismo e democrazia*. Rome: Bulzoni.

Böhm, Irmingard. 1995a. "Agnes Neuhaus (1854–1944)." In Hengst, Brandt, and Böhm, *Geliebte Kirche*, 17–22.

———. 1995b. "Elisabeth Gnauck-Kühne (1850–1917)." In Hengst, Brandt, and Böhm, *Geliebte Kirche*, 147–53.

Boileau, David A. 2003. "Some Reflections on the Historical Perspectives of Catholic Social Teaching." In R. Aubert, *Catholic Social Teaching*, 241–82.

Boismarmin, Christine de. 1985. *Madeline Delbrêl 1904–1964: Rues des villes chemins de Dieu*. Paris: Nouvelle Cité.

Bokenkotter, Thomas S. 1998. *Church and Revolution: Catholics in the Struggle for Democracy and Social Justice*. New York: Doubleday.

Bonafoux-Verrax, Corinne. 2004. *À la droite de Dieu: La fédération nationale catholique, 1924–1944*. Paris: Fayard.

Bornewasser, Hans. 1992. "De groei van het sociaal-ideologisch denken in katholiek Nederland." In Lamberts, *Een kantelend tijdperk*, 65–87.

Bosmans, Louis. 1978. *August Schaurhofer 1872–1928: Ein Leben im Dienst der christlichen Sozialarbeit*. Vienna: Geyer.

Boswell, Jonathan S., Francis P. McHugh, and Johan Verstraeten, eds. 2000. *Catholic Social Thought: Twilight or Renaissance?* Leuven: Leuven University Press and Peeters.

Bourdais, Henri. 1995. *La J.O.C. sous l'occupation allemande: Témoignages et souvenirs d'Henri Bourdais*. Paris: Éditions de l'Atelier and Éditions ouvrières.

Boyer, John W. 1994. "Religion and Political Development in Central Europe around 1900: A View from Vienna." *Austrian History Yearbook* 25: 13–57.

———. 1995. *Culture and Political Crisis in Vienna: Christian Socialism in Power, 1897–1918*. Chicago: University of Chicago Press.

———. 2001. "Catholics, Christians, and the Challenges of Democracy: The Heritage of the Nineteenth Century." In Gehler, Kaiser, and Wohnout, *Christdemokratie in Europa*, 23–59.

———. 2005. "Political Catholicism in Austria, 1880–1960." In *Religion in Austria*, edited by Günter Bischof, Anton Pelinka, and Hermann Denz, 6–35. New Brunswick, N.J.: Transaction.

———. 2010. *Karl Lueger (1844–1910): Christlichsoziale Politik als Beruf; Eine Biographie*. Cologne and Vienna: Böhlau Verlag.

Brachin, Pierre, and L. J. Rogier. 1974. *Histoire du catholicisme hollandais depuis le XVIe siècle*. Paris: Aubier Montaigne.

Bragard, Lucie, et al. 1990. *La jeunesse ouvrière chrétienne: Wallonie-Bruxelles 1912–1957*. 2 vols. Brussels: Vie Ouvrière.

Bragard, Lucie, Marguerite Fiévez, and Jacques Meert. 1990. "La JOC? Une utopie qui se vit tous les jours." In Bragard et al., *Jeunesse ouvrière chrétienne*, 1:25–52.

Bragard, Lucie, Marguerite Fiévez, and Guy Zelis. 1990. "Le jocisme se place sur orbite." In Bragard et al., *Jeunesse ouvrière chrétienne*, 1:105–59.

Brauns, Heinrich. 1976. *Katholische Sozialpolitik im 20. Jahrhundert: Ausgewählte Aufsätze und Reden von Heinrich Brauns*. Edited by Hubert Mockenhaupt. Mainz: Grünewald.

Bredohl, Thomas M. 2000. *Class and Religious Identity: The Rhenish Center Party in Wilhelmine Germany*. Milwaukee: Marquette University Press.

Bressan, E. 1990. "'L'Osservatore Romano' e le relazioni internazionali della Santa Sede (1917–1922)." In *Benedetto XV e la pace—1918*, edited by Giorgio Rumi, 233–53. Brescia: Morcelliana.

Briefs, Goetz. 1921. "Der soziale Volksstaat und der Sozialismus." In *Soziale Arbeit im neuen Deutschland. Festschrift zum 70. Geburtstage von Franz Hitze*, edited by August Pieper, 61–84. Mönchengladbach: Volksvereins-Verlag.

———. 1951. "Pesch and His Contemporaries: Nationalökonomie vs. Contemporary Economic Theories." *Social Order* 1: 153–60.

Briemle, Theodosius, ed. 1928. *Der Zweifrontenkrieg der katholischen Kirche gegen Kapitalismus und Sozialismus: Die wichtigsten Hirtenschreiben unserer Bischöfe über brennende soziale Fragen der Gegenwart*. Wiesbaden: Hermann Rauch.

Brose, Eric Dorn. 1985. *Christian Labor and the Politics of Frustration in Imperial Germany*. Washington, D.C.: The Catholic University of America Press.

Brotherton, Anne, ed. 1992. *The Voice of the Turtledove: New Catholic Women in Europe*. New York: Paulist.

Brucculeri, Angelo. 1933. "Problemi internazionali." *Civiltà Cattolica* 82: 255–64.

Brunori De Siervo, Maria Teresa. 1981. "L'Istituto Cattolica di Attività Sociali dalla nascita alla seconda guerra mondiale." *Storia Contemporanea* 12: 737–91.

Bruyn, Severyn. 1991. *A Future for the American Economy: The Social Market*. Stanford, Calif.: Stanford University Press.

Buchanan, Tom, and Martin Conway, eds. 1996. *Political Catholicism in Europe, 1918–1965*. Oxford and New York: Clarendon Press.

Burke, Edmund. 1999. *The Portable Edmund Burke*. New York: Penguin.

Cadiot, Jean-Michel. 2006. *Francisque Gay et les démocrates d'inspiration chrétienne 1885–1963*. Paris: Salvator.

Calvez, Jean-Yves. 1999a. *L'Église et l'économie: La doctrine sociale de l'église*. Paris: Harmattan.

———. 1999b. *Les silences de la doctrine sociale catholique*. Paris: L'Atelier.

———. 2002. *Chrétiens penseurs du social*. Vol. 1, *Maritain, Mounier, Fessard, Teilhard de Chardin, de Lubac*. Paris: Cerf.

———. 2006. *Chrétiens penseurs du social*. Vol. 2, *L'après-guerre (1945–1967): Lebret, Perroux, Montuclard, Desroche, Villain, Desqueyrat, Bigo, Chambre, Bosc, Clément, Giordani, Courtney Murray, Ellul, Mehl*. Paris: Cerf.

Camp, Richard L. 1969. *The Papal Ideology of Social Reform: A Study in Historical Development, 1878–1967*. Leiden: Brill.

Campanini, Giorgio. 1981. "De Gasperi, Alcide (1881–1954)." In *DSMCI* 2:157–68.

———. 1998. "I cattolici e il fascismo italiano." In *BASMSCI* 33: 199–211.

Canavero, Alfredo. 1982. "La Cil, il Partito popolare e l'occupazione delle fabbriche." In Zaninelli, *Sindacalismo bianco*, 95–124.

———. 1985. "De Gasperi e l'Italia nel primo dopoguerra (1919–1921)." In *De Gasperi e il Trentino tra la fine dell'800 e il primo dopoguerra*, edited by Alfredo Canavero and Angelo Moioli, 697–760. Trent: Luigi Reverdito.

———. 1995. "Cinquant'anni di storiografica sul 'movimento cattolico' italiano." In *Mezzo secolo di ricerca storiografica sul movimento cattolico in Italia dal 1861 al 1945: Contributo a una bibliografia*, edited by Eleanora Fumasi, 7–72. Brescia: La Scuola.

———. 2003. "Die christliche Arbeiterbewegung in Italien: Von den Anfängen im 19. bis zur Mitte des 20. Jahrhunderts." In Hiepel and Ruff, *Christliche Arbeiterbewegung*, 218–39. Stuttgart: Kohlhammer.

Carlen, Claudia, ed. 1981. *The Papal Encyclicals*. 5 vols. Wilmington, N.C.: McGrath.

———. 1990. *Papal Pronouncements: A Guide, 1740–1978*. Ann Arbor, Mich.: Pierian Press.

Carlyle, Thomas. 1849. "Occasional Discourse on the Negro Question." *Fraser's Magazine for Town and Country* 40: 672.

Cary, Noel D. 1996. *The Path to Christian Democracy: German Catholics and the Party System from Windthorst to Adenauer*. Cambridge, Mass.: Harvard University Press.

Casanova, José. 1994. *Public Religions in the Modern World*. Chicago: University of Chicago Press.

Casella, Mario. 1981. "L'azione cattolica del tempo di Pio XI e di Pio XII (1922–1958)." In *DSMCI* 1, pt. 1:84–101.

———. 1992. *L'azione cattolica nell'Italia contemporanea (1919–1969)*. Rome: A.V.E.

———. 1996. "Pio XI e l'azione cattolica italiana." In *Achille Ratti*, 605–40.

Castel, Robert. 2003. *From Manual Workers to Wage Laborers: Transformation of the Social Question*. New Brunswick, N.J.: Transaction.

Catholicisme: hier, aujourd'hui, demain. Edited by Gérard Mathon and G.-H. Baudry. 15 vols. Paris: Letouzey et Ané, 1948–2000.

Cathrein, Victor. 1890. *Der Sozialismus*. Freiburg: Herder.

Caudron, André. 1990. *Lille—Flandres*. Vol. 4 of *Dictionnaire du monde religieux*; see *DMR*.

———. 1991. "Eugène Duthoit et la première génération de catholiques sociaux." *Revue du Nord* 73: 315–20.

Cavalin, Tangi, and Nathalie Viet-Depaule. 2007. *Une histoire de la Mission de France: La riposte missionnaire, 1941–2002*. Paris: Karthala.

Cella, Gian Primo. 2004. *Il sindacato*. New ed. Rome and Bari: Laterza.

Chabot, Joceline. 1992. "Tribolati, Madeleine." In *DBMOF* 42:322–23. Paris: Éditions ouvrières.

———. 1993. "Les syndicats féminins chrétiens et la formation militante de 1913 à 1936: 'Propagandistes idéales' et 'héroïne identitielle.'" *Mouvement social* 165: 7–21.

———. 2003. *Les débuts du syndicalisme féminin chrétien en France, 1899–1944*. Lyon: Presses universitaires de Lyon.

Chadwick, Kay, ed. 2000. *Catholicism, Politics and Society in Twentieth-Century France*. Liverpool: Liverpool University Press.

Chélini, Michel-Pierre. 2000. "Belin, René." In *DHFO* 69.

Chenaux, Philippe. 1990. *Une Europe vaticane? Entre le Plan Marshall et les Traités de Rome*. Brussels: Ciaco.

———. 1999. *Entre Maurras et Maritain: Une génération intellectuelle catholique (1920–1930)*. Paris: Cerf.

———. 2003. *Pie XII: diplomate et pasteur*. Paris: Cerf.

———. 2006a. *"Humanisme intégral" (1936) de Jacques Maritain*. Paris: Cerf.

———. 2006b. "L'influence du personnalisme dans les débuts de la construction de l'Europe (1932–1950)." In *Agir avec Mounier: Une pensée pour l'Europe*, edited by Jean-François Petit and Rémy Valléjo, 33–48. Lyon: Chronique sociale.

———. 2009. *L'Église catholique et le communisme en Europe (1917–1989): De Lénine à Jean-Paul II*. Paris: Cerf.

Chenu, Marie-Dominique. 1955. *Pour une théologie du travail*. Paris: Cerf.

———. 1966a. "Une constitution pastorale de l'Église." In Chenu, *Peuple de Dieu*, 11–34.

———. 1966b. *Peuple de Dieu dans le monde*. Paris: Cerf.

———. 1966c. *The Theology of Work: An Exploration*. Chicago: Regnery.
———. 1967. "Les signes des temps: Réflexion théologique." In Congar and Peuchmaurd, *L'Église dans le monde*, 2:205–25.
———. 1979. *La doctrine sociale de l'Eglise comme idéologie*. Paris: Cerf.
Chiron, Yves. 2004. *Pie XI (1857–1939)*. Paris: Perrin.
Cholvy, Gérard. 1982. "Patronages et oeuvres de jeunesse dans la France contemporaine." In *RHE* 48: 235–56.
———. 1985a. "De l'homme d'oeuvre au militant: Une évolution dans la conception du laicat catholique en France depuis le xix_e siècle." In *Miscellanea Historiae Ecclesiasticae*, 7:215–42. Brussels: Nauwelaerts; Leuven: Revue d'histoire ecclésiastique.
———, ed. 1985b. *Mouvements de jeunesse chrétiens et juifs, 1799–1968: Sociabilité juvénile dans un cadre européen 1799–1968*. Paris: Cerf.
———. 1999. *Histoire des organisations et mouvements chrétiens de jeunesse en France (xixe–xxe siècles)*. Paris: Cerf.
———. 2000. "Aux origines de la JOC française: Le temps de la conquête (1927–1943)." In *RHE* 95: 107–35.
Cholvy, Gérard, and Yves-Marie Hilaire, eds. 2002a. *La France religieuse: 1945–1975*. Toulouse: Privat.
———, eds. 2002b. *Religion et société en France: 1914–1945*. Toulouse: Privat.
Christensen, Torben. 1962. *Origin and History of Christian Socialism, 1848–54*. Aarhus, Denmark: Aarhus University Press.
Christophe, Paul. 1986. *Les catholiques et le Front populaire*. Paris: Desclée.
Ciampani, Andrea. 1990. *La buona battaglia: Giulio Pastore e i cattolici sociali nella crisi dell'Italia liberale*. Milan: F. Angeli.
———. 1991. *Lo statuto del sindacato nuovo (1944–1951): Identità sociale e sindacalismo confederale alle origini della Cisl*. Rome: Edizioni Lavoro.
Ciampani, Andrea, and Massimiliano Valenti. 2005. "The Social and Political Dynamics of the Christian Workers in Unified Trade Union Movements: The Experiences of Italy and West Germany after World War II." In Heerma van Voss, Pasture, and De Maeyer, *Between Cross and Class*, 203–23.
Clark, Martin. 2008. *Modern Italy, 1871 to the Present*. 3rd ed. Harlow, UK, and New York: Pearson Longman.
Clément, Jean-Louis. 1999. *Les évêques au temps de Vichy: Loyalisme sans inféodation*. Paris: Beauchesne.
———. 2003. "Civisme épiscopal, civisme démocrate-chrétien en France: Une divergence (1919–1939)." In *RHE* 98: 80–105.
Coffey, Joan L. 2003. *Léon Harmel: Entrepreneur as Catholic Social Reformer*. Notre Dame, Ind.: University of Notre Dame Press.
Cointet, Michèle. 1998. *L'Église sous Vichy (1940–1945): La repentance en question*. Paris: Perrin.
Cole-Arnal, Oscar L. 2001. "The *Témoignage* of the Worker Priests: Contextual Layers of the Pioneer Epoch (1941–1955)." In Horn and Gerard, *Left Catholicism 1943–1955*, 118–41.
Coleman, John. 1978. *The Evolution of Dutch Catholicism, 1958–1974*. Berkeley: University of California Press.
———. 1991a. "Neither Liberal nor Socialist: The Originality of Catholic Social Teaching." In Coleman, *One Hundred Years*, 25–42.
———, ed. 1991b. *One Hundred Years of Catholic Social Thought: Celebration and Challenge*. Maryknoll, N.Y.: Orbis.
———. 2000. "Retrieving or Re-Inventing Social Catholicism: A Transatlantic Response." In Boswell, McHugh, and Verstraeten, *Catholic Social Thought*, 265–92.
———. 2005. "The Future of Catholic Social Thought." In Himes et al., *Modern Catholic Social Teaching*, 533–44.
Colombo, Maria Assunta. 1982. "Coari, Adelaide." In *DSMCI* 2:109–12.
Colsen, Jozef Petrus. 1922. "De Jonge Werkman." In *HJS* 300–305.

———. 1955. *Poels*. Roermond-Maaseik: J. J. Romen.
Compagnoni, Francesco, and Helen J. Alford, eds. 2007. *Preaching Justice: Dominican Contributions to Social Ethics in the Twentieth Century*. Dublin: Dominican Publications.
Comte, Bernard. 1992. "Rapport de synthèse." In Durand et al., *Cent ans de catholicisme social*, 381–90.
———. 1998. *L'honneur et la conscience: Catholiques français en Résistance (1940–1944)*. Paris: Éditions ouvrières.
Comte, Bernard, Jean-Marie Domenach, Christian Rendu, and Denise Rendu, eds. 1998. *Gilbert Dru: Un chrétien résistant*. Paris: Beauchesne.
Congar, Yves. 2012. *My Journal of the Council*. Collegeville, Minn.: Liturgical Press.
Congar, Yves, and Michel Peuchmaurd, eds. 1967. *L'Église dans le monde de ce temps: Constitution pastorale Gaudium et spes*. Paris: Éditions du Cerf.
Connelly, John. 2007. "Catholic Racism and Its Opponents." *Journal of Modern History* 79: 813–47.
Conway, Martin. 1990. "Building the Christian City: Catholics and Politics in Inter-War Francophone Belgium." *Past and Present*: 117–51.
———. 1996. "Belgium." In Buchanan and Conway, *Political Catholicism in Europe*, 187–218.
———. 1997. *Catholic Politics in Europe 1918–1945*. London and New York: Routledge.
———. 2001. "Left Catholicism in Europe in the 1940s: Elements of an Interpretation." In Horn and Gerard, *Left Catholicism 1943–1955*, 269–81.
———. 2003. "The Age of Christian Democracy: The Frontiers of Success and Failure." In Kselman and Buttigieg, *European Christian Democracy*, 43–67.
Coppa, Frank J., ed. 1999a. *Controversial Concordats: The Vatican's Relations with Napoleon, Mussolini, and Hitler*. Washington, D.C.: The Catholic University of America Press.
———. 1999b. "Mussolini and the Concordat of 1929." In Coppa 1999a, *Controversial Concordats*, 81–119.
Corbin, Alain, Nicole Lemaitre, Françoise Thelamon, and Catherine Vincent, eds. 2007. *Histoire du christianisme: Pour mieux comprendre notre temps*. Paris: Seuil.
Corlieu, Cécile de. 1970. *Carnets d'une chrétienne moderniste, de 1898 à nos jours*. Toulouse: Privat.
Corrin, Jay P. 2002. *Catholic Intellectuals and the Challenge of Democracy*. Notre Dame, Ind.: University of Notre Dame Press.
Coste, René. 2000. *Les dimensions sociales de la foi: Pour une théologie sociale*. Paris: Cerf.
Coutrot, Aline. 1982. *"Sept," un journal, un combat: Mars 1934–août 1937*. Paris: Cana.
Cova, Anne. 1992. "Femmes et catholicisme social: trois mouvements nationaux d'initiative lyonnaise." In Durand et al., *Cent ans de catholicisme social*, 307–22.
Cox, Robert H. 1993. *The Development of the Dutch Welfare State: From Workers' Insurance to Universal Entitlement*. Pittsburgh: University of Pittsburgh Press.
Craeybeckx, Jan. 2000. "From the Great Depression to World War II." In Witte, Craeybeckx, and Meynen, *Political History of Belgium*, 105–63.
Crouch, Colin. 1993. *Industrial Relations and European State Traditions*. Oxford: Clarendon.
Curran, Charles E. 2002. *Catholic Social Teaching, 1891–Present: A Historical, Theological, and Ethical Analysis*. Washington, D.C.: Georgetown University Press.
———. 2003a. *Change in Official Catholic Moral Teaching*, ed. Charles E. Curran. Readings in Moral Theology 13. New York: Paulist Press.
———. 2003b. "The Changing Anthropological Bases for Catholic Social Teaching." In Curran 2003a, 171–94.
Curran, Charles E., and Richard A. McCormick, eds. 1986. *Official Catholic Social Teaching*. Readings in Moral Theology 5. New York: Paulist Press.
Curtis, David. 1997. *The French Popular Front and the Catholic Discovery of Marx*. Hull: University of Hull Press.
D'Agostino, Peter R. 2004. *Rome in America: Transnational Catholic Ideology from the Risorgimento to Fascism*. Chapel Hill: University of North Carolina Press.
Daly, Lew. 2009. *God's Economy: Faith-Based Initiatives and the Caring State*. Chicago: University of Chicago Press.

Damberg, Wilhelm. 1997. *Abschied vom Milieu? Katholizismus im Bistum Münster und in den Niederlanden 1945–1980*. Paderborn: Schöningh.

Damberg, Wilhelm, and Patrick Pasture. 2010. "Restoration and Erosion of Pillarised Catholicism in Western Europe." In Kenis, Billiet, and Pasture, *Transformation of the Christian Churches*, 55–76.

Dau Novelli, Cecilia. 1998. "L'associazionismo femminile cattolico (1908–1960)." In BASMSCI 33: 112–37.

Davids, Karel, Greta Devos, and Patrick Pasture, eds. 2007. *Changing Liaisons: The Dynamics of Social Partnership in Twentieth-Century West-European Democracies*. New York: Peter Lang.

Dawes, Helena. 2011. "The Catholic Church and the Woman Question: Catholic Feminism in Italy in the Early 1900s." *Catholic Historical Review* 97: 484–526.

DBMOF (*Dictionnaire biographique du mouvement ouvrier français*). 1964–97. Edited by Jean Maitron. Paris: Editions ouvrières.

Debès, Joseph. 1982. *Naissance de l'Action catholique ouvrière*. Paris: Éditions ouvrières.

Debès, Joseph, and Emile Poulat. 1986. *L'Appel de la J.O.C. (1926–1928)*. Paris: Cerf.

Deck, Alan Figueroa. 2005. "*Populorum progressio*." In Himes et al., *Modern Catholic Social Teaching*, 292–314.

De Clercq, Bertrand Juliaan. 2007. "A Social Scientist in the Service of the Workers: Georges Ceslas Rutten (1875–1952)." In Compagnoni and Alford, *Preaching Justice*, 51–61.

De Decker, Annie, Nathalie Ista, and Denise Keymolen. 1994. "Le mouvement ouvrier chrétien féminin." In *HMOCB* 2:324–423.

Deferme, Jo. 2007. *Uit de ketens van de vrijheid: Het debat over de sociale wetgeving in België, 1886–1914*. Leuven: Leuven University Press.

De Haan, Peter. 1994. *Van volgzame eliteststrijder tot kritische gelovige: Geschiedenis van de Katholieke Actie in Nederland (1934–1966)*. Nijmegen: KDC/KSC.

De La Bedoyère, Michael. 1958. *The Cardijn Story*. Milwaukee: Bruce.

Delbreil, Jean-Claude. 1990. *Centrisme et Démocratie-Chrétienne en France: Le parti démocrate populaire des origines au M.R.P. 1919–1944*. Paris: Publications de la Sorbonne.

———, ed. 1997. *Marc Sangnier: Témoignages*. Paris: Beauchesne.

———. 1999. "Le contexte français et européen des débuts de l'action internationale de Marc Sangnier après la première guerre mondiale." In *Marc Sangnier: La guerre, la paix (1914–1939)*, 21–51. Paris: Institut Marc Sangnier.

———. 2004. "Christian Democracy and Centrism: The Popular Democratic Party in France." In Kaiser and Wohnout, *Political Catholicism in Europe*, 116–35.

———. 2008. *La revue La vie intellectuelle: Marc Sangnier, le thomisme et le personnalisme*. Paris: Cerf.

Delbrêl, Madeleine. 2000. *We, the Ordinary People of the Streets*. Grand Rapids, Mich.: Eerdmans.

Delors, Jacques. 2004. *Mémoires*. Paris: Plon.

Delprat, Raymond, and Denis Pelletier. 1994. "Lebret, Louis." In *DMR* 6:270–71.

Delville, Jean-Pierre. 2009a. "Antoine Pottier (1849–1923), le 'Docteur de la démocratie chrétienne': Ses relations internationales jusqu'à son exil à Rome en 1902." In Zelis et al., *Intellectuels catholiques*, 209–60.

———. 2009b. "Réseaux démocrates chrétiens: L'action de Mgr Antoine Pottier (1849–1923) à Rome, sous Léon XIII et Pie X." In *La papauté contemporaine (xixe–xxe siècles): Hommage au chanoine Roger Aubert*, edited by Jean-Pierre Delville and Marko Jacov, 195–228. Louvain-la-Neuve: Bibliothèque de la R.H.E.

De Maeyer, Jan. 1994. *De rode baron: Arthur Verhaegen, 1847–1917*. Leuven: Leuven University Press.

———. 2003. "Katholische Soziallehre und Christliche Arbeiterorganisationen in Belgien von der Freiburger Union (1884–1888) zur Union von Mechelen (1921–1960)." In Hiepel and Ruff, *Christliche Arbeiterbewegung*, 99–119.

———. 2005. "The Formation of a Christian Workers' Culture in Pillarized Societies: Belgium, Germany and the Netherlands, c.1850–1950." In Heerma van Voss, Pasture, and De Maeyer, *Between Cross and Class*, 81–102.

Denk, Hans Dieter. 1980. *Die christliche Arbeiterbewegung in Bayern bis zum Ersten Weltkrieg*. Mainz: Grünewald.

Derks, Marjet. 1993. "Dienende Liefde en Feminsterij." In *De dynamiek van religie en cultuur: Geschiedenis van het Nederlands katholicisme*, edited by Marit Monteiro, Gerard Rooijackers, and Joost Rosendaal, 181–208. Kampen: J. H. Kok.

Derks, Marjet, Catharina Halkes, and Annelies Van Heijst, eds. 1992. *"Roomse Dochters": Katholieke vrouwen en hun beweging*. Baarn: Arbor.

Derks, Marjet, and Marijke Huisman. 2002. *"Edelmoedig, fier en vrij": Katholieke arbeidersvrouwen en hun beweging en de twintigste eeuw*. Hilversum: Verloren.

De Rosa, Gabriele. 1979. *Il partito popolare italiano*. Bari: Laterza.

———. 1982. "Sturzo, Luigi." In *DSMCI* 2:615–24.

DHFO (*Dictionnaire historique de la France sous l'Occupation*). 2000. Edited by Michèle Cointet and Jean-Paul Cointet. Paris: Tallandier.

DHGE (*Dictionnaire d'histoire et de géographie ecclésiastique*). 1912–. Paris: Letouzey et Ané.

Diamant, Alfred. 1960. *Austrian Catholics and the First Republic: Democracy, Capitalism, and the Social Order, 1918–1934*. Princeton: Princeton University Press.

Didry, Claude. 2007. "Thoughts on France's Industrial Relations System: From Strike Action to Representative Democracy?" In Davids, Devos, and Pasture, *Changing Liaisons*, 85–113.

Diébolt, Evelyne. 2000. "Les femmes catholiques: Entre Église et société." In Chadwick, *Catholicism, Politics and Society*, 219–43.

DMR (*Dictionnaire du monde religieux dans la France contemporaine*). 1985–2013. Edited by Jean-Marie Mayeur and Yves-Marie Hilaire. Paris: Beauchesne. Currently 11 vols.; vol. 12 forthcoming.

Dokumente: Etappen der katholisch-sozialen Bewegung in Österreich seit 1850: 130 Jahre Katholische Arbeitnehmerbewegung in Österreich. 1980. St. Pölten: Katholische Arbeitnehmerbewegung Österreichs.

Donoso Cortés, Juan. 1862. *Essay on Catholicism, Liberalism and Socialism Considered in Their Fundamental Principles*. Philadelphia: J. B. Lippincott.

Döring, Diether. 2004. *Sozialstaat*. Frankfurt: Fischer Taschenbuch Verlag.

Dorr, Donal. 1983. *Option for the Poor: A Hundred Years of Vatican Social Teaching*. Maryknoll, N.Y.: Orbis Books; Dublin: Gill and Macmillan.

———.1986. "Pope John XXIII—A New Direction?" In Curran and McCormick, *Official Catholic Social Teaching*, 77–109.

———. 1991. *The Social Justice Agenda: Justice, Ecology, Power, and the Church*. Maryknoll, N.Y.: Orbis Books; Dublin: Gill and Macmillan.

———. 1992. *Option for the Poor: A Hundred Years of Vatican Social Teaching*. Maryknoll, N.Y.: Orbis Books.

Drapac, Vesna. 1998. *War and Religion: Catholics in the Churches of Occupied Paris*. Washington, D.C.: The Catholic University of America Press.

Dreyfus, François-Georges. 1988. *Histoire de la démocratie chrétienne en France, de Chateaubriand à Raymond Barre*. Paris: Albin Michel.

Droulers, Paul. 1969. *Politique sociale et christianisme: Le père Desbuquois et l'Action populaire; Débats, syndicalisme et intégristes (1903–1918)*. Paris: Éditions ouvrières.

———. 1981. *Politique sociale et christianisme: Le père Desbuquois et l'Action populaire; Dans la gestation d'un monde nouveau (1919–1946)*. Paris: Éditions ouvrières; Rome: Università Gregoriana Editrice.

———. 1982a. *Cattolicesimo sociale nei secoli XIX e XX: Saggi di storia e sociologia*. Rome: Storia e Letteratura.

———. 1982b. "Catholiques sociaux et Révolution Nationale (été 1940–avril 1942)." In Montclos et al., *Églises et chrétiens*, 213–25.

DS (*Enchiridion symbolorum, definitionum et declarationum de rebus fidei et morum*). Edited by Heinrich Denzinger and Adolf Schönmetzer. New York: Herder, 1965. Originally published by Denzinger in Wurzburg, 1854.

DSMCI (*Dizionario storico del movimento cattolico in Italia 1860–1980*). 1981–84. Edited by Francesco Traniello and Giorgio Campanini. Turin: Marietti. 3 vols. in 5 parts.

DSMCI 1997. (*Dizionario storico del movimento cattolico: Aggiornamento 1980–95*). 1997. Turin: Marietti.
DTC (*Dictionnaire de théologie catholique*). 1909–72. Edited by Alfred Vacant, E. Mangenot, and Emile Amann. Paris: Letouzey et Ané.
Duchini, Francesca. 1990. "Dal primo dopo-guerra all'interruzione degli anni trenta." In *Le Settimane sociali nell'esperienza della Chiesa italiana (1945–1970): Atti del 60| corso di aggiornamento culturale dell'Università Cattolica, Pisa 9–14 sett. 1990*, 49–87. Milan: Vita e Pensiero.
Duffhues, Ton. 1992. "Een wending naar boeren, middenstanders en arbeiders? De katholieke volksbewegingen in Nederland." In Lamberts, *Een kantelend tijdperk*, 175–97.
Duffhues, Ton, Albert Felling, and Jan Roes. 1985. *Bewegende patronen: Een analyse van het landelijk netwerk van katholieke organisaties en bestuurders, 1945–1980*. Publicaties van het Katholiek Documentatie Centrum (Nijmegen) 12. Baarn: Ambo.
Duffy, Eamon. 1997. *Saints and Sinners: A History of the Popes*. New Haven: Yale University Press.
Dumons, Bruno. 1994. "Rochebillard, Marie-Louise." In *DMR* 6:373–74.
Dumoulin, Michel. 1997. "The Socio-Economic Impact of Christian Democracy in Western Europe." In Lamberts, *Christian Democracy in the European Union*, 369–74.
Duquesne, Jacques. 1986. *Les Catholiques français sous l'occupation*. 2nd ed. Paris: Grasset.
Durand, Jean-Dominique. 1990. "L'Italie." In *HC* 12:349–402.
———. 1994. "Rerum novarum dans l'enseignement social de l'Église catholique en Italie, au lendemain de la Deuxième Guerre Mondiale." In Furlong and Curtis, *Church Faces the Modern World*, 181–90.
———. 1995. *L'Europe de la démocratie chrétienne*. Brussels: Éditions Complexe.
———. 2002. "Christian Democracy." In *The Papacy: An Encyclopedia*, edited by Philippe Levillain, 304–12. New York: Routledge.
———, ed. 2006. *Les Semaines Sociales de France: Cent ans d'engagement social des catholiques français 1904–2004*. Paris: Parole et Silence.
Durand, Jean-Dominique et al. eds. 1992. *Cent ans de catholicisme social à Lyon et in Rhône-Alpes: La postérité de Rerum novarum*. Paris: Éditions ouvrières.
Duriez, Bruno. 2001. "Les services du MPF: La fin d'un projet intégral." In Duriez et al., *Chrétiens et ouvriers*, 215–29.
———. 2003. "Zwischen Apostolat und sozialer Umgestaltung: Die katholische Arbeiterbewegung in Frankreich." In Hiepel and Ruff, *Christliche Arbeiterbewegung*, 199–217.
Duriez, Bruno et al., eds. 2001. *Chrétiens et ouvriers en France, 1937–1970*. Paris: Éditions de l'Atelier and Éditions ouvrières.
Duriez, Bruno, Étienne Fouilloux, Denis Pelletier, and Nathalie Viet-Depaule, eds. 2005. *Les catholiques dans la République 1905–2005*. Paris: Les éditions de l'Atelier and Éditions ouvrières.
Dutton, Paul V. 2002. *Origins of the French Welfare State: The Struggle for Social Reform in France, 1914–1947*. Cambridge: Cambridge University Press.
Dyson, Kenneth, and Stephen Padgett, eds. 2006. *The Politics of Economic Reform in Germany: Global, Rhineland or Hybrid Capitalism?* Abingdon and New York: Routledge.
Eaton, Evelyn Thayer. 1955. *The Belgian Leagues of Christian Working-Class Women*. Washington, D.C.: The Catholic University of America Press.
Ederer, Rupert J. 2011. *Pope Pius XII on the Economic Order*. Lanham, Md.: Scarecrow Press.
Eppstein, John. 1935. *The Catholic Tradition of the Law of Nations*. London: Burns, Oates, and Washbourne; Washington, D.C.: Catholic Association for International Peace.
Epstein, Klaus. 1959. *Matthias Erzberger and the Dilemma of German Democracy*. Princeton: Princeton University Press.
Esser, Albert. 1990. *Wilhelm Elfes 1884–1969*. Mainz: Grünewald.
Evans, Ellen L. 1999. *The Cross and the Ballot: Catholic Political Parties in Germany, Switzerland, Austria, Belgium and the Netherlands, 1785–1985*. Boston: Humanities Press.
Ewing, Jack, and Bill Vlasic. Oct. 11, 2013. "VW Plant Opens Door to Union and Dispute." *New York Times*, B1.
Fappani, Antonio. 1982. "Miglioli, Guido." In *DSMCI* 2:379–84.

Farrugia, Peter. 1992. "French Religious Opposition to War, 1919–1939: The Contribution of Henri Roser and Marc Sangnier." *French History* 6: 279–302.
Fattorini, Emma. 2007. *Pio XI, Hitler e Mussolini: La solitudine di un papa*. Turin: Giulio Einaudi.
———. 2011. *Hitler, Mussolini and the Vatican: Pope Pius XI and the Speech that Was Never Made*. Malden, Mass., and Cambridge: Polity Press.
Fayet-Scribe, Sylvie. 1990. *Associations féminines et catholicisme: XIXe–XXe siècle*. Paris: Éditions ouvrières.
Feldman, Gerald D. 1993. *The Great Disorder: Politics, Economics, and Society in the German Inflation, 1914–1924*. New York: Oxford University Press.
Ferber, Walter. 1973. "Hedwig Dransfeld (1871–1925)." In *ZGiLB* 1:129–36.
Ferrari, Liliana. 1989. *Una storia dell'Azione cattolica: Gli ordinamenti statutari da Pio XI a Pio XII*. Genoa: Marietti.
Fiévez, Marguerite. 1990. "Droit de cité pour la jeunesse ouvrière! 1924–1927." In Bragard et al., *Jeunesse ouvrière chrétienne*, 89–103.
Fiévez, Marguerite, and Jacques Meert, eds. 1978. *Cardijn*. 3rd ed. Brussels: EVO.
Fine, Sidney. 1969. *Sit-Down: The General Motors Strike of 1936–1937*. Ann Arbor: University of Michigan Press.
Finn, Daniel K., ed. 2010. *The True Wealth of Nations: Catholic Social Thought and Economic Life*. New York: Oxford University Press.
———. 2013. *Christian Economic Ethics: History and Implications*. Minneapolis: Fortress Press.
Fischer, Conan. 2003. *The Ruhr Crisis, 1923–1924*. Oxford and New York: Oxford University Press.
Flannery, Austin, ed. 1996. *Vatican Council II: The Basic Sixteen Documents*. Northport, N.Y.: Costello; Dublin: Dominican Publications.
Focke, Franz. 1978. *Sozialismus aus christlicher Verantwortung: Die Idee eines christlichen Sozialismus in der katholisch-sozialen Bewegung und in der CDU*. Wuppertal: Hammer.
Fogarty, Gerald P. 1989. *American Catholic Biblical Scholarship: A History from the Early Republic to Vatican II*. San Francisco: Harper and Row.
Fogarty, Michael P. 1957. *Christian Democracy in Western Europe, 1820–1953*. London: Routledge and Kegan Paul. Repr. 1974. Westport, Conn.: Greenwood Press.
Fontana, Sandro. 1981. "Confederazione italiana sindacati lavoratori (CISL)." In *DSMCI* 1, pt. 2:216–26.
Fonzi, Fausto. 1981. "Mondo cattolico, Democrazia Cristiana e sindacato (1943–1955)." In *Il Sindacato nuovo: Politica e organizzazione del movimento sindacale in Italia negli anni 1943–1955*, edited by Sergio Zaninelli, 717–820. Milan: F. Angeli.
Foot, John M. 1997. "'White Bolsheviks'? The Catholic Left and the Socialists in Italy, 1919–1920." *Historical Journal* 40: 415–33.
Ford, Caroline. 1993. "Religion and Popular Culture in Modern Europe." *Journal of Modern History* 65: 152–75.
Formigoni, Guido. 1997. "Le Associazioni cristiane dei lavoratori italiani dopo il 1980." In *DSMCI* 1997, 165–69.
Forster, Bernhard. 2003. *Adam Stegerwald (1874–1945): Christlich-nationaler Gewerkschafter, Zentrumspolitiker, Mitbegründer der Unionsparteien*. Düsseldorf: Droste.
Fouilloux, Étienne, ed. 1990a. "Le catholicisme." In *HC* 12:116–239.
———. 1990b. *Les communistes et les chrétiens: Alliance ou dialogue? Madeleine Delbrêl (1904–1933–1964)*. Paris: Cerf.
———. 1990c. "Traditions et expériences françaises." In *HC* 12:451–522.
———. 1997. *Les chrétiens français entre crise et libération, 1937–1947*. XXᵉ Siècle. Paris: Seuil.
———. 1998. *Une église en quête de liberté: La pensée catholique française entre modernisme et Vatican II 1914–1962*. Paris: Desclée de Brouwer.
Fry, Karl. 1949–1952. *Kaspar Decurtins: Der Löwe von Truns 1855–1916*. 2 vols. Zurich: Thomas.
Furlong, Paul, and David Curtis, eds. 1994. *The Church Faces the Modern World: Rerum Novarum and Its Impact*. Humberside, UK: Earlsgate.

Gaines, Jena M. 1993. "Alsatian Catholics against the State, 1918–25." *Contemporary European History* 2: 207–24.

Gaiotti de Biase, Paola. 2002. *Le origini del movimento cattolico femminile*. Brescia: Morcelliana.

Gallagher, John A. 1990. *Time Past, Time Future: An Historical Study of Catholic Moral Theology*. New York: Paulist.

Gascoigne, Robert. 2009. *The Church and Secularity: Two Stories of Liberal Society*. Washington, D.C.: Georgetown University Press.

Gatti, Angelo, and Giovanni Allara, eds. 1993. *Pensiero sociale della chiesa e impegno politico dei cattolici democratici: I testi della Rerum novarum, del Codice de Camaldoli e della Centesimus Annus*. Rome: Cinque Lune.

Gavignaud-Fontaine, Geneviève. 2011. *Les catholiques et l'économie sociale en France: XIXe–XXe siècles*. Paris: Indes savantes.

Gehler, Michael, and Wolfram Kaiser, eds. 2004. *Christian Democracy in Europe since 1945*. London and New York: Routledge.

Gehler, Michael, Wolfram Kaiser, and Helmut Wohnout, eds. 2001. *Christdemokratie in Europa im 20. Jahrhundert; Christian Democracy in 20th Century Europe ; La Démocratie chrétienne in Europe au XXe siècle*. Vienna: Böhlau.

Gellott, Laura. 1987. *The Catholic Church and the Authoritarian Regime in Austria, 1933–1938*. New York: Garland.

———. 1988. "Defending Catholic Interests in the Christian State: The Role of Catholic Action in Austria, 1933–1938." *Catholic Historical Review* 74: 571–89.

Georgi, Frank. 1995. *L'invention de la CFDT 1957–1970: Syndicalisme, catholicisme et politique dans la France de l'expansion*. Paris: Éditions de l'Atelier and CNRS.

———, ed. 2003. *Autogestion: La dernière utopie?* Paris: Publications de la Sorbonne.

Georgi, Frank, and Lex Heerma van Voss. 2005. "Christian Trade Unionism and the Organization of Industry: From the Organized Profession to Democratic Planning and Self-Management." In Heerma van Voss, Pasture, and De Maeyer, *Between Cross and Class*, 225–49.

Gerard, Emmanuel. 1981. "Het Algemeen Christelijk Werkersverbond, omstreden standsorganisatie (1921–1940)." In *De kracht van een overtuiging. 60 jaar ACW (1921–1981)*, edited by Emmanuel Gerard, 11–59. Zele: S. V. Reinaert.

———. 1983. "Cardijn, arbeidersbeweging en Katholieke Actie (1918–1945)." In *Cardijn, un homme, un mouvement*, 119–47. KADOC Jaarboek, 1982. Leuven: Leuven University Press.

———. 1985. *Katholieke partij en crisis: Partijpolitieke leven in België (1918–1940)*. Leuven: Kritak.

———. 1986. "Tussen apostolaat en emancipatie: de christelijke arbeidersbeweging en de strijd om de sociale werken 1925–1933." In *Voor kerk en werk: Opstellen over de geschiedenis van de christelijke arbeidersbeweging, 1886–1986*, edited by Emmanuel Gerard and Jozef Mampuys, 203–60. KADOC Jaarboek, 1985. Leuven: Leuven University Press.

———, ed. 1990. *Église et mouvement ouvrier chrétien en Belgique: Sources inédites relatives à la direction générale des oeuvres sociales, 1916–1936*. Brussels: Nauwelaerts.

———. 1994a. "Adaptation en temps de crise 1921–1944." In *HMOCB* 1:174–245.

———. 1994b. "L'épanouissment du mouvement ouvrier chrétien 1904–1921." In *HMOCB* 1:114–73.

———. 1994c. "Le MOC-ACW." In *HMOCB* 2:565–631.

———. 1994d. "Les mutualités chrétiennes." In *HMOCB* 2:68–149.

———. 1998. "The Christian Workers' Movement as a Mass Foundation of the Flemish Movement." In *Nationalism in Belgium: Shifting Identities, 1780–1995*, edited by Kas Deprez and Louis Vos, 127–38. London: St. Martin's; New York: Macmillan.

———. 2001. "The Emergence of a People's Party: The Catholic Party in Belgium 1918–1945." In Gehler, Kaiser, and Wohnout, *Christdemokratie in Europa*, 98–121.

———. 2003. "Les Congrès sociales de Liège (1886, 1887, et 1890), carrefours du catholicisme social international." BASMSCI 39: 303–39.

———. 2004a. "Le mouvement ouvrier chrétien: Le modèle belge." In Sorrel, *L'engagement social*, 163–76.

———. 2004b. "Religion, Class and Language: The Catholic Party in Belgium." In Kaiser and Wohnout, *Political Catholicism in Europe*, 94–115.
Gerard, Emmanuel, and Steven Van Hecke. 2004a. "European Christian Democracy in the 1990s: Towards a Comparative Approach." In Van Hecke and Gerard, *Christian Democratic Parties in Europe*, 297–318.
———. 2004b. "European Christian Democracy in the 1990s: Towards a Framework for Analysis." In Van Hecke and Gerard, *Christian Democratic Parties in Europe*, 9–19.
Gérin, Paul. 1992. "Les mouvements populaires en Belgique. In Lamberts, *Een kantelend tijdperk*, 143–73.
Giblin, Marie J. 1994a. "Corporatism." In *NDCST* 244–46.
———. 1994b. "Quadragesimo Anno." In *NDCST* 802–13.
Gillingham, John. 1991. *Coal, Steel and the Rebirth of Europe, 1945–1955: The Germans and French from Ruhr Conflict to Economic Community*. New York: Cambridge University Press.
Giuntella, Maria Cristina. 1981. "Federazione universitaria cattolica italiana (FUCI) e laureati cattolici." In *DSMCI* 1, pt. 2: 295–301.
Gleason, Philip. 1968. *The Conservative Reformers: German-American Catholics and the Social Order*. Notre Dame, Ind.: University of Notre Dame Press.
Glossner, Christian Ludwig. 2010. *The Making of the German Post-War Economy: Political Communication and Public Reception of the Social Market Economy after World War II*. London: Tauris Academic Studies; New York: Palgrave Macmillan.
Godin, Henri, and Yvan Daniel. 1943. *La France, pays de mission?* Paris: Abeille (Cerf).
Gramsci, Antonio. 1977. *Il Vaticano e l'Italia*. 3rd ed. Rome: Riuniti.
Grebing, Helga. 1985. *History of the German Labour Movement*. Dover, N.H.: Berg.
Gremillion, Joseph B. 1961. *The Catholic Movement of Employers and Managers*. Rome: Gregorian University Press.
Greshake, Gisbert. 2008. *Selig die nach Gerechtigkeit Dürsten: Hildegard Burjan—Leben—Werk—Spiritualität*. Innsbruck: Tyrolia.
Gribling, J. P. 1978. *Willem Hubert Nolens 1860–1931: Uit het leven van een Priester-Staatsman*. Assen: Van Gorcum.
Grootaers, Jan. 1997. "The Drama Continues between the Acts: The 'Second Preparation' and its Opponents." In Alberigo and Komonchak, *History of Vatican II*, 2:359–514.
Größl, Franz, ed. 1975. *Die christlichen Gewerkschaften in Österreich*. Vienna: Europaverlag.
GS (Gaudium et spes). 1965. Vatican II: *Pastoral Constitution on the Church in the Modern World*. In Flannery, *Vatican Council II*, 163–282.
Guérend, Jean-Pierre. 2011. *Cardinal Emmanuel Suhard, archevêque de Paris (1940–1949): Temps de guerre, temps de paix, passion pour la mission*. Paris: Les Éditions du Cerf.
Gulick, Charles A. 1948. *Austria from Habsburg to Hitler*. Berkeley: University of California Press.
Gundlach, Gustav. 1929a. "Klasse." In *Staatslexikon der Görres-Gesellschaft*, 3:383–92. 5th ed. Freiburg: Herder.
———. 1929b. "Klassenkampf." In ibid., 3:394–99.
———. 1929c. "Stand und Klasse." *Stimmen der Zeit* 117: 284–93.
———. 1964. *Die Ordnung der menschlichen Gesellschaft*. Cologne: J. P. Bachem.
Haffert, Claus. 1995. *Die katholischen Arbeitervereine Westdeutschlands in der Weimarer Republik*. Essen: Klartext.
Hales, E. E. Y. 1965. *Pope John and His Revolution*. Garden City, N.Y.: Doubleday.
Halls, Wilfred D. 1995. *Politics, Society and Christianity in Vichy France*. Oxford and Providence, R.I.: Berg.
Hanisch, Ernst. 1994. *Der lange Schatten des Staates: Österreichische Gesellschaftsgeschichte im 20. Jahrhundert*. Vienna: Ueberreuter.
Hanschmidt, Alwin. 1988. "Eine christlich-demokratische 'Internationale' zwischen den Weltkriegen: Das 'Secrétariat International des Partis Démocratiques d'Inspiration Chrétienne' in Paris." In Becker and Morsey, *Christliche Demokratie in Europa*, 153–88.

Harbulot, Jean-Pierre. 2000. "Service de travail obligatoire (STO)." In *DHFO* 645–46.
Haupt, Heinz-Gerhard, and Jürgen Kocka, eds. 2009. *Comparative and Transnational History: Central European Approaches and New Perspectives.* New York: Berghahn.
Hause, Steven C., and Anne R. Kenney. 1981. "The Development of the Catholic Women's Suffrage Movement in France, 1896–1922." *Catholic Historical Review* 67: 11–30.
———. 1984. *Women's Suffrage and Social Politics in the French Third Republic.* Princeton: Princeton University Press.
HC (*Histoire du christianisme des origines à nos jours*). 1990–2001. Edited by Jean-Marie Mayeur, Charles Pietri, André Vauchez, and Marc Venard. 14 vols. Paris: Desclée-Fayard.
HDTFR (*Historical Dictionary of the Third French Republic, 1870–1940*). 1986. Edited by Patrick J. Hutton. Westport, Conn.: Greenwood Press.
Hebben, Gerh. J. 2001. "Poels, Henricus." In *Biografisch Woordenboek van het Socialisme en de Arbeidersbeweging in Nederland (BWSA)*, 8:193–203. The Hague; see http://www.iisg.nl/bwsa/bios/poels.html.
Hebblethwaite, Peter. 1993. *Paul VI: The First Modern Pope.* New York: Paulist.
Heerma van Voss, Lex. 1995. "The Netherlands." In *The Force of Labour: The Western European Labour Movement and the Working Class in the 20th Century*, edited by Stefan Berger and David Broughton, 39–70. Oxford and Herndon, Va.: Berg.
Heerma van Voss, Lex, Patrick Pasture, and Jan De Maeyer, eds. 2005. *Between Cross and Class: Comparative Histories of Christian Labour in Europe, 1840–2000.* Bern and New York: Peter Lang.
Hehir, J. Bryan. 1995a. "Catholic Social Teachings." In *The HarperCollins Encyclopedia of Catholicism*, edited by Richard P. McBrien, 280–84. San Francisco: HarperCollins.
———. 1995b. "Social Justice." In *The HarperCollins Encyclopedia of Catholicism*, edited by Richard P. McBrien, 1203–4. San Francisco: HarperCollins.
Heitzer, Horstwalter, ed. 1991. *Deutscher Katholizismus und Sozialpolitik bis zum Beginn der Weimarer Republik.* Paderborn: Schöningh.
Hengsbach, Friedhelm. 1990. "Die Sache katholischer Arbeiter hat ihn gepackt: Werk, kirchliches Umfeld und politische Resonanz." In *Ein unbekannter Behannter: Eine Auseinandersetzung mit dem Werk von Oswald von Nell-Breuning, SJ*, edited by Friedhelm Hengsbach, Matthias Möhring-Hesse, and Wolfgang Schroeder, 18–61. Cologne: Ketteler.
Hengst, Karl, Hans Jürgen Brandt, and Irmingard Böhm, eds. 1995. *Geliebte Kirche—Gelebte Caritas: Agnes Neuhaus—Christian Bartels—Elisabeth Gnauck-Kühne—Wilhelm Liese.* Paderborn: Schöningh.
Heynsbroek, Louis. 1991. "Corporatisme in de katholieke zuil: Katholieke opvattingen over het loonoverlegstelsel na Rerum novarum." *Tijdschrift voor Sociale Geschiedenis* 17: 172–96.
Hiepel, Claudia. 1999. *Arbeiterkatholizismus an der Ruhr: August Brust und der Gewerkverein christlicher Bergarbeiter.* Stuttgart: Kohlhammer.
Hiepel, Claudia, and Mark Ruff, eds. 2003. *Christliche Arbeiterbewegung in Europa 1850–1950.* Stuttgart: Kohlhammer.
Higgins, George G. 1993. *Organized Labor and the Church: Reflections of a "Labor Priest."* New York: Paulist.
Hilaire, Yves-Marie. 1994. "Rerum Novarum et la presse catholique sociale dans la région du Nord de la France (1891–1914)." In Furlong and Curtis, *Church Faces the Modern World*, 139–48.
———. 2010. "L'émergence du militantisme catholique (1914–1962)." In *Histoire générale du christianisme*, edited by Jean Robert Armogathe, 2:885–916. Paris: PUF.
Hilden, Patricia Penn. 1993. *Women, Work and Politics: Belgium, 1830–1914.* Oxford: Clarendon.
Hill, Steven. 2010. *Europe's Promise: Why the European Way Is the Best Hope in an Insecure Age.* Berkeley: University of California Press.
Himes, Kenneth R., Lisa Sowle Cahill, Charles E. Curran, David Hollenbach, and Thomas Shannon, eds. 2005. *Modern Catholic Social Teaching: Commentaries and Interpretations.* Washington, D.C.: Georgetown University Press.
Hinze, Christine Firer. 2005. "Commentary on *Quadragesimo anno* (After Forty Years)." In Himes et al., *Modern Catholic Social Teaching*, 151–74.

HJS (*Honderd jaar social: Teksten uit honderd jaar sociale beweging en sociaal denken in Nederland 1891–1991*). 1998. Edited by Jan M. Peet, L. J. Altena, and C. H. Wiedijk. Amsterdam: SDU.

HMOCB (*Histoire du Mouvement Ouvrier Chrétien en Belgique*). 1994. Edited by Emmanuel Gerard and Paul Wynants. 2 vols. Leuven: Leuven University Press.

Hoffmann, Peter. 1996. *The History of the German Resistance 1933–1945*. 3rd English ed. Montreal: McGill-Queen's University Press.

Holland, Joe. 2003. *Modern Catholic Social Teaching: The Popes Confront the Industrial Age 1740–1958*. New York: Paulist.

Hollenbach, David. 1979. *Claims in Conflict: Retrieving and Renewing the Catholic Human Rights Tradition*. New York: Paulist.

———. 2005. "Gaudium et spes." In Himes et al, *Modern Catholic Social Teaching*, 266–91.

Hollerbach, Alexander. 1974. "Das Verhältnis der katholischen Naturrechtslehre des 19. Jahrhunderts zur Geschichte der Rechtswissenschaft und Rechtsphilosophie." In Langner, *Theologie und Sozialethik*, 61–112.

Holmes, J. Derek. 1981. *The Papacy in the Modern World 1914–1978*. New York: Crossroad.

Hömig, Herbert, ed. 2003. *Katholiken und Gewerkschaftsbewegung 1890–1945*. Paderborn: Schöningh.

Hong, Young-Sun. 1998. *Welfare, Modernity, and the Weimar State, 1919–1933*. Princeton: Princeton University Press.

———. 2009. "Weimar Welfare System." In McElligott, *Weimar Germany*, 175–206.

Horn, Gerd-Rainer. 2008. *Western European Liberation Theology: The First Wave (1924–1959)*. Oxford: Oxford University Press.

Horn, Gerd-Rainer, and Emmanuel Gerard, eds. 2001. *Left Catholicism 1943–1955: Catholics and Society in Western Europe at the Point of Liberation*. KADOC Studies 25. Leuven: Leuven University Press.

Hornsby-Smith, Michael P. 2006. *An Introduction to Catholic Social Thought*. Cambridge: Cambridge University Press.

Hünermann, Peter. 2006. "The Final Weeks of the Council." In Alberigo and Komonchak, *History of Vatican II*, 5:363–483.

Hürten, Heinz. 1992. *Deutsche Katholiken 1918 bis 1945*. Paderborn: Schöningh.

———. 2003. *Kirche auf dem Weg in eine veränderte Welt: Ein Versuch über die Auseinandersetzung der Katholiken mit der Gesellschaft des 19. und 20. Jahrhunderts*. Münster: LIT.

IESS (*International Encyclopedia of the Social Sciences*). 1979. Edited by David L. Sills. 19 vols. New York: Macmillan.

"In Face of the World's Crisis." 1942. *Commonweal* 36: 415–21.

International Labour Organisation: The First Decade. 1931. London: Allen and Unwin.

Jackson, Julian. 1988. *The Popular Front in France: Defending Democracy, 1934–38*. Cambridge: Cambridge University Press.

———. 2001. *France, the Dark Years, 1940–1944*. Oxford: Oxford University Press.

———. 2003. *The Fall of France: The Nazi Invasion of 1940*. Oxford: Oxford University Press.

———. 2005. "'Mal embarqué bien arrivé': The Strange Story of François Perroux." In *Vichy, Resistance, Liberation: New Perspectives on Wartime France*, edited by Hanna Diamond and Simon Kitson, 155–69. Oxford and New York: Berg.

Jadoulle, Jean-Louis. 1991. *La pensée de l'abbé Pottier (1849–1923): Contribution à l'histoire de la démocratie chrétienne en Belgique*. Louvain-la-Neuve: Collège Erasme; Brussels: Nauwelaerts.

———. 1992. "La question sociale, une question religieuse avant tout: Réponse d'un démocrate-chrétien—Antoine Pottier (1849–1923)." In *Le monde catholique et la question sociale (1891–1950)*, edited by Françoise Rosart and Guy Zelis, 47–66. Brussels: Editions Vie Ouvrière.

Jagschitz, Gerhard. 1983. "Der österreichische Ständestaat 1934–1938." In Weinzierl and Skalnick, *Österreich 1918–1938*, 497–515.

JCSW (*Jahrbuch für christliche Sozialwissenschaften*). 1960–. Münster: Regensberg.

Joblin, Joseph. 1990. "L'appel de l'Union de Fribourg à Léon XIII en faveur d'une législation internationale du travail: Son lien avec 'Rerum Novarum.'" *Archivum Historiae Pontificiae* 28: 357–72.

John XXIII. 1961. *Mater et magistra*. In Carlen, 5:59–90.
Joret, Bernadette. 1990. "Préludes à une organisation de la jeunesse travailleuse 1912–1924." In Bragard et al., *Jeunesse ouvrière chrétienne*, 55–88.
Judt, Tony. 2005. *Postwar: A History of Europe since 1945*. New York: Penguin.
———. 2008. *Reappraisals: Reflections on the Forgotten Twentieth Century*. New York: Penguin Press.
———. 2010. *Ill Fares the Land*. New York: Penguin Press.
Kaelble, Hartmut. 1990. *A Social History of Western Europe 1880–1980*. Dublin: Gill and Macmillan.
Kaiser, Josef, ed. 1996. *Der Deutsche Gewerkschaftsbund 1949–1956*. Quellen zur Geschichte der Deutschen Gewerkschaftsbewegung im 20. Jahrhundert 11. Cologne: Bund.
Kaiser, Wolfram. 2007. *Christian Democracy and the Origins of European Union*. Cambridge and New York: Cambridge University Press.
Kaiser, Wolfram, and Helmut Wohnout, eds. 2004. *Political Catholicism in Europe, 1918–45*. London and New York: Routledge.
Kalb, Don. 1997. *Expanding Class: Power and Everyday Politics in Industrial Communities, The Netherlands, 1850–1950*. Durham, N.C.: Duke University Press.
Kalyvas, Stathis N. 1996. *The Rise of Christian Democracy in Europe*. Ithaca, N.Y.: Cornell University Press.
Kaufmann, Franz-Xaver. 2000. "Towards a Theory of the Welfare State." *European Review* 8: 291–312.
Keller, Franz. 1918. "Der moderne Kapitalismus." In *Deutschland und der Katholizismus: Gedanken zur Neugestaltung des deutschen Geistes- und Gesellschaftslebens*, edited by Max Meinertz and Hermann Sacher, 345–66. Freiburg: Herder.
Kelly, J. N. D. 2005. *The Oxford Dictionary of Popes*. Oxford: Oxford University Press.
Kenis, Leo, Jaak Billiet, and Patrick Pasture, eds. 2010. *The Transformation of the Christian Churches in Western Europe 1945–2000 / La transformation des églises chrétiennes en Europe occidentale*. Leuven: Leuven University Press.
Kertzer, David I. 2001. *The Popes against the Jews: The Vatican's Role in the Rise of Modern Anti-Semitism*. New York: Alfred A. Knopf.
Kettern, Bernd. 1998. "The Development of the Concept 'Iustitia' from Thomas Aquinas through the Social Encyclicals." In *Principles of Catholic Social Teaching*, edited by David A. Boileau, 85–102. Milwaukee: Marquette University Press.
Keymolen, Denise. 1985. "Baers, Maria-Gabriella." *Biographie nationale* 44: 5–16. Brussels.
———. 2001. *Victoire Cappe (1886–1927): Une vie chrétienne, sociale, féministe*. Leuven: Leuven University Press.
Keynes, John Maynard. 1920. *The Economic Consequences of the Peace*. New York: Harcourt, Brace, and Howe.
Kitchen, Martin. 1980. *The Coming of Austrian Fascism*. London: Croom Helm; Montreal: McGill-Queen's University Press.
Klein, Wolfgang, Heinrich Ludwig, and Karl-Josef Rivinius, eds. 1976. *Texte zur katholischen Soziallehre*. Vol. 2, *Dokumente zur Geschichte des Verhältnisses von Kirche und Arbeiterschaft am Beispiel der KAB*. Kevelaer: Butzon and Bercker.
Klose, Alfred. 1983. "Die Interessenverbände." In Weinzierl and Skalnick, *Österreich 1918–1938*, 331–41.
Klostermann, Ferdinand. 1967. "Das organisierte Apostolat der Laien und die Katholische Aktion." In *Kirche in Österreich 1918–1965*, edited by Erika Weinzierl, 2:68–137. Vienna: Herold.
Kluwick, Christl. 1975. "Die Christlichen Gewerkschaften im Ständestaat." In Größl, *Christlichen Gewerkschaften*, 235–64.
Knapp, Thomas A. 1975. "The Red and the Black: Catholic Socialists in the Weimar Republic." *Catholic Historical Review* 61: 386–408.
Köhler, Joachim. 1984. "Katholische Aktion und politischer Katholizismus in der Endphase der Weimarer Republik." In *Kirche im Nationalsozialismus*, edited by Rudolf Reinhardt, 141–53. Sigmaringen: Jan Thorbecke.
Kolb, Eberhard. 2005. *The Weimar Republic*. London and New York: Routledge.

———. 2010. *Deutschland 1918–1933: Eine Geschichte der Weimarer Republik*. Munich: Oldenbourg.
Komonchak, Joseph A. 1995. "The Struggle for the Council during the Preparation of Vatican II (1960–1962)." In Alberigo and Komonchak, *History of Vatican II*, 1:167–356.
———. 1999. "Returning from Exile: Catholic Theology in the 1930s." In *The Twentieth Century: A Theological Overview*, edited by Gregory Baum, 35–48. Maryknoll, N.Y.: Orbis; London: Chapman; Ottawa: Novalis.
———. 2003. "Augustine, Aquinas, or the Gospel *sine glossa*? Divisions over *Gaudium et Spes*." In *Unfinished Journey: The Church 40 Years after Vatican II*, edited by Austen Ivereigh, 102–18. London and New York: Continuum.
Kossmann, Ernst Heinrich. 1978. *The Low Countries, 1780–1940*. Oxford: Clarendon.
Kosthorst, Erich. 1975. "Jakob Kaiser (1888–1961)." In *ZGiLB* 2:143–58.
Kreins, Jean-Marie. 2003. "Le père Joseph Arendt, S.J. (1885–1952): Une vie au service de l'action sociale catholique." In *Angles d'approches: Histoire économique et social de l'espace wallon et de ses marges; XVe–XXe siècles*, by V. Fillieux et al., 193–211. Dossiers d'histoire économique et social 1. Louvain-la-Neuve: Bruylant-Academia.
Krenn, Dorit-Maria. 1991. *Die christliche Arbeiterbewegung in Bayern vom Ersten Weltkrieg bis 1933*. Mainz: Grünewald.
Kreukels, L. H. M. 1986. *Mijnarbeid: Volgzaamheid en strijdbaarheid; Geschiedenis van de arbeidsverhoudingen in de Nederlandse steenkolenmijnen, 1900–1940*. Assen and Maastricht: Van Gorcum.
Krieg, Robert A. 1992. *Karl Adam: Catholicism in German Culture*. Notre Dame, Ind.: University of Notre Dame Press.
———. 1999. "Karl Adam, National Socialism, and Christian Tradition." *Theological Studies* 60: 432–56.
Kselman, Thomas, and Joseph A. Buttigieg, eds. 2003. *European Christian Democracy: Historical Legacies and Comparative Perspectives*. Notre Dame, Ind.: University of Notre Dame Press.
KSL (*Katholisches Soziallexikon*). 1980. Edited by Alfred Klose, Wolfgang Mantl, and Valentin Zsifkovits. 2nd ed. Innsbruck: Tyrolia; Graz: Styria.
Kuiper, Cornelis Johannes. 1951–53. *Uit het rijk van de arbeid: Ontstaan, groei en werk van de Katholieke Arbeidersbeweging in Nederland*. Utrecht.
Kwanten, Godfried, ed. 1986a. *Cent ans de syndicalisme chrétien 1886–1986*. Brussels: Confédération des Syndicats Chrétiens.
———, ed. 1986b. *Honderd jaar christelijke vakbeweging 1886–1986*. Brussels: A.C.V.
———. 1994. "Les cooperatives chrétiennes." In *HMOCB* 2:278–423.
Lagrée, Michel. 1992. *Religion et cultures en Bretagne (1850–1950)*. Paris: Fayard.
Lamb, Matthew L. 1994. "Solidarity." In *NDCST* 908–12.
Lamberts, Emiel, ed. 1992. *Een kantelend tijdperk. Une époque en mutation. Ein Zeitalter im Umbruch: De wending van de Kerk naar het volk in Noord-West-Europa. Le catholicisme social dans le Nord-Ouest de l'Europe. Die Wende der Kirche zum Volk im nordwestlichen Europa (1890–1910)*. KADOC Studies, 13. Leuven: University Press.
———, ed. 1997. *Christian Democracy in the European Union 1945–1995*. KADOC Studies 21. Leuven: Leuven University Press.
———, ed. 2002. *The Black International: The Holy See and Militant Catholicism in Europe / L'internationale noire: Le Saint-Siège et le catholicisme militant en Europe, 1870–1878*. KADOC Studies 29. Leuven: Leuven University Press.
———. 2006. "Belgium since 1830." In Blom and Lamberts, *History of the Low Countries*, 319–91.
Langner, Albrecht, ed. 1974. *Theologie und Sozialethik im Spannungsfeld der Gesellschaft: Untersuchung zur Ideengeschichte des deutschen Katholizismus im 19. Jahrhundert*. Paderborn: Schöningh.
———, ed. 1980. *Katholizismus, Wirtschaftsordnung und Sozialpolitik, 1945–1963*. Paderborn: Schöningh.
———, ed. 1988. *Adam Müller 1779–1829*. Paderborn: Schöningh.
Laudouze, André. 1989. *Dominicains français et Action française, 1899–1940: Maurras au couvent*. Paris: Éditions ouvrières.

Laufen, Veronika. 2011. *Der Verband katholischer kaufmännischer Vereinigungen Deutschlands 1877–1933*. Frankfurt am Main: Peter Lang.

Launay, Michel. 1982. "Le syndicalisme chrétien et la Charte du travail." In Montclos et al., *Églises et chrétiens*, 189–212.

———. 1984. *Le syndicalisme chrétien en France de 1885 à nos jours*. Paris: Desclée.

———. 1985. "Réflexions sur les origines da le J.O.C." In Cholvy, *Mouvements de jeunesse chrétiens et juifs*, 223–31.

———. 1986. *La C.F.T.C.: Origines et développement 1919–1940*. Paris: Publications de la Sorbonne.

———. 1990. *Le Syndicalisme en Europe*. Paris: Imprimerie nationale.

Lavigne, Jean-Claude, and Hugues Puel. 2007. "For a Human-Centered Economy: Louis Joseph Lebret (1897–1966)." In Compagnoni and Alford, *Preaching Justice*, 100–125.

The Lay Apostolate: Papal Teachings. 1961. Boston: St. Paul.

Le Crom, Jean-Pierre. 1995. *Syndicats nous voilà! Vichy et le corporatisme*. Paris: Éditions de l'Atelier / Éditions ouvrières.

———. 2003. *L'introuvable démocratie salariale, le droit de la représentation du personnel dans l'entreprise (1890–2002)*. Paris: Syllepse.

Lécrivain, Philippe. 1990. "Les Semaines sociales de France." In Maugenest, *Mouvement social catholique*, 151–65.

———. 1993. "Semaines sociales de France." In *Catholicisme* 13: 1051–56.

Ledure, Yves, ed. 1991. *Rerum novarum en France: Le père Dehon et l'engagement social de l'Église*. Paris: Éditions universitaires.

———. 2005. *Le père Leon Dehon, 1843–1925: Entre mystique et catholicisme social*. Paris: Cerf.

———, ed. 2009. *Catholicisme social et question juive: Le cas de Léon Dehon (1843–1925)*. Paris: Desclée de Brouwer; Lethielleux.

Leo XIII. 1891. *Rerum novarum*. In Carlen, 2:241–58.

Leprieur, François. 1989. *Quand Rome condamne: Dominicains et prêtres-ouvriers*. Paris: Plon and Cerf.

Letterhaus, Bernard. 1976. "Die Wertung des Lohnarbeiters in der heutigen Wirtschafts- und Gesellschaftsordnung im Lichte der katholischen Weltanschauung." In Klein, Ludwig, and Rivinius, *Texte zur katholischen Soziallehre*, 2:1042–79. "Die Wertung" originally published in 1928.

Liebmann, Maximilian. 1987. "Innitzer." In *StL* 3:90–92.

Lienkamp, Andreas. 2001. "Socialism out of Christian Responsibility: The German Experiment of Left Catholicism (1945–1949)." In Horn and Gerard, *Left Catholicism 1943–1955*, 196–227.

Lijphart, Arend. 1975. *The Politics of Accommodation: Pluralism and Democracy in the Netherlands*. 2nd rev. ed. Berkeley: University of California Press.

Lindt, Andreas. 1981. *Das Zeitalter des Totalitarismus: Politische Heilslehren und ökumenischer Aufbruch*. Stuttgart: Kohlhammer.

Loew, Jacques. 1994. *Vivre l'Evangile avec Madeleine Delbrêl*. Paris: Centurion.

Lönne, Karl-Egon. 1986. *Politischer Katholizismus im 19. und 20. Jahrhundert*. Frankfurt: Suhrkamp.

———. 1996. "Germany." In Buchanan and Conway, *Political Catholicism in Europe*, 156–86.

Lorwin, Val R. 1954. *The French Labor Movement*. Cambridge, Mass.: Harvard University Press.

Ludwig, Heiner, and Wolfgang Schroeder, eds. 1990. *Sozial- und Linkskatholizismus: Erinnerung—Orientierung—Befreiung*. Frankfurt: Knecht.

Lugmayer, Karl. 1924. *Das Linzer Programm der christlichen Arbeiter Österreichs*. Vienna: Typographische Anstalt.

Lutz, Heinrich. 1962. *Demokratie im Zwielicht: Der Weg der deutschen Katholiken aus dem Kaiserreich in die Republik 1914–1925*. Munich: Kösel.

Luykx, Paul. 1994. "A Century of Dutch Catholicism and *Rerum Novarum*. In Furlong and Curtis, *Church Faces the Modern World*, 123–38.

———. 1996. "The Netherlands." In Buchanan and Conway, *Political Catholicism in Europe*, 219–47.

Luyten, Dirk, and Guy Vanthemsche, eds. 1995. *Het Sociaal Pact van 1944: Oorsprong, betekenis en gevolgen*. Brussels: VUB.

MacMillan, Margaret Olwen. 2002. *Paris 1919: Six Months that Changed the World*. New York: Random House.

Maderthaner, Wolfgang. 2002. "12 February 1934: Social Democracy and Civil War." In *Austria in the Twentieth Century*, edited by Rolf Steininger, Günter Bischof, and Michael Gehler, 45–71. New Brunswick, N.J.: Transaction.

Magraw, Roger. 1992. *A History of the French Working Class*. Vol. 2, *Workers and the Bourgeois Republic*. Oxford: Blackwell.

Maier, Charles S. 1975. *Recasting Bourgeois Europe: Stabilization in France, Germany, and Italy in the Decade after World War I*. Princeton: Princeton University Press.

Malgeri, Francesco. 1980. "Il partito popolare italiano." In Malgeri, *Storia*, 3:1–201 and 321–57.

———, ed. 1980–81. *Storia del movimento cattolico in Italia*. 6 vols. Rome: Il Poligono.

———. 1983. "I rapporti fra Sturzo e Valente." In Traniello, *Dalla prima democrazia cristiana*, 503–17.

Mampuys, Jozef. 1994. "Le syndicalisme chrétien." In *HMOCB* 2:150–277.

Mann, Charles F. 1996. *Madeleine Delbrêl: A Life Beyond Boundaries*. San Francisco: New World Press.

Mann, Michael. 2004. *Fascists*. New York: Cambridge University Press.

Maraviglia, Mariangela. 1994. *Achille Grandi fra lotte operaie e testimonianza cristiana*. Brescia: Morcelliana.

Margotti, Marta. 2000. *Preti e operai: La Mission de Paris dal 1943 al 1954*. Turin: Paravia Bruno Mondadori.

Maritain, Jacques. 1996. *Integral Humanism: Temporal and Spiritual Problems of a New Christendom*. In *The Collected Works of Jacques Maritain*, 11:143–345. Notre Dame, Ind.: University of Notre Dame Press. *Integral Humanism* was originally pubished in 1936.

Maritain, Jacques, and Raïssa Maritain. 1982–. *Oeuvres complètes: Jacques et Raïssa Maritain*. 17 vols. Fribourg Suisse: Éditions universitaires.

Martin, Benjamin F. 1978. *Count Albert de Mun, Paladin of the Third Republic*. Chapel Hill: University of North Carolina Press.

Marx, Reinhard. 2008. *Das Kapital: Ein Plädoyer für den Menschen*. Munich: Pattloch.

Masson, Catherine. 2001. *Le Cardinal Liénart, évêque de Lille, 1928–1968*. Paris: Cerf.

Mattiazzo, Antonio. 1983. "Le internazionali cattoliche: origini e programmi." In *Genesi della coscienza internazionalista dei cattolici fra '800 e '900*, 59–168. Padua: Gregoriana.

Maugenest, Denis, ed. 1990. *Le mouvement social catholique en France au XXe siècle*. Paris: Cerf.

Mayeur, Jean-Marie. 1968. *Un prête démocrate, l'abbé Lemire (1853–1928)*. Tournai: Casterman.

———. 1980. *Des partis catholiques à la démocratie chrétienne, XIXe–XXe siècles*. Paris: Colin.

———. 1988. "Les années 30 et Humanisme intégral." In Allard et al., *L'humanisme intégral de Jacques Maritain*, 17–36.

———, ed. 1990. *HC 12: Guerres mondiales et totalitarismes (1914–1958)*.

———. 2007. "L'encyclique *Rerum novarum* (1891) et la doctrine sociale de l'Église catholique." In Corbin et al., *Histoire du christianisme*, 415–18.

———. 2009. "Léon Dehon et l'antisémitisme." In Ledure, *Catholicisme social et question juive*, 105–9.

Mazower, Mark. 1999. *Dark Continent: Europe's Twentieth Century*. New York: A. A. Knopf.

McElligott, Anthony, ed. 2009. *Weimar Germany*. Short Oxford History of Germany. Oxford: Oxford University Press.

———. 2014. *Rethinking the Weimar Republic: Authority and Authoritarianism, 1916–1936*. London and New York: Bloomsbury.

McGreevy, John T. 2003. *Catholicism and American Freedom: A History*. New York: W. W. Norton.

McHugh, Francis P. 2008. *Catholic Social Thought Renovating the Tradition: A Keyguide to Resources*. Annua Nuntia Lovaniensia 55. Leuven; Dudley, Mass.: Peeters.

McHugh, Francis P., and Samuel M. Natale, eds. 1993. *Things Old and New: Catholic Social Teaching Revisited*. Lanham, Md.: University Press of America.

McLeod, Hugh, ed. 1995. *European Religion in the Age of Great Cities 1830–1930*. London and New York: Routledge.

McMillan, James F. 1981. "Clericals, Anticlericals and the Women's Movement in France under the Third Republic." *Historical Journal* 22: 361–76.

———. 1995. "French Catholics: *Rumeurs infames* and the Union Sacrée, 1914–1918." In *Authority, Iden-*

tity and the Social History of the Great War, edited by Frans Coetzee and Marilyn Shevin-Coetzee, 113–32. Providence, R.I., and Oxford: Berghahn.

———. 1996a. "Catholicism and Nationalism in France: The Case of the *Fédération nationale catholique*." In *Catholicism in Britain and France since 1789*, edited by Nicholas Atkin and Frank Tallett, 151–63. London: Hambledon Press.

———. 1996b. "France." In Buchanan and Conway, *Political Catholicism in Europe*, 34–68.

Mee, Charles L., Jr. 1980. *The End of Order: Versailles, 1919*. New York: Dutton.

MEGA (Karl Marx, Friedrich Engels Gesamtausgabe). 1972–. Berlin: Dietz.

Mengus, Raymond, ed. 1991. *Cent ans de catholicisme social en Alsace: De l'encyclique Rerum novarum (1891) à la fin du 20e siècle*. Strasbourg: Presses Universitaires.

Menozzi, Daniele, and Renato Moro, eds. 2004. *Cattolicesimo e totalitarismo: Chiese e culture religiose tra le due guerre mondiali (Italia, Spagna, Francia)*. Brescia: Morcelliana.

Mertens, P. J. J., et al. 1981. *Terugblikken bij het vooruitzien: De Katholieke Arbeiders Beweging in herinneringen en beschouwingen. Een Liber Amicorum voor KAB/NKV*. Baarn: Ambo.

Messner, Johannes. 1936. *Die berufständische Ordnung*. Innsbruck: Tyrolia.

Mich, Marvin L. Krier. 1998. *Catholic Social Teaching and Movements*. Mystic, Conn.: Twenty-Third.

———. 2005. "*Mater et magistra*." In Himes et al., *Modern Catholic Social Teaching*, 191–216.

Misner, Paul. 1990. "Adam Müller and Adam Smith: A Romantic-Catholic Response to Modern Economic Thought." In *Religion and Economic Ethics*, 175–98, edited by Joseph F. Gower. Annual Publication of the College Theology Society, 31. Lanham, Md.: University Press of America.

———. 1991. *Social Catholicism in Europe: From the Onset of Industrialization to the First World War*. New York: Crossroad.

———. 1994a. "Antecedents of Rerum Novarum in European Catholicism." In *On the Condition of Labor and the Social Question One Hundred Years Later: Commemorating the 100th Anniversary of Rerum Novarum, and the Fiftieth Anniversary of the Association for Social Economics*, edited by Thomas O. Nitsch, Joseph M. Phillips Jr., and Edward L. Fitzsimmons, 211–20. Lewiston, N.Y.: Edwin Mellen Press.

———. 1994b. "The Emergence of an International Organisation of Christian Labour after *Rerum Novarum*." In Furlong and Curtis, *Church Faces the Modern World*, 241–56.

———. 1994c. "Opera dei Congressi." In *NDCST* 692–93.

———. 1994d. "Paternalism." In *NDCST* 712–13.

———. 1994e. "Volksverein." In *NDCST* 975–76.

———. 2000. "Catholic Anti-Modernism: The Ecclesial Setting." In *Catholicism Contending with Modernity: Roman Catholic Modernism and Anti-Modernism in Historical Context*, edited by Darrell Jodock, 56–87. Cambridge: Cambridge University Press.

———. 2003. "Christian Democratic Social Policy: Precedents for Third-Way Thinking." In Kselman and Buttigieg, *European Christian Democracy*, 68–92.

———. 2004a. "Catholic Labor and Catholic Action: The Italian Context of *Quadragesimo Anno*." *Catholic Historical Review* 90: 650–74.

———. 2004b. "Christian Trade Unionists Conference, Switzerland 1908." In *St. James Encyclopedia of Labor History Worldwide: Major Events in Labor History and Their Impact*, 157–60, edited by Neil Schlager. Detroit: St. James Press and Thomson Gale.

———. 2005. "The Roman Catholic Hierarchy and the Christian Labor Movement: Autonomy and Pluralism." In Heerma van Voss, Pasture, and De Maeyer, *Between Cross and Class*, 103–25.

MM (Mater et magistra). John XXIII, 1961. In Carlen, 5:59–90.

Mockenhaupt, Hubert. 1973. "Heinrich Brauns (1868–1939)." In *ZGiLB* 1:148–59.

———, ed. 1977. *Weg und Wirken des geistlichen Sozialpolitikers Heinrich Brauns*. Paderborn: Schöningh.

Molette, Charles. 1970. *Albert de Mun, 1872–1890: Exigence doctrinale et préoccupations sociales chez un laïc catholique*. Paris: Beauchesne.

Moloney, Deirdre M. 2002. *American Catholic Lay Groups and Transatlantic Social Reform in the Progressive Era*. Chapel Hill: University of North Carolina Press.

Molony, John N. 1977. *The Emergence of Political Catholicism in Italy: Partito popolare 1919–1926*. London: Croom Helm; Totowa, N.J.: Rowman and Littlefield.

Mommsen, Hans. 1996. *The Rise and Fall of Weimar Democracy*. Chapel Hill: University of North Carolina Press.

———. 2003. *Alternatives to Hitler: German Resistance under the Third Reich*. London: I. B. Tauris.

Montclos, Xavier de, Monique Luirard, François Delpech, and Pierre Bolle, eds. 1982. *Églises et chrétiens dans la IIe Guerre mondiale: La France; Actes du Colloque national tenu à Lyon du 27 au 30 janvier 1978*. Lyon: Presses universitaires de Lyon.

Monti, Giuseppe, ed. 1924. *International Handbook of Catholic Organisations*. Paris: Spes.

Moody, Joseph N., ed. 1953. *Church and Society: Catholic Social and Political Thought and Movements 1789–1950*. New York: Arts, Inc.

Moore, Bob, ed. 2000. *Resistance in Western Europe*. Oxford and New York: Berg.

Moro, Renato. 1979. *La formazione della classe dirigente cattolica (1929–1937)*. Bologna: Il Mulino.

———. 1981a. "Azione cattolica, clero e laicato di fronte al fascismo." In Malgeri, *Storia*, 4:87–377.

———. 1981b. "Azione cattolica italiana (ACI)." In *DSMCI* 1, pt. 2:180–91.

Morsey, Rudolf. 1966. *Die Deutsche Zentrumspartei 1917–1923*. Düsseldorf: Droste.

———. 1973. "Adam Stegerwald (1874–1945)." In *ZGiLB* 1:206–19.

———. 1979. "Helene Weber (1881–1962)." In *ZGiLB* 3:223–34.

———, ed. 1988. *Katholizismus, Verfassungsstaat und Demokratie: Vom Vormärz bis 1933*. Paderborn: Schöningh.

———. 2002. "1918–1933." In *Lexikon der Christlichen Demokratie in Deutschland*, edited by Winfried Becker, Günter Buchstab, Anselm Doering-Manteuffel, and Rudolf Morsey, 35–43. Paderborn: Schöningh.

Mucci, Giandomenico. 1988. *Carlo Maria Curci: Il fondatore della "Civiltà Cattolica."* Rome: Studium.

Mueller, Franz H. 1963. "The Church and the Social Question." In *The Challenge of Mater et Magistra*, edited by Joseph N. Moody and Justus George Lawler, 13–154. New York: Herder and Herder.

———. 1980. *Heinrich Pesch: Sein Leben und seine Lehre*. Cologne: J. P. Bachem.

———. 1984. *The Church and the Social Question*. Washington, D.C.: American Enterprise Institute for Public Policy Research.

———. 1994a. "Pesch, Heinrich." In *NDCST* 738–39.

———. 1994b. "Solidarism." In *NDCST* 906–8.

Mulcahy, Richard E. 1951. "Economic Freedom in Pesch: His System Demands, but Restrains, Freedom." *Social Order* 1: 161–68.

———. 1952. *The Economics of Heinrich Pesch*. New York: Holt.

Muller, Albert. 1933. *Notes d'économie politique. Première série: Production—Répartition—Problèmes sociaux*. 2nd ed. Paris: Spes; Antwerp: Institut supérieur de Commerce St. Ignace.

Müller, Dirk H. 1996. *Arbeiter, Katholizismus, Staat: Der Volksverein für das katholische Deutschland und die katholischen Arbeiterorganisationen in der Weimarer Republik*. Bonn: Dietz, for the Forschungsinstitut der Friedrich-Ebert-Stiftung.

Müller, Guido. 2001. "Das 'Secrétariat International des Partis Démocratiques d'Inspiration Chrétienne' 1925–1939: Ein vorweggenommenes Exil katholischer Demokraten in der Zwischenkriegszeit." In Gehler, Kaiser, and Wohnout, *Christdemokratie in Europa*, 559–73.

———. 2004. "Anticipated Exile of Catholic Democrats: The Secrétariat International des Partis Démocratiques d'Inspiration Chrétienne." In Kaiser and Wohnout, *Political Catholicism in Europe*, 252–64.

Müller, Otto. 1976. "Erinnerungen an die Katholische Arbeiter-Bewegung." In Klein, Ludwig, and Rivinius, *Texte zur katholischen Soziallehre*, 2:840–1026.

Muracciolo, Jean-François. 2000. "Conseil nationale de la résistance (CNR)." In *DHFO* 199–200.

Murphy, Francis J. 1989. *Communists and Catholics in France, 1936–1939: The Politics of the Outstretched Hand*. Gainesville: University of Florida Press.

Musto, Ronald G. 1986. *The Catholic Peace Tradition*. Maryknoll, N.Y.: Orbis.

NCE (*New Catholic Encyclopedia*). 1967–79. New York: McGraw-Hill.

NDB (*Neue Deutsche Biographie*). 1953–. Berlin: Duncker and Humblot.

NDCST (*The New Dictionary of Catholic Social Thought*). 1994. Edited by Judith A. Dwyer. Collegeville, Minn.: Liturgical Press.

Nell-Breuning, Oswald von. 1932. *Die soziale Enzyklika: Erläuterungen zum Weltrundschreiben Papst Pius' XI. über die gesellschaftliche Ordnung*. 2nd ed. Cologne: Katholische Tat-Verlag.
———. 1936. *Reorganization of Social Economy: The Social Encyclical Developed and Explained*. Edited and translated by Bernard W. Dempsey. Milwaukee: Bruce.
———. 1968. "Der Königswinterer Kreis und sein Anteil an 'Quadragesimo anno.'" In *Soziale Verantwortung: Festschrift für Goetz Briefs zum 80. Geburtstag*, edited by J. Broermann and Ph. Herder-Dorneich, 571–85. Berlin: Duncker and Humblot.
———. 1970. "Social Movements." In *Sacramentum Mundi: An Encyclopedia of Knowledge*, edited by Karl Rahner et al., 6:115. New York: Herder and Herder.
———. 1972a. "15.5.1931: Erinnerungen zur Entstehungsgeschichte von 'Quadragesimo anno.'" In *Wie sozial ist die Kirche?*, 127–36.
———. 1972b. "Die katholische Soziallehre—Aufstieg, Niedergang und bleibendes Verdienst: Ein Rückblick auf ihre Leistung und ihr Versagen in acht Jahrzehnten." In *Wie sozial ist die Kirche?*, 71–96.
———. 1972c. "Der Königswinterer Kreis und sein Anteil an 'Quadragesimo anno.'" In *Wie sozial ist die Kirche?*, 99–115.
———. 1972d. "Octogesimo anno." In *Wie sozial ist die Kirche?*, 116–26.
———. 1972e. *Wie sozial ist die Kirche? Leistung und Versagen der katholischen Soziallehre*. Düsseldorf: Patmos.
———. 1980. "Der Beitrag des Katholizismus zur Sozialpolitik der Nachkriegszeit." In Langner, *Katholizismus*, 109–21.
———. 1986. "The Drafting of Quadragesimo Anno." In Curran and McCormick, *Official Catholic Social Teaching*, 60–68.
———. 1990. *Den Kapitalismus umbiegen: Schriften zu Kirche, Wirtschaft und Gesellschaft; Ein Lesebuch*. Düsseldorf: Patmos.
———. 1992. "Einführung." In *Texte zur katholischen Soziallehre*. 8th ed., Bundesverband der Katholischen Arbeitnehmer-Bewegung Deutschlands KAB, vii–xxx. Bornheim: Ketteler Verlag; Kevelaer: Butzon and Bercker.
Nocken, Ulrich. 1978. "Corporatism and Pluralism in Modern German History." In *Industrielle Gesellschaft und politisches System: Beiträge zur politischen Sozialgeschichte*, edited by Dirk Stegmann et al., 37–56. Bonn: Neue Gesellschaft.
Noonan, John T., Jr. 1957. *The Scholastic Analysis of Usury*. Cambridge, Mass.: Harvard University Press.
———. 2003. "Usury: The Amendment of Papal Teaching by Theologians." In Curran 2003a, 80–108.
———. 2005. *Church That Can and Cannot Change*. Notre Dame, Ind.: University of Notre Dame Press.
Nord, Philip. 2006. "Catholic Culture in Interwar France." In *Religious Differences in France: Past and Present*, edited by Kathleen Perry Long, 179–99. Kirksville, Mo.: Truman State University Press.
———. 2010. *France's New Deal: From the Thirties to the Postwar Era*. Princeton: Princeton University Press.
Nuesse, C. Joseph. 1990. *The Catholic University of America: A Centennial History*. Washington, D.C.: The Catholic University of America Press.
O'Brien, David J. 1968. *American Catholics and Social Reform: The New Deal Years*. New York: Oxford University Press.
O'Brien, David J., and Thomas A. Shannon, eds. 2010. *Catholic Social Thought: The Documentary Heritage*. Expanded ed. Maryknoll, N.Y.: Orbis.
O'Leary, Don. 2000. *Vocationalism and Social Catholicism in Twentieth-Century Ireland: The Search for a Christian Social Order*. Dublin: Irish Academic Press.
Oelinger, Josef. 1980. "Schwerpunkte der innerkatholischen Mitbestimmungsdiskussion 1945–1963." In Langner, *Katholizismus*, 153–204.
Offen, Karen. 2000. *European Feminisms, 1700–1950: A Political History*. Stanford, Calif.: Stanford University Press.
O'Malley, John W. 2008. *What Happened at Vatican II*. Cambridge, Mass.: Belknap Press of Harvard University Press.

Osbat, Luciano. 1982. "Movimento cattolico e questione giovanile." In *DSMCI* 1, pt. 2, 84–96.
Otte, Bernhard. 1932. In *Internationales Handwörterbuch des Gewerkschaftswesens*, 817–23. Berlin: Werk und Wirtschaft.
Pankoke-Schenk, Monika. 1982. "Katholizismus und Frauenfrage." In Rauscher, *90 Jahre Rerum novarum*, 2:278–311.
Pankoke-Schenk, Monica, and Gerlinde Mehrle. 1986. "Frauenbewegungen." In *StL*, 668–75.
Papini, Roberto. 1988. *L'Internationale démocrate-chrétienne: La coopération internationale entre les partis démocrates-chrétiens de 1925 à 1986*. Paris: Cerf.
———. 1995. *Il coraggio della democrazia: Sturzo e l'Internazionale popolare tra le due guerre*. Rome: Studium.
———. 1997. *The Christian Democrat International*. Lanham, Md.: Rowman and Littlefield.
Paronetto, Sergio, et al. 1945. *Per la comunità cristiana: Principi dell'ordinamento sociale a cura di un gruppo di studiosi amici di Camaldoli*. Rome: Studium.
Pasini, Giuseppe. 1982. Associazioni cristiane dei lavoratori italiani (ACLI)." In *DSMCI* 1, pt. 2:170–75.
Pasture, Patrick. 1992. *Kerk, politiek en sociale actie: De unieke positie van de christelijke arbeidersbeweging in België 1944–1973*. Leuven and Apeldoorn: Garant.
———. 1993. "The April 1944 'Social Pact' in Belgium and Its Significance for the Post-War Welfare State." *Journal of Contemporary History* 28: 695–714.
———. 1994a. "Adaptation en temps du crise (1921–1944): Redressement et expansion (1944–1960)." In *HMOCB*, 1:174–301.
———. 1994b. *Christian Trade Unionism in Europe since 1968: Tensions Between Identity and Practice*. Aldershot: Avebury; Brookfield, Vt.:Ashgate.
———. 1994c. "Diverging Paths: The Development of Catholic Labour Organisations in France, the Netherlands and Belgium since 1944." In *RHE* 89: 54–89.
———. 1994d. "L'état-providence (1960–1973)." In *HMOCB*, 1:302–54.
———. 1999. *Histoire du syndicalisme chrétien international: La difficile recherche d'une troisième voie*. Paris: Harmattan.
———. 2000. "The Flight of the Robins. European Trade Unions at the Beginnings of the European Integration Process." In *The Past and Future of International Trade Unionism. International Conference, Ghent (Belgium) May 19–20, 2000*, edited by Bart De Wilde, 80–103. Ghent: IALHI.
———. 2001a. "Modèles internationaux d'action ouvrière catholique." In Duriez et al, *Chrétiens et ouvriers*, 245–57.
———. 2001b. "Multi-Faceted Relations between Christian Trade Unions and Left Catholicism in Europe." In Horn and Gerard, *Left Catholicism 1943–1955*, 228–46.
———. 2003. "The Enigma of Christian Labor: A Case of Modernizing Catholicism." In BASMSCI 39: 282–303.
———. 2004. "Window of Opportunities or Trompe l'Oeil? The Myth of Labour Unity in Western Europe after 1945." In *Transnational Moments of Change: Europe 1945, 1968, 1989*, edited by Gerd-Rainer Horn and Padraic Kenney, 27–49. Lanham, Md.: Rowman and Littlefield.
———. 2005a. "Building the Social Security State: A Comparative History of Belgium, the Netherlands, and Germany, from the Nineteenth Century to the 1960s." In Heerma van Voss, Pasture, and De Maeyer, *Between Cross and Class*, 251–84.
———. 2005b. "Introduction: Between Cross and Class: Christian Labour in Europe 1840–2000." In Heerma van Voss, Pasture, and De Maeyer, *Between Cross and Class*, 9–48.
———. 2007. "Christian Social Movements Confronted with Fascism in Europe: Consistency, Continuity, or Flexibility in Principles, Strategies, and Tactics towards Social and Economic Democracy." In *Religion under Siege*, edited by Lieve Gevers and Jan Bank, 1:283–314. Louvain: Peeters.
Patch, William L. 1985. *Christian Trade Unions in the Weimar Republic, 1918–1933: The Failure of "Corporate Pluralism."* New Haven: Yale University Press.
———. 1998. *Heinrich Brüning and the Dissolution of the Weimar Republic*. Cambridge and New York: Cambridge University Press.
———. 2005. "Fascism, Catholic Corporatism, and the Christian Trade Unions of Germany, Austria, and France." In Heerma van Voss, Pasture, and De Maeyer, *Between Cross and Class*, 173–201.

Paul, Harry W. 1967. *The Second Ralliement: The Rapprochement between Church and State in France in the Twentieth Century*. Washington, D.C.: The Catholic University of America Press.
Paul VI. 1967. *Populorum progressio: On the Development of Peoples*. In Carlen, 5:183–99.
Pauley, Bruce. 1992. *From Prejudice to Persecution: A History of Austrian Anti-Semitism*. Chapel Hill: University of North Carolina Press.
Paulhus, Normand J. 1983. "The Theological and Political Ideals of the Fribourg Union." Diss., Boston College. Ann Arbor, Mich.: University Microfilms, 1985.
———. 1994. "Fribourg Union." In *NDCST*, 404–5.
Pavan, Pietro. 1992. "Dalla 'Rerum novarum' alla 'Mater et Magistra.'" In *Scritti*, vol. 4, *La Chiesa luce e fermento dell'umanità*, edited by Franco Biffi, 3–51. Rome: Città Nuova (1989–92).
Paxton, Robert O. 1994. Review of *The Birth of Fascist Ideology*, by Zeev Sternhell. *New York Review of Books*, June 23, 1994, 51–54.
Payne, Stanley G. 1995. *A History of Fascism, 1914–1945*. Madison: University of Wisconsin Press.
Pazos, Antón M., ed. 1993. *Un siglo de catolicismo social en Europa, 1891–1991*. Pamplona: Ediciones Universidad de Navarra (EUNSA).
Pecorari, Paolo. 1991. *Toniolo: Un economista per la democrazia*. Rome: Edizioni Studium.
Pedersen, Susan. 1993. "Catholicism, Feminism, and the Politics of the Family during the Late Third Republic." In *Mothers of a New World: Maternalist Politics and the Origins of Welfare States*, edited by Seth Koven and Sonya Michel, 246–76. New York: Routledge.
Peet, Jan. 1987. *Het uur van de arbeidersjeugd: De Katholieke Arbeiders Jeugd, de Vrouwelijke Katholieke Arbeidersjeugd en de emancipatie van de werkende jongeren in Nederland, 1944–1969*. Baarn: Arbor.
———. 1993. *Katholieke arbeidersbeweging: De KAB en het NKV in de maatschappelijke ontwikkeling van Nederland na 1945*. Baarn: Arbor; Nijmegen: Katholiek Documentatie Centrum.
———. 2003. "Die katholische Arbeiterbewegung in den Niederlanden: Geschichtsschreibung und Geschichte." In Hiepel and Ruff, *Christliche Arbeiterbewegung*, 142–58.
Pelinka, Anton. 1972. *Stand oder Klasse? Die Christliche Arbeiterbewegung Österreichs 1933 bis 1938*. Vienna: Europaverlag.
———. 1998. *Austria: Out of the Shadow of the Past*. Boulder, Colo., and Oxford: Westview Press.
Pelletier, Denis. 1996. *Economie et Humanisme: De l'utopie communautaire au combat pour le tiers-monde (1941–1966)*. Paris: Cerf.
———. 2002. *La crise catholique: Religion, société, politique en France (1965–1978)*. Paris: Payot.
Pesch, Heinrich. 1888. "Zinsgrund und Zinsgrenze." *Zeitschrift für Katholische Theologie* 12: 36–74 and 393–418.
———. 1901. *Liberalismus, Socialismus und christliche Gesellschaftsordnung*. Freiburg: Herder.
———. 1905–25. *Lehrbuch der Nationalökonomie*. 5 vols. Freiburg: Herder.
———. 1921. "Der richtige Weg zur Lösung der sozialen Frage." In *Soziale Arbeit im neuen Deutschland*, edited by August Pieper, 38–60. Mönchengladbach: Volksvereins-Verlag.
———. 1988. *Ethics and the National Economy*. Translated by Rupert J. Ederer. Manila: Divine Word.
———. 1998. *Heinrich Pesch on Solidarist Economics: Excerpts from the Lehrbuch der Nationalökonomie*. Translated by Rupert J. Ederer. Lanham, Md.: University Press of America.
———. 2000–2006. *Liberalism, Socialism, and Christian Social Order*. Translated by Rupert J. Ederer. Lewiston, N.Y.: Edwin Mellen Press.
———. 2002. *Lehrbuch der Nationalökonomie* [*Teaching Guide to Economics*]. Translated by Rupert J. Ederer. Lewiston, N.Y.: Edwin Mellen Press.
———. 2008. *Ethics and the National Economy*. Translated by Rupert J. Ederer. Norfolk, Va.: IHS Press.
Peters, Walter H. 1959. *The Life of Benedict XV*. Milwaukee: Bruce.
Petrie, John. 1956. *The Worker-Priests: A Collective Documentation*. London: Routledge and Kegan Paul.
Pierrard, Pierre. 1984. *L'Eglise et les ouvriers en France 1840–1940*. Paris: Hachette.
———. 1991. *L'Eglise et les ouvriers en France 1940–1990*. Paris: Hachette.
———. 1997. *Georges Guérin: Une vie pour la JOC*. Paris: Éditions ouvrières.
Pigenet, Michel, Patrick Pasture, and Jean-Louis Robert, eds. 2005. *L'apogée des syndicalismes en Europe occidentale 1960–1985*. Paris: Publications de la Sorbonne.

Piketty, Thomas. 2014. *Capital in the Twenty-First Century*. Cambridge, Mass.: Harvard University Press.
Pirotte, Jean, and Guy Zelis, eds. 2003. *Pour une histoire du monde catholique au 20e siècle: Wallonie-Bruxelles*. Louvain-le-Neuve: ARCA-Eglise-Wallonie.
Pius XI. 1922. *Ubi Arcano Dei Consilio*. In *AAS* 14: 673–700.
———. 1925. *Quas primas*. In Carlen, 3:271–79.
———. 1931. *Quadragesimo Anno*. In *AAS* 23: 177–228. English translation in Carlen, 3:415–43.
———. 1985. "Alla Federazione francese dei sindacati cristiani" [Sept. 18, 1985]. In *Discorsi di Pio XI*, 810–16. Vatican City: Libreria editrice vaticana.
Pius XII. 1950. "Address to Those Attending the International Convention of Social Studies in Rome." In *AAS*, 485–88. Vatican City: Vatican Polyglot Press.
Le Plan de la CFTC 1936. Paris: Spes.
Poels, Henry A. 1982. *A Vindication of My Honor*. Edited by Frans Neirynck. Leuven: Leuven University Press and Peeters. Originally published in 1910.
———. 1998. "Onze moderne katholieke standsorganisatie." In *HJS* 290–99. Originally published in 1921.
Polasky, Janet. 1995. *The Democratic Socialism of Emile Vandervelde: Between Reform and Revolution*. Oxford and Washington, D.C.: Berg.
Pollard, John F. 1985. *The Vatican and Italian Fascism, 1929–32: A Study in Conflict*. Cambridge: Cambridge University Press.
———. 1994. "Fascism." In *NDCST* 381–88.
———. 1996. "Italy." In Buchanan and Conway, *Political Catholicism in Europe*, 69–96.
———. 1997. "Religion and the Formation of the Italian Working Class." In *American Exceptionalism: U.S. Working Class Formation in an International Context*, edited by Rick Halpern and Jonathan Morris, 158–80. London: Macmillan; New York: St. Martin's.
———. 1999. *The Unknown Pope: Benedict XV (1914–1922) and the Pursuit of Peace*. London: Geoffrey Chapman.
———. 2002. "The Pope, Labour, and the Tango: Work, Rest, and Play in the Thought and Action of Benedict XV (1914–1922)." In *The Use and Abuse of Time in Christian History*, edited by R. N. Swanson, 369–84. Woodbridge, Suffolk: Boydell Press for the Ecclesiastical History Society.
———. 2005. *Money and the Rise of the Modern Papacy: Financing the Vatican, 1850–1950*. Cambridge: Cambridge University Press.
———. 2008. *Catholicism in Modern Italy: Religion, Society and Politics Since 1861*. London: Routledge.
———. 2009. "Fascism and Catholicism." In *The Oxford Handbook of Fascism*, edited by R. J. B. Bosworth, 166–84. Oxford and New York: Oxford University Press.
Ponson, Christian. 1992. "Joseph Vialatoux, le philosophe lyonnais des Semaines sociales." In Durand et al., *Cent ans de catholicisme social*, 453–84.
———. 1994. "Gonin, Marius." In *DMR* 6:211–12.
Post, Harry H. G. 1989. *Pillarization: An Analysis of Dutch and Belgian Society*. Aldershot: Gower.
Poulat, Emile. 1965. *Naissance des prêtres ouvriers*. Tournai and Paris: Casterman.
———. 1993. "*Humanisme intégral* dans la culture des années trente: Un projet catholique pour le monde." In *Le Supplément: Revue d'Éthique et Théologie Morale* 187: 139–74.
———. 1999. *Les prêtres-ouvriers: Naissance et fin*. Paris: Cerf.
PP (Populorum progressio). Paul VI, 1981. In Carlen, 5:183–201.
Prévotat, Jacques. 2001. *Les Catholiques et l'Action française: Histoire d'une condamnation 1899–1939*. Paris: Fayard.
Problème de la vie internationale. 1927. Semaines sociales de France 18. Paris: Gabalda.
Pulzer, Peter. 2004. "Nationalism and Internationalism in European Christian Democracy." In Gehler and Kaiser, *Christian Democracy in Europe*, 10–24.
QA (Quadragesimo anno). Pius XI, 1931. In Carlen, 3:415–43.
Rauscher, Anton. 1979. "Heinrich Pesch (1854–1926)." In *ZGiLB* 3:136–48.
———, ed. 1981–82. *Der soziale und politische Katholizismus: Entwicklungslinien in Deutschland 1803–1963*. 2 vols. Munich: Günter Olzog.

———, ed. 1982. *90 Jahre Rerum novarum*. Cologne: Bachem.
———. 1986. "Gundlach." In *StL* 2:1150–51.
———. 1988a. *Gustav Gundlach 1892–1963*. Paderborn: Schöningh.
———. 1988b. "Pesch." In *StL* 4:362.
———. 1989. "Subsidiarität." In *StL* 5:386.
———. 2004. "Theodor Brauer (1880–1942)." In *ZGiLB* 11:42–56.
Rémond, René. 1960. *Les catholiques, le communisme et les crises, 1929–1939*. Paris: A. Colin.
———. 1979. *Les crises du catholicisme en France dans les années trente*. Paris: Cana.
———. 1996. *Les crises du catholicisme en France dans les années trente*. Paris: Seuil.
"Rerum novarum": Écriture, contenu et réception d'une encyclique. Actes du colloque international organisé par l'École française de Rome et le Greco no. 2 du CNRS (Rome, 18–20 avril 1991). 1997. Rome: École française de Rome.
RHE (*Revue d'histoire ecclésiastique*). 1990–. Université catholique de Louvain.
Ribaut, Jean-Pierre. 1991. "Les débuts de l'Ecole des Missionnaires du Travail." In *Cent ans de catholicisme social dans la région du Nord: Actes du colloque de Lille des 7 et 8 décembre 1990; Revue du Nord* 73, nos. 290–91: 365–74.
Riccardi, Andrea. 1997. "The Tumultuous Opening Days of the Council." In Alberigo and Komonchak, *History of Vatican II*, 2:1–67.
Righart, Hans. 1986. *De katholieke zuil in Europa: Een vergelijkend onderzoek naar het ontstaan van verzuiling onder katholieken in Oostenrijk, Zwitserland, België en Nederland*. Meppel/Amsterdam: Boom.
Ritter, Emil. 1954. *Die katholisch-soziale Bewegung Deutschlands im 19. Jahrhundert und der Volksverein*. Cologne: J. P. Bachem.
Ritter, Gerhard A. 1989. *Der Sozialstaat: Entstehung und Entwicklung im internationalen Vergleich*. Munich: R. Oldenbourg.
RN (*Rerum novarum*). Leo XIII, 1891. In Carlen, 2:241–61.
Robbiati, Angelo, ed. 1981a. "Confederazione italiana dei lavoratori (CIL)." In *DSMCI* 1, pt. 2:213–16.
———. 1981b. *Confederazione italiana dei lavoratori 1918–1926: Atti e documenti ufficiali*. Milan: Franco Angeli.
———. 1984. "I quadri sindacali." In *DSMCI* 3: 935–40.
———. 1998. *Achille Grandi: Il sindacalista che portò il Vangelo tra i lavoratori*. Milan: Centro Ambrosiano.
Rodgers, Gerry, Eddy Lee, Lee Swepston, and Jasmien Van Daele. 2009. *The International Labour Organization and the Quest For Social Justice, 1919–2009*. Ithaca, N.Y.: Cornell University Press; Geneva: ILO.
Roes, Jan, ed. 1982. *Bronnen van de katholieke arbeidersbeweging in Nederland: Toespraken, brieven en artikelen van Alphons Ariëns, 1887–1901*. Nijmegen: Katholiek Documentatie Centrum; Baarn: Ambo.
———. 1985a. "Katholieke arbeidersbeweging in historische banen. Inleidende beschouwingen over achtergronden, fasen en aspecten." In Roes 1985b, *Katholieke arbeidersbeweging*, 15–77.
———. 1985b. *Katholieke arbeidersbeweging: Studies over KAB en KNV in de economische en politieke ontwikkeling von Nederland na 1945*. Baarn: Ambo.
———. 1990. "Hirtenbrief und Bumerang: Das Mahnwort der katholischen Bischöfe der Niederlande (1954) zur parteipolitischen Tätigkeit von katholischen Christen." *Kirchliche Zeitgeschichte* 3: 116–25.
———. 2004. "A Historical Detour: The Roman Catholic State Party in the Netherlands." In Kaiser and Wohnout, *Political Catholicism in Europe*, 80–93.
Rollet, Henri. 1955. *Sur le chantier social: L'action des catholiques en France, 1870–1940*. Lyon: La Chronique sociale.
———. 1960. *Andrée Butillard et le féminisme chrétien*. Paris: Spes.
Roos, Lothar. 1982. "Kapitalismus, Sozialreform, Sozialpolitik." In Rauscher, *90 Jahre Rerum novarum*, 2:52–158.
Roucou, Christophe. 2001. "La Mission de France." In Duriez et al, *Chrétiens et ouvriers*, 100–114.

Routhier, Gilles. 2006. "Finishing the Work Begun: The Trying Experience of the Fourth Period." In Alberigo and Komonchak, *History of Vatican II*, 5:49–184.
Roux, Jacqueline. 1995. *Sous l'étendard de Jeanne: Les fédérations diocésaines de jeunes filles 1904–1945; Une ACJF féminine?* Paris: Cerf.
Ruffieux, Roland. 1969. *Le mouvement chrétien-social en Suisse romande 1899–1949.* Fribourg: Éditions universitaires.
Ruhnau, Clemens. 1980. *Der Katholizismus in der sozialen Bewährung: Die Einheit theologischen und sozialethischen Denkens im Werk Heinrich Peschs.* Paderborn: Schöningh.
Ruppert, Karsten. 1992. *Im Dienst am Staat von Weimar: Das Zentrum als regierende Partei in der Weimarer Demokratie 1923–1930.* Düsseldorf: Droste.
———. 1993. "Der deutsche Katholizismus im Ringen um eine Standortsbestimmung des Reiches nach dem Ersten Weltkrieg." *Zeitschrift Für Kirchengeschichte* 104: 198–229.
Rüthers, Bernd, and Gerhard Kleinhenz. 1987. "Mitbestimmung." In *StL*, 3:1176–85.
Ryan, John A. 1935. *A Better Economic Order.* New York: Harper.
Saba, Vincenzo. 1983. "Dall'Unione Economico-Sociale alla C.I.L." In *Dalla prima democrazia cristiana*, 477–501.
———, ed. 1994. *Il Patto di Roma: Dichiarazione sulla realizzazione dell'unità sindacale, 3 Giugno 1944; Il movimento sociale cattolico alla ricerca della terza via.* Rome: Edizioni Lavoro.
———. 1996. *Quella specie di laburismo cristiano: Dossetti, Pastore, Romani e l'alternativa a De Gasperi, 1946–1951.* Rome: Edizioni Lavoro.
Salemink, Theo. 1991. *Katholieke kritiek op het kapitalisme 1891–1991: Honderd jaar debat over vrije markt en verzorgingsstaat.* Amersfoort and Leuven: Acco.
Sander, Hans-Joachim. 2005. "Theologischer Kommentar zur Pastoralkonstitution über die Kirche in der Welt von heute *Gaudium et spes*." In *Herders theologischer Kommentar zum Zweiten Vatikanischen Konzil*, edited by Peter Hünermann and Jochen Hilberath, 4:81–886. Freiburg im Breisgau: Herder.
Sassoon, Donald. 1996. *One Hundred Years of Socialism: The West European Left in the Twentieth Century.* London and New York: I. B. Tauris.
Saudejaud, Carole. 1999. *Le syndicalisme chrétien sous l'Occupation.* Paris: Perrin.
Sauvage, Pierre. 1987. *La Cité Chrétienne (1926–1940): Une revue autour de Jacques Leclercq.* Brussels.
Scatena, Silvia, Dennis Gira, Jon Sobrino, and Maria Clara Bingemer, eds. 2012. *Vatican II.* Concilium: International Journal of Theology. London: SCM Press.
Schäfer, Michael. 1990. *Heinrich Imbusch: Christlicher Gewerkschaftsführer und Widerstandskämpfer.* Munich: C. H. Beck.
Scheler, Max. 1918. "Deutschlands Sendung und der katholische Gedanke." In *Gesammelte Werke*, 4:515–40. Bern: Francke.
Schloesser, Stephen. 2005. *Jazz Age Catholicism: Mystic Modernism in Postwar Paris, 1919–1933.* Toronto and Buffalo, N.Y.: University of Toronto Press.
———. 2007. "Against Forgetting: Memory, History, Vatican II." In *Vatican II: Did Anything Happen?* edited by David G. Schultenover, 92–152. New York: Continuum.
———. 2010. "The Rise of a Mystic Modernism: Maritain and the Sacrificed Generation of the Twenties." In *The Maritain Factor: Taking Religion into Interwar Modernism*, edited by Rajesh Heynickx and Jan De Maeyer, 28–39. Leuven: Leuven University Press.
Schmitter, Philippe C. 1974. "Still the Century of Corporatism?" *Review of Politics* 36: 85–131.
Schneider, Michael. 1982a. *Die Christlichen Gewerkschaften 1894–1933.* Bonn: Neue Gesellschaft.
———. 1982b. "Religion and Labour Organisation: The Christian Trade Unions in the Wilhelmine Empire." *European Studies Review* 12: 345–69.
———. 1989. *Kleine Geschichte der Gewerkschaften: Ihre Entwicklung in Deutschland von den Anfängen bis heute.* Bonn: Dietz.
Schoelen, Georg. 1982. *Bibliographisch-historisches Handbuch des Volksvereins für das katholische Deutschland.* Mainz: Grünewald.
Scholl, S. Hermann, ed. 1963–66. *150 jaar katholieke arbeidersbeweging in België (1789–1939).* 3 vols. Brussels: Arbeiderpers.

Schroeder, Wolfgang. 1992. *Katholizismus und Einheitsgewerkschaft: Der Streit um den DGB und der Niedergang des traditionellen Sozialkatholizismus in der Bundesrepublik bis 1960*. Bonn: J. H. W. Dietz.
Schuck, Michael J. 1991. *That They Be One: The Social Teaching of the Papal Encyclicals 1740–1989*. Washington, D.C.: Georgetown University Press.
———. 1994. "Modern Catholic Social Thought." In *NDCST* 611–32.
———. 2005. "Early Modern Roman Catholic Social Thought, 1740–1890." In Himes et al., *Modern Catholic Social Teaching*, 99–124.
Schulmeister, Otto. 1966. "Kirche, Ideologien und Parteien." In *Kirche in Österreich 1918–1965*, edited by Erika Weinzierl, 1:218–40. Vienna: Herold.
Schulte, Karl Joseph. 1925. "Richtlinien zur sozialen Verständigung." In Briemle, *Zweifrontenkrieg der katholischen Kirche*, 1–9.
Schumpeter, Joseph A. 1954. *History of Economic Analysis*. New York: Oxford University Press.
Schwarte, Johannes. 1975. *Gustav Gundlach S.J. (1892–1963): Massgeblicher Repräsentant der katholischen Soziallehre während der Pontifikate Pius' XI. und Pius' XII*. Paderborn: Schöningh.
Scoppola, Pietro. 1971. *La Chiesa e il Fascismo: Documenti e interpretazioni*. Bari: Laterza.
———. 1986. *La "nuova cristianità" perduta*. Rome: Studium.
Semaine sociale de France (22nd, Marseille 1930). *Le problème social aux colonies*. Paris: Gabalda, 1931.
Sen, Amartya. 1999. *Development as Freedom*. New York: Knopf.
Sertillanges, Antonin D. 1930. *Féminisme et Christianisme*. 7th ed. Paris: Gabalda.
Shannon, Thomas A. 2005. "Rerum novarum." In Himes et al., *Modern Catholic Social Teaching*, 127–50.
Sheehan, James J. 2008. *Where Have All the Soldiers Gone? The Transformation of Modern Europe*. Boston: Houghton Mifflin.
Sinyai, Clayton. 2006. *Schools of Democracy: A Political History of the American Labor Movement*. Ithaca, N.Y.: ILR Press.
Smith, Adam. 1976. *An Inquiry into the Nature and Causes of the Wealth of Nations* (1776). 2 vols. Oxford: Clarendon Press.
Smith, Bonnie G. 1981. *Ladies of the Leisure Class: The Bourgeoises of Northern France in the Nineteenth Century*. Princeton: Princeton University Press.
Smith, Paul. 1996. *Feminism and the Third Republic: Women's Political and Civil Rights in France, 1918–1945*. New York: Clarendon Press of Oxford University Press.
Sobrino, Jon. 2012. "The 'Church of the Poor' Did not Prosper at Vatican II." In Scatena et al., *Vatican II*, 75–85.
Somerville, Henry. 1933. *Studies in the Catholic Social Movement*. London: Burns, Oates, and Washbourne.
Sorrel, Christian, ed. 2004. *L'engagement social des croyants: Lignes de force, expériences européennes, itinéraires alsaciens*. Strasbourg: ERCAL.
Spael, Wilhelm. 1964. *Das katholische Deutschland im 20. Jahrhundert: Seine Pionier- und Krisenzeiten, 1890–1945*. Würzburg: Echter.
Spicciani, Amleto. 1984. *Agli inizi della storiografia economica e medioevistica in Italia: La corrispondenza di Giuseppe Toniolo con Victor Brants e Godefroid Kurth*. Rome: Jouvence.
Spieker, Manfred. 1989. "Sozialstaat." In *StL* 5:72–78.
Spiertz, M. G. 1979. "Poels, Henricus A." In *Biografisch Woordenboek van Nederland*, 1:460–62. The Hague: Martinus Mijhoff.
Stacpoole, Alberic, ed. 1986. *Vatican II Revisited: By Those Who Were There*. Minneapolis: Winston Press.
Staudinger, Anton. 1983. "Christlichsoziale Partei." In Weinzierl and Skalnick, *Österreich 1918–1938*, 1:249–76.
Stegmann, Franz Josef. 1974. *Der soziale Katholizismus und die Mitbestimmung in Deutschland: Vom Beginn der Industrialisierung bis zum Jahre 1933*. Paderborn: Schöningh.
———. 1982. "Der sozialpolitische Weg im deutschsprachigen Katholizismus." In Rauscher, *90 Jahre Rerum novarum*, 98–129.

Stegmann, Franz Josef, and Peter Langhorst. 2000. "Geschichte der sozialen Ideen im deutschen Katholizismus." In *Geschichte der sozialen Ideen in Deutschland: Sozialismus—katholische Soziallehre—protestantische Sozialethik; Ein Handbuch*, edited by Helga Grebing, 599–862. 2nd ed. Essen: Klartext.

Stehlin, Stewart A. 1983. *Weimar and the Vatican, 1919–1933: German-Vatican Diplomatic Relations in the Interwar Years*. Princeton: Princeton University Press.

Stern, Fritz. 1961. *The Politics of Cultural Despair: A Study in the Rise of the Germanic Ideology*. Berkeley: University of California Press.

Sternhell, Zeev. 1994. *The Birth of Fascist Ideology: From Cultural Rebellion to Political Revolution*. Princeton: Princeton University Press.

Stjernø, Steinar. 2004. *Solidarity in Europe: The History of an Idea*. Cambridge: Cambridge University Press.

StL (Staatslexikon: Recht, Wirtschaft, Gesellschaft). 1985–93. 7th ed. 5 vols. Freiburg: Herder.

Strikwerda, Carl. 1990. "Corporatism and the Lower Middle Classes: Interwar Belgium." In *Splintered Classes: Politics and the Lower Middle Classes in Interwar Europe*, edited by Rudy Koshar, 210–39. New York: Holmes and Meier.

———. 1995. "A Resurgent Religion: The Rise of Catholic Social Movements in Nineteenth-Century Belgian Cities." In McLeod, *European Religion*, 61–89.

———. 1997. *A House Divided: Catholics, Socialists, and Flemish Nationalists in Nineteenth Century Belgium*. Lanham, Md.: Rowman and Littlefield.

———. 2003. "Die belgische christliche Arbeiterbewegung 1880–2000." In Hiepel and Ruff, *Christliche Arbeiterbewegung*, 83–98.

———. 2005. "'L'organisation, clé du succès!'": European Christian Labor Movements in Comparative Perspective." In Heerma van Voss, Pasture, and De Maeyer, *Between Cross and Class*, 333–77.

Sturzo, Luigi. 1974–76. *Scritti inediti*. Rome: Cinque Lune.

———. 1992. *Il popolarismo*. Edited by Gabriele de Rosa. Rome: Laterza.

Suaud, Charles, and Nathalie Viet-Depaule. 2005. *Prêtres et ouvriers: Une double fidélité mise à l'épreuve, 1944–1969*. 2nd rev. ed. Paris: Karthala.

Suhard, Emmanuel. 1947. *Essor ou déclin de l'Église?* Paris: Éditions du Vitrail.

———. 1948. *Growth or Decline? The Church Today*. Notre Dame, Ind.: Fides.

SWB (Wilhelm Emmanuel von Ketteler: Sämtliche Werke und Briefe). 1977–2001. Edited by Erwin Iserloh. Mainz: Von Hase and Koehler.

Tallett, Frank, and Nicholas Atkin, eds. 1996. *Catholicism in Britain and France since 1789*. London: Hambledon Press.

Talmy, Robert. 1966. *Le syndicalisme chrétien en France (1871–1930): Difficultés et controverses*. Paris: Bloud et Gay.

Tanner, Norman P. 2003. "The Church in the World (*Ecclesia ad extra*)." In Alberigo and Komonchak, *History of Vatican II*, 4:270–386.

———. 2005. *The Church and the World: Gaudium et Spes, Inter Mirifica*. New York: Paulist Press.

Taylor, Charles. 2007. *A Secular Age*. Cambridge, Mass.: Belknap Press of Harvard University Press.

———. 2011. "Magisterial Authority." In *The Crisis of Authority in Catholic Modernity*, edited by Michael J. Lacey and Francis Oakley, 259–69. New York: Oxford University Press.

Tedeschi, Paolo. 2005. "Un nuovo ruolo per il fattore lavoro nel XX secolo: Gli scritti dell'abate Pottier sulla questione operaia e l'evoluzione del sindacalismo 'bianco' in Italia nei primi decenni del novecento." In *BASMSCI* 40: 200–219.

———. 2008. "Un rôle nouveau pour les ouvriers au sein des entreprises après la grande guerre: Les idées de l'Abbé Pottier et le syndicalisme catholique en Italie." In *Italie et Belgique en Europe depuis 1918*, edited by Michel Dumoulin, 149–68. Brussels and Rome: Institut Historique Belge de Rome.

Tihon, André. 1990. "La Belgique." In *HC* 12:538–54.

———. 1996. "Associations de laïcs et mouvements d'Action catholique en Belgique." In *Achille Ratti*, 641–56.

Toniolo, Giuseppe. 1949. *Trattato di economia sociale e scritti economici*. Opera Omnia di Giuseppe Toniolo, ser. 2. 2 vols. Vatican City: Comitato opera omnia di G. Toniolo.
Tramontin, Silvio. 1980. "Il sindacalismo cristiano dall'età giolittiana al fascism." In Malgeri, *Storia*, 3:203–318 and 358–69.
———. 1981. "Opera dei Congressi e dei comitati cattolici in Italia." In *DSMCI* 1, pt. 2:336–47.
Traniello, Francesco, ed. 1983. *Dalla prima democrazia cristiana al sindacalismo bianco: Studi e ricerche in occasione del Centenario della nascita di Giovanni Battista Valente*. Rome: Cinque Lune.
———. 1995. "L'Italia cattolica nell'era fascista." In *Storia dell'Italia Religiosa, III. L'età contemporanea*, 257–99, edited by Gabriele De Rosa. Roma and Bari: Laterza.
Tranvouez, Yvon. 1988. *Catholiques d'abord: Approches du mouvement catholique en France (XIXe–XXe siècle)*. Paris: Éditions ouvrières.
———. 2000. *Catholiques et communistes: La crise du progressisme chrétien, 1950–1955*. Paris: Cerf.
———. 2011a. *Catholicisme et société dans la France du XXe siècle: Apostolat, progressisme et tradition*. Paris: Éditions Karthala.
———. 2011b. "Deux équivoques de l'Action catholique." In Tranvouez, *Catholicisme et société*, 63–84.
Turbanti, Giovanni. 1997. "Il ruolo del P. D. Chenu nell'elaborazione della costituzione *Gaudium et Spes*." In *Marie-Dominique Chenu: Moyen-âge et modernité : colloque organisé à Paris, les 28 et 29 octobre 1995*, présentation de Guy Bedouelle, 173–212. Paris: Centre d'études du Saulchoir.
———. 2000. *Un concilio per il mondo modern: La redazione della costituzione pastorale Gaudium et spes del Vaticano II*. Bologna: Il Mulino.
———. 2006. "Toward the Fourth Period." In Alberigo and Komonchak, *History of Vatican II*, 5:1–47.
Turmann, Max. 1909. *Le développement du catholicisme social depuis l'encyclique "Rerum novarum" (15 mai 1891): Idées directrices et caractères généraux*. 2nd ed. Paris: F. Alcan.
Turner, Lowell. 1998. *Fighting for Partnership: Labor and Politics in Unified Germany*. Ithaca, N.Y.: Cornell University Press.
Union internationale d'études sociales (UIES). 1927. *Code social: Esquisse d'une synthèse sociale catholique*. Paris: Spes.
———. 1931. *La Hiérarchie catholique et le problème social depuis l'encyclique Rerum Novarum 1891–1931: Répertoire bibliographique des documents emanés des souverains pontifes et de l'épiscopat*. Paris: Spes.
———. 1952. *A Code of Social Principles*. Oxford: Catholic Social Guild. Originally published by the UIES in Mechlin, Belgium, in 1929.
Valente, Giovanni Battista. 1978. *Aspetti e momenti dell'azione sociale dei cattolici in Italia (1892–1926)*. 2nd ed. Rome: Cinque Lune.
Van den Berg, Annette. 1995. *Trade Union Growth and Decline in the Netherlands*. Amsterdam: Thesis.
Van der Meersch, Maxence. 1947. *Fishers of Men*. New York: Sheed and Ward.
Van der Velden, Joseph, ed. 1933. *Wirtschafts- und Sozial-Politik in der berufsständischen Ordnung: Erste Soziale Woche des Volksvereins für das katholische Deutschland*. Cologne: Bachem.
Vandeweyer, Luc. 1981. "De Katholieke Arbeiders-Internationale: Standsorganisatie in internationaal perspectief." In Gerard, *Église et mouvement*, 61–80.
Van Duin, Pieter, and Zuzana Poláčková. 2005. "'Against the Red Industrial Terror!': The Struggle of Christian Trade Unions in Austria and Czechoslovakia against Socialist Trade-Union and Workplace Domination, 1918–1925." In Heerma van Voss, Pasture, and De Maeyer, *Between Cross and Class*, 127–71.
Van Hecke, Steven, and Emmanuel Gerard, eds. 2004. *Christian Democratic Parties in Europe since the End of the Cold War*. KADOC Studies on Religion, Culture and Society 1. Leuven: Leuven University Press.
Van Hook, James C. 2004. *Rebuilding Germany: The Creation of the Social Market Economy, 1945–1957*. New York: Cambridge University Press.
Van Kersbergen, Kees. 1995. *Social Capitalism: A Study of Christian Democracy and the Welfare State*. London and New York: Routledge.
Van Kersbergen, Kees, and Philip Manow, eds. 2009. *Religion, Class Coalitions, and Welfare States*. Cambridge and New York: Cambridge University Press.

Van Marrewijk, J. M., ed. 1994. *Blijvende dynamiek: 75 jaar geschiedenis von de Katholieke Land- en Tuinbouwbond LTB*. Haarlem: LTB.

Van Meeuwen, Jos. 1998. *Lijden aan einheid: Katholieke arbeiders op zoek naar hun politiek recht (1897–1929)*. Hilversum: Verloren.

Van Molle, Leen. 1990. *Chacun pour tous: Le Boerenbond Belge 1890–1990*. Leuven: Leuven University Press.

———. 1993. "Croissance économique et éthique catholique: les points de vue de l'Union de Malines dans les années vingt." In *Studia Historica Economica: Liber amicorum Herman Van der Wee*, edited by Erik Aerts, Brigitte Henau, Paul Janssens, and Raymond van Uytven, 317–35. Leuven: Leuven University Press.

Vanthemsche, Guy. 1990. "Unemployment Insurance in Interwar Belgium." *International Review of Social History* 35: 349–76.

Van Til, Kent A. 2008. "Subsidiarity and Sphere-Sovereignty: A Match Made in . . . ?" *Theological Studies* 69: 610–36.

Vecchio, Giorgio. 1981. "Il partito popolare." In *DSMCI* 1, pt 1: 68–79.

———. 1987a. *Alla ricerca del partito: Cultura politica ed esperienze dei cattolici italiani nel primo Novecento*. Brescia: Morcelliana.

———. 1987b. "La costruzione del programma del Partito Popolare Italiano." In Vecchio, *Alla ricerca del partito*, 211–68.

———. 1987c. "Il programma del Partito Popolare Italiano." In *Cristiani in politica: I programmi politici dei movimenti cattolici democratici*, edited by Bartolo Gariglio, 39–98. Milan: Franco Angeli.

Vecchio, Giorgio, Daniela Saresella, and Paolo Trionfini. 1999. *Storia dell'Italia contemporanea: Dalla crisi del fascismo alla crisi della Repubblica (1939–1998)*. Bologna: Monduzzi.

Ventresca, Robert. 2013. *Soldier of Christ: The Life of Pope Pius XII*. Cambridge, Mass.: Belknap Press of Harvard University Press.

Vermeersch, Arthur, and Albert Muller. 1909. *Manuel social: La législation et les oeuvres en Belgique*. 3rd rev. ed. Louvain: A. Uystpruyst; Paris: F. Alcan.

Versluis, W. G. 1949. *Beknopte geschiedenis van de katholieke arbeidersbeweging in Nederland*. Utrecht and Nijmegen: Dekker and Van de Vegt.

Verstraelen, Jules. 1966. "L'aspect international." In Scholl, *150 jaar katholieke arbeidersbeweging*, 481–505.

Vidler, Alec R. 1964. *A Century of Social Catholicism 1820–1920*. London: SPCK.

Viaene, Vincent, ed. 2005. *The Papacy and the New World Order: Vatican Diplomacy, Catholic Opinion and International Politics at the Time of Leo XIII, 1878–1903* [La papauté et le nouvel ordre mondial: Diplomatie vaticane, opinion catholique et politique internationale au temps de Leo XIII, 1878–1903]. Leuven: Leuven University Press.

Viet-Depaule, Nathalie. 1998. "Missionnaires au travail en banlieue parisienne." In *Ouvriers en banlieue, XIXe–XXe siècle*. Paris: Edition de l'Atelier.

———. 2001. "Prêtres ou ouvriers?" In Duriez et al, *Chrétiens et ouvriers*, 117–31.

———. 2005. "Les prêtres-ouvriers ou un engagement sans retour (1944–1969)." In Duriez et al, *Catholiques dans la République*, 253–62.

Vignaux, Paul. 1943. *Traditionalisme et syndicalisme: Essai d'histoire sociale (1884–1941)*. New York: Maison français.

———. 1953. "Christian Trade Unionism since World War II." In Moody, *Church and Society*, 205–22.

———. 1980. *De la CFTC à la CFDT: Syndicalisme et socialisme; "Reconstruction" (1946–1972)*. Paris: Éditions ouvrières.

Vinatier, Jean. 1978. *Le Cardinal Liénart et la Mission de France*. Paris.

———. 1983. *Le cardinal Suhard (1874–1949): L'évêque du renouveau missionnaire en France*. Paris: Centurion.

———. 1985. *Les prêtres-ouvriers, le cardinal Liénart et Rome: Histoire d'une crise (1944–1967)*. Paris: Éditions ouvrières/Éditions Témoignage chrétien.

———. 1991. *Le père Louis Augros: Premier supérieur de la Mission de France (1898–1982)*. Paris: Cerf.

Voog, Roger. 1994. "Guérin, Maurice." In *DMR* 6:220–21.
Vos, Louis. 1994. "La jeunesse ouvrière chrétienne. In *HMOCB* 2:425–99.
Wachtling, Oswald. 1973. "Joseph Joos (1878–1965)." In *ZGiLB* 1:236–50.
———. 1974. *Joseph Joos, Journalist—Arbeiterführer—Parlamentarier: Politische Biographie 1878–1933*. Mainz: Grünewald.
Walckiers, Marc A., ed. 1970. *Sources inédites relatives aux débuts de la J.O.C. 1919–1925*. Louvain/Paris: Nauwelaerts.
Walsh, Michael, and Brian Davies, eds. 1991. *Proclaiming Justice and Peace: Papal Documents from Rerum Novarum through Centesimus Annus*. Rev ed. Mystic, Conn.: Twenty-Third Publications.
Ward, Maisie. 1949. *France Pagan? The Mission of Abbé Godin*. New York: Sheed and Ward.
Warner, Isabel. 1996. *Steel and Sovereignty: The Deconcentration of the West German Steel Industry, 1949–1954*. Mainz: Philipp von Zabern.
Waterman, Anthony Michael C. 1991. *Revolution, Economics and Religion: Christian Political Economy, 1798–1833*. Cambridge: Cambridge University Press.
Waters, William R. 1994. "A Solidarist Social Economy: The Bruyn Perspective." *Review of Social Economy* 52: 108–21.
Wattebled, Robert. 1990. *Stratégies catholiques en monde ouvrier dans la France d'après-guerre*. Paris: Éditions ouvrières.
Weber, Christoph. 1970. *Kirchliche Politik zwischen Rom, Berlin und Trier 1876 bis 1888: Die Beilegung des preussischen Kulturkampfes*. Mainz: Matthias-Grünewald-Verlag.
Weber, Eugen. 1994. *The Hollow Years: France in the 1930s*. New York: Norton.
Webster, Richard A. 1960. *The Cross and the Fasces: Christian Democracy and Fascism in Italy*. Stanford, Calif.: Stanford University Press.
Weiler, Rudolf. 1992. "Zur Frage der Richtungen in der katholischen Soziallehre Österreichs." In *Der Mensch ist der Weg der Kirche: Festschrift für Johannes Schasching*, edited by Herbert Schambeck and Rudolf Weiler, 119–36. Berlin: Duncker and Humblot.
Weinzierl, Erika. 1980. "Österreich, Geschichte der katholischen Sozialbewegung in." In *KSL* 2023–40.
———. 1983. "Kirche und Politik." In Weinzierl and Skalnick, *Österreich 1918–1938*, 1:437–96.
———. 1987. "Austria: Church, State, Politics, and Ideology, 1918–1938." In Wolff and Hoensch, *Catholics, the State, and the European Radical Right*, 3–30.
———. 1995. *Der Februar 1934 und die Folgen für Österreich*. Vienna: Picus.
Weinzierl, Erika, and Kurt Skalnick, eds. 1983. *Österreich 1918–1938: Geschichte der Ersten Republik*. 2 vols. Graz: Styria.
Weitz, Eric D. 2007. *Weimar Germany: Promise and Tragedy*. Princeton: Princeton University Press.
Wells, Sherrill Brown. 2007. *Pioneers of European Integration and Peace, 1945–1963: A Brief History with Documents*. New York: Palgrave Macmillan.
Wentholt, G. J. M. 1984. *Een arbeidersbeweging en haar priesters: Het einde van een relatie*. Nijmegen: Dekker and van de Vegt.
Whitney, Susan B. 2009. *Mobilizing Youth: Communists and Catholics in Interwar France*. Durham, N.C.: Duke University Press.
Wiedijk, Hein. 1998. "Inleiding." In *HJS* 243–46.
Wieviorka, Olivier. 2000. "France." In Moore, *Resistance in Western Europe*, 125–55.
———. 2013. *Histoire de la Résistance: 1940–1945*. Paris: Perrin.
Windmuller, John P. 1969. *Labor Relations in the Netherlands*. Ithaca, N.Y.: Cornell University Press.
Windmuller, John P., C. De Galan, and A. F. Van Zweeden. 1990. *Arbeidsverhoudingen in Nederland*. 7th ed. Utrecht: Het Spectrum.
Winkelman, P. H. 1966. "Les Pays-Bas." In Scholl, *150 jaar katholieke arbeidersbeweging*, 3:351–403.
Winkler, Heinrich August. 1994. *Weimar 1918–1933: Die Geschichte der ersten deutschen Demokratie*. 2nd rev. ed. Munich: Beck.
Winock, Michel. 1996. *Esprit. Des intellectuels dans la cité, 1930–1950*. Paris: Seuil.
Witt, Peter-Christian. 2004. "Matthias Erzberger und die Entstehung des demokratischen Wohlfahrtsstaates (1919–1920)." *RJKG* [*Rottenburger Jahrbuch für Kirchengeschichte*] 23: 201–27.

Witte, Els, Jan Craeybeckx, and Alain Meynen. 2000. *Political History of Belgium: From 1830 Onwards.* Antwerp: Standaard Uitgeverij; Brussels: VUB University Press.

Wittkau, Annette. 1992. *Historismus: Zur Geschichte des Begriffs und des Problems.* Göttingen: Vandenhoeck and Ruprecht.

Wohnout, Helmut. 2003. "A Chancellorial Dictatorship with a 'Corporative' Pretext: The Austrian Constitution between 1934 and 1938." In Bischof, Pelinka, and Lassner, *Dollfuss/Schuschnigg Era*, 143–62.

———. 2004. "Middle-Class Governmental Party and Secular Arm of the Catholic Church: The Christian Socials in Austria." In Kaiser and Wohnout, *Political Catholicism in Europe*, 172–94.

Wolf, Hubert. 2010. *Pope and Devil: The Vatican's Archives and the Third Reich.* Cambridge, Mass.: Belknap Press of Harvard University Press.

Wolff, Richard J. 1987. "Italy: Catholics, the Clergy, and the Church: Complex Reactions to Fascism." In Wolff and Hoensch, *Catholics, the State, and the European Radical Right*, 137–57.

———. 1990. *Between Pope and Duce: Catholic Students in Fascist Italy.* New York: Peter Lang.

Wolff, Richard J., and Jörg K. Hoensch, eds. 1987. *Catholics, the State, and the European Radical Right, 1919–1945.* Boulder, Colo.: Social Science Monographs.

Wynants, Paul. 1984. "La controverse Cardijn-Valschaerts (mars–avril 1931)." *Revue Belge d'histoire contemporaine: Belgisch Tijdschrift voor Nieuwste Geschiedenis* 15: 103–36.

———. Wynants, Paul, and Fabienne Vanneste. 2000. "Jeunesse ouvrière chrétienne ou JOC." In *DHGE* 27:1254–80.

Yerly, Frédéric. 1999. "La morale au secours du politique? L'exemple de l'Union catholique d'études internationales (UCEI)." In *Marc Sangnier: La guerre, la paix (1914–1939)*, 121–48. Paris: Institut Marc Sangnier.

Zamagni, Vera Negri. 1993. *The Economic History of Italy, 1860–1990.* Oxford: Clarendon.

———. 2010. "The Political and Economic Impact of CST since 1891: Christian Democracy and Christian Labour Unions in Europe." In Finn, *True Wealth of Nations*, 95–115.

Zaninelli, Sergio. 1981a. "Il sindacalismo cattolico." In *DSMCI* 1, pt. 1: 55–68.

———. 1981b. "La situazione economica e l'azione sociale dei cattolici." In *DSMCI* 1, pt.1:320–58.

———, ed. 1982. *Il sindacalismo bianco tra guerra, dopoguerra e fascismo (1914–1926).* Milan: Franco Angeli.

Zelis, Guy, Luc Courtois, Jean-Pierre Delville, and Françoise Rosart, eds. 2009. *Les intellectuels catholiques en Belgique francophone (19e–20e siècles): Mélanges offerts a Jean Pirotte.* Louvain-la-Neuve: Arca.

ZGiLB (*Zeitgeschichte in Lebensbildern: Aus dem deutschen Katholizismus des 19. und 20. Jahrhunderts*). 1973–2007. Edited by Rudolf Morsey, Jürgen Aretz, and Anton Rauscher. 12 vols. Mainz: Grünewald; Münster: Aschendorff.

Zirnheld, Jules. 1937. *Cinquante années de syndicalisme chrétien.* Paris: Spes.

INDEX OF NAMES

Aalberse, Petrus J. M. (1871–1948), 25, 46, 89, 92, 96, 231
Adam, Karl (1876–1966), 65
Adenauer, Konrad (1876–1967), 52, 57–58, 270, 277–79
Aengenent, Johannes D. J. (1873–1935), 92
Agartz, Viktor (1897–1964), 284
Albert I (1875–1934), 97
Ambrosetti, Giovanni, 224
Amelink, Herman (1881–1957), 44
Amette, Léon Adolphe (1850–1920), 29–30
Andreotti, Giulio (1919–2013), 225
Anizan, Jean-Emile (1853–1928), 139
Antoine, Charles (1848–1921), 61–62, 77, 83
Arendt, Joseph (1885–1952), 98, 247
Ariëns, Alfons (1860–1928), 89, 159, 254
Arnou, André (1886–1955), 46
Aubert-Picard, Jeanne (1909–2003), 158
Augros, Louis (1898–1982), 264, 269

Baader, Franz Xaver von (1765–1841), 6
Badoglio, Pietro (1871–1956), 221
Baers, Maria (1883–1959), 153, 155–56, 159, 248n63
Balduzzi, Giovanni (1886–1961), 197
Barde, Louis, 99
Bardot, Maria (1883–1927), 149–50
Barelli, Armida (1882–1952), 144–45, 192–93
Bataille, Jules (1864–1937), 111, 116
Bauer, Gustav (1870–1944), 31
Bauer, Otto (1881–1938), 206–8, 229
Bauer, Otto (1897–1986), 208–9, 230
Bazire, Henri (1873–1919), 8, 18
Belin, René (1898–1977), 258–59
Belloc, Hilaire (1870–1953), 149
Belpaire, Jan (1881–1972), 130
Benedict XV (1854–1922), 15–18, 27–30, 33–34, 41, 48, 52, 80, 151, 185, 192
Bernadot, Pierre (1883–1941), 238
Bernanos, Georges (1888–1948), 232
Bernareggi, Adriano (1884–1953), 224–25
Beschet, Paul (1920–), 267n39
Bianchi, Antonio, 188
Bidault, Georges (1899–1983), 58, 136, 232, 262, 270
Biederlack, Joseph (1845–1930), 66

Billot, Louis (1846–1931), 113
Bismarck, Otto von (1815–98), 7
Bloquaux, Joseph (1889–1967), 127–28
Blum, Léon (1872–1950), 239–41
Böckler, Hans (1875–1951), 276–77, 283
Bodart, Jean (1895–1964), 102
Bordet, Charles (d. 1967), 158
Borne, Etienne (1907–93), 232
Bouladoux, Maurice (1907–77), 244, 259
Boulier, Jean (1894–1980), 139–40
Bouxom, Fernand (1909–91), 137
Brandts, Franz (1834–1914), 9, 18
Brants, Victor (1856–1917), 18, 124, 155
Brauer, Theodor (1880–1942), 43–44, 169, 172
Brauns, Heinrich (1868–1939), 10, 37, 45, 58, 162, 166–68, 170–71, 173–77, 203
Briand, Aristide (1862–1932), 49
Briefs, Goetz (1889–1974), 63, 172
Brodier, Jean, 261
Brohée, Abel (1880–1947), 129–31
Broutin, Charlemagne (1884–1963), 112–13, 259
Brüning, Heinrich (1885–1970), 164, 178, 181
Brust, August (1862–1924), 9
Buchez, Philippe (1796–1865), 6
Buozzi, Bruno (1881–1944), 256
Burjan, Hildegard (1883–1933), 146
Buss, Franz Josef (1803–78), 65
Butillard, Andrée (1881–1955), 147–49, 152, 157–58

Callon, Pierre (1882–1959), 137, 139
Canevari, Emilio (1880–1964), 256
Cappe, Victoire (1886–1927), 14, 125, 153–55
Cardijn, Joseph (1882–1967), 61, 98, 103, 121–35, 138–40, 146, 157, 196, 228, 253, 290n29
Carels, René (1897–1928), 98
Carton de Wiart, Henri (1869–1961), 101
Castelnau, Edouard de Curières de (1851–1943), 107
Cathrein, Victor (1845–1931), 62
Catoire, Jules (1899–1988), 259
Cavazzoni, Stefano (1881–1951), 51–52
Cetty, Henri (1847–1918), 18
Chenu, Jeanne (1861–1939), 147

Chenu, Marie-Dominique (*1895–1990*), 232, 266, 269, 290n29
Chollet, Jean-Arthur (*1862–1952*), 110–13
Civardi, Luigi (*1886–1971*), 86
Claudel, Paul (*1868–1955*), 232
Clemenceau, Georges (*1841–1929*), 32, 49
Coari, Adelaide (*1881–1966*), 144
Colens, Louis (*1877–1936*), 56, 98, 100–101, 103–4, 129–30, 153, 247
Colombo, Luigi (*1886–1973*), 193, 197,
Congar, Yves (*1904–1995*), 269, 290n29
Constant, Léonard (*1880–1923*), 18
Cool, August (*1903–1983*), 248–50
Corbillé, François (*1866–1941*), 139–40
Cort, John (*1913–2006*), 164
Coty, François (*1874–1934*), 115
Coux, Charles de (*1787–1864*), 6

Daens, Adolf (*1839–1907*), 124
Dalla Torre, Giuseppe (*1885–1967*), 192–93, 197
Daniel, Yvan (*1909–86*), 264–65
Danset, Achille (*1877–1935*), 113–14, 137, 139
De Bruijn, Adrianus C. (*1887–1966*), 56, 93, 100, 159–60, 231, 251–52
Debruyne, René (*1868–1941*), 12, 98–99, 153, 155
Debussche, Alphonse (*1872–1969*), 111–113
Decurtins, Kaspar (*1855–1916*), 18
Defourny, Maurice (*1878–1953*), 78–79
De Gasperi, Alcide (*1881–1954*), 27, 52, 58, 220, 270, 275
Dehon, Léon (*1843–1925*), 77
De Jong, Johann (*1885–1955*), 160, 253
Della Chiesa, Giacomo. *See* Benedict XV
De Man, Henri (*1885–1953*), 234, 248, 251
De Roo, Madeleine (*1888–1969*), 125–26
De Rossi, Giulio (*1877–1925*), 51–52
Desbuquois, Gustave (*1869–1959*), 10, 46, 48, 78, 139, 149, 151, 266
Dessauer, Friedrich (*1881–1963*), 181
Di Vittorio, Giuseppe (*1892–1957*), 256
Dobretsberger, Josef (*1903–70*), 66, 230
Dollfuss, Engelbert (*1892–1934*), 23, 211, 218, 226–30
Donati, Giuseppe (*1889–1931*), 194
Douterlunghe, Alois (*1863–1945*), 129
Dransfeld, Hedwig (*1871–1925*), 145
Dubois, Louis-Ernest (*1856–1929*), 140
Ducpétiaux, Edouard (*1806–68*), 6
Durkheim, Emile (*1858–1917*), 71, 79
Duthoit, Eugène (*1869–1944*), 78, 81, 108, 112–14, 117, 119, 238
Dutrieux, Nelly, 156

Ebert, Friedrich (*1871–1925*), 20, 31
Einaudi, Luigi (*1874–1961*), 270
Elfcs, Wilhelm (*1884–1969*), 166, 172–74, 178
Erhard, Ludwig (*1897–1977*), 270, 277, 279

Ernst, Georg (*1880–1953*), 166
Erzberger, Matthias (*1875–1921*), 12, 18, 20, 28, 31–32, 36–38, 52
Etcheverlopo, André (*1904–87?*), 261

Fahrenbrach, Heinrich (*1878–1950*), 181
Fanfani, Amintore (*1908–99*), 218
Farinacci, Roberto (*1892–1945*), 189
Faulhaber, Michael von (*1869–1952*), 35
Feltin, Maurice (*1883–1975*), 268–69, 288
Féret, Henri-Marie (*1904–92*), 269
Ferrari, Francesco Luigi (*1889–1933*), 144, 194
Fichaux, Charles (*1869–1944*), 137
Fischer, Antonius (*1840–1912*), 165
Flory, Charles (*1890–1981*), 136
Folliet, Joseph (*1903–72*), 238, 241
Franco, Francisco (*1892–1975*), 239
Frings, Joseph (*1887–1978*), 284, 287
Fumet, Stanislas (*1896–1983*), 241

Garcet, Paul (*1901–45*), 127, 129
Garric, Robert (*1896–1967*), 137, 263–66
Gasparri, Pietro (*1852–1934*), 52–53, 57, 86, 198–99
Gaulle, Charles de (*1890–1970*), 257, 262
Gay, Francisque (*1885–1963*), 233
Gedda, Luigi (*1902–2000*), 221
Gemelli, Agostino (*1878–1959*), 222–23
Gerlier, Pierre-Marie (*1880–1965*), 139, 268
Giesberts, Johannes (*1865–1938*), 13
Giolitti, Giovanni (*1842–1928*), 187
Glorieux, Palémon (*1892–1979*), 157
Gnauck-Kühne, Elisabeth (*1850–1917*), 145–46
Godin, Henri (*1906–44*), 264–66
Godwin, William (*1756–1836*), 6
Gompers, Samuel (*1850–1924*), 42
Gonella, Guido (*1905–82*), 220
Gonin, Marius (*1873–1937*), 119, 238
Gramsci, Antonio (*1891–1937*), 48
Grandi, Achille (*1883–1946*), 36, 188, 197, 256, 270–71
Gronchi, Giovanni (*1887–1978*), 187, 197, 270–71
Gross, Nikolaus (*1898–1945*), 59, 178–79, 283
Guardini, Romano (*1885–1968*), 67
Guérin, Georges (*1891–1972*), 132–40, 157–58, 265n30, 266, 268
Guérin, Maurice (*1887–1969*), 120
Guichard, Jean (*1887–1973*), 158
Gundlach, Gustav (*1892–1963*), 74, 175, 180, 213–16, 218, 237

Habermann, Max (*1885–1944*), 183
Harmel, Léon (*1829–1915*), 8–9, 18, 124
Hartmann, Felix (*1851–1919*), 165
Havard, Georges (*1876–1959*), 118
Haye, Félicie (*1891–1948*), 159
Hayek, Friedrich von (*1899–1992*), 64

Heinen, Anton (1869–1934), 175
Hengsbach, Franz (1910–91), 291
Hermans, Henri (1874–1949), 55–56
Hertling, Georg von (1843–1919), 26
Heyman, Hendrik (1879–1958), 56, 99, 248
Hillen, Willy (1896–1974), 159
Hindenburg, Paul von (1847–1934), 176, 181
Hitler, Adolf (1889–1945), 162, 181–82, 230, 244, 248, 259
Hitze, Franz (1851–1921), 77, 171
Hohoff, Wilhelm (1848–1923), 208
Horthy, Miklós (1868–1957), 218
Houte, Arthur, 115–16
Hoyois, Giovanni (1893–1969), 129

Imbusch, Heinrich (1878–1945), 169, 178, 181–82, 213
Innitzer, Theodor (1875–1955), 209, 227, 230

John XXIII (1881–1963), 4, 285–87
Joos, Joseph (1878–1965), 55–57, 59, 166, 172–74, 181
Journet, Charles (1891–1975), 242

Kaas, Ludwig (1881–1952), 178
Kaiser, Jakob (1888–1961), 166, 169, 181–83, 276
Keller, Michael (1896–1962), 284
Kessler, Harry (1868–1937), 26
Ketteler, Wilhelm von (1811–77), 7
Kolping, Adolph (1813–65), 7
Kuiper, Cornelis Johannes (1875–1951), 93
Kunschak, Leopold (1871–1953), 11, 64, 204–5, 210, 230
Kurth, Godefroid (1847–1916), 18
Kuyper, Abraham (1837–1920), 12

La Brière, Yves de (1877–1941), 49
Lafeuille, Marguerite (1888–1969), 156
Lassalle, Ferdinand (1825–64), 7
La Tour du Pin, René de (1834–1924), 8, 82, 110, 237
Lebret, Louis-Joseph (1897–1966), 118
Legien, Carl (1861–1920), 21, 167
Lehmkuhl, August (1834–1918), 62
Lemire, Jules (1853–1928), 17
Lenin, Vladimir (1870–1924), 57
Leo XIII (1810–1903), 8–10, 15–16, 54, 57, 62, 68, 141, 176, 185, 219, 293
Leopold III (1901–1983), 249
Le Play Frédéric (1806–82), 146
Lesage, Pierre (1881–1960), 113
Letterhaus, Bernhard (1894–1944), 57, 59, 178–80, 283
Leurent, Jacques (1892–1961), 139
Ley, Désiré (1883–1967), 110–12, 114–16
Liagre, Louis (1883–1955), 157–58
Liberatore, Matteo (1810–92), 62
Liénart, Achille (1884–1973), 114–17, 259, 267–69, 287–89

Longinotti, Giovanni Maria (1876–1944), 42, 187
Lorin, Henri (1857–1919), 10, 18, 108, 119, 148
Lubac, Henri de (1896–1991), 232
Lugmayer, Karl (1892–1972), 64
Luytgaerens, Eduard (1863–1946), 131

Maistre, Joseph de (1754–1821), 82
Malthus, Thomas Robert (1766–1834), 6
Maritain, Jacques (1882–1973), 113n28, 223, 232, 241–42, 247, 271
Marx, Karl (1818–83), 182
Marx, Wilhelm (1863–1946), 176–78
Mathon, Eugène (1860–1935), 110–15
Maugeret, Marie (1844–1928), 146
Mauriac, François (1885–1970), 232
Maurras, Charles (1868–1952), 106, 120, 243
Meda, Filippo (1869–1939), 52
Meert, Jacques (1902–2001), 127, 129
Melun, Armand de (1807–77), 6
Menthon, François de (1900–1984), 139
Mercier, Désiré (1851–1926), 14, 62, 79, 96, 98, 124, 126, 130–32, 141, 153
Mertens, P. J. J. (1916–2000), 208, 251
Messner, Johannes (1891–1984), 66, 83, 209, 230
Metzger, Max Joseph (1887–1944), 49
Michaux, Georges (1888–1940), 102–3
Michonneau, Georges (1899–1983), 266
Miglioli, Guido (1879–1954), 11, 36, 188–90
Milani, Fulvio, 52
Monnet, Jean (1888–1979), 270, 278
Montini, Giambattista. See Paul VI
Montini, Lodovico (1896–1990), 197
Morandat, Léon Yvon (1913–72), 261
Moro, Aldo (1916–78), 225
Moulin, Jean (1899–1943), 262
Mounier, Emmanuel (1905–50), 232, 238
Muller, Albert (1880–1951), 62, 77
Müller, Hermann (1876–1931), 176
Müller, Otto (1870–1944), 54, 56–57, 59, 165–75, 178–79, 283
Müller-Armack, Alfred (1901–78), 277
Mun, Albert de (1841–1914), 8, 18, 54, 82, 138, 148
Murri, Romolo (1870–1944), 9, 11, 144
Mussolini, Benito (1883–1945), 57, 84, 116, 130, 191–94, 198–202, 216, 220, 227, 229, 256

Naillod, Louis, 261
Nell-Breuning, Oswald von (1890–1991), 212–15, 217, 279, 283–85
Nolens, Willem Hubert (1860–1931), 45–47, 58, 89–90, 92, 231

Orel, Anton (1881–1959), 64, 204, 207
Ottaviani, Alfredo (1890–1979), 287
Otte, Bernhard (1883–1933), 45, 59, 166
Owen, Robert (1771–1858), 6

Pacelli, Eugenio. *See* Pius XII
Papen, Franz von (1879–1969), 58, 178, 181
Paronetto, Sergio (1911–45), 225
Pastore, Giulio (1902–69), 275
Paul VI (1897–1978), 187, 200, 220, 223, 289–90
Pauwels, Henri (1890–1946), 45–46, 99, 248–50, 274
Pavan, Pietro (1903–94), 287
Péguy, Charles (1873–1914), 18
Pérès, Jean (1897–), 234, 260
Perquy, Jules L. (1870–1946), 155–56
Perroux, François (1903–87), 237
Pesch, Heinrich (1854–1926), 60–63, 65–77, 79, 83, 95, 146, 171, 213–14, 279
Pétain, Philippe (1856–1951), 244, 257–59
Pfliegler, Michael (1891–1972), 208–9, 230
Philippovich, Eugen von (1858–1917), 70
Picard, Louis (1886–1955), 129, 131
Pieper, August (1866–1942), 175
Piffl, Gustav (1864–1932), 206, 209
Pius IX (1792–1878), 16, 185
Pius X (1835–1914), 10–11, 15–16, 33, 48, 84, 144, 151
Pius XI (1857–1939), 57, 60, 84–87, 102, 106, 113, 116, 120, 131, 141, 144, 191–99, 201–2, 212–23, 238, 242–43, 253
Pius XII (1876–1958), 56–57, 212, 218, 243, 268, 278
Pizzardo, Giuseppe (1877–1970), 221, 288
Plenge, Johann (1874–1963), 65
Poels, Henry (Hendrik, Henri, Henricus; 1868–1948), 13, 55–57, 61, 85–86, 89–90, 96, 100, 121–22, 129–30, 159, 228, 251, 253, 271–72
Poimboeuf, Marcel (1889–1974), 260–61
Pottier, Antoine (1849–1923), 9, 154
Poullet, Prosper (1868–1937), 132
Prelot, Marcel (1898–1972), 58

Quiclet, Georges (1899–1981), 137–38
Quilliet, Hector-Raphael (1859–1928), 111, 114

Rampolla, Mariano (1843–1913), 15
Renner, Karl (1870–1951), 205
Reynold, Gonzague de (1880–1970), 48
Righetti, Igino (1904–39), 220, 222–25
Rochebillard, Marie-Louise (1857–1936), 147, 153
Romani, Mario (1917–75), 275
Roosevelt, Franklin D. (1882–1945), 248
Roscam, Jules, 250
Roussel, Nelly (1878–1922), 152
Ruijs de Beerenbrouck, C. J. M. (1873–1936), 25, 58
Rutten, Georges Ceslas (1875–1952), 97–99, 103–4, 130, 153, 155–56

Salazar, António de Oliveira (1889–1970), 23
Saliège, Jules-Géraud (1870–1956), 260
Sangnier, Marc (1873–1950), 8, 18, 27, 48–50, 52, 119, 124, 137, 204
Sbarretti, Donato (1856–1939), 113–15

Schaepman, Herman (1844–1903), 88, 254
Schaurhofer, August (1872–1928), 208
Scheler, Max (1874–1928), 26, 65
Scherrer, Josef (1891–1965), 44
Schindler, Franz (1847–1922), 66, 203,
Schleicher, Kurt von (1882–1934), 181
Schmitt, Hermann Josef (1896–1964)
Schmitz, Mia, 159
Schmitz, Richard (1885–1954), 58, 66, 203, 230
Schmoller, Gustav von (1838–1917), 147
Schöpfer, Aemilian (1858–1936), 66
Schulte, Karl Joseph (1871–1941), 165–66, 172–73, 175
Schultze-Delitzsch, Hermann (1808–83), 7
Schuman, Robert (1886–1963), 58, 107, 270, 278
Schumpeter, Joseph Alois (1883–1950), 64
Schuschnigg, Kurt (1897–1977), 227–30
Schutte, Johannes Antonius, 56
Seipel, Ignaz (1876–1932), 26, 58, 66, 206, 211, 225
Serrarens, P. J. S. (1888–1963), 43–44, 46–47, 58, 92–94, 231, 243, 284
Sertillanges, Antonin-Dalmace (1863–1948), 29–30, 151
Sibenaler, Marie-Antoinette (1898–1982)
Six, Paul (1860–1936), 17, 112, 116
Smith, Adam (1723–90), 5, 71
Sombart, Werner (1863–1941), 214
Sonnenschein, Carl (1876–1929), 57
Spalowsky, Franz (1875–1938), 205, 230
Spann, Othmar (1878–1950), 64–65, 68, 70, 211
Spengler, Oswald (1880–1936), 67
Staud, Johann (1882–1939), 227, 230
Stegerwald, Adam (1874–1945), 9, 13, 21, 37, 43–45, 161, 163–64, 167–69, 173, 175–78, 181, 277
Steinbüchel, Theodor (1888–1949), 65
Stinnes, Hugo (1870–1924), 21, 167
Stokman, Jacobus Gerardus (Siegfried, OFM; 1903–70), 160
Sturzo, Luigi (1871–1959), 9, 11, 27, 33–37, 50–54, 87, 185–87, 192, 194
Suenens, Léon-Joseph (1904–96), 279
Suhard, Emmanuel (1874–1949), 263–65, 268–69

Talamo, Salvatore (1844–1932), 63
Taylor, Charles (1931–), 1–2, 105, 280–81, 292–93, 295
Tessier, Gaston (1887–1960), 108, 150, 233, 242–44, 258–59, 261–62
Teusch, Christine (1888–1968), 171
Thomas, Albert (1878–1932), 45–46
Thorez, Maurice (1900–1964), 239, 241
Tiberghien, Pierre (1880–1960), 112
Tocqueville, Alexis de (1805–59), 22
Togliatti, Palmiro (1893–1964), 275
Toniolo, Giuseppe (1845–1918), 11, 18, 62–63, 77, 191
Tonnet, Fernand (1894–1945), 127, 129
Tönnies, Ferdinand (1855–1936), 67

Torcq, Georges, 112
Troelstra, Pieter J. (1860–1930), 91
Tromp, Sebastian (1889–1975), 287

Valente, Giovanni Battista (1872–1944), 11, 17, 42, 145, 185–87
Valois, Georges (1878–1945), 110
Van den Plas, Louise (1877–1968), 153–54
Vande Putte, Philippe (1903–63), 248n63
Vandervelde, Emile (1866–1938), 46, 132, 232
Vanistendael, August (1917–2003), 284, 290n31, 294
Vanhove, Marcel (1908–), 261
Van Nispen tot Sevenaer, Maria (1903–99), 160
Vanneufville, Gaston (1866–1936), 113
Van Roey, Jozef-Ernest (1874–1961), 98, 105, 132, 141, 246, 250, 279
Veraart, Johannes A. (1886–1955), 94–96, 231
Verdier, Jean (1864–1940), 148, 150, 239–40, 243, 264
Verhaegen, Arthur (1847–1917), 18
Verheeke, Emiel (1881–1963), 248
Vermeersch, Arthur (1858–1936), 12, 62, 77, 114
Verneyras, Paul, 261

Vialatoux, Joseph (1880–1970), 120, 238
Viellefon, Léon (1873–1942), 112–13
Vignaux, Paul (1904–87), 234, 237, 242, 261, 275
Villeneuve-Bargemont, Alban de (1784–1850), 6
Vogelsang, Karl von (1818–90), 8, 64, 66, 77, 203–4, 206

Wagner, Adolph (1835–1917), 69
Waitz, Sigismund (1864–1941), 206
Walterbach, Carl (1870–1952), 54, 57, 166
Weber, Helene (1881–1962), 145
Weber, Max (1864–1920), 70
Weiss, Albert Maria (1844–1925), 62
Waitz, Sigismund (1864–1941), 66
Wieber, Franz (1858–1933), 169
Wilhelm II, 31, 35
Wilson, Woodrow (1856–1924), 28, 30, 32, 34–35, 49
Winter, Ernst Karl (1895–1959), 64, 229–30
Wirth, Joseph (1879–1956), 38, 52, 181

Zamanski, Joseph (1874–1962), 148,
Zirnheld, Jules (1876–1940), 41–45, 108, 150, 238, 243–44, 258–59

GENERAL INDEX

Action catholique ouvrière (ACO), 271–72, 279, 290
Action française (AF), 106, 110, 113, 119, 198, 238
Action populaire (AP), 10, 99, 116–18, 137, 139, 148–49, 239–40
Ad beatissimi apostolorum, 15–17, 28
Africa, 266
agriculture, 33, 35, 88–89, 99, 104, 131, 175, 188–90
Ahlen Program, 276
Algemeen Christelijk Vakverbond (ACV; Belgium). *See* Confederation of Christian Trade Unions
Algemeen Christelijk Werkersverbond (ACW; Belgium). *See* National League of Christian Workers
Alsace, 18, 29, 117–19, 260
Amsterdam, 89, 159
Angers, 61–62, 238
anticlericalism, 106, 152, 185
anti-Semitism, 67, 204–5, 245
Antwerp, 45, 153, 155
apostolate, 122, 272, 282, 290n31
Arbeiterstand, 213–14, 228
Arbeitervereine, 14, 93, 164–67, 173, 205. *See also* milieu organizations
arbitration, 148–150
Assemblée des cardinaux et archevêques (ACA), 264, 271
Association catholique de la jeunesse belge (ACJB and ACJBF), 122–23, 129–31, 133, 245
Association catholique de la jeunesse française (ACJF), 8, 18, 122, 136–40, 148
Associazioni cristiane dei lavoratori italiani (ACLI), 270–71, 275
L'Aube, 233, 238, 259
Austria, 2, 4, 15, 19, 23, 26–27, 29, 42, 44, 53–54, 58, 83, 146, 172, 184, 202–11, 215, 218, 225–30, 273–74
Austrian Trade Union Federation (ÖGB), 274
authoritarianism, 58, 79, 161, 211, 226, 246
autonomy issues, 33–34, 138–40, 143, 174, 178, 185–86, 272, 280

Bavaria, 20, 54, 57
bedrijfsorganisatie (industrial organization), 94. *See also* concertation; corporatism
Belgian Catholic Union, 96, 101
Belgian Labor Party, 97, 100, 248
Belgium, 2, 12, 19, 24–25, 27, 29–30, 41–44, 46, 48, 53–54, 83, 87–88, 93, 96–105, 112, 119, 121–35, 153–58, 172, 210, 232, 244–50, 255–56, 270–71
Benelux, 4
Bergamo, 192, 224
Berlin, 20, 183, 212
Beveridge Plan, 3
bishops, 111, 113–17, 206–7, 246, 253, 257, 259, 262–66, 279–80, 281–83, 286–92
Bochum, 277
Boerenbond, 99, 101, 128, 131–32
Bologna, 35
Bonn, 169
bourgeoisie, 100–102, 104, 153–55
Britain, 3, 7, 19, 27, 244, 257, 274
Brittany, 117–18
Brussels, 53, 101, 123, 125–29, 137, 139, 153–59, 244, 256
Bund religiöser Sozialisten, 208–9

Camadoli, 225
Cambrai, 110–11
capitalism, 1–3, 47, 63, 172, 203–7, 217–18, 237, 270, 285
Catholic Action, 60, 83–87, 102, 116, 121–23, 129–32, 144, 159, 176, 191–202, 212, 219–25, 242, 245, 251–53, 271–72, 283
Catholic social thought, 1, 16, 60–83, 114, 212–19, 232–33, 242, 279, 285–86
Catholic Worker International, 54–59, 83, 116, 196
Center Party (Germany), 11, 37, 52, 161–63, 166, 174, 178
charities, 4, 111, 146, 262
Charleroi, 102, 106
Charte du travail, 258–61
Christendom, 1, 241–42
Christian Democratic Union, 276–77
Christian democrats, Christian democracy, 4, 51–52, 62, 116, 119, 154, 206, 229, 233, 237

337

Christian Social Party (CSP; Austria), 11, 203–5, 226, 228
Christian Unions of Germany (CGD), 284
Chronique social de France, 118–20
church-state relations, 101, 197, 226
class, classes, 1, 5–14, 16–17, 33, 45, 56, 80, 91, 121–22, 130, 180, 197, 213–14, 228, 237, 245, 273, 293–96
clergy, chaplains, 17–18, 110–17, 165, 263–69, 288–89
codetermination. See Mitbestimmung
collective bargaining, 150, 162
collectivism, 47
Cologne, 43, 56, 89, 166, 172, 179–80, 284
common good, 47, 237, 245, 274
Commonweal, 67
communism, 20–21, 35, 238–41, 243, 255–56
communitarianism, community, 62, 64, 67–71, 175
Como, 145
Compiègne, 20
concertation, consultation (*overleg*), 92, 96, 213, 231, 235–37, 249–52, 255–56, 282, 285n11
concordats, 179, 181, 198–202, 220–21
Confédération française des travailleurs chrètiens (CFTC), 43, 108–17, 120, 149–50, 231, 233–38, 258–62, 268, 274–75
Confédération française et démocratique du travail (CFDT), 276, 279
Confédération générale du travail (CGT), 108–10, 113, 147, 234, 236–37, 239–41, 244–45, 258–60, 268, 274, 276
Confédération générale du travail unitaire (CGTU), 110, 115–16
Confédération internationale des syndicats chrétiens (CISC), 40–47, 59, 94, 99, 156, 243, 247, 284
Confederation of Christian Trade Unions (CSC/ACV; Belgium), 98–100, 128, 156, 245–50, 274–75, 279
Confederazione Generale Italiana del Lavoro (CGIL), 256, 274–75
Confederazione italiana dei lavoratori (CIL), 36, 48, 145, 184–88, 193, 196–98, 220
Confederazione italiana sindacati lavoratori (CISL), 275
confessionality, 33, 55, 89, 92, 167–68, 176
cooperatives, 101, 150
corporatism, 19–24, 44, 61, 74–77, 92, 94–96, 169, 196, 206, 215, 217, 226, 231, 234–38, 244, 248
Cremona, 188–89
La Croix, 113–14, 119, 239–40
Curia. See Vatican
Czechoslovakia, 44, 53, 56, 202

deconfessionalization, 294
Delft, 94
democracy, 1–3, 19, 31–36, 80, 82, 104, 161–63, 184, 225–27, 230, 245, 255, 273–74
depression, 56, 92, 96, 218, 241, 247, 252

Deutscher Gewerkschaftsbund (DGB), 163–64, 167–69, 174, 181, 247, 277, 283–84
Divini redemptoris, 243, 253
Düsseldorf, 179
Dutch Labor Federation (FNV), 283

Ecclesiam suam, 290
École normale sociale (ENS), 148, 151, 155
economic council, 80, 251–52
economic policy, 6–7, 36, 47, 79–80, 270, 278, 282
economics, 69–70, 72, 214
Economic-Social Union (UES), 11, 17, 191–92
education, 16, 25, 84, 86, 101, 117, 121–24, 135, 152, 154, 175, 180, 220
Eindhoven, 12
employers, 172–73
enquêtes, 124–35, 146
Études, 114
European Coal and Steel Community (ECSC), 58, 270, 278, 286

family, 72, 79–80, 101, 111, 151–52, 257, 262–63
fascism, 11, 24, 58, 81–83, 85, 87, 144, 189–91, 215, 220–27
Fédération nationale catholique (FNC), 107, 118, 238
Federazione universitaria cattolica italiana (FUCI), 191, 202, 220, 223–25
feminism, 143, 146–48, 150–52
Le Figaro, 115
financial institutions, 33, 35
Flanders, Flemish, 97, 99–101, 123–25, 153, 246
Florence, 224
France, 2, 7–9, 15, 17–19, 23–24, 27, 42–50, 53, 56, 83, 88, 122–23, 136–42, 144, 146–52, 157–58, 172, 231–45, 256–69
Frankfurt, 7
Freiburg, 49
Freiheitsbund, 210
Fribourg, 8, 40, 48, 155

garment workers, 147–50
Gaudium et spes (GS), 4, 288–92, 295
Geneva, 45–46, 50
Genoa, 17
Germany, 2–4, 15, 17–23, 25–2, 53–59, 83, 118, 144–46, 213, 228–30, 232, 244, 256–59, 267, 270–74, 276–79, 283–85
Gesamtverband der christlichen Gewerkschaften (GcC; Germany), 37, 45, 163, 167–69, 174, 181
Gewerkschaftsbund (Austria), 228
Ghent, 11, 90, 99, 147
Gioventù Cattolica, 191
Gioventù Italiana di Azione Cattolica (GIAC), 220–22
Godesberg Program, 284–85
government intervention, 74–75, 161–64, 246–50
Graz, 66
Grenoble, 107, 147

338   GENERAL INDEX

Haarlem, 90
The Hague, 44
Halluin, 113–14, 116
Le Havre, 41, 48, 96
Heidelberg, 172
Heimwehr, 205, 211
history, historical change, 62, 69–70, 77, 225
human needs, 68–73
human rights, 4, 47, 82, 180, 199, 245, 289
Hungary, 26, 44, 202, 218

individualism, 62
industrialization, industrialism, industry, 5–6, 9, 11–14, 72, 203, 237, 243
inequality, economic, 1, 287
Innsbruck, 44, 47, 66
insurance associations, mutual, 96, 102
integrism, 8, 15–16, 105, 117, 195
interest on loans, 66
intermediary bodies, 79
international aspects, 13, 27, 39, 40–59, 130, 197, 234–45, 249, 269–70, 293–96
International Federation of Christian Trade Unions (IFCTU). *See* Confédération internationale des syndicats chrétiens
International Federation of Trade Unions (IFTU), 46
International Labour Organization (ILO), 41, 45–48, 50, 153, 156
International Trade Union Confederation (ITUC), 294n5
intransigentism, 15–16
Istituto cattolico di attività sociali (ICAS), 197, 201, 224–25
Istituto per la Ricostruzione Industriale (IRI), 222
Italy, 2, 4, 24–25, 27–29, 32–36, 42, 44, 53, 56, 83–87, 123, 130, 144–45, 184–202, 218–25, 242, 245, 256, 270–71, 273–76

Jesuits, 10, 62
Jeunesse ouvrière chrétienne (JOC and JOCF), 14, 98, 121–23, 127–42, 156–58, 179, 196, 219, 233, 240–41, 245–46, 251, 263–65, 268, 271–72, 290
Jonge Werkman, 122, 251
journalism, 33, 55, 200, 233, 238
justice, 4. *See also* social justice

Katholieke Arbeidersbeweging (KAB), 160, 271–72, 284
Katholieke Arbeidersjeugd (KAJ), 128, 133. *See also* Jeunesse ouvrière chrétienne
Katholieke Arbeidersvrouwenbeweging (KAV), 156–58
Katholikentag, 112, 191, 212, 226, 277
Katholischer Deutscher Frauenbund, 145
Kristelijke arbeiders vrouwenbeweging (KAV), 156–60. *See also* Ligues ouvrières féminines chrétiennes

Königswinter, 169, 213
Krefeld, 173–74

labor, 73–77, 224, 296
labor actions, 239. *See also* strikes
labor apostolate, 55, 111, 263–69
labor internationals. *See* Catholic Worker International; Confédération internationale des syndicats chrétiens; International Federation of Trade Unions
labor-management negotiations, 110, 187–88, 235–37, 240–41, 245, 251, 269–79, 291–92. *See also* Zentralarbeitsgemeinschaft
labor requisitions, 43, 266–68
labor secretariats, 166
labor unions, 21, 41, 80, 92–94, 165–70, 192, 196, 227, 231–54, 244, 260, 282–84; Christian, 21, 33, 40–48, 64, 87, 89–94, 97–105, 110–17, 126–29, 205–7; socialist, 91–92, 110, 205–6; unitary, 273–78, 283–85. *See also individual organizations by name*
laity, 122, 165, 191, 272, 289–90
Lateran Pacts, 57, 199
Latin America, 242, 291–92
Latvia, 42
League of Christian Trade Unions (Germany). *See* Gesamtverband der christlichen Gewerkschaften
League of Nations, 27–30, 32, 35, 50, 202
legislation, 77–78, 91–92, 119, 148–52, 169–71
liberalism, 35, 61–62, 162, 295
liberal market economy, 22
Liège, 40, 61–62, 153–54
Ligue Nationale des Travailleurs Chrétiens (LNTC; Belgium). *See* National League of Christian Workers
Ligue ouvrière chrétienne (LOC), 263
Ligues ouvrières féminines chrétiennes (LOFC), 157–58. *See also* Kristelijke arbeiders vrouwenbeweging
Liguria, 185
Lille, 10–11, 110–16, 157, 238, 244, 259
Limburg, 46, 89–90, 100
Limoges, 149, 269
Linz, 64, 206, 228
Lisieux, 263–66, 269
Lithuania, 42, 53
liturgical movement, 67, 287
Lombardy, 144, 185
London, 256
Louvain, 79, 153, 155
Lucerne, 42, 54
Luxembourg, 278
Lyon, 10, 117–20, 147–48, 238, 260

Malines (Mechlin, Mechelen), 60, 114, 126, 153, 225, 279
Mandement, 281–83

Manifest des Douze, 244–45, 258–59
markets, 74–76, 270
Marne, 18
Marseilles, 147
Marshall Plan, 1, 270, 279
Marxism, 46, 114, 207, 214, 232, 247, 270
Mater et magistra, 285–87
Matignon Agreements, 232, 237, 240–41
Metz, 107, 112
Milan, 144–45, 218, 223
milieu organizations, 14, 41, 54–59, 60, 84, 86, 164–66, 228, 245–47, 270–72, 273n64, 294n5. *See also standsorganisatie*
mining, 5, 9, 89, 169, 181
Mission de France, 257, 263
Mission de Paris, 263, 265–66
Mitbestimmung, 47, 95, 170, 188, 206, 213, 277–78
Mit brennender Sorge, 243
mobilization, 2, 80, 281–85, 293–96
modernism, Roman Catholic, 11, 16, 90, 197
Mönchengladbach, 10, 89, 155, 165, 174
Mortalium animos, 219
Mouvement populaire des familles (MPF), 263, 271, 279
Mulhouse, 18, 238
Münster, 284

Nancy, 152
Naples, 197
nationalism, 16, 19, 81–83, 210
nationalization, 248
National League of Christian Workers (ACW/LNTC; Belgium), 93, 98, 100–105, 112, 129–31, 153, 156–57, 245–47
Nazism, 56, 58, 177–79, 181–83, 210–11, 227–29, 243, 255–56
Nederlands Katholieke Vakverbond (NKV), 251
Nederlands Verbond van Vakverenigingen (NVV), 251
Netherlands, 20, 24–25, 42–47, 53–59, 84, 87–96, 121, 158–60, 210, 231–32, 244, 250–54, 270–71, 273–75, 281–83
Non abbiamo bisogno, 201–2
Nord (France), 110–17, 137, 149, 244, 259
North Atlantic Treaty Organization (NATO), 276

Opera dei Congressi, 191
organicism, 61–62, 65, 67, 73, 175, 213
organization(s), 80, 114; in 19th century, 6–12
Osservatore Romano, 114, 201, 220
Ouest-Eclair, 118
overleg. *See* concertation

Pacem in terris, 4, 30, 285
Padua, 224
papal magisterium, 197
Paris, 10, 18, 41–42, 148–52, 239, 241, 259, 261, 263–66

Parti démocrate populaire (PDP), 118–19
Partito popolare italiano (PPI), 33–36, 52–53, 87, 118, 130, 184–87, 193–94, 197, 200–201, 220, 222
party politics, 55–56, 91–92, 95, 97, 132, 161–64, 187, 238–39, 245–47, 282–85. *See also individual parties by name*
Pascendi dominici gregis, 144
Patrons du Nord, 106, 110–17
peace, 15, 18–21, 27–30, 32, 35, 38–39, 48–50
personalism, 47, 71, 236, 247, 279
philosophy, 68–73
Piedmont, 185
pillarization, 96, 106; in Belgium, 100–105; in the Netherlands, 93, 96, 282–83
Plan de la CFTC, 234–35
pluralism, 1–3, 210, 254, 281–84, 292
Poland, 42, 53, 202, 244, 292
political economy, 68, 71, 215, 248, 270, 282
Pontigny, 269
Popular Democratic Party (PDP), 233, 237
Popular Front, 233–34, 238–41
Popular Union (UP), 185, 191–92
Populorum progressio, 118, 292n35
Portugal, 215, 218
poverty, the poor, 6, 61
Presbyterorum ordinis, 288–89
priests. *See* clergy; worker priests
proletariat, 6
promotion, promoters, 138, 140, 148, 155
property, 5, 47, 291
Protestants, 25, 31, 44, 145, 284
Prussia, 7, 161, 168

Quadragesimo anno, 56, 60, 75, 77, 82, 96, 199–200, 202, 211, 212–19, 226–27, 229, 240, 251, 253, 282, 286
Quod iam diu, 30

re-Christianization, 121, 130, 221, 245
Reims, 263
religious congregations of women, 146, 149, 154
Rennes, 118
Rerum novarum, 9–10, 60, 62, 64, 66, 88–89, 96, 149, 205–7, 212, 219, 285, 287
resistance movements, 179, 183, 257
Rhineland, 7, 23, 54, 172–74, 179
Rivista internazionale delle scienze sociali, 62–63
Roermond, 159
romanticism, 64–65, 67
Rome, 145, 256. *See also* Vatican
Rooms-Katholiek Werkliedenverbond (RKWV), 93, 159, 251–54
Rotterdam, 43–44
Roubaix, 106, 110–13, 115, 157
Ruhr, 21, 49–50, 56, 172, 181–82, 278
Russia, 15, 20, 179, 239

Saar, 182
Saint-Étienne, 108
Saint-Malo, 118
Sankt Gallen, 44
Secrétariat international des partis démocratiques d'inspiration chrétienne (SIPDIC), 50–54
secularization, 1, 80, 136, 272, 280–81
Semaines sociales. *See* Social Weeks
Serbia, 15
Service du travail obligatoire (STO). *See* labor requisitions
Sillon, 10, 119, 137
social assistance, 33, 103, 114, 262–63
Social Democratic Party (SPD; Germany), 176, 277, 284–85
social democrats, Social Democratic parties, 18, 20, 31, 202, 206, 209, 277, 284, 286
socialism, 1, 35, 61, 114, 162, 162, 207, 218, 239, 241, 247–49, 251, 282
socialism, Christian, 65, 162, 276–77
socialization, 285–86
social justice, 13, 47, 69–70, 235, 238, 289
social market economy, 270, 285n11
Social Pact, 256
social partnership, 2, 180, 213
social secretariats, 33, 107, 111, 114–15, 118, 238
social security, 119, 170–71, 186
social state, 1, 181
Social Weeks, 10–12, 48, 112, 114, 119, 148–49, 152, 197, 202, 223–25, 238
social work, 159
sociology, 65, 68–69, 79, 214
solidarism, 65, 68–77, 82, 92, 169–71, 206, 213–14
solidarity, 63, 70–72, 292
Spain, 42, 44, 56, 218, 239, 241
Ständestaat, 226–30
standsorganisatie, 13–14, 55–56, 83–84, 86, 92–94, 100–101, 121–22, 206, 246, 251–54
Strasbourg, 117
strikes, 115–16, 239–41, 243
Studium, 224
St. Vincent de Paul Society, 262
subsidiarity, 74–75, 79–80, 216–17
suffrage, 25–26, 91, 148, 150, 161
Sulpicians, 137, 148, 264
Sweden, 3
Switzerland, 18, 42, 44, 53–54, 273
Syndicat des employés du commerce et de l'industrie (SECI), 11, 41. *See also* Confédération française des travailleurs chrétiens

Témoignage chrétien, 261
textile industry, 44, 89, 110–17, 153, 169, 179, 193, 232
Third Way, 61, 67–68, 80, 94, 180, 222
Thomism, 60, 62, 68–69

totalitarianism, 58, 161
Toulouse, 260–61
Tourcoing, 110, 112, 157
Tournai, 129
trade associations, 73–76, 80
training, 7, 10, 13, 55, 112, 138, 147–50
Treaty of St. Germain, 184, 202

Ubi arcano Dei consilio, 122, 196
unemployment compensation, 90
Union Démocratique Belge (UDB), 274
Union des travailleurs manuels et intellectuels (UTMI), 250
Union féminine civique et sociale (UFCS), 150–52
United States, 90
Utrecht, 43, 56, 92

Vanves, 18
Vatican, 15, 27, 110, 113–17, 184, 232, 240, 268–69, 287
Vatican Council II, 4, 279, 287–92
Veneto, 185
Venlo, 89
Verdun, 18
Versailles, 32, 49, 162, 184
Vichy, 244, 257, 259–60, 262, 267, 273
Vienna, 49, 64, 66, 82, 203, 210, 226–27, 229–30
vocational order, 23, 75–77, 169, 206, 213–14, 282, 286
Volksbund, 66, 203–5
Volksverein, 9–10, 37, 52, 66, 89, 118, 145, 173, 175–76, 203
Vrouwelijke katholieke arbeidersjeugd (VKAJ), 157

wages, 64, 146–47, 248
Wallonia, 97, 100, 122, 132–34, 153, 246
Washington, D.C., 90, 153
Weimar Republic, 25, 31, 38, 162–64, 166
Westdeutsche Arbeiter-Zeitung (WAZ), 164–65, 173–74, 177–80
women's issues, organizations, 122, 125–26, 143–60, 175, 192
worker priests, 266–69, 288–89
workers' leagues (non-union). *See* milieu organizations
working conditions, 92, 123–27, 133, 148, 170, 187, 240–41, 243, 248
Wurzburg, 50, 56

youth issues, organizations, 67, 117–18, 121–42, 143–45, 156–58, 191–93, 204, 208, 221, 225, 251, 263. *See also* Jeunesse ouvrière chrétienne
Yugoslavia, 202

Zentralarbeitsgemeinschaft (ZAG), 20–21, 37, 76–77, 92, 167, 170, 174, 182, 213

Catholic Labor Movements in Europe: Social Thought and Action was designed in Filosofia with Hypatia Sans display and composed by Kachergis Book Design of Pittsboro, North Carolina. It was printed on 60-pound Sebago and bound by Maple Press of York, Pennsylvania.